Economic and Social Aspects of Unemployment

Economic and Social Aspects of Unemployment

Dr. L.S.N. Prasad

SERIALS PUBLICATIONS
NEW DELHI (INDIA)

First Published – 2010

ISBN: 978-81-8387-299-7

Published by

SERIALS PUBLICATIONS
4830/24, 1st Floor, Ansari Road
Darya Ganj, New Delhi-110002 (India)
Phone : 23245225. Fax : 91-11-23272135
E-mail: serials@satyam.net.in

CONTENTS

PREFACE

The term "full employment" is a formal concept. It does not mean literally any unemployment. Classical economists defined "full employment" is an absence of "Involuntary unemployment". According to Prof. Pigou "full employment" is a condition when "Everybody at the ruling rate of wages wishes to be employed is in fact employed". According to him, "it is a situation in the economy in which an expansion of effective demand fails to bring about an expansion of output and employment. The most widely accepted definition for "full employment" was given by William H. Beveridge. According to him, it is a situation in which the normal lag in between losing one job and finding another job will be very short".

In the situation of globalization in the International arena and liberalization in the Indian economy, the authorities have many challenges in providing the employment to all the eligible who wish to do job. The National Rural Employment Bill, which was finalized in the Parliament (24-08-05) made it that there should be transparency in creating employment opportunities. The honorable Union Minister for Commerce announced that the Central Government proposes freedom to States to formulate their own labour laws in respect of Special Economic Zones (SEZs) involving many issues that include both labour rights and economic policy. The Government of India has failed to address long overdue Simplification, updating and reform of labour laws, enforcement of the rights and the changing needs of both employees and employers.

India being a rapidly growing population coupled with a still backward economy, proper management and efficient utilization of its work force is essential with unbalanced relationship between the rate of economic development and the rapid population growth. In this respect, the capacity of the economy in absorbing the potential labour force needs to monitor regularly. For this purpose, appropriate employment policies should be consequently adopted Situation in India in general, and in Andhra Pradesh in particular is discussed in this book. A thorough review of the unemployment problem both Social and Economic in our economy and to tackle in our economy by discussing the present situation and difficulties and future changes is presented in this book. Some of the thought provoking solutions were also presented by different authors.

This book is broadly divided in 3 parts. The first part is related to the structure and nature of unemployment in India. In this part 12 papers are included. The second part deals with unemployment situation in various sectors. In this section 13 papers were included and the third and last part deal with measurement and remedies of unemployment. There are 17 papers in this part.

Most of the papers in this book are written by well experienced and research oriented academicians. I am greatly thankful to all of them.

I am greatly thankful to my mentor, former student of London School of Economics and former member of Rajya Sabha Dr. Y. Sivaji for his constant encouragement in all my personal and academic activities.

I am also thankful to the President of the Hindu College Committee, Sri S.V.S. Somayaji. The Secondary and Correspondent Sri MVRK. Mutyalu for their encouragement. I am grateful to Sri N. Kameswara Rao, (Rtd) former Principal, Dr. R. Varanuchi, Principal, Dr. T. Nageswara Rao and Mr. S. Ravi Babu Vice-Principals for their Co Operation. I am greatly indebted to Prof. N. Sudhakara Rao, Pro. I. Satyasundaram, Dr. R. Nagi Reddy, for their encouragement.

I am greatly indebted to the people of Ethiopia and particularly the people of Awassa. I am thankful to the president of Debub University, where I worked. Dr. Zenabu and the Head of the department of Economics Dr. Ato. Getachew for their encouragement and love towards my family.

I am also thankful the colleagues in the department, Dr. A. Rajasekhar, Dr. P. Vasudeva Rao, Smt K. Vedehi, Dr. P Venu Gopal and Dr. M. Syamala for their involvement in the preparation of the book.

I am also thankful to Mrs. Ch. Rama Lakshmi, who helped me in typing the manuscripts. I am greatly indebted to my wife Dr. Y. Sunandamma Asst. Professor in Acharya Nagarjuna University and my son L. Vishnu and my family members for their cooperation.

Finally I am greatly indebted to the MD of Serials Publications Mr. S.K. Jha and Mr. Vijaya Kumar for accepting the manuscript for publication and their encouragement.

L.S.N. Prasad

LIST OF CONTRIBUTORS

Prof. C. Ratnam, Vice Chancellor, S.V. University, Tirupathi

P. Lakshmi Narayana, Research Scholar, Department of Economics, Andhra University, Visakhapatnam – 03

Geetha Mohan, Research Scholar, Department of Economics, Andhra University Visakhapatnam – 03

Dr. A. Ranga Reddy, Professor, Department of Economics, Sri Venkateswara University, Tirupati – 517 502

Dr. S.N. Tripathy, Gokhale Institute of Politics and Economics, (Deemed University), BMCC Road,Pune, Maharashtra-411004

Dr. I. Satya Sundaram, Research Director in Economics,2, 354-I, Rustumbada, Machilipatnam – 521 001

Dr. P. Kothandarami Reddy, Associate Professor, Academic Staff College, Sri Venkateswara University, TIRUPATI

Dr. P. Vasudeva Rao, Senior Lecturer, Dept. of Economics Hindu College, Guntur

Dr. S. Ramanjaneyulu, Reader, Department of Economics, V.S.M. College, Ramachanddrapuram, East Godavari Dist – 533 255

Dr. C. Basavaiah, Head & Associate Professor, Dept. of Economics S.V. University Post Graduate Centre, Kavali–524201

Dr. I. Malyadri, Associate Professor, P.B.R. Viswodaya Institute of Technology & Science, Kalavli 524 201

Dr. N. Koti Reddy, Reader and Head, Department of Economics, G.B.R. Degree College, Anaparthi, East Godavari Dist

D. Venkata Rao, Research Scholar, Department of Economics, Andhra University, Visakhapatnam

Mr. N. Srihari, Department of Commerce & Life Sciences, St. Ann's College for Women, Gorantla, Guntur, A.P., India – 522 035

Mr. S.H.K.R. Prasad, Department of Commerce & Life Sciences, St. Ann's College for Women, Gorantla, Guntur, A.P., India – 522 035

Mr. D. Rajasekhar, Department of Commerce & Life Sciences, St. Ann's College for Women, Gorantla, Guntur, A.P., India – 522 035

Dr. K. Rajeswari, Principal, Govt. Degree College, Chebrole, Guntur

Smt. V. Naveena Devi, Govt. Degree College for Women, District-Ongole Prakasam

M. Sankara Reddi, C/o. Prof. M. Sundara Rao, Dept. of Economics, Andhra University, Visakhapatnam - 530003

Prof. M. Sundara Rao, Professor, Dept of Economics, Andhra University, Visakhapatnam- 530003

Prof. K. Siva Prasad, Professor of Economics, Dept. of Economics, Andhra University, Visakhapatnam530003

K. Kiran, Research Scholar, Dept. of Economics, Andhra University, Visakhapatnam530003

Prof. M. Koteswara Rao, Professor of Economics, Department of Economics & Applied Economics, A.N.U., Nagarjuna Nagar

Dr. P. Venu Gopal, Lecturer in Economics, Hindu College, Guntur

Prof. M. Samnasiva Rao, Professor, Dept. of Geography, S.K. University, Anantapur

Dr. G. Venkata Ramana, Associate Professor, Dept. of Sociology, S.K. University, Anantapur

A. Venkateswara Rao, Lecturer in Economics, K.B.N. College, Vijayawada

Dr. Shaik Ameer, Lecturer in Economics, A.M. College, Guntur

S. Narasimha Reddy, Lecturer in Economics, SS&N College, Narasaraopet

B.V. Raghavendar, Ph.D. Scholar in Economics, ACHARYA Nagarjuna University, Guntur – 522 510

Miss. M.N. Swarna, Ph.D. Scholar in Economics, Acharya Nagarjuna University, Guntur – 522 510

Prof. B.S. Rao, Professor, Dept. of Economics, Acharya Nagarjuna University, Guntur – 522 510

G. Uma, Lecturer in Economics, Dept. of Comm.& Busi. Admi, Acharya Nagarjuna University.

Dr. A. Bhavani, Asst. Professor, Sivan Institute of Management, NH-7 Hyderabad

Dr. N.T.K. Naik, Associate Professor, Dept. of Economics, S.K. University, P.G. Centre, Kurnool – 2

Mr. Y. Maddileti, Research Scholar, Dept. of Economics, S.K.U. P.G. Centre, Kurnool – 2

K.V.R. Srinivas, Research Scholars, Political Science & Pub. Admn., Acharya Nagarjuna University.

A. Srinivasa Charyulu, Research Scholars, Political Science & Pub. Admn., Acharya Nagarjuna University.

K. Hari Babu, Research Scholars, Political Science & Pub. Admn., A.N.U.

Mrs. Swapna. V, Lecturer in Dept. of Economics, Maris Stella College, Vijayawada – 8

Dr. Lal B. Suresh, Faculty of Economics, University Arts & Science College, Kakatiya University, Warangal – 506 001

A.P. India, G. Sujatha, Research Scholar, Dept. of Economics, KU, Warangal

G. Kavitha, Research Scholar, Dept. of Economics, KU, Warangal

V. Jaya, Lecturer in Botany, Hindu College, Guntur

V. Sowjanya, Department of Life Sciences & Commerce, St. Ann's College for Women, Gorantla, Guntur - 522 035

D. Rajasekhar, Department of Life Sciences & Commerce, St. Ann's College for Women, Gorantla, Guntur – 522 035

S.H.K.R. Prasad, Dept. of Life Sciences & Commerce, St. Ann's College for Women, Gorantla, Guntur – 522 035

N. Srihari, Department of Life Sciences & Commerce, St. Ann's College for Women, Gorantla, Guntur – 522 035

Prof. N. Sudhakara Rao, Professor, Head of the Department of Economics, A.N.U.

Dr. R. Nagi Reddy, Reader in Commerce, Govt. Women's College, Guntur

M. Sankara Reddi, Doctoral Fellow, Dept. of RD, Etcherla, Srikakula

Prof. M. Sundara Rao, Professor, Dept. of Economics, A.U. Campus, Visakhapatnam-530003

Dr. M. Lakshmi Narasaiah, Professor of Economics, Sri Krishnadevaraya University, P.G. Centre, Kurnool–518 002

Prof. Chandraiah Miriyala, Prof. in Rural Development, A.U. Dr. B.R. Ambedkar University, Etcherla, Srikakulam

Dr. Suryanarayana Neduri, H.O.D. and Associate Professor, Department of Economics, M.R.P.G. College, Vizianagaram

Dr. Hariprakash Poojari, Associate Professor, School of Distance Education, Andhra University, Visakhapatnam

S. Ramachandran, Research Officer, Dr. Ambedkar Centre for Economics Studies, University of Madras, CHENNAI

Dr. T.M. Rajendra Prasad, Jr. Lecturer in Civics (Contract), SPW Jr. College (TTD), Tirupati

Dr. D. Purushotham Naidu, Lecturer in Economics (Contract), S.V. Arts College, Tirupati

Dr. B. Lilly Grace Eunice, Assistance Professor, Department of Economics, A.U. Campus, Etcherla, Srikakulam

Dr. G. Paidi Raju, Reader & H.O.D. of Economics, A.M.A.L. College, Anakapalle–1, Visakhapatnam Dist

P. Mercy Kumari, Research Scholar, Dept. of Economics, A.N.U., Guntur – 522 510

K. Mahendra Kumar, Research Scholar in Ph.D., Dept. of Economics, A.N.U., Guntur – 522 510

Dr. P. Madhavi, Reader, Dept. of Commerce, Kasturba Gandhi College for Women, West Marred ally,Secunderabad – 500 026

Mr. C. Singa, Dr. M. Syamala, Lecturer, Dept. of Economics, Hindu College, Guntur, Retd. English Lecturer, Govt. College, Nellore

Dr. M. Srinivasa Narayana, Principal & Professor, Nalanda Institute of Technology & Management, Sattenapalli(M), Guntur

Dr. K. Lalitha, Principal, B.H. Degree College, Guntur.

Dr. N. Tyagaraju, Director, Chreestu Jayanthi College of Management, Guntur.

Mrs . M.Kusuma Kumari, Dept of Social work, Govet college for Women, GUNTUR 522 002

Dr. T.D.Vimala Ph.D, HOD.,Dept.of Psychology, Govt. College for Women, Guntur.

A.V.V. Siva Prasad, Associate Professor, Nalanda Institute Engineering and Technology, Kantepudi(V), Sattenapalli(M), Guntur Dist. A.P.

PART – I

STRUCTURE AND NATURE OF UNEMPLOYMENT IN INDIA

1

STRUCTURAL CHANGES IN THE ECONOMY OF ANDHRA PRADESH–A STUDY OF SHIFTS IN EMPLOYMENT AND OUTPUT

C. Ratnam
P.Lakshmi Narayana
GeethaMohan

The study of the changes in the structure of the economy started in the 19th century evolved on a systematic theory, known as "Structural Change Theory". Basically it focuses on the study of mechanism by which economies transform their domestic economic structure from a heavy emphasis on traditional substance agriculture to a more modern and industrially diverse manufacturing and service economy. The structural shifts are best-exemplified in terms of changing sectoral shares of agriculture, industry and services in gross domestic product. Along with shifts in the output shares, shifts in employment shares may also occur because of changes either in the final demand or due to differential productivity across the sectors. If the shifts in employment shares are not in tune with the shifts in output shares, income inequalities in the economy occur and some sections of the society may be thrown into distress. Therefore the study of the patterns of the shifts in sectoral output and employment shares assume importance in the context promoting development in the back ward regions. In this study, an attempt has been made to examine the pattern of shifts in the shares of output and employment at the major sector level in the economy of Andhra Pradesh and analyze the employment elasticity's with respect to output. Against such a background, an attempt has been made to identify the major issues of concern relating to employment

METHODOLOGY

The major sectors of the economy constitute Primary sector, Secondary sector and Tertiary sector. As per the C.S.O classification, the Primary sector includes Agriculture, Livestock, Forestry & logging, Fishing, Mining& Quarrying. Secondary sector includes Registered Manufacturing, Unregistered Manufacturing, Electricity, and Construction. The Tertiary sector includes Trade, Hotels & Restaurants, Railways, Transport, Communications, Banking and Insurance, Real Estate & Ownership of Dwelling, Public Administration and Other services.

In this study, the sectoral share of output and employment are measured in terms of percentages. The employment elasticity's with respect to output are estimated by using the Log-linear regression models. The database for this study constitutes C.S.Os National Accounts Statistics, NSS Sample surveys and the Hand Book of Statistics, Published by Directorate of Economics and Statistics, Govt of Andhra Pradesh. It covers the period 1980-81 to 2004-05. How ever, due to constraints on employment data, the analysis of employment elasticities is confined to the period 1990-91 to 2002-03.

STRUCTURAL CHANGES IN ANDHRA PRADESH: SHIFTS IN OUTPUT

For analyzing the structural changes in an economy, an understanding of the experiences of prominent countries on this matter is useful. Therefore the present study started with an attempt to gain such an understanding. All the present day developed countries experienced more or less the same pattern of structural changes-first a shift from agriculture to industry and then from industry to services.

In other wards, historically the share of agriculture has seen a steady decline in total output that of industry registered an increase for a considerably long period and then has shown decline, where the share of services has steadily increased, all through and with an accelerated rate during the period, industry has seen a decline. But the timing of different phases of structural change and the speed of such changes are different among different countries. Different economists explain the pattern of these shifts in different ways. Classical economists like Fisher argued that shifts from agriculture to industry takes place as a result of low income elasticity of demand for agricultural products and high income elasticity of demand for manufactured goods. High-income elasticity of demand for services in turn cause shift from industry to services. Economists like Baumal, particularly in regard to the shift of labour forces to services, question the demand side explanation based on differences in income elasticity of demand. His main contention was employment shifts do not result from changing final demand, but from differential productivity growth.

Siman Kuznets(1966) sees the driving force for changes in sectoral composition of output in differences in income elasticity of demand for products of different sectors, but caused by differential growth of productivity in different sectors. Changing structure of demand with increasing per capita income induces changes in production structure, but at the same time, changes in technological conditions of production and institutional arrangements necessitated by changes in location of production. Changes in population size also have significant influence on the pattern of these changes [Bela Kadar(Ed) 1984].

The pattern of structural changes that took place in India is fund to be different from the experiences of the present day developed countries. As per the study of TS Papola (2005), the most striking features of the structural changes in the Indian economy in recent decades have been the pre-eminence of service sector as the major contributor to growth. Industry, particularly manufacturing, which has observed historically to be the main contributor of growth, at least in the initial period of development has played only a minor role in India's economic growth in recent years. Thus it appears that Indian economy passes through a transition from agriculture to a service economy by passing industrial development and the growth path is characterized by services-led rather than industry-led growth. Another significant feature of the Indian economy is that the decline in employment share in agricultural sector is much lower than the decline in its output share. This pattern of structural changes may have implications for sustainability, and macro economic imbalances like incompatibility between production and consumption demand, employment, income inequalities etc., The pattern of structural changes and their implications especially for employment, that have been occurring in Andhra Pradesh may not be same as those observed at the All India Level. Let us examine the experiences of Andhra Pradesh in this regard

Table 1
The Sectoral Shares of NSDP (At Constant 1993-94 Prices) in Andhra Pradesh Economy

	Year			
Sector	*1980-81 to 1991-92*	*1991-92 to 2005-06*	*1981-82 to 2005-06*	*Chow Test Values*
Primary	2.20**	3.89*	3.02*	0.5629
Secondary	5.19*	5.96*	5.52*	2.6721
Tertiary	5.29*	7.83*	6.98*	11.8282
Economy as a whole	4.04*	5.96*	4.82*	4.9614

* Significant at the 1% level
** Significant at the 5% level

The structural changes in the economy of Andhra Pradesh at the major sectoral level and at the sub-sectoral levels are examined here in terms of the output shares, for the period 1980-81 to 2005-06. In 1980-81 the largest sector in the state was the Primary sector with a share of 43.7 percent in the NSDP and it was followed by Tertiary sector with a share of 37.2 percent and Secondary sector with a share of 18.7 percent. The dominance of the Primary sector continued up to 1985-86 and there after Tertiary sector turned out to be the major sector (Table 1). Although there have been some positive and negative year to year variations in the shares of these three major sectors of the economy, the overall trend is that there has been a decline in the contribution of Primary sector, and an increase of the Tertiary sector while the contribution of secondary sector remained more or less the same. By the year 2005-06, the contribution of the Primary sector to the total output declined to 27.79 percent, while the contribution of the Tertiary sector increased to 52.35 percent. The contribution of the Secondary sector increased only marginally to 19.86 percent.

Table 2
Trends in the Major Sectoral Incomes (At Constant 1993-94 Prices) in Andhra Pradesh Economy

	Period		
Sector	*1980-81 to 1991-92*	*1991-92 to 2005-06*	*1981-82 to 2005-06*
Primary	0.902399 (21.34)	1.16734 (19.57)	1.03315 (20.81)
Secondary	0.96749 (22.95)	1.19036 (19.95)	1.04606 (21.07)
Tertiary	2.28394 (56.55)	3.60862 (60.50)	2.88602 (58.13)
NSDP	4.038796 (100.00)	5.964023 (100.00)	4.964687 (100.00)

The changes in the relative sectoral contribution to NSDP are due to the differences in the rates of growth of output. During the study period, the output of the Primary sector grew at a rate of 2.7 percent (overall annual compound growth rate), Secondary sector grew at a rate of 5 percent and Tertiary sector grew at a rate of 6.2 percent. The "Chow – Test" confirms that there has been an improvement in the performance of all these sectors during the reform period. The rates of growth of output of Primary sector, secondary sector and Tertiary sector during the reform period are respectively 3.3 percent, 5.64 percent and 7.35 percent, while they were respectively, 2.2 percent, 5.19 percent and 5.79 percent during the post reform period. (Table.2)

The decomposition results of growth of output reveals that, to the 4.6 percent of NSDP growth rate, the Primary sectors contribution is 0.97 percent, (20.81%), Secondary sector contribution is 0.98 percent (21.06%) and the Tertiary sector contribution is 2.72 percent (58.13%). Thus Andhra Pradesh economy is a service sector–led growth economy and this characteristic feature of the economy has been further strengthened during the reform period. (Table.3)

Table 3
Sectoral Contribution to the Overall Growth of the State Economy

		Major Sectors		
Period	*Primary*	*Secondary*	*Tertiary*	*All Sectors*
		Employment		
1983-84	72.61	9.40	18.10	100.00
1993-94	65.42	13.23	21.35	100.00
2004-05	60.18	17.04	22.86	100.00
		Output		
1983-84	45.60	17.90	36.45	100.00
1993-94	38.02	18.8	43.21	100.00
2004-05	28.30	20.08	51.62	100.00

In the Primary sector the major sub-sector is Agriculture and Livestock with a contribution ranging between 88 percent and 79 percent. The major sub sector in the Secondary sector is the registered manufacturing, followed by unregistered manufacturing and construction. The contribution of these sub-sectors to Secondary sector income respectively varied between 37% and 45%, 24% and 34%, and 25%-34% during the study period. In the Tertiary sector, the major sub-sectors are Trade, Hotels and Restaurants with a contribution ranging from 29 percent to 34 percent and Real Estate and Ownership of Dwelling with a contribution ranging from 15 percent to 17.7

percent. Although the contribution of Banking & Insurance sector is relatively low, it has been the fastest growing sub-sector in the Tertiary sector during the study period. (Table.7)

STRUCTURAL CHANGES – SHIFTS IN EMPLOYMENT

Along with the shifts in output shares, employment shares may also occur. An attempt has been made here to study whether the employment shifts are in tune with shifts in output.

Table 4
Sectoral Shares of Employment* and Output in Andhra Pradesh

	Year			
Sector	*1980-81*	*1990-91*	*2000-01*	*2005-06*
Primary	43.7	37.5	33.1	27.8
Secondary	18.7	20.8	18.9	19.9
Tertiary	37.2	41.93	48.0	52.9

Source: CSO National Accounts Statistics,NSSO Surveys
• Usual principal and subsidiary status

As the NSSO employment data are available only for specific periods of time, output data are also considered for the same periods. Here the periods considered for studying the shifts are 1983-84, 1993-94 and 2004-05. In 1983-84, 72.61 percent of the total work force in the State was engaged in the Primary sector, whose contribution to the NSDP was only 45.60 percent. On the other hand the Tertiary sector with a contribution of 36.45 percent to NSDP engaged only 18.10 percent of the work force and the Secondary sector with a contribution of 17.90 percent, engaged 9.40 percent of work force. The participation of a disproportionately, large part of work force in agriculture is mainly responsible for the existence of high poverty levels and income inequalities in the State. The structural changes have been taking place in the state, and by 2004-05, the Primary sector shares of employment and income declined to 60.18 percent and 28.30 percent respectively (Table.4). Thus the decline in the share of income is much larger than the decline the share of employment indicating an increase in the distress of the people engaged in Primary sector. On the other hand, the Tertiary sector's shares of employment and income were increased during that period and the increase in income share was much higher than the increase in employment share indicating jobless growth in the sector. Contrary to this trend, in the Secondary sector, increase in employment share is found to be much higher than the increase in output share. Thus, the structural changes that have been taking place in the State with fast declining income share of agriculture with no corresponding decline in employment and the fast rising income share of the Tertiary sector with no corresponding increase in labour absorption may pose serious employment problems. Although the changes in the Secondary sector have positive employment, effects, its potentiality measured in terms of its contribution to NSDP, may not be sufficient to address the employment problems arising out of the changes in the Primary and Tertiary sectors.

THE SECTORAL EMPLOYMENT ELASTICITY'S AND OUTPUT GROWTH

To examine more closely the impact of structural changes on employment in the State, the employment elasticity's with respect to output and the growth of output at the major sectoral level and sub-sectoral level are analyzed here. The concept of employment used here is the employment in the public sector and private sectors including the employment in the units engage 10 or more workers. This employment data are drawn from the reports of the Statistical Abstracts of Andhra Pradesh. It covers the period 1990-91 to 2002-03. In 1990-91, the share of employment in the primary sector was 7.79 percent and it was 20.87 percent for Secondary sector and 63.34 percent for Tertiary sector. The overall trends in the employment shares of these three sectors were, a decline in the primary sector a continuous increase in the Tertiary sector, and Secondary sectors. By 2000-01, the share declined to 5.85 percent in the Primary sector, and increased to 64.53 percent in the Tertiary sector and 29.62 percent in Secondary sector. (Table.5). Thus Tertiary sector has emerged as major sector providing regular employment in the State.

Table 5
The Sectoral Shares of Employment in Public and Private Sectors in Andhra Pradesh

Year	*Employment*				*Output*			
	Primary Sector	*Secondary Sector*	*Tertiary Sector*	*Total*	*Primary Sector*	*Secondary Sector*	*Tertiary Sector*	*Total*
1990	7.79	28.87	63.34	100.00	39.68	19.00	41.32	100.00
1991	7.83	28.65	63.52	100.00	37.43	20.74	41.84	100.00
1992	7.62	29.44	62.94	100.00	37.49	20.03	42.48	100.00
1993	7.48	29.08	63.44	100.00	36.76	20.73	42.51	100.00
1994	7.11	29.12	63.77	100.00	38.01	18.78	43.21	100.00
1995	6.98	29.28	63.74	100.00	36.44	19.02	44.54	100.00
1996	6.85	29.43	63.72	100.00	36.60	19.47	43.93	100.00
1997	6.44	31.01	62.55	100.00	33.30	20.89	45.81	100.00
1998	6.23	30.21	63.56	100.00	30.32	22.17	47.51	100.00
1999	6.16	30.44	63.39	100.00	34.09	20.33	45.58	100.00
2000	5.92	30.28	63.80	100.00	31.64	20.34	48.02	100.00
2001	5.85	29.62	64.53	100.00	33.14	18.85	48.00	100.00

The results of the log-linear regression models of employment on output are presented in Table.6. The employment elasticity of the Primary sector is statistically significant and negative. A one percent increase in output leads to 0.39 percent decline in regular employment. The statistically significant negative response of employment to output is also found in the Mining and Quarrying sector. But in the major sub-sector of the Primary sector viz., "Agriculture, Hunting, Forestry and Fishing" employment is not responsive to the change in the output. All the sub-sectors in the Primary sector recorded a significant positive growth of output and the rate of growth is much higher in the Mining and Quarrying sub-sector, but it is only a jobless growth.

In the Secondary sector, employment elasticity is significant and positive. A one percent increases in output in this sector results in 0.40 percent increase in output. The employment-creating sub-sector in the Secondary sector is manufacturing. Its employment elasticity is 0.62. The employment creation in response to increase in output in the other sub-sectors in the Secondary sector is relatively low. But unfortunately the manufacturing sector is growing at a lower rate than the other sub-sectors within the Secondary sector. (Table.7)

Table 6
The Estimated Values of the Parameters of the Log-linear Regression of Employment on Output for Various Sectors in Andhra Pradesh

Sector	*a*	*b*	t_b	R^2	*F*	*Output Elasticity of Employment*
Primary Sector	6.78	-0.39	-5.91*	0.78	34.88	-0.39
Agriculture, Hunting, Forestry and Fishing	3.28	0.28	1.81	0.25	3.29	0.28
Mining and Quarrying	5.70	-0.23	-7.29*	0.84	53.18	-0.23
Secondary Sector	4.13	0.40	7.03*	0.83	49.42	0.40
Manufacturing	3.30	0.62	5.88*	0.78	34.54	0.62
Electricity, Gas and Water	4.46	0.05	1.81	0.25	3.27	0.05
Construction	6.17	-0.37	-5.98*	0.78	35.72	-0.37
Tertiary Sector	4.91	0.27	6.89*	0.83	47.55	0.27
Wholesale and Retail Trade, Restaurant and Hotels	4.11	0.12	1.59	0.20	2.54	0.12
Transport, Storage and Communications	4.78	0.19	2.03**	0.29	4.11	0.19
Financing, Insurance, Real Estate and Business Services	3.26	0.47	8.52*	0.88	72.56	0.47
Community, Social and Pension Services	4.88	0.27	8.36*	0.88	69.82	0.27

* Significant at the 1 percent level
** Significant at the 5 percent level
*** Significant at the 10 percent level

Table 7
Trends in the Growth of Sectoral Incomes of Andhra Pradesh 1980-81 to 2004-05

(in %)

Sector	*1980-81 to 1990-91*	*1990-91 to 2002-03*	*1980-81 to 2002-03*	*Chow Test Values*
Primary Sector	2.20**	3.89*	3.02*	0.57
Agriculture	2.3**	2.65	2.48*	5.09**
Forestry	0.22	0.41	1.71**	0.59
Fishing	1.05	7.7*	3.7*	100.21*
Mining and Quarrying	3*	9.04**	6.97*	17.41*
Secondary Sector	5.19*	5.96*	5.52*	2.67
Registered Manu.	8.7*	4.77*	5*	6.24*
Unregistered Manu.	2*	5.65*	3*	41.49*
Electricity, Gas.	41*	6.2*	20*	13.86*
Construction	3.9*	6.7*	5.2*	3.35
Tertiary	5.29*	7.83*	6.98*	11.83
Trade	6*	7.02*	6*	4.81**
Railways	4*	6.2*	6*	3.2
Storage	7	6*	8*	0.04
Communication	6.5*	19.4*	10.8*	109.04*
Banking	16*	10*	10.5*	19.44*
Real Estate	5*	5.5*	5.1*	5.36**
PAD	6*	6.2*	7.4*	4.09**
Other Services	2*	6.68*	4*	51.17**
Economy as a Whole	4.04*	5.96*	4.82*	4.96

* Significant at 1 percent level
** Significant at 5 percent level

In the Tertiary sector the employment elasticity is statistically significant and positive, but relative to Secondary sector it is lower. A one percent increase in the output of this sector leads to only 0.27 percent increase in employment. The employment elasticities are observed to differ across the sub-sectors in the Tertiary sector. Finance, Insurance and Real Estate is the only sub-sector in which the responsiveness of employment to output is high. In the other sub-sectors the employment elasticities are much lower. In regard to creation of employment in the state, a positive feature is that the output in the Finance, Insurance and Banking sub-sector is growing at a much faster rate relative to the other sub-sectors.

On the whole the changes that are taking place in the various sectors of the State economy are not conducive for creation of more employment. The major contributor to NSDP and its growth is Tertiary sector and its employment creation potentiality is relatively low. On the other hand, the Secondary sector with a relatively high potentiality for creating employment is growing at a relatively lower rate and its size in terms of contribution to NSDP is relatively low.

CONCLUSIONS

The type of structural changes taking place in the economy of Andhra Pradesh are a shift from primary sector to the tertiary sector by passing the Secondary sector, a pattern different from the experience of the present day developed countries where a shift took place from primary sector to Secondary sector, and then to Tertiary sector. The Tertiary sector is not only the major contribution to NSDP but also the fastest growing one. Although, the Secondary sector is also growing at a faster rate, its contribution to NSDP is rather low. The primary sector's contribution to NSDP is fast declining and its rate of income growth is also low. These changes indicate that Andhra Pradesh economy is a service sector led growth economy.

The study of sectoral employment in relation to income shares show that a disproportionately large work force is engaged in the primary sector and withdrawal of work force is not taking place in tune with the decline in its contribution to NSDP. It creates distress in the farm sector through the decline in incomes of the people engaged in agriculture.

The employment elasticity with respect to output is negative in the primary sector while it is positive in both the Secondary and Tertiary sectors. But the size of the coefficient is low in the fastest growing Tertiary sector. Therefore the growth of output taking place in the state economy may be a jobless growth and it is a serious cause of concern. The Secondary sector has more potential for employment creation in the State, but its size in terms of contribution to NSDP is rather low and it is also growing at a relatively lower rate. Therefore for strengthening the state economy through the creation of employment, the manufacturing sector, the major sub-sector in the Secondary sector, should be strengthened. In this connection, promotion of agro based industries and other small-scale enterprises assume importance. It also helps in the withdrawal of surplus labour from agriculture and strengthening agricultural sector.

REFERENCES

Siman Kuznets (Ed) (1966), "Modern Economic Growth Rate, Structure and Spread" Oxford & IBM Publishing Company, New Delhi

Bala Kadar (Ed) (1984), "Structural Changes in the World Economy", Akademiai Kiado Budapest

T.S. Papola (2005), "Emerging Structure of Indian Economy-Implications of Growing Inter Sectoral Imbalances"Presidential Address, 88th Annual Conference of Indian Economic Association, Dec 27-29, 2005

B.B. Bhattacharya & Arup Mitra (1990), "Excess Growth of Tertiary Sector in Indian Economy: Issues and Implications"Economic and Political Weekly, Nov-3

B.B. Bhattacharya & Arup Mitra (1997), "Changing Composition of Employment in Tertiary sector" Economic and Political Weekly, March-15

Ajit k. Ghose (2000), "The Employment Challenge in India"Economic and Political Weekly, April, 1

2

UNEMPLOYMENT: TIME FOR CONVERSION OF CURSE INTO COMMON-WEAL

A. Ranga Reddy

The paper highlights the place of unemployment in India, in general and Andhra Pradesh, in particular, and conversioning it into productive use in near future.

INTRODUCTION

Amartya Sen, Nobel laureate, felt that development can be seen as a process of expanding the real freedoms that people enjoy. Mugbul Huq' Pakistan economist, viewed that development is to create an enabling environment in which people can enjoy long, healthy and creative life. V.R. Panchamukhi observed that increasing role of market forces and competition, globalization etc will have to be suitably tempered so as give due consideration to the employment dimensions of development. The visionary perspective is India should achieve the full employment goal by 2020.[1]

Every household has to employ the people in positive productive use that State and Society has to support it.

UNEMPLOYMENT IN PARADOXICAL SITUATION IN ASIA

The latest 21st century development is that Asian countries will face emerging labour shortages and other social and economic consequences of their ageing workforces. Key challenge in these countries is to extend working life and enhance the employability of older workers through *lifelong learning* in such a way that promotes decent work at later stages in the life cycle, while also providing a mechanism for skills and knowledge transfer to the next generation of workers. Japan's labour force is projected to contract 7 *per cent* between 2006 and 2015 due to ageing[2].

Providing "gainful and high quality employment at least to addition to the labour force" is one of the monitorable targets of the Tenth Five Year Plan in India. However, in the first three years of the plan period (2002-005), the pace of creation of employment opportunities may not exceed the addition to the labour force. The Tenth Plan envisaged the creation of 50 million employment opportunities over the plan period, against a total addition to the labour force of 35 million persons. "Unemployment condition of a person who is able to work, is actively seeking work, but is unable to find any. Statistics on unemployment are collected and analysed by Government Labour Office in most countries and are considered an important indicator of economic health"[3].

DREAM OF MANMOHAN SINGH, PRIME MINISTER, ON EMPLOYMENT

India at 60 is a nation of young people. To realise our true potential, we must invest in the health and education of every child. We must create new employment opportunities for all, especially for the less privileged sections of society, and for those living in rural areas. We must eliminate the rural-urban divide in development indicators. We must also ensure that the process of industralisation generates enough jobs for our youth, in urban, semi–urban and rural areas. In the past 60 years, people moved to where work was available; in the next years, work must move to where people live[4].

SOLUTION OF UNEMPLOYMENT BY MAYAWATHI, CHIEF MINISTER, U.P

Mayavathi's gesture of extending voluntary reservations to the socially excluded is definitely need of the hour. It is a tragedy that even after 60 years of independence the State failed to address the basic needs of education and employment of a large segment of society, despite all claims of socialism and welfare. If implemented in right earnest, will go a long way in evolving a new India where no one will be seriously disadvantaged. In this direction ASSOCHAM – an industry Association has already created a corpus of Rs.5 crore for skill development and providing basic higher education to children from backward Communities, including SCs/STs. Over the past couple of months they have already imparted skill training to over 3,000 youth from these sections[5].

HUMAN CAPITAL AN UNRIVALLED RESOURCE

Educated, skilled, hardworking and English speaking managers, scientists, engineers and workers, represent the greatest strength of India. The Country has the youngest workforce of any large economy, a status that will be maintained for long. According to a recent World Competition year Book prepared by IMD, Switzerland, India ranks 11th among 60 nations in terms of the extent that the University education system meets the competitive needs of the economy in terms of availability of skilled labour, especially engineers, India ranks 7th. India was ranked first for availability of qualified engineers (China is 57th and US ranks 9th). India ranks among the top three of 30 nations in terms of availability of skilled labour [6].

EMPLOYMENT AND UNEMPLOYMENT IN INDIA

To the landless worker in an India village, of one of the world's most unfortunate individuals, unemployment is not even a misfortune. It is his normal fortune[7].

The National Sample Survey Organisation Survey, (NSSO) namely 61st round conducted during July 2004–June 2005 constitutes an important source of information on employment

Table 1
Employment and Unemployment in India (By Usual Principal Status)

	1983	*1993-94*	*1199-2000*	*2004-05*	*1983 to 1993-94*	*1993-94 to 1999-2000*	*1999-2000 to 2004-05*
	In Million				*Growth in Per cent Per Annum*		
Labour force	277.34	343.56	377.88	428.37	2.06	1.60	2.54
Work force	269.36	334.54	367.37	415.27	2.09	1.57	2.48
Number of unemployed	7.98	9.02	10.51	13.10	—	—	—
	As a Proportion of Labour Force in Per cent						
Unemployment rate	2.88	2.62	2.78	3.06			

Source: Government of India (2007) Economic Survey 2006-2007, P. 208.

and unemployment. The 61st round of the NSSO survey reveals a faster increase in employment during 1999–2000 to 2004–05 as compared to 1993–94 to 1999–2000. The following table analyses it.

The table 1 has proved that as labour force and workforce are rising, unemployment rate is also raising from 2.88 in 1983 to 3.06 in 2004-05, which is not significantly high. Female unemployment has increased both in rural and urban areas[8].

The share of agriculture in total employment has come down from 61.67 per cent in 1993-94 to 58.54 per cent in 1999-2000, and further to 54.19 per cent in 2004-05. With the declining share in agriculture in GDP, the scope for absorbing substantial additional labour force in agriculture appears limited. Employment in the organized sector, however, has decreased in 2001-2003 years in both Public and Private sectors[9]. Service sector employment opportunities are rising very fast in Indian economy than agriculture and Industry; as in advanced economies.

Employment and Unemployment in Andhra Pradesh

Labour force participation rates during the year 2004-05 increased when compared with 1999-2000. Labour force participation Rate of Andhraw Pradesh was higher when compared with all India. Which is presented in Table 2?

Table 2
Labour Force Participation Rates

	Andhra Pradesh			*India*		
Year	*Males*	*Females*	*Persons*	*Males*	*Females*	*Persons*
1999-2000 Rural	582	387	484	515	220	370
2004-05 Rural	586	399	492	531	237	387
1999-2000 Urban	517	158	341	528	123	335
2004-05 Urban	567	210	388	561	150	364

Source: Govt. of A.P. (22007) Socio-Economic Survey 2006-2007, P. 248

The Table 2 reveals that males and females labour Participation in rural Andhra Pradesh are found more than in all India rural level. Unfortunately, urban female labour participation is also higher than all India urban Population. This is a positive trend in Andhra Pradesh labour force.

RAISING WORKFORCE IN ANDHRA PRADESH

Work force participation rate among males and females in rural areas of Andhra Pradesh declined during 2004-05, when compared to 1999–2000. Whereas in urban areas of Andhra Pradesh, it was increased. Work force participation rates in general are high in Andhra Pradesh when compared with all India. Which is analyed in table 3?

Table 3
Work Force Participation Rates

	Andhra Pradesh			*India*		
Year	*Males*	*Females*	*Persons*	*Males*	*Females*	*Persons*
1999-2000 Rural	535	355	445	478	204	344
2004-05 Rural	528	350	439	488	216	355
1999-2000 Urban	480	144	315	490	111	309
2004-05 Urban	523	192	358	519	133	334

Source: Govt. of A.P. (2007) Socio-Economic Survey 2006-07, P... 249

The Table 3 explains that both rural and urban work force participation is higher than all India level. Unfortunately, in urban work force participation is very little higher than all India level.

UNEMPLOYMENT RATE ON DECLINE IN ANDHRA PRADESH

Higher the Unemployment rate leads to higher the violence and unrest in the Society. Naxalism is a bye product of it. Then violent organisation has emerged from this angle only. The uneven behaviour and Policy of employment also generated vengeance. Suppose upper caste got more jobs than BCs, SCs and STs. The unemployment gap between rural and urban also made Indian economy or Andhra Pradesh economy in an ugly and unfortunate situation. A.P.J. Abdul Kalam, formerly president often suggested public amenities for rural area (PURA) to fill the gap between rural and urban India. Caste and unemployment discrimination also added more woes in rural level. The following table gives a comprehensive picture of unemployment in State.

Table 4
Unemployment Rate (Current Daily Status)

	Andhra Pradesh			*India*		
Year	*Males*	*Females*	*Persons*	*Males*	*Females*	*Persons*
1999-2000 Rural	81	81	81	72	70	71
2004-05 Rural	100	122	109	80	87	82
1999-2000 Urban	72	89	76	73	94	77
2004-05 Urban	78	83	79	75	116	83

Source: Govt. of A.P. (2007) Socio-Economic Survey 2006-07, P. 251

The table 4 analyses that, in general, unemployment in rural and urban Andhra Pradesh is higher than all India level. At all India level, urban unemployment is found higher than Andhra Pradesh. It is found that in agriculture sector, women even prefer crop cutting, harvesting and some menial Jobs, whereas men like non-farm jobs, to get higher wage rates. This is the late transition in Andhra Pradesh Agriculture labour marketing.

DOMINANCE OF STATE IN PUBLIC SECTOR

Employment is a birth right of every citizen and constitutionally guaranteed. State should be more liberal in generating employment potential in private sector than public sector. Wage rates are to be enhanced to compensate their standard of living. The following table provides a bird's eye view of it.

Table 5
Employment in Public and Private Sectors in Andhra Pradesh

Years	*Public Sector*	*Private Sector*	*Total*
March 1966	656003	300738	956741
March 1976	933878	258391	1192269
March 1986	1259098	340339	1599437
March 1996	1464097	484580	1948677
March 2006	13,74,735	6,26,719	220,01,454

Source: Govt. of A.P. (2007) Socio-economic Survey 2006-07, P. 250

Table 5 denotes that Government of Andhra Pradesh in the last four decades consistently added more employees in public sector than private sector. Even after economic reforms 1991 also public sector was a leader in providing regular employment. Private sector offered only below fifty per cent in public sector. Comparing 7.5 crore population for the 2001 census, creating 20 lakh persons employment is highly insignificant. State has to encourage more rural private institutions for generating more size and quality employment.

NEW INITIATIVES OF ANDHRA PRADESH

The State computerized all Employment Exchanges by providing online services to the job seekers and employers. In view of slowly decreasing public employment, four new initiatives were taken up.

(a) 8670 candidates were placed under pre-recruitment training for Defense and Para– military forces during the year 2004 and 1052 up to September 2006.

(b) 1132 candidates were placed through *job melas* during 2004 and 1281 during 2005 and 1739 candidates in September 2006.

(c) 6554 candidates were guided under adoption of one Government High School and one Junior college in each district for providing career guidance to the students of terminal class during 2004 and 61,227 during 2005 and 24,109 candidates in September 2006.

(d) Training was arranged for 994 urban unskilled unemployed during 2004 and 609 during 2005 and 652 in September 2006.

When private sector was emerging in the State Private Employment Exchanges were also entered by taking premiums, especially Information Technology areas.

An overseas Manpower Company has been launched in Andhra Pradesh in March 2006 to help the unemployed youth and to bring Overseas Employers and the aspirants together. 2128 candidates have registered till 30th September 2006 at this company. Two programmes have been organised in English Language proficiency for the Job seekers desirous of going abroad. Two Malaysian Induction Training programmes have been organised by the Company so far for the Job seekers desirous of taking up job in Malaysia[10].

In 2006, Government of Andhra Pradesh introduced *"Udyogshree"*. In this connection, a Job *mela* was organized on August 19, 2007 to give employment for 6464 jobs. Around 40 thousand unemployed attended. Finally they failed to interview the candidates, because of organizational lapses[11].

Further State proposed an Employment Generation and Marketing Mission (EGMM) to provide employment to rural youth by constructing Transit homes in and around city. Specialized Training will be provided through 86 Industrial Training Institutes. The Mission will provide employment for 10 lakhs youth.[12]

SUGGESTIONS FOR REDUCING UNEMPLOYMENT

(a) It is right time to educate the girl child compulsorily first and make the family to trim it. It reduces population growth in long term.

(b) Under the globalization wave, agriculture is going towards Corporatisation and farmers are to be shareholders, especially marginal and small farmers.

(c) Special Economic Zones (SEZs) are indicators for transforming the disguised unemployed to productive employees and transferring the ownership and agriculture.

(d) Rural industries are to be promoted like Agri-business, Textile, and Dairy.

(e) Rural infrastructure facilities like *pucca* roads, power, education, health, water, transport, and internet are to be guaranteed.

(f) Rural greenery is to be promoted and protected i.e. eco-system at any cost. Mass afforestation programmes with wildlife protection are too encouraged at every village level.

(g) People participation through Non-governmental organizations, (NGOs) Voluntary Organizations, (V.O) Charity Trusts, Educational ad Health Institutions are encouraged, than State employees.

(h) State should play the role of low-maker and monitor only, than provider. Producer private sector is to be encouraged with proper guidelines.

(i) Unfair, dishonesty and corrupt practices are very much in Political hierarchy, outdated rule minded bureaucracy, intermediaries involvement at all levels have made the development into complex, not encouraged meritorious products to generate any innovative and inventive ideas.

(j) Quality Training Institutions are to be established and nurtured with incentives.

(k) Collaboration with foreign – institutions, investors, banks, industries are to be promoted.

(l) People are to be motivated as positive thinkers and workaholic in day to day life.

(m) Able bodied, skilled, professional employees should *have lifelong employment* opportunities like in Japan economy, to fill the generation gaps for making strong knowledge society.

(n) NEAP, IRDP, Self-employed programmes are strengthened and encouraged. Ethics ad *Nyaya panchayats* are to be established to oversee the development both inn rural and urban areas.

CONCLUSION

Development fruits should have to percolate to all sections of Society, especially rural. Through Quality education and training people are to be made workaholic. It is found that female empowerment and workforce is very low at all India level. As share of agriculture in the GDP is falling very sharply, the employment opportunities are also, fallen drastically. Andhra Pradesh is a leader in many economic indicators also fallen very low in creating employment. More unemployment is found in rural areas than urban even among women workforce. State has not encouraged employment potential in Private sector. State initiatives for generation of jobs are very insignificant. Rural development through people participation and NGOs, VOs is highly needed. Next sixty years, Jobs have to knock the door of the unemployed, convert chronic curse into commonweal.

NOTES

1. *Current Daily Status (CDS):* The CDS indicates the Unemployment status of a person without gainful employment and seeking employment during all the seven days in a week. The rate of unemployment is the ratio of unemployed days per week to the total labour supply per week.
2. *Labour Force Participation Rate:* (LFPR) Is defined as the number of persons in the labour force per 1000 persons. Persons categorized as working (employed) and those who are seeking or available for work (unemployed) together constitute labour force.
3. *Work Force Participation Rate (WFPR)*: Persons who were engaged in any economic activity constitute work force. The number of persons employed per 1000 persons
4. *Unemployee:* Persons who owing to lack of work has not worked but either sought through employment exchanges, intermediaries, making applications to prospective employers were considered as unemployed. Unemployment rate is defined as the number of persons unemployed per 1000 persons in the labour force.
5. *Types of Unemployment:* 1. Voluntary unemployment, 2. in voluntary unemployment, 3. Disguised unemployment, 4. Cyclical unemployment, 5. Seasonal unemployment and six. Frictional unemployment.
6. *Underemployment:* It is used to describe the situation of those who are able to find employment only for shorter than normal periods–for example, part-time workers and seasonal workers and may also describe the condition of workers whose education or training makes them overqualified for their jobs.
7. *Full employment:* Is conventionally defined not as zero unemployment but as that level of employment where unemployment has fallen to the irreducible minimum.

8. *PURA:* Providing Urban Amenities in Rural Area (PURA): APJ Abdul Kalam's intervention made to introduce this programme by Planning Commission at All India level in Tenth plan.

REFERENCES

1. V.R. Panchamukhi (2000), India: Vision 2020, 4th *Annual Conference of the Economic Association of Bihar*, May 27-29, p.19).
2. *Kyodo (2007), Japanese Labour Force to Shrink 7%*, The Economic Times, *Aug, 17, p.14)*
3. Britannica (2005), Britannica Ready Reference Encyclopedia, Vol.10, p.52.
4. Manmohan Singh (2007), India @ 60, *The Economic Times*, August 15, p.2
5. D.S. Rawat (007), Is UP Job Quota Policy Sensible ? *The Economic Times*, August 15, 2007, p.18.
6. G.Vijaya Raghavan and U.S.M. Nair (2007), The Great Indian Boom – The Renaissance of Manufacturing, *Manorama year Book 2007*, p. 48.
7. John Kenneth Galbraith (1958), The Affluent Society, Mentor Books, NewYork, p.91.
8. Planning Commission (2007), *Economic Survey* 2006-07, P. 208.
9. Planning Commission (2006), Mid-Term Appraisal of 10th Five Year Plan (2002-2007), p. 264)
10. Government of Andhra Pradesh (2007), Socio-economic Survey 2006-07, p. 161.
11. Correspondent (2007), Unemployed India, *Andhra Jyothi*, Chittoor edition, August 20, p.9
12. Correspondent (2007), Transit Homes for Rural Youth, *The Hindu*, August 21, p.4.

3

PROBLEMS OF UNEMPLOYMENT IN THE GLOBALIZING INDIAN ECONOMY

S. N. Tripathy

The Government of India (GOI) introduced economic reforms in 1991. The reforms were triggered by a balance of payments crisis continued with the need to correct an unsustainable high fiscal deficit. The reforms package included the abolition of industrial licensing for most industries, liberalization of rules pertaining to FDI and foreign technology agreements, disinvestments, privatisation, financial sector liberalisation, private investment in infrastructure and removal of restriction on trade. The purpose was to enable increased economic growth and existing reductions in controls and restrictions. The assumption was that this would lead to significant economic growth which finally will lead to poverty reduction.

In 1996, the working class of the world received an average 3% increase in wages while the heads of multinational corporations received a 67% increase. The five largest multinationals, mostly American, together earn more in a year than all the domestic earnings of India, Pakistan, and Bangladesh put together.

Governments have to cut expenditure on health care, education and even food subsidies. But at the same time, governments are offering multinationals lower taxes and subsidies such as reduced electricity rates. In sum, the "free" market economy of capitalism is not free at all – it is controlled to benefit only the rich at the cost of the poor. The breaking down of all barriers of the national boundaries has opened up the markets for the multinational enterprises. The impact of globalization has been widespread encompassing all segments of society and sectors of employment and work. Since most of the laborers fall under the broad category of working class, vulnerable sections, workers both in formal and informal sectors, it has been conceived that to reduce labour cost is possible compared to other costs on other inputs, cost minimization is done through pressure on labour costs. As a result, there has been decentralization of production, disparity in the distribution of wealth and income, decline in real wages, reduction of expenditure on social security, breakdown of joint family system, growing ownership in natural resources, institutionalization of corruption and violation of human rights.

IMPACT OF GLOBALIZATION ON LABOR AND EMPLOYMENT

Anyone who is able and willing to work but does not find work is involuntarily unemployed. India as a nation is confronted with massive problem of unemployment which has been a steadily rising after 1990's.

Table 1
Number Unemployed and Incidence of Unemployment in Rural Areas (1973-74 to 1999-2000)

	1973-74	*1974-78*	*1983-84*	*1987-88*	*1993-94*	*1999-2000*
Number of Unemployed (in millions)	3.98	7.14	5.95	9.14	7.49	9.15
Incidence of Unemployment (Percent)	1.64	2.58	1.93	2.74	1.96	2.25

Source: NSSO surveys on Employment and unemployment.

Thus, while both growth in labour force and employment registered a decline in the last 20 years and also in aggregate terms (and especially between 1993-94 and 1999-2000), the decline in the growth of employment outstripped decline in the growth of the labour force (Desai and Das, 2004, pp.3045-51).

Table 2
State-wise Number and Growth of Unemployed in India
(Dcs basis)

	'Number of Unemployment (CDS) (in million)	
States	*1993-94*	*1999-00*
Andhra Pradesh	2.13 (3)	2.66 (4)
Assam	0.60 (12)	0.67 (12)
Bihar	1.86 (4)	2.38 (5)
Gujarat	0.98 (8)	0.90 (11)
Haryana	0.37 (13)	0.29 (15)
Karnataka	0.97 (9)	0.98 (9)
Kerla	1.64 (7)	2.36 (6)
Madhya Pradesh	0.94 (10)	1.34 (8)
Maharashtra	1.72 (5)	2.68 (3)
Orissa	0.88 (11)	0.95 (10)
Punjab	0.23 (15)	0.34 (14)
Rajasthan	0.26 (14)	0.65 (13)
Tamilnadu	2.91 (1)	3.09 (2)
Uttar Pradesh	1.64 (6)	2.13 (7)
West Bengal	2.46 (2)	3.99 (1)
All. India*	19.58	25.41
All India**	20.24	26.44

Notes:
* Implies all India consisting of 15 major states only;
** Implies all India considering all states and territories.
Figures in parenthesis are ranks among 15 major states.

It is found that the growth rate of employment for the period 1987-88 was 2.03, which further declined to 0.58 percent in 1993-94 as per NSSO data. Also, it has been observed that at the All India level, number of unemployed on current daily status basis has increased from 19.5 million during 1993-94 to 26.44 million in 1999-2000(Table No.2). The planning commission has estimated that unemployment rate for the economy as a whole has increased from 8.87 to 9.11 percent in 2004-05.

The annual growth rate of unemployment during the period 1993-94 to 1999-200 has been estimated as 4.5 percent. The vast majority of unemployed have been from rural areas in India. The share of rural unemployed was 73 percent during 1999-2000 in India. States like Bihar, Orissa, Andhra Pradesh, Assam, West Bengal, Kerla, Rajasthan, Haryana, Gujarat and Tamilnadu are reported to have more than 70 percent of rural unemployment in India (Bhaumik, S.K, 2003).

EMPLOYMENT AND ITS GROWTH IN INDIA

Employment and its growth in various sectors have been exhibited in table No.3. It is revealed from the table that next to agriculture, though manufacturing sector provides substantial employment has not indicated desired growth. Along with other Sectors manufacturing sector should be accorded priority as a vital source of employment. It is further revealed from the table No.3 that there has been a decline in self-employment and an increase in casual employment during the period 1993-2000

The proportion of regular salaried employment has remained more or less unchanged. An increasing trend of Casuals employment has been depicted during the period under review. This phenomenon of increasing casual employment is because of non-availability of regular employment as well as their incapability of being absorbed in self-employment. Further, with the abundant supply of labour and extremely limited scope of organized sector employment, the employers will be in a position to employ at a lower wages.

The macro data clearly demonstrates that the unskilled labour absorption in future is more likely to take place in this sector in the absence of increase in organized sector employment. The usual status unemployment among the rural youth with secondary education and above was estimated at 12.5% (Radhakrishna, 2002).

Table 3
Employment and Growth by the Sectors

	Employed Workers (million)		
Industry	*1999-00*	*1983*	*1993-94*
Agriculture	207.23	242.46	237.56
Mining & quarrying	1.76	2.70	2.27
Manufacturing	34.03	42.50	48.01
Electricity	0.85	1.35	1.28
Construction	6.78	11.68	17.62
Trade,	19.22	27.78	37.32
Transport, storage &Common	7.39	10.33	14.69
Financial services	1.70	3.52	5.05
Community, social & personal services	23.80	32.13	33.20
Total Employment	302.76	374.45	397.00

Source: NSSO surveys on Employment and unemployment

There is wide spread concern that the acceleration in GDP growth in the post reforms period has not accompanied by a commensurate expansion in employment. Because of withdrawals from the public sector, there will be slow expansion of employment leading to a rise in unemployment rates.

Besides, relevance of unemployment among educated females in rural areas is about three times more than that of their male counterparts, presumably due to limited chances being open to them for migration to urban areas for securing employment.

Though women are increasingly employed in the post-reform period but they are by and large employed in low skill jobs, usually non-unionized, and experience adverse working conditions like low wages and long working hours (Dev, Mohendra 2000).

The characteristics features of the structure of the female work force in the nineties are an increasing feminization of the urban work force on account of an increased WPR for urban women, a declining share for women in rural non-farm employment largely in community and other services (Kalpagam, 2001).

UNEMPLOYMENT IN AGRICULTURE IN RURAL INDIA

In rural India the deplorable fact is that due to the inadequacy of employment opportunities, scarcity of land, over dependence on agriculture, dependent on the gambling of monsoon; resulting in disguised unemployment declines in agricultural productivity.

Thus, agriculture in India provides seasonal employment to our population and as a result, the agricultural workers compete in the labour market in the informal services sectors. As a matter of fact the marginal product of labour determines their wages, but marginal product of labour depends largely on the efficiency of the technology and on the land- to- labour ratio. Any change that would move labour from agriculture to other sectors would increase the land-to-labour ratio in agriculture and thus, ameliorate their economic conditions. Appropriate technologies with their enormous potentialities in enhancing the productivity of agriculture-based enterprises would help in creating employment opportunities. But over the years there has been decline in village industries on the wake of globalization and strong competitions at global level has made it a great problem for their survival and continuation.

A comparative analysis of NSS employment-unemployment surveys for 1993-94 and 1999-2000 reveals that between these periods, there has been a significant decline in the crude worker population ratio resulting in a slower growth of workforce relative to the growth in population and an absolute reduction in the number of women workers in rural India.

In terms of labour productivity, except for the construction sector, the gross value added per worker has grown significantly with a 6% per annum growth in the economy as a whole. This significant growth in labour Productivity has translated into an equally significant and wide spread growth in daily average wage earnings of casual wage labourers in rural India. In turn, this growth in real wage earnings has been significant to more than offset a reduction in the crude worker–population ratio to raise average wage earnings per capita at over 2.5% per annum in rural India during the period 1993-94 to 1999-2000.

Given the predominance of the agricultural Sector in the national economy in terms of employment, a meaningful employment strategy for rural India should accord high priority to the development of agriculture and allied rural sectors. In our country, 55% of population depends for their livelihood on agricultural sector, though this sector provides barely one-fifth of the GDP.

Deceleration in the growth of employment during post-liberalization period from 1993-94 to 1999-00 has not been uniform across sectors of the economy. An important development that has been manifested is the sharp decline in employment growth in agriculture during 1990s (Table 4).

Rapid agricultural growth generally triggers a higher growth in output and employment in non-farm sectors. In India, the emergence of numerous growth poles, including corridors of development along highways, and above all, public expenditure on anti-poverty and other rural development programmes and on rural infrastructure have been playing instrumental role in increasing output and employment in non-farm sectors.

This positive achievement in terms of rising productivity in agriculture and the process of diversification away from agriculture have been slow and halting. As has been evident from the table No 4, that from 1972-73 to 1999-2000, the share of agricultural labourers in the total labour force has declined only marginally from 73.9% to 60.2 %.

There are several reasons for the near brink of employment growth during 1990s in agriculture. One of the important factors was a sharp deceleration in the growth rate of agriculture in general and crop production in particular. The second reason for the decline of employment in agriculture is increasing capitalization.

On the contrary, in rural area, the non-agricultural sector has recorded a higher growth rate in employment than agriculture. Growth rate of employment in the non-agricultural sector was appreciably higher than that in agriculture over the period from 1972-73 to 1999-00. As a result, manufacturing, trade, transport and other service sectors have been emerging as important sources of rural employment.

Table 4
Growth Rates of Population, Workers (Employment) & Labour Force in Rural India

	2000-1994	*1994-83*	*2000-83*	*2000-1978*	*2000-1973*
Population	*1.956*	*2.103*	*2.049*	*2.077*	*2.088*
Workers (employment)					
(a) UPS	1.557	2.105	1.905	1.919	Na
(b) UPSS	1.030	2.037	1.670	1.789	1.936
No. of unemployed					
(a) UPS	1.363	2.095	1.828	-0.247	Na
(b) UPSS	1.482	3.316	2.645	1.138	3.136
Labour force					
(a) UPS	1.551	2.105	1.903	1.842	Na
(b) UPSS	1.040	2.063	1.690	1.774	1.960

Source: NSSO surveys for 1972-73, 1977-78, 1978, 1987-88, 1993-94 and 1999-2000.

Na: Not available

With farming fast becoming increasingly less rewarding than other sectors, farming households are likely to release an increasingly large share of workers every year for non-agricultural activities. After a long period of job shedding, the manufacturing sector has been expanding but to remain competitive against global manufacturers this sector has had to drop prices while becoming more cost and labour efficient. The services sector contributing 55% of the GDP has been considered for scope of employment but here too, competitive advantage in the sphere of education and skill will play a big role in determining employability.

Table 5
Employment Scenario in Indian States (CDS Basis)

Selected States	*Employment (,000) 1999-00*	*Employment Growth 1993-94 to 1999-00 (% p.a.)*	*Unemployment Rate 1999-00 (%)*	*Unemployment Rate 1993-94 (%)*	*Gdp (% per annum) 1993-94 to 1999-00*
Andhra Pradesh.	30614	0.35	8.03	6.69	5.2
Assam	7647	1.99	8.03	8.03	2.7
Bihar	30555	1.59	7.32	6.34	4.5
Gujarat	18545	2.31	4.55	5.70	7.3
Haryana	5982	2.43	4.77	6.51	5.8
Himachal Pradesh.	2371	0.37	2.96	1.80	7.1
Karnataka	20333	1.43	4.57	4.94	7.6
Kerala	8902	0.07	20.97	15.51	5.5
Madhya Pradesh	28725	1.28	4.45	3.56	4.7
Maharashtra	34979	1.25	7.16	5.09	5.8
Orissa	11928	1.05	7.34	7.30	4.0
Punjab	8013	1.96	4.03	3.10	4.6
Rajasthan	19930	0.73	3.13	1.31	7.0
Tamil Nadu	23143	0.37	11.78	11.41	7.1
Uttar Pradesh	49387	1.02	4.08	3.45	5.5
West Bengal	22656	0.41	14.99	10.06	7.3
All India	336736	1.07	7.32	5.99	6.7

Source: Planning Commission

However, agricultural growth ought to act as an important engine of growth for other sectors of the economy, especially in rural areas. Thus, for rural employment a policy packages should be aimed at: a) Accelerating the rates of sectoral and national economic growth) Reversing the trend of deceleration of agricultural growth and public investment in agriculture, c) Promotional policies for labour intensive and higher income generating allied agriculture and non-agricultural activities in rural areas for domestic markets, and d) Diversification of agriculture towards hitherto neglected dry land areas in central and eastern regions are highly imperatives in order to boosting up agricultural production and rural employment and finally, assaulting on rural poverty.

It goes without saying that increased concern for human rights has provided a momentum for increased access to information right to work and abuses for denial of rights. If human welfare is the ultimate goal of development, providing basic human needs for all and guarantying decent work for the poor laborers must be the fundamental objectives. There should be rethinking about right in the context of work. The realization of rights in a broader economic, social and political context of development has emerged (Nayyar, 2003, pp.11-12)

Globalization and Working Poor/Agricultural Labourers

India, characterized by pervasive poverty (300 million below the poverty line) has been implementing several poverty alleviation programmes over the passed decades. These programmes have been in the form of "Garibi Hatao" (eradicate poverty), self-employment creation (SEC), Food for Work (FFW), asset building programmes and wage employment creation (WEC) programmes. These programmes were mainly targeted towards the poor or very poor families on the basis of income threshold. However, a feature of most programmes is that they are financed by the state and, as such, periodic funding inadequacies often lead to either abandonment or reduced effectiveness of the schemes. However, with the onset of globalisation the resource allocations to these programmes in real terms are badly hit (Streeten, 2001, p.56). There is now substantial evidence that India's success at reducing the incidence of poverty during the 1970s and 1980s was halted, if not reversed, during the globalisation era of 1990s. Estimates made at the World Bank show that the incidence of poverty, which between 1972-73 and 1989-90 fell from 55.5 per cent to 34.3 per cent in rural India and from 54.3 to 34.1 per cent nationally, has in subsequent National Sample Survey (NSS) rounds, up to 1997 (when the incidence was 34.2 per cent national and 35.8 per cent rural) never gone below the 1989-90 level and has in fact risen to much higher levels in individual years. These estimates made from time to time indicate that the gap between rural and urban areas, which had decreased during the 1980s and the 1970s, increased considerably during the 1990s (Streeten, 2001, p.73)

In addition to the decline in the purchasing power of the incomes of the rural poor, the rate of growth of per capita rural income in real terms has sharply decelerated. This fall in rural income is, however, not just because the share of agricultural income in national income has fallen. The share in non-agricultural incomes in total rural incomes, which rose sharply between 1977-78 and 1990-91, has stagnated since then. The reason behind all this is the inefficiency and corrupts practices inherent in the governance system of the Indian Government, which does not enhance productivity, competitiveness and development.

Given that India accounts for about a third of the world's absolute poor, the nature of her integration with the international economy has critical implications for liberalization and globalisation reducing world poverty. India can be described as a relatively large, closed or protected economy, in the threshold of industrialization, with trade and foreign investment plating a limited role, low per capita income, and a significant agrarian sector, marked by sharp inequality.

The issue of poverty and inequality is far more important for India both because of the alarming and overwhelming proportion of the population living below the poverty line (however measured) and also because inequality halting growth usually leads to the self-perpetuation of a low-level equilibrium. In regard to the distributive effect in particular, economists are worried over a noticeable empirical phenomenon that suggests a considerable decline in the income of unskilled labour and/or a decline in their employment relative to the more skilled segment of the work force (Acharya and Marji, 2000)

Under the globalization, policies such as trade liberalization, cutbacks in price supports and subidies for food producers, privatization of credit, commercialization of agriculture, excessive export promotion and promotion of research in expensive technologies such as genetic engineering etc., undercut the economic viability of the smaller and poorer farmers. The onslaught of these policies adversely affects the small farmers leading to high failure rates, sell-offs, increased landlessness, land concentration, even intensified land degradation, and rural-urban migration.

One of the major adjustment mechanisms to the agrarian crisis by the poor peasantry and rural labour could be seen in the form of distressed migration to urban centers and nearby cities without social security provisions, which have serious implications for rural labour. Moreover, factors like demographic pressure, low land men ratio, uncertain monsoon, poverty of the farmers, low infrastructure and global competition etc., have resulted in deterioration in agricultural income of the farmers. This has been evident from the fact that during 1990s the proportion of rural labour among the rural poor increased from 49 per cent to 54 per cent. The distress in the agricultural sector resulting in under-employment and unemployment has its adverse impact on wages too.

The suicides of thousands of farmers around the country tell poignant and revealing tales of our country, and the desperation that marks the lives of so many millions. Disastrous policies, woeful access to affordable credit, greedy and corrupt middlemen, and indifferent administrations are among the factors that have pushed farmers to their breaking point. Thus, as an impact of globalization, an agrarian crisis particularly in cotton growing regions of Andhra Pradesh, Karnataka, and Maharashtra in India, has precipitated a spate of suicide death among farmers. This has been of public policy concern and therefore, the present study based on secondary sources of data makes an effort to analyze various socio-economic aspects to understand processes and identify risk factors which would help in formulating policy suggestions.

To this magnitude human problem of farmers' suicide, WTO trade negotiators should exhibit their sensitiveness with the commitment to redress the problem. It has been recognized that removing state support to agriculture and diluting import restrictions in developing countries during the last 15 years has led to degradation of farming, instead of accelerating growth and development especially in India. Between the period 1996-97 and 2003-04, agricultural imports have hiked by 270 per cent by volume and 300 per cent in value terms. A food surplus economy has been transferred to be an importer of food has been a dangerous signal, because the latter has adverse effect on balance of payment situation and likely to aggravate the problem of unemployment.

A critical analysis of post-globalization scenario reveals that the root of the problem is 'jobless growth' in the Indian economy, that is, despite acceleration in the growth rate in India; the pace of creation of work opportunities has not kept pace with the growing requirement. In the post-globalization period, unemployment on a Current Daily Status basis rose from 6.0 percent in 1993-94 to 7.3 percent in 1999-2000 resulting in an additional 27 million job seekers. The most disturbing fact is that of these, 74 percent are in the rural areas and 60 percent among them are educated. There is substantial decline in employment elasticity (e.g. increase in employment for every unit rise in GDP) in almost all the major productive sectors, except for transport and finance. In agriculture, the employment elasticity has dropped to near zero. The reason for the phenomenon of jobless growth could be that growth in India has essentially been capital intensive. Further, the public sector is in the process of shedding excess labour in the name of downsizing for meeting the efficiency challenges of market competition.

Team Lease Services in its 'India Labour Report 2006' says by 2020, if the current trends of employment generation continue, India will face an "unemployment explosion" with substantial negative socio-economic ramifications. There will be over 211 million unemployed in 2020, which works out to an unemployment rate of 30 per cent. Unemployment will largely be a youth problem: nine out of 10 unemployed people will be in the 15 to 29 age bracket. India's working population in 2020 will be equal to India's total population (846 million) when economic reforms started in 1991. The report further says that the potential working age population in the 20 to 59 years group in 2020 is estimated to be over 761 million. About half of all Indians (about 567 million in 2006) currently fall into the 20 to 59 age bracket, which in itself is no small advantage. And this segment is increasing by 2.4 per cent every year. But, in 2020, in terms of the share of this group in our total population; we are looking at a working age population of 56 per cent of the total estimated population of 1.35 billion. The overall labour force that will come up in 2020 will be around 716 million.

Recently, the global economic slowdown has it's deter mental impact on Indian economy despite its resilience. There has been deceleration in exports of labour intensive products, particularly textiles, leather, marine products, carpets, sports goods and handicrafts during 2007-08 as compared to the previous year. The situation is unlikely to get better in the current year with other segments too tottering. RBI data, up to March 2007, indicate there are more than 1.14 laky sick micro and small enterprises. And from 2006 up to August 2008, nearly 280 units have closed down rendering at least 12,000 people jobless.

The growth in domestic industry is reported to be poor with a negative central excise collection of minus 3.8% recorded for the quarter ending September. The lower excise collection came soon after results of the Index of Industrial Production (IIP) pointed a 10-year low in growth of industrial output based on the results for August. The industrial growth, measured in terms of IIP, came down from 11.6% in 2006-07 to 8.3% in 2007-08 which led to a slower growth in the capital goods sector that makes equipment consumed by other sectors.

Both the intermediate and consumer goods sector witnessed massive downfall. While the intermediate goods came down to 8.9% in 2007-08 from 12% the previous year, consumer goods fell a steep 6.1% from 10.1%. Another major employment generating sector, the information technology and BPO industry, has reported slower growth with many banking and financial companies in US and European countries going bust or reporting massive financial crunch

Policy Paradigms

A strong basic education system has been necessary preconditions to undermining India's efforts to enhance further the productivity and efficiency of its economy (Singh & Sagar, 2004). Investments in basic education are thus crucial for improving the productivity and quality of labour and deliver the manpower needed for their development efforts (Singh, 1997)

This has been emphasized because economic growth is not only a function of capital formation but also of investment in human capital. South Asian countries like Sri Lanka, Singapur, Hongkong, Malaysia, and Korea have adopted appropriate policy and made remarkable success in eradicating human deprivation and creating human capabilities. These countries underwent social transition because of noteworthy progress in the sphere of education, health, sanitation and water supply. Human capabilities enhance increased participation of people in production and thus, establish synergic relationship between rural development and social development. In the context of globalization, we need to emphasize on twin factors like education and health, which will not only create an enormous potentialities for our knowledge economy but also leads to gain from the process of globalization.

With regard to adverse impact of globalization on farm labour, as we know, the farmer's problem has been rooted in his exposure to risk–yield as well as price shocks. Insurance schemes may be devised to mitigate these. Credit insurance can look into the credit default. Policy packages like management of water, control of excessive use of fertilizers, intercropping, integrated pest management, organic farming, non-farm employment–mostly agro based to augment the income of the farmers will go a long way in mitigating the problem of farmers' suicides.

In the context of the global economic slowdown hitting employment, which has deepened because of government's deceleration in labour intensive segments as revealed from the in recent data, there is a need to evolve a suitable policy strategy to tackle the grim situation. The on-going employment schemes like NREGA should have effective delivery mechanism and corruption should be dealt stringently. In view of the above-facts, for creating employment in agricultural sector, we need to develop indigenous technology, raise non-farm employment, sustainable development of agriculture, integrated pest management, development of competitive skills, employment in horticulture sector, biotechnology and other related activities for rural livelihood supports. .

REFERENCES

Bhaumik, S.K (2003), Unemployment in India in the Post Liberation Era, *The Journal of Labour Economics*, Vol.46, No.1, p.726

Desai, Sonalde and Das, Maitreyi Bordie (2004), Is Employment Driving India's Growth Surge? A Reality Check, *Economic and Political Weekly*, vol.27, July 3-9, pp.3045-515

Kalpagam, U (2001), Globalisation, Liberalization and Women Workers in the Informal Sector, in Amitabh Kundu and Alakh N. Shrma edited, "*Informal Women Labour in India*" Institute for Human Development, New Delhi.

Mohendra Dev, S (2000), Economic Liberalization and Employment in South Asia-i&ii, *Economic and Political Weekly*, vol.35, Nos.1, 2&3

January 8- 15, pp.40-51 and pp.135-147

Nayyar, Deepak (2003), Work Livelihoods and Rights, *the Journal of Labour Economics*, Vol.46, January- march, pp.11-12

Radhakrishna, R (2002), Agricultural Growth, Employment and Poverty: A Policy Perspective, The *Journal of Labour Economics*, Vol.45, No.1, p.9

Rajat Acharya and Sugata Marji (2000), "Globalisation and Inequality":, EPW, 23 September, p. 3503

Singh, Surjit and Sagar, Divyashi (2004), "Education, Human Capital and Labour Market: Some Regional Features", the Indian Journal of Labour Economics, October-December.

Singh, Surjit (1997), "Issues in Indian Educational Development", Anvesak, Vol. 27, No.1-2, p.p. 125-137

Streeten Paul, "Globalisation: Threat or Opportunity", Copenhagen Business School Press, 2001

4

RURAL UNEMPLOYMENT: CHALLENGES AHEAD

I. Satya Sundaram

Employment is the primary source of livelihood for the majority, particularly in their rural areas. How to create productive employment on a sustainable basis is the real challenge facing our planners and policy makers. In India, rural employment matters because 70 per cent of the population lives in rural areas.

Growing unemployment has serious implications from the point of view of growth. According to the ILO, If we can reduce the youth unemployment rate by just half, we will add at least $ 2-2 trillion to the global economy".*,

This paper has been divided into two parts: (i) Rural Unemployment: Current Trends; and (ii) Rural Unemployment: Measures Needed.

RURAL UNEMPLOYMENT: CURRENT TRENDS

There has been a significant decline in wage employment in general but a substantial rise in self-employment among all categories of workers in India. The increase has been sharpest among rural women where seif employment now accounts for nearly two-thirds of all jobs.

The over-all rate of growth of employment per annum declined in the post- liberalisation phase, but the decline was faster in the case of women than men. For rural males, it declined from 1.94 per cent during 1983 to 1993-94 to 0.94 per cent during 1993-94 to 1999-2000, and for females, it went down from 1.41 per cent to a mere 0-15 per cent. Whatever addition to female employment has taken place during this period ha largely been confined to the informal sector.

Of course, there is some improvement in recent years, During the period, June 2000 to December, 2002, employment growth has been over 2 per cent per annum, with an average of 8-4 million jobs added per year, as revealed by the preliminary results of the 58" Round Survey of NSSO.

According to the 60th round survey conducted by NSSO, the unemployment rate in urban areas was more than double the rate in rural areas during January - June, 2004. While it was 2.3 per cent for the rural areas, it was 5.3 per cent in the urban areas. But, the urban workers are better placed in terms of monthly per capita expenditure (MPCE). Whi91e 57 per cent of urban households had MPCE of Rs-775 or more, the corresponding figure for rural areas was 15 per cent less.

The latest NSS data shows that employment growth at 2.5 per cent outpaced the growth rate of population between 1999 to 2005. However, this was also accompanied by a deceleration of real wages among the regular rural and urban workers.

Based on current daily status, rural unemployment rate for males increased from 7.2 per cent in 1999-2000 (55th Round of NSSO) to 8.0 per cent in 2004-2005 (61s1 Round). In the case of females, it increased from 7.0 per cent to 8.7 per cent. II. Rural Unemployment: Measures Needed the ILO lays stress on promotion of entrepreneurship, innovation and productivity, small enterprise and training of workforce.

Of course, there is some diversification of the agricultural sector, and the entire rural economy, a result of this, the share of non-farm sector employment rose from about 14 per cent in 19977-78 to nearly 24 percent in 1999-2000.

There are many sectors and sub-sectors which have high employment potential which needs to be exploited- For instance, food-processing is very important in the context of diversification of Indian agriculture. Tourism has strong backward and forward linkages. According to reliable estimates, tourism alone can generate more than 20 million additional Jobs within a decade.

We have been implementing employment (wage employment as well as self employment) generating programmes in rural areas, but the results are not encouraging. The delivery mechanism is weak. In addition, the incidence of leakages is high- The special schemes should form an integral part of the block plan so as the enhance to quantum of productive assets. Also, the schemes should be concentrated in the more depressed regions where poverty is endemic rather than in all area of the country.

The labour force available in rural areas is mostly unskilled. In the context of globalisation, the demand for skilled labour increases- The problem of skill obsolescence needs to be tackled carefully. The stress should be on continual reselling through retraining.

Rural infrastructure needs our immediate attention. Studies show states with better infrastructure support exhibit lower poverty as also greater non-farm employment opportunities.

Rural prosperity is the key to economic growth in India. Top priority should therefore be given to diversification of agricultural sector, and also the entire rural economy. Agri-business and bio-energy can change the status of rural India. With better irrigation facilities, farmers can have two or three crops. This also enhances the employment of the farm sector.

Rural development offers many employment opportunities. But, rural schemes should be so designed that the assets created should strengthen the rural economy. Also, rural real wages should be kept at a reasonable level.

REFERENCES:

ILO (2006), Global Employment Trends Brief.

Gopal Prasad (2007), Employment: Recent Trends, YoJana, May, p.50.

Manish Sabharwal (2007), Create A Ministry of Employment, Business Standard, June.

—(2005), Business Standard, November, 22.

M.K.Venu (2007), Don't Ignore the New Aspiring Class, The Economic Times, March.

—(2007), Ministry of Finance, Government of India: Economic Survey 2006-2007, p.210.

—(2006), I-L.O : op.cit.

Arvind Singhat (2004): Jobless Growth. Business Standard, March. 20/21.

I.Satya Sundaram (1984): Anti-Poverty Rural Development in India, B.R.Publishing Corporation, New Delhi.

Alakh N.Sharma (2004), Globalisation, Labour Markets and Poverty: Energing Perspectives in India, D.T. Lakdawala Memorial Lecture, 87th Conference of the Indian Economic Association, Banaras Hindu University, Varanasi, December, 21.

Rahav Gaiha and Vani S Kulkarni (2007), Non-Farm Employment and Poverty Reduction, Business Standard, April, 26.

5

SOME DIMENSIONS OF UNEMPLOYMENT IN INDIA

P. Kothandarami Reddy

NATURE OF UNEMPLOYMENT

Unemployment in India is a major economic and social problem. It is the root cause of absolute poverty of the masses. But the nature and character of unemployment in India is quite different from that of an advanced industrial economy like the U.K. or the U.S.A. According to Keynes involuntary unemployment in such an economy is caused by deficiency in aggregate demand. He, therefore, advocated demand inducing fiscal policy for economic stabilization. But in underdeveloped economies unemployment is caused by capital deficiency and choice of capital biased technologies which are growth oriented. Therefore, a different policy framework is needed to counter the unemployment problem. In rural areas, unemployment is disguised rather than open, seasonal rather than perennial. The rural social structure tends to provide a sort of social security for the unemployed which is utterly lacking in the advanced industrial countries. We may say that unemployment is caused by technological factors in those countries and therefore it is frictional unemployment or technological unemployment. In underdeveloped countries like India it is more structural rather than technological. In the modern urban sector there is open unemployment like the one witnessed in industrial countries. In this context it is proposed to discuss some dimensions of unemployment in India.

EMPLOYMENT STRUCTURE

The structure of the employment in any economy reveals its economic status and indicates its economic development. Table 1 gives the distribution of workers by category of employment.

Table 1
Percentage Distribution of Workers by Category of Employment

Category	*1972-73*	*1983*	*1993-94*	*1999-2000*
Self employment	61.4	57.3	54.8	52.9
Regular Salaried employment	15.3	13.8	13.2	13.9
Casual wage employment	23.3	28.9	32.0	33.2
Total	100.0	100.0	100.0	100.0

Source: NSSO Surveys

It can be seen from table 1 that there is a decline from 61 to 53 percent in the proportion of self-employed during the 17 years period. There is also a marginal decline from 15 to 14 percent of regular salaried employment. There is a corresponding increase in the casual wage employment from 23 to 33 percent. The increase in casual wage employment is an index of capitalist development in Indian economy. The decline in self-employment was converted into casual labour. Since the casual labour is not associated with job security and associated benefits generally increase in the proportion of casual labour is treated as an index of deterioration in the quality of employment.

UNEMPLOYMENT ESTIMATES

(i) Chronic unemployment or usual principal status (UPS) employment is measured in number of persons i.e., persons who remained unemployed for a major part of the year. This measure is more appropriate to those in search of regular employment e.g., educated and skilled persons who may not accept casual work. This is also referred to as 'open unemployment'.

(ii) Weekly status unemployment (measured in number of persons) i.e., persons who did not find even an hour of work during the survey week.

(iii) Daily status unemployment (measured in person days or person years, i.e., persons who did not find work on a day or some days during the survey week.

The weekly status and daily status unemployment estimates bring out the seasonal and part-time unemployment and under-employment effectively. These represent the average number of person unemployed per week and per day respectively during the survey period. Daily status unemployment is considered to be the most inclusive and significant indicator of the magnitude of unemployment.

Table 2
Magnitude and Rate of Unemployment in India

		1980		
Category	*1977-78%*	*Millions*	*%*	*1999-2000%*
Usual status	4.23	12.02	4.48	–
Weekly status	4.48	12.18	4.54	–
Daily status	8.18	20.74	7.84	7.32
Total labour force		268.05		

Source: Sixth and Tenth Five Year Plans

From the data given in table 2 it is obvious that no serious dent has been made into the problem of unemployment. Nearly 12 million persons fall in the category of usual status or open unemployment. The overall rate of usual status unemployment for the country as a whole has risen from 4.23 percent in 1977-78 to 4.48 percent in 1980. The rate of unemployment for the year 1999-2000 on current daily status basis is estimated at 7.3%.

LABOUR FORCE PARTICIPATION RATES

Table 3 summarizes the crude Labour Force Participation Rates (LFPR) estimates separately by rural urban residence and gender.

Table 3
Labour Force Participation Rates: 1972-73 – 1993-94

Sector/Gender		*1972-73*	*1983*	*1993-94*
Rural	Males	55.1	55.5	56.1
	Females	32.1	34.2	33.0
	All	43.9	45.2	44.9
Urban	Males	52.1	54.0	54.3
	Females	14.2	15.9	16.5
	All	34.5	36.2	36.3
India	Males	54.5	55.1	55.6
	Females	28.6	30.0	28.7
	All	42.0	43.0	42.7

Source: ILO site on Unemployment estimates

The LFPRs show a reasonable stability in the rates for rural males around 55-56 percent and for urban males around 52-54 percent. The rates for females have tended to fluctuate between 32-34 percent in rural areas and between 14 and 16 percent in urban areas.

Worker population ratio is also an important indicator of unemployment levels in the economy. Data collected in this regard through census and NSS surveys(50th round) are presented in Table-4.

Table 4
Workers Population Ratios by Gender and Rural-Urban Residence (1951 to 1993-94)

	India			*Rural*			*Urban*		
Item	*Persons*	*Male*	*Female*	*Persons*	*Male*	*Female*	*Persons*	*Male*	*Female*
1951 Census	39.1	53.9	23.4	39.5	53.5	25.0	37.1	56.4	14.7
1971 Census	34.0	52.7	13.9	36.1	53.6	15.5	29.6	48.9	7.1
1981 Census	36.8	52.6	19.8	38.9	53.8	23.2	30.0	49.1	8.3
1991 Census	37.5	51.6	22.3	40.0	52.5	26.7	30.2	48.9	9.2
1993-94 (NSS)	42.0	54.5	28.6	44.4	55.3	32.8	34.7	52.0	15.4

Source: ILO Opcit.

Table 5
Incidence of Unemployment by Gender and Residence (1987-88 to 1993-94)

Item		*India*			*Rural*			*Urban*		
		Persons	*Male*	*Female*	*Persons*	*Male*	*Female*	*Persons*	*Male*	*Female*
Usual Status	1987-88	2.7	2.6	2.9	2.0	1.8	2.4	5.4	5.2	6.2
	1993-94	1.9	2.2	1.4	1.1	1.4	0.8	4.4	4.0	6.2
Weekly Status	1987-88	4.8	4.8	5.0	4.2	4.2	4.3	7.0	6.6	9.2
	1993-94	3.6	3.5	3.8	3.0	3.0	3.0	5.8	5.2	8.4
Daily Status	1987-88	6.0	5.6	7.5	5.2	4.6	6.7	9.4	8.8	12.0
	1993-94	6.0	5.9	6.3	5.6	5.6	5.6	7.4	6.7	10.5

Source: ILO optic.

The data suggest a reasonable stability since 1970's in worker population ratios for rural males around 54 percent, for rural females between 15-33 percent, for urban males between 49-52 percent and for urban females between 7-15 percent. The worker population ratio for the total population of the country has been stable around 34-42 percent.

INCIDENCE OF UNEMPLOYMENT

Data on the incidence of unemployment in rural and urban India are presented in Table 5.

The data presented in Table 5 shows the unemployed as percentage of the labour force in terms of the relevant concept. The 1993-94 survey data suggest a decline in the level of open unemployment in the country between 1987-88 and 1993-94. A decline of the order of 1 percentage point is seen in the rates of unemployment in terms of both usual and current weekly status in rural as well as urban areas. The rates based on current weekly status indicate a decline of one percentage point among both males and females (but the corresponding estimate for rural males shows a rise of 1 percentage point). It is possible that the drought relief works started by several State Governments during the period had contributed to a reduction in the level of rural unemployment among males.

UNEMPLOYMENT AMONG EDUCATED

In view of the higher unemployment rates among the educated Table-6 presents data according to surveys of 1987-88 and 1993-94. In terms of usual principal status the decline in unemployment is quite marked except among the urban graduate female. The rate for urban females has remained almost constant at 21 percent, while that for rural females has dropped sharply from 37 to 34 percent.

The data relating to the graduates and higher educated also show a decline in unemployment in terms of the usual principal status, although the drop is negligible and insignificant in the case of urban females. The decline in unemployment rates seems surprising in view of the slow growth of employment opportunities in the organised sector in which the educated seek work.

Table 6
Incidence of Unemployment Among Educated Persons (Graduates & Above) :1981 to 1993-94

		Persons		*Males*		*Females*	
Item		*1987-88*	*1993-94*	*1987-88*	*1993-94*	*1987-88*	*1993-94*
RURAL	UPS	16.9	15.2	15.0	13.2	37.3	34.6
	CWS	NA	14.2	NA	12.2	NA	32.0
URBAN	UPS	9.8	8.9	7.4	6.4	21.0	20.6
	CWS	NA	8.8	NA	6.3	NA	20.2

Source: ILO opcit.

CHANGING DIMENSIONS OF UNEMPLOYMENT

Table 7
Unemployment Rates: Alternative Measures (% of Labour Force)

Year	*UPS*	*CWS*	*CDS*
1977-78	4.23	4.47	8.18
1983	2.77	4.51	8.28
1987-88	3.77	4.80	6.09
1993-94	2.56	3.63	6.03
1999-00	2.81	4.41	7.32

Source: Ruddar Dutt & Sundharam, Indian Economy, 2006

From the data provided in Table 7 certain disturbing trends in the unemployment rates become evident in the post-reform period. Although the reforms were introduced in 1991, yet the year 1991-92 was particularly a depressed year and the reform process really got a going by 1993-94. Thus, 1993-94 to 1999-2000 the 6 years period can be considered as the period of liberalisation. It may be noted that open employment as measured by UPS criterion declined from 4.23 percent in 1977-78 to 2.56 percent in 1993-94, but indicated an increase to 2.81 percent in 1999-2000. The current weekly status (CWS) unemployment rate which was 4.48 percent in 1977-78 declined to 3.63 percent in 1993-94, but rose to 4.41 percent in 1999-2000. Even the most comprehensive measure of unemployment, Viz. Current Daily Status (CDS) unemployment rate declined from 8.18 percent in 1977-78 to 6.03 percent in 1993-94 but, the declining trend reversed to 7.32 percent in

1999-2000. UPS measures open unemployment throughout the year, but CDS besides taking into account open unemployment also measures under-employment. It has becomes obvious that whereas the UPS rates are modest, CDS rates are quite high. In other words, the major problem of the Indian Economy is not open unemployment but under-employment.

CONCLUSION

The high rates of unemployment particularly youth unemployment need serious attention by the policy makers not only to mitigate the frustrations faced by the new entrants into the workforce but also to minimize the likely attention and wide-spread evidence of deviant behavior of the youth throughout the country. The unemployed youth have partly been responsible for the tensions and unrest in several parts including the border states of the country. Ever since the initiation of planning in 1950, the government has stressed the goal of increasing employment opportunities and eventually eradicating unemployment from the country. Some of the special employment schemes have been aimed specifically at the youth to improve their training and skills to promote self-employment and entrepreneurship. Several schemes initiated by the planners during the past merit a careful scrutiny to assess and evaluate their impact on the employment situation in the country. Hence it is high time that the planners and policy makers should take appropriate measures to reduce the unemployment levels and poverty in the country by strengthening the existing schemes and by introducing the innovative schemes following the Chinese model where they have been successful in these areas.

REFERENCES

—Planning Commission, Sixth, Seventh & Tenth Five Year Plans.

—(1973), Government of India, Report of the Committee on Unemployment.

Runddar Dutt & Sundaram (2006), Indian Economy, S.Chand & Co.

—ILO site relating to Unemployment estimates.

6

RURAL EMPLOYMENT SITUATION IN INDIA

S. Ramanjaneyuylu

Most of the unemployment in India is definitely structural. During the 1961-2001 period, population in this country had grown at an alarming rate of around 2.15 percent per annum and with it the number of people coming to the labour market in search of jobs had also increased rapidly, whereas employment opportunities did not increase most of the time correspondingly due to slow economic growth. Hence, there has been an increase in the volume of unemployment from one plan period to another.

EMPLOYMENT IN RURAL SECTOR

In rural sector, most of the employment is in agriculture and allied activities. Employment away from agriculture and primary activities, towards secondary and tertiary sectors is rather small. During the 1980s there was diversification of employment away from agriculture. It was generally considered to be a positive feature because it had resulted in overall growth of rural employment in most regions of the country and was associated with a decline in the incidence of rural poverty. The main dynamic source of rural employment generation in this period was expansion of the government expenditure rather than forces internal to the rural economy.

During the 1980s along with a rapid increase in subsidies, there was a steep rise in expenditure on the rural sector, by the State and Central Governments. As a result of conscious policy of rural development nearly 80 per cent of all new government jobs created during the decade occurred in rural areas. Hence, flow of government resources into rural areas must have been substantially large.

The 55th Round NSS date (referring to 1999–2000) suggested marked slowdown in the rate of job generation in both agriculture and non-agriculture. According to the NSS, primary sector employment declined for both men and women in rural areas between 1992-93 and 1999-2000 and the decline was sharp in the case of men. However, for men's share of tertiary sector employment rose significantly.

Apparently, this appears to be a welcome tendency. But, in fact, the decline in primary sector employment over the period 1992-93 to 1999-2000 was less a sign of rural dynamism than a reflection of the collapse of productive employment opportunities in rural areas generally. Growth rates of employment in both rural and urban areas are shown in table 1.

Table 1
Growth Rates of Employment
(Per cent Change Per Annum)

Period	*Rural*	*Urban*	*Rural Urban Combined*
1982-83 to 1987-88	1.36	2.77	1.54
1987-88 to 1993-94	2.03	3.39	2.43
1993-94 to 1999-2000	0.66	2.27	0.98

Source: GOBI, *Economic survey 2001 – 2002,* P.240.

Employment in Organsied Sector

Organised sector employment in 1999-2000 was 28.11 million i.e., about 7.08 per cent of the total employment of about 397 million (Table 2). Interestingly, despite economic reforms employment in the organised sector has been declining in percentage terms. In absolute terms, employment in the organised sector was 24.01 million in 1983. It steadily rose to reach the level of 27.37 million in 1994 and further to 28.11 million 1999-2000. This cannot be considered as a satisfactory development, because in percentage terms employment kept on declining since 1983. The organised sector had accounted for 7.83 per cent of the employment in 1983. Thereafter it steadily declined to 7.3 per cent in 1994 and further to 7.08 per cent in 1999-2000. Moreover, growth rate of employment in the organised sector has shown a tendency to decline. Employment in the organised sector had increased at the rate 1.2 per cent per annum during the period 1983-1994. Thereafter most of economic growth in the organised sector has been jobless, as a result of which annual average rate of employment growth declined to 0.53 per cent during the period 1994-2000.

Table 2
Employment in Organised and Unorganised Sectors

	Employment (Million)			*Growth Rate per cent per annum*	
Sector	*1993-83*	*1993-94*	*1999-2000*	*1983-94*	*1994-2000*
Total Employment	302.75	374.45	397.00	2.04	0.98
Organised Sector Employment	24.01	27.37	28.11	1.20	0.53
Public Sector	16.46	19.44	19.41	1.52	-0.03
Private Sector	7.55	7.93	8.70	0.45	1.87
Unorganised Sector Employment	278.70	347.08	368.89	2.01	1.02

Source: GOI, *Economic Survey 2001-2002*, P.240.

The public sector had accounted for 68.55 per cent of the employment in the organised sector in 1983. Its share in employment in the organised sector had increased during the period 1983 to 1994 and stood at 71.03 per cent. Thereafter the government consciously pursued the policy of reducing employment in the public sector and as a result, employment declined from 19.44 million in 1994 to 19.41 million in 1999-2000.

UNORGANISED SECTOR EMPLOYMENT

The Unorganised sector in the economy is quite large. Whole of agriculture is in Unorganised sector. It provides employment to around 93 per cent of the labour force. In 1983, employment in the Unorganised sector was 278.7 million. It rose at the annual rate of 2.01 per cent during the period 1983 to 1994 and touched the level of 347.08 million. There-after, there was a slowdown in employment growth in the Unorganised sector. The annual rate of employment growth declined to 1.02 per cent during the period 1994 to 2000 which was almost half of the growth rate during the previous period.

Reasons for Declining Employment

Over the 1990s, under neoliberal economic reforms the government reversed several of its polices which had contributed to more employment in rural areas. Macro-economic strategy from 1991 involved cuts in Central Government revenue expenditure on rural development in per capita terms. There were substantial reductions in public investments in infrastructure which adversely affected non-agricultural employment in rural areas. Moreover, reduced transfers to State Governments meant facing financial crunch they also cut down their spending, particularly on social sectors like education, health and sanitation, which in turn undermined public employment. Financial reforms effectively cut down availability of rural credit reducing scope for rural enterprise development. Thus possibilities of self-employment were curtailed.

The private sector has always accounted for less than one-third of the employment in the organised sector. The government had erroneously pinned its hopes on the private sector for substantial employment generation. But it is now well established that the profit maximizing business corporate would never generate the amount of employment that the public sector generated in the past. Growth in the organised sector employment is now dependent on the employment growth in the private sector.

The most probable reason for the decline in the Unorganised sector employment growth is non-availability of employment opportunities because of jobless growth. Agriculture's potential to absorb increasing labour force seems to have exhausted. Small scale industries unable to withstand competition from imported goods have suffered closure and the workers employed in these industries have lost their jobs. Even in other segments of the Unorganised sector, employment elasticity is low. All these factors taken together adequately explain the decline in Unorganised sector employment growth rate during the period 1994-2000.

Special programmes for poverty eradication and employment creation were started from the 5th Five Year Plan. They are MNP, IRDP, NREP, RLEGP, MFAL, DPAP, CSRE, TRYSEM, JRY, NRY, SJSRY, PMY, FWP, INDIRAMMA etc. The present most important employment programme in rural sector is National Rural Employment Guarantee Programme.

NATIONAL RURAL EMPLOYMENT GUARANTEE SCHEME (NREGS)

The National Rural Employment Guarantee Act was notified on September 7, 2005. But the scheme was launched on Feb 2, 2007 in Ananthapur District in Andhra Pradesh. The implementation of the NREG Act calls for the formulation of the NREGSs by the State Governments. The Act provides that within five months from the promulgation of the Act, every State Government shall by notification make a scheme for providing not less than 100 days of guaranteed employment in a financial year to every household in the rural areas. The NREGS covers 200 districts identified in the initial stage. It will cover all the districts with in five years. The objective of the NREG Act 2005 is to enhance the livelihood security of the people in rural areas by guaranteeing employment through works that develop infrastructure base of that area. The choices of the work suggested are such that they might help in tackling the problem of chronic poverty.

NREGA in Rajastan

Among all major States, Rajastan comes first in terms of employment generation per rural household under the NREGA. In 2006-07, the average rural household in Rajastan's six NREGA Districts worked for as many as 77 days under this programme, earning nearly Rs. 4,000 in the process. This is an unprecedented achievement in the history of social security in India.

Further, disadvantaged sections of the population are the main gainers. The share of women in NREGA employment is around two-thirds in Rajastan, and that of Scheduled Caste and Scheduled Tribe house holds is as high as 80 per cent. In this and other ways, the Act contributes to social equity and economic redistribution.

According to the official data of the Ministry of Rural Development, the average wage rate paid under the NREGA in 2006–07 was lower in Rajastan (Rs.51 a day) than in any other State, and much below the national average of Rs.65 a day.

NREGP in Andhra Pradesh

Far from the general perception that Andhra Pradesh is a model in implementation of NREGP, its rank in utilisation of funds is 22nd among 27 States according to the information given by the Union Ministry of Rural Development. The State was able to utilise Rs.680.20 crore out of the Rs.1,298.11 crore of total available funds (Central funds, State's share and Misc. receipts) working out to 52.40 per cent by March 2007 as against all India average of 71.56 per cent.

It compares poorly with big backward States like Bihar (71%), Orissa (72.32%) and Madhya Pradesh (82.19%) and even smaller States like Uttaranchal (72%) Jharkhand (79%) and Chhattisgarh (84.56%).

There is large–scale diversion of NREGA funds for schemes like Indiramma housing. Civil society groups and activists feel so and assert that the diversion has resulted in dilution of the employment guarantee scheme in the State. The percentage of utilisation of funds would have been worse but for large scale misuse of funds at the village level. A study of first year's performance showed that only a quarter of those who registered for job cards were offered work, that too for 30 days against the guaranteed 100 days. Distress migration continues.

NREGS in East Godavari

NREGS works well launched on May 24, 2007 in East Godavari District. As many as 211 works well launched in 180 villages under the NREGS in Indiramma villages in the first phase all over the district. NREGS works were grounded in all the mandals in the district except kothapet Mandal. The reason for non-starting of works in kothapet was that coolies did not come forward to take up the works. Since the work measurements so far showed that there was every chance of workers getting up to Rs.100 daily as against the minimum wage of Rs.80 prescribed by the Government, the District Collector wanted the officials to create awareness among workers so that they availed themselves of the opportunity in large numbers.

Regarding the facilities at the work spots, first aid boxes were arranged and 6000 crowbrs were distributed to various mandals for giving free to the workers who worked for 10 days without break. If the coolies brought their own baskets for doing the work, they would be paid Rs.2 additionally. For purchasing the spades,axes, cutters required for NREGS works, rates of each item were decided at the district level purchase committee and the MDOs made the purchage locally at those rates. The Collector said that each mandal was divided into three clusters for the purpose or preparing the estimates of NREGS works and each cluster was placed under the control of one assistant engineer.

Both men and women of all ages above 18 years were eligible to enroll their names for securing work under the scheme. Crèches would be organised for children of coolies keeping one of the workers as in–charge. In addition to the normal works like laying roads, de silting drains and irrigation and drinking water tanks, the Collector said that development of lands assigned to SCs/STs could also be taken up.

Horticulture works would also be encouraged. Of the estimated work, 60 per cent should be wage component and the rest material component. Under the scheme, each family would get Rs.8,000 per annum. Employment would be guaranteed to all agriculture labourers.

No Scope for Misuse

The District Collector said that every work would be computerised and there would be no irregularity. Every beneficiary should open any account in post office or bank so as to enable the administration to deposit wages by 15th of every month. Post offices in East Godavari district have registered a good business, thanks to the NREGS. According to the Superintendent of Post offices, Rajahmundry, the MPDO and the VAO would issue job cards to labourers who in turn would come to post offices and open an account. The government will bear Rs.50 towards charges for opening of the account. The Government will provide 100 days work to the labourers and make payments through the post offices.

For this, the Government will deposit certain amount in post offices in advance. In East Godavari, Rs.20 lakhs was deposited in kakinada, Rs.10 lakhs each in Amalapuram and Rajahmundry post offices. Weekly balance sheets or fortnightly balance sheets will be prepared to ensure transparency. The post offices will get a commission of Rs.1 lakh to Rs.3 lakhs in each district on the accounts opened.

Progress of NREGS

The East Godavari Zilla Parishad at its special general body meeting held on July 15, 2007 unanimously accorded approval for taking up as many as 6,783 works costing Rs.108.09 crores in 42 mandals under the NREGS. The progress under the scheme, the district was the first in the State in taking up a maximum number of works. So far, Rs.5.30 crores was paid to workers towards wage component, the highest among the districts where the scheme was being implemented. On an average, each worker was getting Rs.89 towards minimum wages. The maximum was Rs.100 under the scheme.

From the above analysis, it is concluded that the NREGS is a novel scheme in preventing migration of labour by assuring 100 days of work to each family. It will reduce rural unemployment in future.

REFERENCES

—(2007), Employment Guarantee : Unfinished Agenda, *The Hindu*, Vol.130, No.166, July 13.

—(2002), GOI, *Economic Survey 2001-02*, New Delhi.

—(1992), GOI, *8th Five Year Plan 1992-97 Vol. I*, New Delhi.

—(2007), Job Scheme works get Z.P.nod, *The Hindu*, VOL. 130, No.168, July 16.

Lekhi R.K. (1994), *Indian Economic Problems*, Kalyani Publishers, New Delhi.

Misra SK & Puri V.K., (2006), *Indian Economy*, Himalaya Publishing House, Mumbai.

—(2007), NREGA Funds to Indiramma ? *The Hindu*, Vol.130, No.126, July1.

—(2007), NREGS works launched, *The Hindu*, Vol. 130, No131, June 2.

—(2007), NREGS: It's Advantage Post Offices, *The Hindu*, Vol.130, No.168, July 16.

Ramanjaneyulu S., (2006), Studies on Urban Poverty in India, *A.P.E.A. Second Pre–Annual Conference Volume*, Nov 26.

Ruddar Datt & Sundaram K PM., (2005), *Indian Economy* S.Chand & Co, New Delhi.

—Rural Job Scheme will check Migrations, says Minister, *The Hindu*, vol.130, No.124, May 24, 2007.

—(2007), State Lags in Job Scheme, *The Hindu* Vol.130, No.143, June 16.

Thakur S., (1990), *Indian Economic Development : Retrospect & Prospect*, Sterling Publishers, New Delhi.

Vinod Kumar P K. *et.al.*,(1992), *Indian Economy* Dhillon Publications, New Delhi.

—(2007), Weed Removal Under Job Scheme, *The Hindu* Vol.130, No.20, May 20.

7

EMPLOYMENT AND UNEMPLOYMENT STATUS IN INDIA

C. Basavaiah
I. Malyadri

As a whole, the world's population is growing by about 100 million new additions each year. Most of the population increase is concentrated in low-income countries. This poses a serious challenge to developing countries, particularly in terms of their capacity to sustain adequate investments in human capital. Slower population growth will not solve the problems, but it may reduce the pressures and they additional time to work on solving the problems.

Like for poverty, the latest and seventh quinquennial NSS survey, namely the 61st round conducted during July 2004-June 2005,constitutes an important source of information on employment and unemployment. The 61st round of the NSSO survey reveals a faster increase in employment during 1999-2000 to 2004-2005 as compared to 1993-94 to 1999-2000.The following table shows the data.

The Tenth Five Year Plan (2002-07) aimed at provision of gainful and high quality employment in excess of addition to the labor force to reduce the number of unemployed significantly by the end of the Plan. The Tenth Plan advocated the need to increase the employment content of growth by promoting sectors and activities, which employ more labor per unit of output. On the whole, the Tenth Plan aimed at the creation of approximately 50 million employment opportunities-30 million from the normal process of growth and additional 20 million from special initiatives-during a period of five years. The results of the 61st NSSO round show that above 47 million persons were provided employment during 2000 to 2005.

Net annual addition to employment on Usual Principal Status (UPS) basis went up from 5.47 million during 1993-94 to1999-2000 to 9.58 million during 1999-2000 to 2004-05, Simultaneously, however, according to the 61st round estimates, during 1999-2000to 2004-2005, labor force grew even faster at an annual 2.54 per cent compared to annual employment growth of 2.48 per cent. As a result, despite the faster growth of employment, unemployment (on UPS basis) was higher at 3.06 per cent of the labor force in 2004-2005 compared to 2.78 in 1999-2000. Incidence of unemployment had come down from 2.88 per cent in 1983 (38th round) to 2.62 per cent in 1993-1994 (50th round).

This deceleration happened in spite of acceleration in annual employment growth in the private sector from 0.44 per cent to 0.61 per cent during the reference periods, as this acceleration was not enough to make up for the corresponding decline of employment in the public sector. However, the latter decline was mainly due to a decrease in employment in public sector establishments, whereas the pace of growth in employment from 0.44 per cent to 0.61 per cent per annum. While the rightsizing of the public sector, whose primary objective is to deliver essential services such as education, health, roads and irrigation and not for providing direct employment, is a welcome development and should continue, there is an urgent need to step up employment growth in the organized private sector.

The Approach paper to the Eleventh Plan targets generation of additional employment opportunities in services and manufacturing, in particular, labour intensive

Table 1

Employment and Unemployment (by Usual Principal Status)

	1983	1993-94	1999-2000	2004-2005	1983 to 1993-94	1993-94 to 1999-2000	1999-2000 to 2004-05
	In million				*Growth in Per cent per annum*		
Labor Force	277.34	343.56	377.88	428.37	2.06	1.60	2.54
Workforce	269.36	334.54	367.37	415.27	2.09	1.57	2.48
No of Unemployed	7.98	9.02	10.51	13.10	–	–	–
	As a Proportion of Labor Force in Per cent Unemployment						
Rate	2.88	2.62	2.78	3.06	–	–	–

Source: Various rounds of NSSO Survey on employment and unemployment

manufacturing sectors such as food processing, leather products, footwear and textiles and in service sectors such as tourism and contraction. It calls for elimination of distorting fiscal incentives which foster capital intensity; infrastructure investment; removal of distortions that hinder competition, prevent entry and discourage graduation from unorganized to organized status; and greater emphasis on vocational training and skill development to improve employability of youth. As Village and Small Scale Enterprises (VSE) will have to provide most of the new employment during the Eleventh Plan, the Approach Paper also calls for redressing the problems faced by VSE units and home based workers, particularly women, such as non-availability of timely and adequate credit, unreliable or absence of power supply, requirement of permission from a number of government agencies and burden of multiple inspections. Some direct employment will also be available in the social sectors like health and education. Moreover, wage employment programmes like the NREGS will help.

OPTIONS FOR ACCELERATING EMPLOYMENT GROWTH IN INDIA

Under the present system, India has achieved rising real wages, job security and other protections and benefits for existing organized sector workers even in a labor-abundant economy. These accomplishments should be recognized. However, the present system appears to be costly in terms of slow growth of employment in the manufacturing sector as a whole, the debilitating affects of labor problems, and incentives skewed towards capital intensification, especially in the organized sector and in small-scale firms access to subsidized credit. Given India's huge need for productive employment generation over the next several decades, these costs seem very high.

REFERENCES

—(2006-2007), Economic Survey, (Government of India, Ministry of Finance Economic Division)

—Ernesto M. Pernia, Urban Poverty in Asia, A Survey of Critical Issues.

George Psacharopoulos, Education for Development, A World Bank Publication, Oxford University Press –P.No:XIII.

—India Poverty, Employment and Social services, A world bank country study, The world bank Washington, D.C., U.S.A

8

WORK FORCE PARTICIPATION IN TRIBAL AREAS OF ANDHRA PRADESH

N. Koti Reddy
D. Venkata Rao

INTRODUCTION

The Indian planners have accorded top'priority for generating adequate employment opportunities during the five-year plans. Moreover, the twin objectives of expanding opportunities for gainful employment and progressive reduction of social and economic disparities fed to the execution of many employment schemes in the country. This has changed the total scenario of working population. The severe growth of population is causing massive unemployment and underemployment in all corners of the nation. As rightly pointed by some academicians "employment in the modern sector lagged behind output and population. Open unemployment and the informal sector, the latter more than the former, increased absolutely and relatively to the population".

Agriculture has been found to be having a steadily declining employment potential and organized industry has been experiencing stagnation in employment. Whatever little employment growth that has been taken place in the entire organized sector is contributed virtually by the public sector. However, rural non-farm employment and the urban informal sector accounted for relatively high employment growth.

It is generally agreed that the new employment that will get generated, would mainly be in the unorganized sector. Issues like rural labour, female workers and workers in the weaker sections such as scheduled caste workers and scheduled tribe workers emerged as a distinct and important subject of study and drawn the attention of many researchers.

PRESENTATION OF THE PROBLEM

India has the highest number of tribal population in the world next to Africa. Similarly in Andhra Pradesh also more number of tribals is living. Andhra Pradesh is the fifth largest State in the country in terms of both population and area. The State claims to have ay area of 2.75-lakh sq.km, forming 8-37 percent of the total geographical area of the country. The population of the state reached to 7, 57, 27, 541 crores. The tribal population of the state has reached to 50, 24, 104 by 2001.

Un-employment and under-employment are the two most prominent problems confronting the economy of the State of Andhra Pradesh. The overall employment growth seems to be not enough to take care of the growth in labour force.

Workforce participation rate is an important means to achieve the end of economic well-being- Work participation is a basic source of human dignity and self-respect.

In the process of reducing regional imbalances, the total workers' participation rates go a long way. As such an attempt is made here to examine the distribution of total workers and non-workers among the tribal areas of the state of Andhra Pradesh.

The present study is confined to the work force participation rates in the tribal areas of Andhra Pradesh- The data have been collected from various sources like Census reports. Economic Survey, Publications of Directorate of Economics and Statistics, Government of Andhra Pradesh, Hyderabad. The district is chosen as the unit of analysis. The data of 2001 Census are employed here.

VOLUME OF TRIBAL POPULATION IN A-P.

The data relating to the volume of tribal population of the state of Andhra Pradesh are presented in Table 1. This reveals that there are many differences in the tribal population in the districts. Khammam district is thickly populated with many tribals ie, 6, 82, 617 and stood first while the Hyderabad district consists of fewer tribals, i.e. 34, 560. Other districts like Adilabad, Visakhapatnam, Warangal also consists more number of tribal population. The government-of Andhra Pradesh is now engaged in providing more and more employment opportunities through the establishment of Girijan Co-operative corporations and Integrated Tribal' Development Agencies (I.T-D.As.)- These organizations are implementing many employment generation programmes including self-employment schemes- The higher volume of tribal population in any district indicates of effective functioning of these organizations that are working for the welfare of tribal community.

Table 1
Tribal Population of Andhra Pradesh

District	*Total Population*	*Total Scheduled Tribe Population*	*Voage of Tribal Population*
Srikakulam	2528491	151249	5.98
Vizianagaram	2245103	214839	9.57
Visakhapatnam	3789823	557572	14.71
East Godavari	4672622	191561	4.1
West Godavari	3796144	96659	- J 2.55
Krishna	4218416	107611	2.55
Guntur	4405521	208157	4.72
Prakasam	3054941	118241	3.87
Nellore	2659651	242257	9.11
Chittoor	3735202	128085	3.43
Kadapa	2573481	61371	2.38
Ananathapur	3639304	127161	3.49
Kurnool	3512266	69635	1.98
Mahabubnagar	3506876	278702	7.95
Rangareddy	3506670	146057	4.17

Contd.

District	Total Population	Total Scheduled Tribe Population	Voage of Tribal Population
Hyderabad	3686460	34560	0.94
Medak	2662296	134533	5.05
Nizamabad	2342803	165735	7.07
Adilabad	2479347	416511	16.8
Karimnagar	3477079	90636	2.61
Waranga!	3231174	457679	14.16
Khammam	2565412	682617	26.61
Algona	3238449	342676	10.58
Andhra Pradesh	75727541	5024104	'6.63

Source: Directorate of Census operations, Andhra Pradesh-

WORK FORCE PARTICIPATION AMONG THE TRIBALS OF A.P.

The government of Andhra Pradesh is formulating and implementing many tribal welfare programmes. As a result, the workforce participation among the tribal population of the state has gone up. The particulars of tribal workers and non-workers are presented in the Table 2.

This table clearly shows that in the state of Andhra Pradesh out of the total scheduled tribe population of 50, 24, 104 many people i.e. 27, 05, G36 are actively engaged in productive activities (53.85%). From this table some more observations can also be presented here. Vizianagaram district tops the list in the percentage of workers (55-84%) in the total ^scheduled tribe population followed by Guntur (56.29%), Waranga) (<5.84%). Similarly the lowest percentage of workers in the total scheduled population of the district is Mahabubnagar (5.32%) followed by Hyderabad (32.7%) and Ranga Reddy (48.54%) districts.

This clearly indicates that some districts like Mahabubnagar. Hyderabad are not able to provide more employment opportunities for tribal population. The rulers of the state should consider this issue and corrective steps might be included in future employment plans.

Table 2
Workforce Particulars of Tribal Population in A.P.

District 1	*Total No. of Workers*	*%age of Total No-of Workers*	*Total No. of Non-workers*	*%age of Total No. of Non-workers*
Srikakulam	79516	52.57	71733	47
Vizianagaram	124179	57-80	90660	42
Visakhapatnam	307845	55.21	249727	44
East Godavari	100049	52.23	91512	47
West Godavari	52676	54.5	43983	45
Krishna	56179	52-21	51432	47
Guntur	117171	56.29	90986	43
Prakasam	62881	53-18	55360	46
Nellore	135034	55.74	107223	44
Chittoor	68561	53.53	59524	46
Kadapa	30756	50.11	30615	49
Ananathapur	66687	52.44	60474	47
Kumool	34775	49.94	34860	50
Mahabubnagar	14829	5.32	263873	94
Kangareddy	70897	48,54	75160	51
Hyderabad	11302	32-70	23258	67
Medak	69626	51.75	64907	48
Nizaripabad	87436	52.76	78299	47
Adilabad	214162	51.42	202349	48
Karimnagar	48840	53.89	41796	46
Waranqal	255584	55.84	202095	44
Khammam	378176	55.4	304441	44
Nalgonda	-185295	54.07	157381	45
Andhra Pradesh	2705636	53.85	2318468	46

Source: Directorate of Census operations, Andhra Pradesh.

SECTORAL COMPOSITION OF TRIBAL POPULATION

It is observed that among the total workers of agricultural sector is contributing much for the livelihood. The data relating to the sectoral composition is presented in Table 3

As can be seen from the Table 3, the highest percentage distribution in the category of cultivators to total scheduled tribe workers of the district is found in Visakhapatnam (62.14), followed by Nizamabad (50.32), and Warangal (48.52), while the lowest percentage of cultivators is noticed in the district of Hyderabad (0.71).

Similarly, in the case of agricultural laborers, the highest percentage of workers in the total scheduled tribe workers of the district is registered in Nellore (74.50). followed by Guntur (69.81), and Chittoor (68.92). In this category of -agricultural labourers the lowest percentage of scheduled tribe workers is recorded in the district of Hyderabad (0.50).

The analysis of workers in Household Industry revealed that, while the highest percentage is registered in Kurnool (17.50), followed by Kadapa (12.22) and "Anantapur (6.16), it is interesting to note that all the remaining districts recorded less than six percentage of scheduled tribe workers to total scheduled tribe workers of its district.

The analysis of workers in the category of other than Household Industry revealed that the highest percentage of scheduled tribe workers In the total Scheduled tribe workers of the district is concentrated in Hyderabad (94.12), while the lowest percentage of scheduled tribe workers to total scheduled tribe workers is noticed in Visakhapatnam,

Thus, the above analysis reveals that of all the four categories of workers, the percentage of Scheduled Tribe workers in the total Scheduled Tribe population of that district is predominantly high in all the districts of Andhra Pradesh with the exception of Hyderabad and Ranga Reddy in the category of agricultural labourers.

POLICY PRESCRIPTIONS AND CONCLUSION

As India is marching towards the sustainable development continuous planned efforts are to be made from time to time to utilize the labour force of the country more effectively in the developmental programs of the nation- This calls for an understanding of work participation rates of males and females in tribal areas. From the above analysis, the following policy presentations can be made for improving. Economic status of Scheduled Tribe population, which enable them to participate more actively in the process of nation building.

- The analysis of the distribution of total workers in scheduled tribe workers revealed that there is a high concentration of workers in the category of agricultural labourers. This also acts as an alarm for the enhancement of rural non-farm sector activities in the coming years, which can prove to be a safety net for the millions of aspirant workers at the grass root level.

- The Rural Development Policy aiming at assigning a significant role to the allied rural farm and rural non-farm activities in the overall strategy of development in the economy should be reconstructed to provide more employment to the weaker sections of the society.
- As the participation of weaker sections like scheduled caste workers and scheduled tribe workers in the development activities is the most effective tool for the promotion of these workers to get the benefits of development, special programs have to be launched to shape their destinies by making them accessible to skills and resources supports.
- On the lines of Swarnajayanthi Gram Swarozgar Yojana (SGSY) self-employment programme for the rural poor may be extended by bringing in a greater coverage of self-employed persons by providing them income-generating assets through bank credit and Government subsidy. Banks should also realize the targets fixed for them in the priority sector to encourage prospective borrowers in the weaker sections of the society who are engaged in agriculture and allied activities.
- Concerted efforts should be made to expand and strengthen the tertiary sector, which has been exhibiting the potential to absorb the excess labour. In order to better utilize the stock of human capital, there is further need for launching special progarmmes to improve the skills of the labour.

Thus, from the above study it is concluded that the districts of Andhra Pradesh have been experiencing different workforce participation rates and different levels of concentration of marginal workers and scheduled tribe workers. This analysis focuses attention on the need for structural improvements by launching differential programmes in Andhra Pradesh by involving the Scheduled Tribe workers. Planned efforts must be made to generate adequate employment opportunities in the non-farm rural sector in view of the growing population in the rural areas in general and to the weaker sections of the society in particular.

REFERENCES

Ramanadham, V.V.(1959), Economy of Andhra Pradesh, Asia Publishing House,Bombay.

Ruddar Datt. K.P.M. Sundharam (2004), "Indian Economy" forty-ninth revised edition, S.Chand & Company Ltd. Ram Nagar, New Delhi.

Hanumantha Rao, Ch. & Hans Linneman, (1998), Economic Reforms and Poverty Apevation in India", Sage Publications, New Delhi.

K.C.Reddy, millennium edition (2000), "Economic and Public Policy" Himalaya Publishing House.

Dasgupta, (1991), "Manpower Problems in South Asia" Committee on Studies for

—Corporation in Development In South Asia (CSCD).

—(2005), UNDP, Human Development Report.

—(2004), Planning Commission Reports on Labour and Employment.

9

PROBLEM OF UNEMPLOYMENT–AN OVER VIEW

N. Srihari
S. H. K. R. Prasad
D. Rajasekhar

INTRODUCTION

The employment situation in the country is marred by a number of ugly marks. Large numbers of people are underemployed. Many are without work. In this context we take up the subject of unemployment to explain its concept, causes, unemployment position in India, effects of unemployment, suggestions to promote employment. We also dwell upon the much debated problem of how to use the vast surplus labour of the country.

CONCEPT OF UNEMPLOYMENT

An unemployed person is defined as *"one who is out of work and who has actively looked for work or is waiting to be recalled to a job after having been laid off or is waiting to report to a new job"*. The person is actively interested in a job, and not merely pretending or expressing an interest. Those who are of working age, but are not in the labour force, might be old people, spouses working in the home, or people who would like to work but are discouraged by lack of success in locating a job. There are flows in and out of the unemployment pool. The description of different types of unemployment that exists is as follows

- *Natural unemployment:* 'Natural' unemployment may be defined as that which exists overall demand for labour in the economy is equal to its supply at the prevailing level of real wages. Consider the following categories of unemployment, which can be described, as natural unemployment. Those are Frictional Unemployment, Structural Unemployment, Seasonal Unemployment, Transitional Unemployment, Residual Unemployment.
- *Demand-deficient Unemployment:* It is a general form of unemployment, which influence the economy as expand the level of aggregate demand for all goods and services. Demand–deficient unemployment is often associated with the depression or slump phase of the trade cycle.

CAUSES FOR UNEMPLOYMENT

The major causes, which have been responsible for the widespread unemployment, can be spelled out as under:

- *Underdevelopment:* In the context of vast and varied unutilized natural resources state the underdevelopment. The volume of economic activities at present is determined largely by agriculture, is low and the rate of rise in such activities is small. The non-agricultural sector, in particular the modern industrials sector, which was to provide increasing avenues of employment, is growing at a very slow pace.
- *Inadequate Employment Planning:* Overall inadequate of planning may be added the weak manpower planning i.e., balancing of manpower needs and supplies in the various branches of production, in the various regions of the country and in various skills.

In some sectors of the economy there is more than we need, while in others there is less than required.

- *Rapid Population Growth:* The rapid growth of population has adversely affected the unemployment situation largely in two ways. In the first place, it has directly affected it by making large addition to labour force. Of course, how much of the evil of unemployment can be ascribed to this factor depends upon the rate of growth of job-opportunities. The second consequence of the rapid population growth has been to worsen indirectly the unemployment situation by reducing the resources for capital formation. This means large additional expenditure on their rearing up, maintenance, education etc..
- *Decay of handicrafts:* Decay of handicrafts in the rural and urban area .is the reasons for unemployment. This leads to the economic burden for all.

UNEMPLOYMENT POSITION IN INDIA

A large number of workers are forced to remain jobless both at rural and urban areas in India. The Dantwala Committee on Unemployment states, "In an economy like India, there is very little open or outright unemployment but there would be considerable seasonal unemployment and under-employment". How many workers are generally unemployed in India in different types of possibly given any factual information with confidence.

- *Unemployment in the Rural Sector:* unemployment in India manifests itself in the rural areas. Rural unemployment has two aspects–seasonal and perennial. Agriculture, which is the principal occupation in the countryside, is by nature a seasonal occupation. The period of seasonal unemployment varies from State to State depending upon the methods of farming, the condition of the soil, the type of crops grown, the possibility of double estimated that for at least five to seven months in a year, a sizeable portion of the population engaged in agriculture remains idle.

The second aspect of rural unemployment is the perennial under-employment or chronic disguised unemployment that prevails in India agriculture. This fast increase of population dependent upon land without a corresponding increase in the area of cultivation has resulted in a surplus population engaged in agriculture. Even if this surplus population is withdrawn from agriculture, total production will not be affected. In the Nurksian language, the marginal productivity of surplus labour is zero.

- *Unemployment in the Urban Sector:* The problem of urban unemployment is mainly of two kinds– (i) unemployment among industrial labourers, and (ii) unemployment among the educated middle class. With the spread of urbanization, people from the rural areas have been shifting to the urban areas. Moreover, during the off-season quite a good number of workers in agriculture come to the industrial centres to seek employment. The rate at which the expansion of industries has been taking place is not keeping pace with the growth of unemployment among industrial workers. The second type of urban unemployment exists among the educated middle class. The Royal Commission on Labour emphasized that the problem of educated unemployment is of an all-India character. The result of an educational system, which is highly, loaded in favour of liberal or general education and partly the result of a slower rate of industrial expansion. Consequently, the numbers of persons seeking employment in clerical posts far exceed those seeking employment for technical posts.

EFFECTS OF UNEMPLOYMENT

We explain below how unemployment effects the economic, social and healthy life of the people.

- *Increases the open unemployment:* The structural changes in increases open unemployment strongly in rural area and small changes in urban area. This means that there is a shift from the state of widespread noteworthy. The Second feature is that the open unemployment rate has increased much faster in the case of women than men.

- *Increase unproductive consumers:* Increase in the number of unproductive consumers or dependent on the work force. With productivity of the workers already how this will affect adversely the enterprise and efficiency of the labour force.
- *Reduce the Resources for Capital Formation:* A higher rate of capital formation is crucial to the development of the country. But unemployment makes it difficult to achieve this objective. It is fact reduces the resources for capital formation. This is done in following two ways.
    - *Eats away Investment Resources:* The investment resources used for maintained in a present level of per capita income of the rising unemployment is a minus item which reduced the total resources for capital formation. The amount involved is quite sizeable in public goods like drinking water, educational, medical and transportation facilities the requiring government spending.
    - *Lower Saving:* Unemployment adversely affects savings and therefore capital formation because of the rise in consumption without producing and earning. Given the level of income, an increase in consumption means less saving. The consumption needs for private goods and services like food, clothing, and shelter etc involving private expenditure.
- *Effect on National Income:* Effect of unemployment leads to Decline GDP of Nations. All natural resources are not properly inputted in production causes increase cost of production. Its results low income. People not in a position to buy even necessities, it effect on the standard of living. This leads to decline per labour production capacity.

SUGGESTIONS TO PROMOTE EMPLOYMENT

In the light of the above-mentioned causes of unemployment, we now discuss the measures that can help us in eradiating this evil.

- *Expanding volume of work:* The one and the foremost solution to the problem of unemployment lies in enlarging the opportunities for work. The work to be expanded has to be in both the sphere of wage-employment and the self-employment, which is substantial, this needs to be done rapidly and at an increased scale so as to clear the backlog of unemployment.
- *Raising Capital Formation:* It is also necessary that the accumulation of capital is stepped up. It helps employment expansion in two principal ways. One, it becomes possible to maintain the existing activities, as also to expand the current activities and set up new ones, the maintenance and replacement of the existing capital stock are necessary to keep up the present level of production. Secondly, capital formation directly generates employment in the capital goods sector. The production of 'mother machines' i.e., machines that produce machines give rise to employment. This also provides capital goods for the production of various other types of goods like consumer goods and services.
- *Special Employment Programmes:* The different types of people for whom special employment programmes are needed are landless agricultural labourers, marginal farmers, village artisans, and tribal people living in remote areas of the country as also people in the hilly areas. The programmes may be in the form of direct employment as on rural capital works. These may be in the form of providing assets like animals, sewing machines, hand/ power driven looms and the supply of infrastructural facilities like marketing, credit etc

- *Efficient Manpower Planning:* For achieving employment for all, it is also necessary to manage human resources in a scientific manner. This is essential to ensure while employment is promoted. *One,* labor planning relate to the demand and supply of skilled personnel, it is essential to adopt effective remedies to cut down the growth rate of population. This will no doubt reduce the growth rate of labour supply. *Two,* the supply of skilled labour needs to be tailored to the requirements of the rate and pattern of employment- oriented development. This should also take care of the imbalances which mark the current scene wherein one finds excess in certain lines and shortages in others. ***Three,*** while high-level skill-formation through education and training will be confined to a small proportion of labour-force; it is essential to improve upon the capabilities. This requires several inter-related measures such as provision of adequate and nutritive foods, health facilities, elementary education, and training for some hobs etc.
- *Changes in the structure of institutional framework:* To promote the employment changes requires in the structure of industry or in the institutional framework of the economy; Improvement of information services provided by employment offices; setting up of retraining schemes and provision of financial help for those prepared to move to high-employment areas; giving grants or tax concessions to firms who locate in depressed areas are helpful to reduce unemployment.

CONCLUSION

The problem of unemployment is causing a great concern to all in recent years. The introduction of Information Technology (IT) has reduced the number of job opportunities in the country. When the educated people are raising in number, it is obvious that the unemployment of youth is increasing over the years.

The government has to study the problem of unemployment and take necessary action to overcome the problem. The educated youth, it is suggested should not depend on government jobs, but find out alternative self-employment overcome for their livelihood. The government should increase wide awareness on the self-employment opportunities available for the youth and encourages them to get benefits from the schemes. Banks also should liberally provide finance to the technically qualified unemployed youth to set by some industrial units and thereby generate further employment opportunities. The organizations should also discourage outsourcing contract work and employ people on regular terms for the benefit of the youth. The government should train the youth with the necessary technical skills to get them employed.

REFERENCES

Nihal Singh.S, (2005), "The Wages of Indo-US Pact", Deccan Chronicle, Sep 22, Vijayawada.

Aarti Dhar (2007), "National Wage Policy Sought", The Hindu, May 2, Vijayawada.

—"Employment News", Various Editions

—"HRD Times", Monthly Journal, Chennai Various Editions.

Ruddar Datt, Sundharam.K.P.M,. "Indian Economy", 26th Edition.

Kewal Krishen Dewett, Adarsh Chand (1999), "Modern Economic Theory", Edition.

10

POVERTY AND UNEMPLOYMENT-AN ANALYTICAL APPROACH

K. Rajeswari
V. Naveena Devi

On the one hand. We have the glittering Lights, luxury apartments, cars, Hotels and race courses-while on the other, We have the slums and the pavement Dwellers.

The study of poverty and unemployment is central to the understanding of the various phenomena with which we daily interact. The entire debate of development and under-development decides for us, not only our approach to history, but how we hope to consciously intercede in it; and for whose benefit. Poverty Before beginning any serious discussion, it might be useful to examine the individualistic theories of poverty. The traditional Hindu doctrine of Karma tries to explain poverty mostly in terms of action in previous lives. It has served a purpose in reconciling the poor to their poverty and in keeping social peace in spite of unpardonable inequalities. Even on a this-worldly and rational basis, poverty is often explained in individual terms, not only in India but in all parts of the world. The poor are poor, it is said, because of lack of education, character or morals. Even those who are more charitable, attribute poverty to individual causes like bodily defect or disease or lack of information and skills. Needless to say, such explanations are true to a very limited extent. But they cannot explain the phenomenon of .mass and continuing poverty, which is what we face and which can only be explained in some social terms. We arc, therefore, of the view that the common tendency to over-emphasize the individual causes of poverty should be played down. In fact, this over-emphasis oh individual aspect is common among the poor themselves and is an integral part of the culture of poverty. It has to be fought against, deliberately and effectively, in all programmes of the conscientiousness of the poor.

We have to develop a more holistic view, one encompassing social processes, within which the autonomy of the individual is maintained. It should also be stressed that poverty is not an absolute concept, but rather a relative one, i.e., the position of an individual vis-à-vis his entire group. Poverty is deprivation, but not only deprivation. It is deprivation for the many and affluence for the few. A simple erythematic concept helps us only in an appreciation of the magnitude of the problem - leading us to seek solutions in the speeding up of growth rates without enough attention to either the product composition or the distribution of benefits.

Poverty and unemployment are not static concepts and dynamiting them involves much more than generating numbers at different points on the time-scale. Both the cut-off point studies, as well as the Characteristics studies suffer from this major handicap. The problem thus has to be looked upon as a process, a necessary outcome of a distorted pattern of distribution of resources, both human and non-human, within a society. It is this interaction between the structure of the economy (the manner in which resources are owned and controlled) and the working of the economy (the organization of economic activity, and consequently the use of resources within the structure), which give rise to a process leading to affluence for a few and deprivation for the many. The problem has to be viewed, in a historical perspective as well as in its multi-dimensionality. The poor and the unemployed are the rejects of our society and consequently they are weak. Concentration of capital provides power, leaving the people without assets, dependent A capturing of this dependency, the manner in which it is perpetuated, and its consequent impact upon those with power and those without power, need's to be looked at much more deeply.

For instance, though the earlier studies attempted to assess the public provision » of essential and non-essential services (ranging from public distribution of food grains, supply of drinking water, to transport and possibly entertainment) at no time was any emphasis placed on (a) at whose cost is this entire infrastructure built up (b) How do the entire socio-cultural programmes of the Government and non-Governmental agencies result in the suppressing of the 'intrinsic assertiveness' of the poor. leaving them hopelessly ill- equipped to fight the battle at the market terms, and even build into them a repugnance for what is rightfully their own? It may also be pointed out that very often the poor are co-opted into the values and culture of the better-off sections of society. This is a process in which they lose both ways. If co-opted, they are alienated from their own environment. If they reject the culture of the better-off sections of society, their development is stunted because they are not in tough with their own culture, and they are also made to feel like 'drop-outs' of the cultural environment. They become subhumans with little or no right to demand anything.

UNEMPLOYMENT

What exactly do we mean, when we say that a man is unemployed? What is the theoretical justification in building up single multiple cut-off points on the time, income, willingness, and productivity scales? Similarly, how far does a study on the characteristics of the employed, or the unemployed carry us? The generation of various correlates telling that the unemployed have fewer skills, less education, belong to lower castes, or to a particular sex or religion provides little wisdom on the key question-"Why is it like this"?

The problems of 'social valuation of time', for instance, are rarely highlighted. Is the given wage and income structure purify a question of demand and supply? Is it only the innate skill within the person which decides the value society places on his time? A skewed asset distribution creates a set of needs, which can get satisfied only by certain kinds of skills. These skills, per se, either are maintained, in short supply, or are made high prices under conditions of restricted entry. Even if there is access to the teaching centers of these skills, in the given atmosphere, the poor cannot succeed there. The poor, the "Unskilled", either thus, are unemployed, or poorly paid employees.

The notion of the reserve army of labour also fits in here. Specialized needs, satisfied by specialized skills, form an interlocking circuit, leaving the rest to fend for them. This might explain the tendency of locking up huge resources in the creation of the IIM's and such other institutions of higher learning, while keeping the centers of basic learning started. The issue of who is 'gainfully employed' also needs to be sorted out. Given the distorted structure of needs and valuation, a house-wife who slaves the whole day at sweeping and cooking, is never considered* a part of the employed set. Her work is not considered economic activity. A serious examination of her problems is thus never considered and the key question which is inbuilt into all the definitions of a cut-off variety is rarely examined.

It should thus be stressed that poverty and unemployment mean different things to different scholars. From the initial perception of a material deprivation (lack of basic necessities), we graduate on to an awareness of a super structural dimension - the 'culture of poverty', i.e., there is a given mental attitude associated with such economic level. If we peel away still another layer and start asking the question of causation, we run into the problems of expropriation of surplus-exploitation. Our horizon widens to include cases of hardworking people/groups that somehow never seem to have enough, given the existence of the intermediary.

These deepening perceptions stilt remains at the level of studying an event, at an individual or social level. Carrying the logic further, we come to the realization, that associated with a given structure of distribution of material assets, both within a country, and between countries, and the manner in which they are used, a process is unleashed which gives rise to the various phenomena of deprivation, a pathology of poverty, and exploitation. This might sometimes be interpreted as deterministic. However, the choice of a development path. which is a combination of planned initiatives, within the limits of freedom accorded to us by history, Is in the final analysis what needs to be determined to get an overview of the system.

POVERTY AND UNEMPLOYMENT IN INDIA; THE COLONIAL PERIOD

To understand the roots of the problems of poverty and unemployment in a third world country tike India, it is important to examine the process of the development of capitalism as a world system. The world. before the industrial revolution, was an altogether different place. Even though the countries of the world were at different stages of development and there were established trade relationships between them they were not dropped into the world economy governed by the invisible market forces, which made inroads not only in their economy but also penetrated the social and cultural fabric. The industrial revolution in Europe, which unleashed a vast production potential, made it necessary to see new land» for extracting raw materials to feed the large scale factories and new markets to earn profits on the factory products. The transportation revolution made it possible. to reach distant nations. Today's third world was transformed by the industrially advanced countries into colonies or semi-colonies extracting slaves, minerals, and agricultural raw materials. A relation of dominance and dependency was established which continues to the present day.

The Process of Domination was Characterized by

(i) Extraction of industrial raw material on an organized and systematic basis which resulted in a destruction of the ecological balances in the dominated country leading to the impoverishment of natural resources; the erosion of soil, the indiscriminate cutting down of forests. It also resulted in a change in the cropping pattern in favour of commercial crops like jute, cotton, indigo, tea, rubber and coffee. The consequent decline in food grains production, coupled with the deterioration in natural resources base, led to a widespread incidence of famines, and impoverishment of the peasantry on an unprecedented scale. The extension of commercial crops made way for the penetration of commercial capital, and exposed the local markets to the fluctuations in the world market. This increased the vulnerability of the local producers to incidents taking place well outside the realm of their control. This is well illustrated by the sharp fluctuations of the area under cotton during the American Civil War and in jute during the two World Wars.

Unfortunately, it is not yet realized fully even in political circles that unless the faulty economic policies that are responsible for the present situation are radically changed, there can be no redemption: any number of government job or the rural works programme or slum clearance schemes, etc., do not provide" a lasting or complete remedy of the cancer of unemployment that is eating into the vitals of the nation. After all, the ultimate objective of policy is not just to provide any kind of programme or jobs, but to provide work that is economically productive and yields enough income for a reasonable standard of living Jobs should primarily aim at producing more goods and services for the people and not merely provide wages for unwanted or untrained hands at the tax-payer's expense, which will add to inflation.

Charan Singh

(ii) The dominated country was also looked upon and used as a market for finished goods. This resulted in a destruction of handicrafts and household and cottage industries and a consequent flow of workers from the towns to villages and increase in dependency on land. The earlier interactive relationship between a large number of households and cottage industry, service and commerce based towns and the rural hinterland was replaced by an exploitative relationship, and led to the destruction of the rural-urban continuum. The history of the conversion of small fishing villages to major ports like Bombay, the systematic development of railways, simultaneously destroying our Shahi Saraks and waterways, displays concretely the well laid out mechanisms for both a transfer of raw materials out of the country, and the inflow of cheap manufactures from the West.

(iii) The cities, thriving essentially on this trade, unlike their Western counterparts, never really developed as centers of manufacturing activity, and this is adequately reflected in their skewed occupational distribution. This domination also resulted in an increasing technological dependence of the poor nations on the rich countries. We thus had to borrow not only the technology but also the educational infrastructure and the culture of the rich nations. A self-reliant industrial sector could never develop in India and this acted as a serious constraint on the intersectional transfer within the working force from the primary to the secondary sectors. The importance given to the "borrowed culture" cut our cities off from their traditional roots, and produced an imitative and rootless ethos. No wonder, our cities rarely became centers of anything creative. This was then the story of our cities-their gradual metamorphosis into parasitic glands living essentially on the fruits of labour of the toiling. peasantry.

(iv) The study of our rural tend is just as pathetic. With the destruction of our handicrafts, there was an over-crowding on land turning a situation of land surplus to labour surplus. While earlier it was difficult to drive the exploitation too far because the peasants could flee to other areas, now in the event of land scarcity, the control of land became, the major source of exploitation.

Having been brought into the trade nexus, and forced to pay a fixed, high amount of cash, rent, the peasantry mere increasingly got into the group of the moneylenders and traders. This started the process of alienation from land resulting in:

(a) an increase in the number of landless labourers and poor peasantry;

(b) a regularization through the zamindari system of 'absentee land-lordisim' which because of its interests in revenue and not in production, resulted in the siphoning off of so much surplus that our agriculture was left completely stagnant. This surplus was utilized by the landed sections in either luxury goods consumption or was fed once again into money lending and trading. The non-development of productive forces in the agrarian set-up resulting in differential excess profits in the above-mentioned activities as compared to profit from production only consolidated the entire phenomenon.

In this queer constellation of circumstances, we get an appropriation of surplus through:

(a) A high rate of land-rent;

(b) An increasing phenomenon of consumption loans, which given the high interest rates, results in a rapid increase in indebtedness;

(c) The phenomenon of distress sales, where the poor peasant is forced to sell his produce when he is at his weakest, to pay both his cash rent, as well as the interest via the price mechanism;

(d) a gradual system of 'enforced bondage' building up in the rural areas, which also provides over-riding political power to the landed interests; and

(e) a steady transference of capital resources from production to money lending and trading. What we had then was stagnant agriculture, characterized by multiple forms of exploitation-the poor peasantry having little chance to grow, having to carry an increasingly larger number of people on their already strained backs.

It is this distorted structure of a weak and stagnant agriculture, an under-developed industry and a bloated tertiary sector that we inherited at independence. Poverty and Unemployment in India: The Post-independence Period

Has the process of development since 1947, in its essence, changed? Outwardly, the various forms of domination have changed, both in form and content. For instance, the relationship between the rich nations and India, is no longer characterized by direct foreign rule. But the wide differential in their relative economic strength gets reflected in:

(a) Unfavorable terms of trade, with our still having to rely on export of agricultural and mineral raw materials, while importing manufactured items;

(b) A large quantum of surplus being transferred through the transportation, communication, banking and insurance links.

(c) An extending shift from exploitation through an unequal trade in commodities to trade in services-particularly in technological processes;

(d) The linking up of aid trade, bringing in the phenomena of tied aid, consultancy services, procuring of spares, etc.

(e) The historical 'progress' in form and content had not decreased our dependency to any significant extend In fact, some would tend to argue that the dependency has actually increased.

The intrusion of multi-nationals into this scene further complicates the picture. Any illusion that we had got rid of the foreigner with the declaration of political independence is soon shattered. The extensive domination of foreign goods/ technology over not only our luxury consumer goods sector, but also essentials, such as drugs, oil and capita) goods like transport equipment and machinery, only points to increasing inroads that foreign capital is making into our country.

The use of 'reality available" technology, developed in the West under the conditions of scarcity of labour, in the growth of modern industry and transportation in India has many serious implications for the economy. The technology being a borrowed one increases our dependence on the West and makes for flow of funds to the West in terms of royalties tied purchase of spares, consultancy, etc. The technology is highly capital-intensive. The employment of labour per unit of output is small. As a result the employment generation for a given capital investment is very limited. However, the number of workers thrown out of employment or employable for the production of the same output of, say, cloth or soap is very large. Thus, the borrowed capital-intensive technology does not take into account the factor endowment of the country and fails to meet the social needs. In the context of the learning, process implicit in the development of indigenous technology and the gradual shift to advanced technology to enable the economy to adjust to the changes, the induction of borrowed technology results in enclave growth. The technology is accessible by and large, to the big industrial and business houses in the country, and this restricted access helps Strength en their monopoly position. The borrowed technology demands specialized skill and thus makes for expansion of institutions and other services catering to the needs of these modern industries. This creates high incorrte pockets and demand for luxury, goods and services of the Western variety, which in turn require specialized skills. The entire process, boosted up by sales promotion and vigorous advertising techniques, helps the development of a 'consumer society'. More and more of our investible funds get locked up to meet the demand of the 'elite' in society.

The concentration of assets and an oligopolistic structure in our industry have a number of development implications. The prices are set by the producers in industries where oligopolies dominate. Pricing is often used to forestall entry of new producers. Because of technological discontinuities, given a price, varying degrees of profitability are associated with firms using different technologies. With the possibility of differentiating products, the profitability of the bigger firms improves, as they build up well-entrenched consumer preferences for their products. Due to concentration of assets, the larger producers enjoy considerable market power acquiring resources, credit, scarce skills and scarce inputs. This often influences their choice of technology. Considerable resources are devoted to product differentiation, on sales organization, and marketing units with a well-paid staff. Much of the investment in Research and Development is concerned with finding out consumer preferences rather than on the technological aspects of production. The firms also go on for prestigious expenditure to built up their image and normalize excess profit by adding to administration costs. Because of the oligopolistic position of the industry, high profit can be maintained without much effort being made to develop indigenous technology.

This development process results in wider income differential expanding the market for commodities and services stimulated through the demonstration effect. This feeds into the 'culture of our cities'. On the one hand, we have the glittering lights, luxury apartments, cars, hotels and race courses-white on the other, we have the slums and the pavement dwellers. The functioning of the organized industry in our restrictive monopoly-oligopoly situations eats into the viability of our poverty production centers, which are unable to survive in the face of such organized competition.

The widening differential of these two sectors attracts a large number of 'possible migrants' into our cities, who more often than not, land up in the 'underworld nexus'. It is here, in organized vice. That smuggling, illicit liquor, prostitution, etc..

Find a haven. This sector serves the purpose of not only sheltering the organized sector from the 'storming unemployed", but also comes in handy to the ruthless politicians in their power games. A word on our 'social services sector', would not be out of plea here. The institutions of higher learning, the big hospitals, and the cinema houses - are meant to serve our elite. On the poor they have a different impact. Other than not permitting less costly versions of similar

Institutions catering to the poor, they also play a critical part in the game of cultural suppression.

Even in the rural areas, the situation has only changed its forms. Various legislations have been passed on land ceilings, on tenancy, on minimum wages, etc. This has altered the forms of bondage, and new 'informal relations' have appeared. Modern technology too has made its inroads, though only in limited pockets. In such areas the importance of rent and interest has gone down, while the surplus expropriation through the wage link is becoming more important. Of course, the intrusion of 'modern inputs' has been of tremendous benefit to multinationals and the local industrial groups who supplied these inputs. They, of course, are not in the least bothered about the 'increasing risk' which the poor farmer faces with this new package. If the exchange between rural and urban areas is unequal then the surplus flows to the metropolitan center. If appropriated (though the support price measure) by the rural bourgeoisie, it is used either for luxury goods and service consumption, or for usury, trade and other forms of unproductive exploitation. The rich peasantry is not driven to expand productive forces, as they can increase absolute surplus by increasing exploitation. The parasite exploitation by the rural big landowners restricts the growth of productive forces, not only in agriculture, but also in industry by restricting the demand for industrial goods.

It is in such a scenario, that the evaluation of the various strategies of rural development have to be studied. From Community Development to the Green Revolution to Integrated Rural Development, who has really benefited, and at whose cost, needs to be looked at much more carefully, this then is our present picture-a tremendous concentration of assets, reflecting clearly a monopoly situation In land, capital, and trade services. What thirty years of planning has done to it needs to be worked out. It is, therefore, vital to understand the distribution of assets which goes on re-directing investment and the choice of technology the appropriation of surplus, and its utilization which tends to be used up more and moir6 in the upper sector and leads to increases in the size of the unproductive sector, retarding further the development possibilities, limiting the growth of employment expansion and raising of productivity only in a small sector and keeping low the earnings of the majority, so that the dynamics of poverty and unemployment become clear.

CONCLUSION

According to newspaper reports, jobless migrants are once again trickling into Calcutta. They have descended upon over-crowded Calcutta from the districts in the interior - in search of work, money and food. They are the landless labour hit by the lean season,. They are just one more vivid manifestation of India's quiet crisis: rural unemployment. It is India's biggest crisis. Even if all the land were re-distributed properly, and the yield per acre were to be obtained at its optimum, and there were to be enough food to feed ail, the crisis of rural unemployment would not be resolved.

There is only one answer. Jobs, many jobs, have to be created in rural India. This should be the nation's one-pint programme. The Government cannot help ... But-the affluent sections of the public can help. Businesspersons can reorient manufacturing methods for many of their ancillary products-even if it means slight inconvenience to begin with-to create more employment in the cottage sector, whenever possible In the rural area. The Government should help remove all tax and excise hindrances to investments and donations which help create self-employment and generate new jobs. Creating more jobs for others, even on a no-profit no-loss basis for themselves, would, one imagines, be a far more satisfying exercise for businessmen than simply donating to charities and temples.

11

SOCIO-ECONOMIC CONDITIONS OF SCHEDULE TRIBE WOMEN WORKERS IN AGRICULTURE: A CASE STUDY IN ANDHRA PRADESH

P. Vasudeva Rao
P. Venu Gopal

INTRODUCTION

The term Tribe as originated at the time of Greeklity states and the early formation of Roman empire. The Latin term, Tribes has science being transformed to mean a group of persons a forming a community and claming descent from a common ancestor. There is no clear definition or criteria for considering a human group a tribe. Different scholars defined it indifferent ways. Sometimes they are called as "Aboriginals" or "depressed class" or Advises. The dictionary meaning of Term Tribe is a group of people in a Primitive stage of development. Acknowledging the authority of chief and usually regarding them as having a common ancestor. As per the Imperial Gazetteer of India. Tribe is a collection of family bearing a common name, speaking a common dialect aid occupying a common directly.

Before discussing the methodology adopting in this study, it is pertinent to explain the use of the term scheduled tribes in lieu of tribals. It may be argued that the term 'Tribe is more scientific as it provides a set of objective criteria'. It is used in the Indian census as a standard term of references for all purposes. The present age of technology and a life of consumable goods. People with varied life styles living in modern society hardly related that in remote part of country Tribal Communities are living along with them and that there development is still primitive. These tribal communities are retaining the original creator of their habitat, habits and culture. Although quantitatively these tribal communities constitute a minor part of society. Their contribution to its variety, vitality and richness is distinctive never before in the history of mankind. The need of understanding the socio-economic life of the tribes is more relevant them today. The present study throws a light on the socio-economic status of women tribes . In this connection an attempt is made in this present paper to examine socio-economic conditions, levels of earnings and levels of living of ST women workers in agricultural sector in selected districts of Andhra Pradesh

SOURCES OF DATA

Research can be conducted by using either primary data or secondary data or both. In the present study both primary and secondary data are used. The study is mostly based on primary data collected for the purpose. By conducting a survey in the three districts of A.P namely, Annathapur, Khamam, and Vishakapatnam the primary data was collected. Interview schedule was used to collect the primary data from the respondents. The units of observation and analysis for this study are rural Schedule Tribe households. The total number of rural households selected in the sample is 450 (of which 68 were non-responsive) spread over 35 villages, 13 mandals, and 03 districts in the state of A.P Covering 382 house holds.

METHODOLOGY

Research can be conducted either through deductive method or inductive method. In the present study inductive method of analysis is used. The study is concerned with Andhra Pradesh which is the major States having large number of ST population in India. Random sampling technique is used in the survey. The trends of schedule tirbe population among different districts shows interesting results. It is found that some are recorded with continuous rise , while in others have erratic growth. However, that ST population rise growth in various socio–economic, infrastructural, medical and health aspects etc., are examine at regional level. Broadly, the state of AP, is dived in three regions namely coastal Andhra, Rayalaseema and Telengana. Among these regions three districts are identified which are having highest share of ST population in total population of the district. These districts are Vishakhapatnam in coastal region, Khammam in Telangana region and Anantapur in Rayalaseema region. There are 63 mandals in Anantapur 46 mandals in Khammam and 43 mandals in Vishakhapatnam on the basis of share of ST population to the total population, five mandals form each district totaling 15 mandals have been selected for the present study. Again for the village level data one village form each mandal is selected. Thus altogether 15 villages are included in the present study. It observed that there are 11 major communities in those villages. On the basis of their concentration in the village 5 per cent of the total selected for this study. Samples are selected by using simple random sampling techniques. Thus we arrive at 382 samples (details have been in Table A). A pre tested questionnaire is canvassed to solicit the information on various socio-economic cultural aspects of ST women in the study area.

SOCIO-ECONOMIC PROFILE

An attempt is made in this part to examine the economic conditions of the surveyed Scheduled Tribe population. Various economic variables such as assets, income ownership occupation etc are examined in detail in the following pages.

House Ownership

An attempt is made to know whether the respondents possess any house. Alternatively, not. Out of the 382 respondents, 360

Table A
Distribution of Respondents by Village and Caste

District	Mandal	Village	Bag-ata	Chin-chu	Gond	Lam-bada	Konda Dora	Koya	Par-oja	Sug-ali	Val-miki	Yan-adi	Yanadi Challa	Yeru-kula	Yeru-kula Kapp-aralla-tippa	Village Total
Ananthapur	Gorantla	Madana Palli	–	3	2	1	1	4	1	1	–	3	–	3	–	19
	Nallamada	Nallamada	–	1	2	2	2	10	1	1	–	3	–	3	–	25
	Mudugabba	Dorigallu	–	1	1	2	2	9	1	2	–	2	–	4	–	24
	Tanakal	Tavalarm	–	2	1	1	1	6	2	1	–	3	–	3	–	20
	Kadiri	Muthyala cheruvu	–	1	1	2	1	7	1	1	–	4	–	6	–	24
	Total															112
Khammam	Tekupalli	Bethampudi	–	4	–	–	2	8	1	–	–	5	–	5	–	27
	Yellindu	Rompaid	–	2	–	–	1	4	1	–	–	6	–	6	–	18
	Singareni	Vsirikayalapalli	–	1	2	–	1	5	2	–	–	6	–	6	–	25
	Kothagudem	Kamkonda	–	2	–	1	2	7	2	–	–	4	–	4	–	22
	Chintur	Chatti	–	2	–	–	2	8	1	–	–	4	–	4	–	22
	Total															114
Vishaka-Patnam	Arukuvalli	Konta banusuguda	9	2	–	-	5	9	2	–	1	1	-	4	–	33
	Paderu	Gudivada	11	3	–	–	2	4	3	–	–	2	–	3	–	28
	Chintapalli	Chintapalli	5	1	–	1	3	6	2	–	1	1	–	5	–	25
	Hukumpeta	Kontapalli	6	1	–	–	9	11	1	–	1	2	–	2	–	33
	Pedabayalu	Rogulu	10	2	3	–	6	6	2	–	1	1	–	6	–	37
	Total															156
	Total		41	28	12	10	40	104	23	06	04	50		64		

(94.2 per cent) have houses. Majority i.e. 356 (98.8 per cent) have houses in rural areas and 4 (1.2 per cent) respondents have houses in urban areas.

Table 1
House of Ownership

Type of House	*Number of Respondents*	*Percent*	*Valid Percent*
RCC	91	23.8	25.3
Mud	47	12.3	13.1
Asbestos	77	20.2	21.4
Thatched	89	23.3	24.7
Tiled sheds	56	14.7	15.6
Total	360	94.2	100.0
No	22	5.8	
Grand Total	382	100.0	

Source: Computed

With respect to the type of houses they possess, data shows that out of 360 respondents, majority i.e. 91 (25.3 per cent) have houses with of RCC Roof. 89 (24.7 per cent) have Thatched houses, 77 (21.4 per cent) have asbestos houses, 56 (15.6 per cent) have tiled houses and 47 (13.1 per cent) have mud houses. It is noticed during the study that most of the houses were constructed by the government under various welfare schemes. It is also noticed that most of these house owners do not have legal rights over their houses. They are constructed in occupied vacant lands of the government

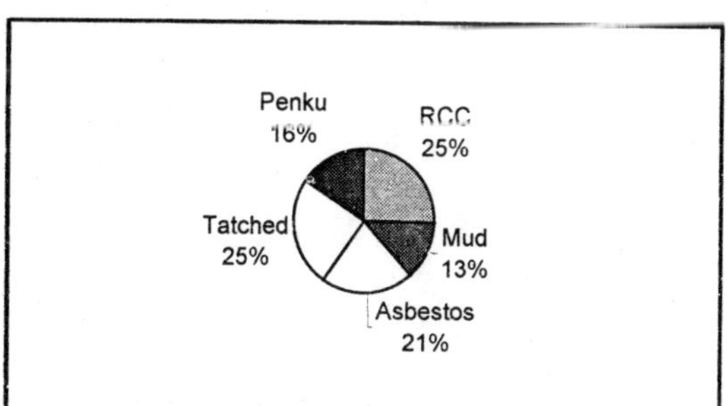

Diagram 1: Type of House
Source: Table 1

Value of the House(in Rupees)

The value of the owned house is more important since it is one factor that determines the economic status of the respondents. The value of the owned house varies widely in the present Study. Out of 360 respondents who are having houses, majority 93 (25.8 per cent) have houses the value of which is less than Rs. 5000 only. Another 41 (11.4 per cent) have houses valuing between Rs. 5000-10000. Only 39 (10.8 per cent) have houses whose value is than Rs. 50000. The average value of the houses is Rs. 37979. The value of houses range form a minimum of Rs 4000 to a maximum of Rs 8,00,000.

Table 2
Value of Owned House

House Value (Rs.)	*Number of Respondents*	*Percent*	*Valid Percent*
>5000	93	24.3	25.8
5000-10000	41	10.7	11.4
10000-15000	38	9.9	10.6
15000-20000	28	7.3	7.8
20000-25000	15	3.9	4.2
25000-30000	26	6.8	7.2
30000-35000	9	2.4	2.5
35000-40000	31	8.1	8.6
40000-45000	6	1.6	1.7
45000-50000	34	8.9	9.4
50000+	39	10.2	10.8
Total	360	94.2	100.0
No	22	5.8	
Grand Total	382	100.0	

Source: Computed

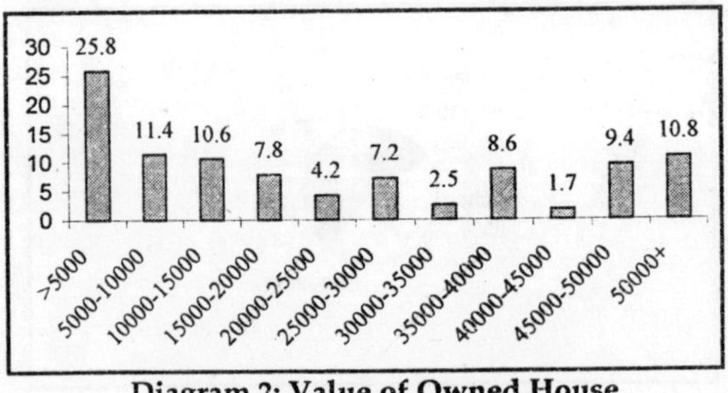

Diagram 2: Value of Owned House
Source: Table 2

Possession of Animals

Table 3 shows the number of animals possessed by the respondents. In the rural areas possession of domestic animals is a common phenomenon. But unfortunately in the study it is observed that 83 per cent of the respondents do not possess animals at all. Only 65 respondents have animals and out of them 40 (61.5 per cent) have 2 and 9 (13.8 per cent) have 1 only. About 80 per cent of the respondents have 3 or less number of animals.

Table 3
Possession of Animals by the Respondents
(Cows, Oxen and Buffaloes)

Number of Animals	*Number*	*Per-cent*	*Valid Percent*	*Number Buffalos*	*Per-cent*	*Valid Percent*
1	9	2.4	13.8	35	9.2	41.1
2	40	10.5	61.5	26	6.8	30.5
3	3	0.8	4.6	12	3.1	14.1
4	6	1.6	9.2	5	1.3	6.0
5	2	0.5	3.1	4	1.0	4.8
6+	5	1.3	7.7	3	0.8	3.5
Total	65	17.0	100.0	85	21.7	100.0
No	317	83.0		299	78.3	
Grand Total	382	100.0		382	100.0	

Source: Computed

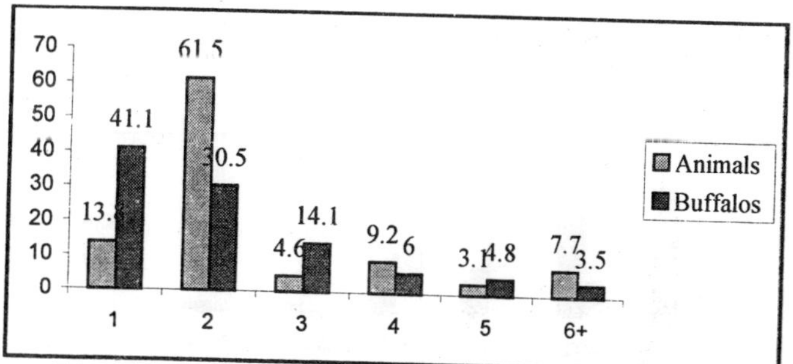

Diagram 3: Possession of Animals by the Respondents
(Cows, Oxen and Buffaloes)
Source: Table 3

The present study is also tried to know the number of buffalos possessed by the respondents. Out of 382 respondents majority i.e., 299 do not have at least a buffalo. Out of 85 respondents, having buffalos, majority i.e. 35 (41.1 per cent) respondents have only one each, followed by 26 (30.5 per cent) having 2, and 3 (3.5 per cent) respondents have 6 and above.

Value of the Animals

Analysis on the value of the animals which the respondents possess proves that out of 65 respondents having animals, majority i.e., (35 per cent) have animals whose value is between Rs. 10000-15000, followed by 16 (24.2 per cent) respondents having animals of the value of Rs. 5000-1000 each and only one respondent has animals whose value is more than Rs. 25000.

Table 4
Value of the Animals (Cows or Oxen)

Value (Rs.)	*Number Cows/ Oxen*	*Per-cent*	*Valid Percent*	*Number Buffalos*	*Per-cent*	*Valid Percent*
Below 5000	12	3.1	18.2	32	8.4	37.6
5000-10000	16	4.2	24.2	28	7.3	32.9
10000-15000	23	6.0	34.8	12	3.1	14.1
15000-20000	12	3.1	18.2	7	1.8	8.2
20000-25000	1	0.3	1.5	3	0.8	3.5
25000+	1	0.3	1.5	3	0.8	3.5
Total	65	17.0	100.0	85	22.3	100.0
No	317	83.0		297	77.7	
Grand Total	382	100.0		382	100.0	

Source: Computed

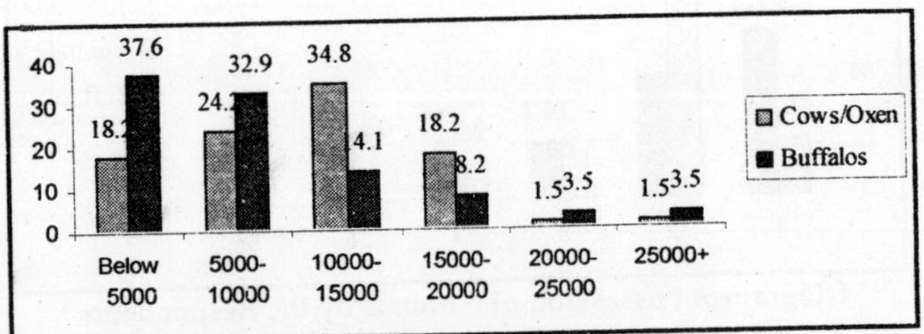

Diagram 4: Value of Animals (Cows or Oxen)
Source: Table 4

Out of 85 respondents having buffalos, majority i.e., 32 (37.6 per cent) have buffalos of the value of less than Rs. 5000, followed by 28 (32.9 per cent) respondents having buffalos of the value of Rs. 5000-10000 and only 3 respondents, having buffalos of the value of more than Rs. 25000. The average value of animals is Rs. 11,759. The value of the animals possessed by the respondents is presented in diagram .

Possession Gold Ornaments

With respect to the quantity of gold possessed by these respondents in grams, the following table shows that majority i.e., 331 (86.6 per cent) of the respondents do not possess gold at all. Out of 51 respondents possessing gold majority i.e., 19 (37.2 per cent) respondents possess 80 grams, 15 (29.4 per cent) of the respondents possess 50 grams. Only one respondent has 90 grams.

Table 5
Gold Possessed by the Respondents

Quantity (Tulas)	*Number*	*Percent*	*Valid Percent*
20	2	0.5	4.0
30	6	1.5	11.7
50	15	3.9	29.4
60	1	0.3	2.0
70	19	4.9	37.2
80	7	1.8	13.7
90	1	0.3	2.0
Total	51	13.4	100.0
No	331	86.6	
Grand Total	382	100.0	

Source: Computed

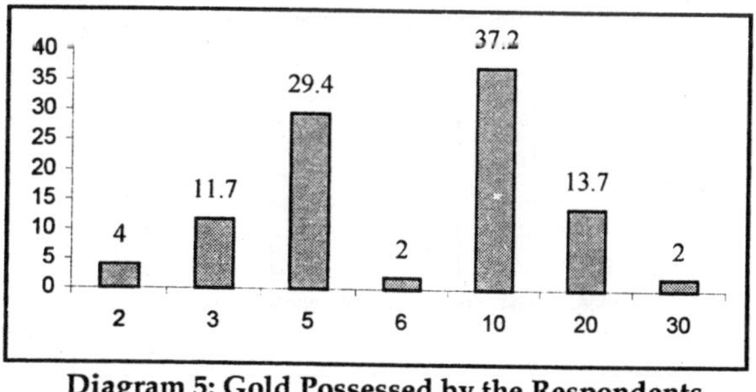

Diagram 5: Gold Possessed by the Respondents
Source: Table 5

Study also attempted to know the value of gold possessed by the respondents. Out of 51 respondents, majority i.e., 14 (27.5 per cent) respondents possess gold the value of which is in between Rs 5000-10000 and another 11 (21.6 per cent) possess gold valuing in between Rs. 10000-15000. Only 14 respondents have gold the value of which is Rs. 30000 and above. The average value of gold possessed is Rs. 23350. The minimum value of the gold is Rs 5000 per the maximum is Rs 70,000. The value of the gold possessed by the respondents is presented in diagram.

Table 6
Value of Gold Possessed by the Respondents

Value of Gold (Rs.)	*Number*	*Percent*	*Valid Percent*
1000-5000	1	0.3	2.0
5000-10000	14	3.7	27.5
10000-15000	11	2.9	21.6
15000-20000	3	0.8	5.9
20000-25000	7	1.8	13.7
25000-30000	1	0.3	2.0
30000+	14	3.7	27.5
Total	51	13.4	100.0
No	331	86.6	
Grand Total	382	100.0	

Source: Computed

Possession of Durable Goods

The durable goods possessed by these respondents proves the status of the respondent. It can be observed from the Table 7

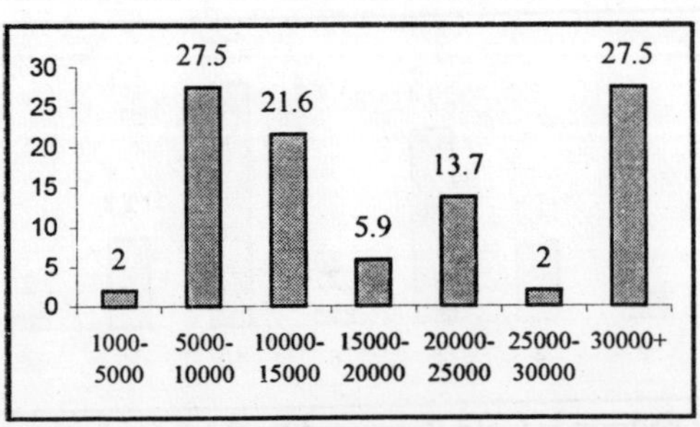

Diagram 6: Value of Gold Possessed by the Respondents
Source: Table 6

that out of 382 respondents, 192 respondents do not possess T.V and only 190 respondents possess T.V. Out of the people possessing T.V., majority i.e., 116 (61.0 per cent) possess T.V value of which is Rs. 1000-5000, followed by 62 respondents who possess T.V having value between Rs. 5000-10,000 and only 12 respondents are having T.V between Rs 10,000-15,000. The average value of the T.V is Rs. 5576. The minimum value is Rs 190 and the maximum value is Rs 35,000.

Table 7
Value of Durable Goods Possessed by the Respondents

Value (Rs.)	*No. T.V*	*Per-cent*	*Valid Per-cent*	*No. Cycle/ Motor-cycle*	*Per-cent*	*Valid Per-cent*	*No. Frizz*	*Per-cent*	*Valid Per-cent*
>1000	–	–	–	14	3.7	23.3	–	–	–
1000-5000	116	30.4	61.0	11	2.9	18.3	–	–	–
5000-10000	62	16.2	32.6	7	1.8	11.7	–	–	–
10000-15000	12	3.2	6.3	3	0.8	5.0	4	1.0	100.0
15000-20000	–	–	–	4	1.0	6.7	–	–	–
20000-25000	–	–	–	1	0.3	1.7	–	–	–
25000-30000	–	–	–	14	3.7	23.3	–	–	–
30000+	–	–	–	6	1.6	10.0	–	–	–
Total	190	49.7	100.0	60	15.7	100.0	4	1.0	–
No	192	50.3	–	322	84.3	–	378	99.0	–
Grand Total	382	100.0	–	382	100.0	–	382	100.0	–

Source: Computed

In the present study, out of 382 surveyed respondents, 322 respondents do not possess cycle/motorcycle. Out of the 190 respondents possessing cycle/motor cycle, 14 (23.3 per cent) possessed the value of which is less than Rs. 1000 and another 14 (23.3 per cent) possessed cycle/motor cycle of the value of between Rs. 25,000-30,000, followed by 11 (18.3 per cent) respondents whose value is between Rs. 1000-5000 and only 6 respondents are having cycle/motorcycle of value above Rs. 30,000. The average value of the motorcycle is Rs. 21,681. The average value of the cycle is Rs 95. Out of 382 respondents, only 4 respondents possessed refrigerator in the range of Rs. 10000-15000. The average value of the refrigerator is Rs. 15000.

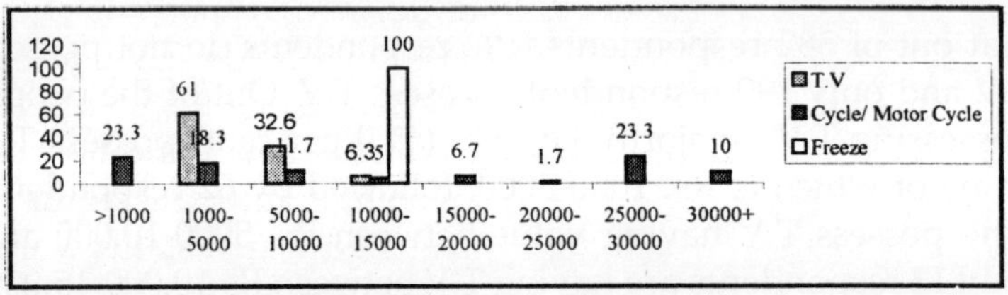

Diagram 7: Value of Durable Goods Possessed by the Respondents
Source: Table 7

Possession of Other Consumer Goods

With respect to the data on possession of the other consumer goods data in the Table 8 reveals that out of 382 respondents, 352 respondents do not possess air cooler and only 30 respondents out of the total surveyed respondents possessed air cooler. Out of the people possessing cooler, majority 18 (60.0 per cent) possessed air cooler whose value is Rs. 1000-5000, followed by 8 respondents whose.

Table 8
Value of Cooler Possessed by the Respondents

Value of Cooler (Rs.)	*Number Cooler*	*Per-cent*	*Valid Percent*	*Number Gas*	*Per-cent*	*Valid Percent*
>1000	4	1.0	13.3	18	4.7	22.5
1000-5000	18	4.7	60.0	61	16.0	76.3
10000-15000	8	2.1	26.7	1	0.3	1.3
Total	30	7.9	100.0	80	20.9	100.0
No	352	92.1		302	79.1	
Grand Total	382	100.0		382	100.0	

Source: Computed

Table 9
Distribution of the Respondents by Possession of Land (Acres)

Acres	*No. Total*	*Per-cent*	*Valid Percent*	*No. Dry*	*Per-cent*	*Valid Percent*	*No. Wet*	*Per-cent*	*Valid Percent*
1	48		21.1	18	4.7	29.5	30	7.9	34.9
2	50		32.2	25	6.5	41.0	25	6.5	29.1
3	23		18.6	13	3.4	21.3	10	2.6	11.6
4	6		3.4				6	1.6	7.0
5	7		10.2	1	0.3	1.6	6	1.6	7.0
6	1		3.4				1	0.3	1.2
8	2		5.9	1	0.3	1.6	1	0.3	1.2
9	9		0.8	3	0.8	4.9	6	1.6	7.0
10	1		4.2				1	.3	1.2
Total	147		100.0	61	16.0	100.0	86	22.5	100.0

Source: Computed

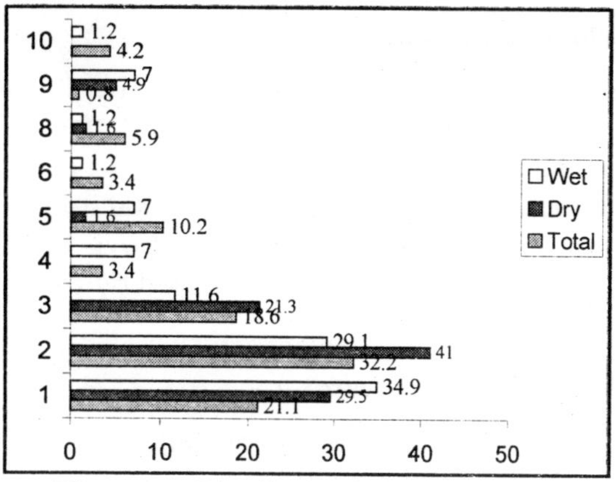

Diagram 8: Distribution of the Respondents by Possession of Land (Acres)
Source: Table 8

Possession of Land

Land is one of the important assets and majority of the people in the developing economics depend on land for their livelihood. In this connection, an attempt is made in Table 9 to examine the possession of land by the respondents in the study area. The extent of land possessed by the respondents. Out of 382 respondents, 235 respondents do not possess any land at all. Out of the 147 respondents possessing land majority i.e., 50 possess 2 acres of land, followed by 48 possessing one acre of land. 75 per cent of the respondents have less than 4 acres of land only. The table also depicts the type of land possessed by the respondents. Generally wet lands are more valuable and productive than the dry lands. In the present study, out of the 61 respondents having dry land, majority, i.e., 25 (41.0 per cent) have 2 acres of dry land each followed by 18 (29.5 per cent) having the 1 acre of dry land. The average of the dry land possessed by them is 2.33 acres. Similarly out of the 86 respondents having wet land, majority, i.e., 30 (34.9 per cent) have 1 acre of wetland, followed by 25 (29.1 per cent) are having 2 acres of wetland. The average number of the wetland possessed is 2.76 acres.

Value of the Land Possessed

Table 10 shows the value of land possessed by the respondents in the study area both for wet and dry. Out of 61 respondents having dry land majority 13 (21.0 per cent) possess land the value of which is between Rs. 15000-20000 and 31 (50.8 per cent) respondents have land valuing above Rs. 25000. The average value of dry land value possessed by the respondents is Rs. 35871only.

Tax Paid by the Respondents

An attempt is also made in the present study to know the amount of annual land tax paid.

Table 10
Tax Paid by the Respondent on Land

Annual Tax Rs.	*Number*	*Percent*	*Valid Percent*
>20	6	1.6	10.7
20-30	3	0.8	5.4
30-40	1	0.3	1.8
40-50	7	1.8	12.5
50-60	19	5.0	33.9
70-80	1	0.3	1.8
80-90	7	1.8	12.5
90-+	12	3.1	21.4
Total	56	14.7	100.0

Only 22 respondents in the study area invested more than Rs. 5000 on land irrigation and land development. The average

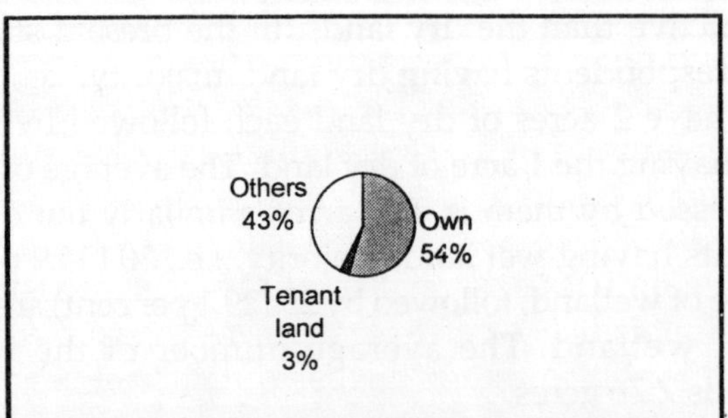

Diagram 9: Working on Land

Table 11
Investment on Land Improvement and Irrigation

Investment	*No of Respondents who Invested on Land*	*Percent*	*Valid Percent*	*No of Respondents who Invested on Irrigation*	*Percent*	*Valid Percent*
>500	19	5.0	28.8	39	10.2	42.4
500-1000	11	2.9	16.7	19	5.0	20.7
1000-1500	4	1.0	6.1	5	1.3	5.4
1500-2000	6	1.6	9.1	2	0.5	2.2
2000-2500	3	0.8	4.5	2	0.5	2.2
2500-3000	5	1.3	7.6	2	0.5	2.2
3500-4000	3	0.8	4.5	1	0.3	1.1
4000-4500	2	0.5	3.0			
5000+	13	3.4	19.7	22	5.8	23.9
Total	66	17.3	100.0	92	24.1	100.0
No	316	82.7		290	75.9	
Grand Total	382	100.0		382	100.0	

investment on irrigation was Rs. 4113 only. The minimum is Rs 200 and the maximum is Rs 30,000. The investment made on land and on irrigation is presented in diagram 9.

Investment on land Improvement and Irrigation

The study also highlighted the data on the investments made on land as well as on irrigation by the respondent in the study area. Out of 382 respondent 316 (82.7 per cent) state that there is no investment on land. Out of 66 respondents who made investment on land, majority i.e., 19 (28.8 per cent) invested Rs. 500 and another 11 (16.7 per cent) between Rs. 500-1000. Only 13 respondents have invested more than Rs. 5000. The average investment on land is Rs. 3058 only. The minimum is Rs 200 and the maximum is Rs 13,000.

Out of 382 respondents, 290 (75.9 per cent) said that they have not invested on irrigation. Out of 92 respondents who invested on irrigation, majority i.e., 39 (42.4 per cent) invested Rs. 500 and another 19 (20.7 per cent) between Rs. 500-1000.

Investment on Fertilizers and Other Inputs

An attempt is also made to know the investment on fertilizers and other inputs. Out of 382 respondents, 290 (75.9 per cent) stated that there was no investment on fertilizers. Out of 92 respondents who made investment on fertilizers, majority i.e., 32 (34.8 per cent) invested more than Rs. 5000 and another 13 (14.1 per cent) between Rs. 500-1000. The average investment on land was Rs. 7713 only.

Production of Paddy, Pulses and Other Food Products

An attempt is made in the study to examine the cropping pattern of the respondent. In the most of the studies, it is concluded that small and medium farmers produce food crops. In the present study also it is proved and revealed that out of the total 147 responds, who are having lands, 122 are producing food crops and the remaining producing non food crops. An analysis shows the number of bags of paddy produced by the respondents. Out of 382 respondents, 346 respondents or not produce paddy. Only 36 respondents report that they produce paddy. Out of them, majority i.e., 9 (25.0 per cent) produce paddy between 5-10 bags and another 9 produce between 20-25 bags. The highest quantity of bags is produced by 3 respondents ranging between 40-50 bags. The average number of bags is 21 bags.

Occupation of Respondents

Occupation is one of the important economic variables. The economic status and income level of an individual depends upon his or her occupational status. Persons in organized employment are more respected and enjoy better salaries as compared to people working in unorganized sector. The occupational structure also influences the social structure.

Table 12
Type of Occupation

Category	*Number*	*Percent*
Farmer	129	33.7
Non farmer	74	19.4
Both	34	8.9
Labour	145	38.0
Total	382	100.0

An analysis of Table 10 shows the occupational structure of the respondents. The study is conducted in the rural areas and hence naturally most of the people are engaged in agricultural or allied activities. An analysis of Table 21 shows that out of 382 respondents, majority i.e., 38.0 per cent are working as labourers and 29.0 per cent are working in different miscellaneous occupations. Unfortunately only 18 (4.7 per cent) are working as farmers and 34 (8.9 per cent) are working as farmers cum agricultural labour. This study clearly shows that the STs don't have land of their own and majority are only working as agricultural labourer for their livelihood.

Daily Wages of the Earners

The examination on mode of wages that they are earning give perfect picture of the earnings of the sample respondents. Hence an attempt is made in Table 12 to know the amount of wage they get per day. Out of 382 respondents, 253 (66.2 per cent) work as laborers of daily wage earners. Out of them, majority i.e., 61 (24.1 per cent) are getting Rs. 50 a day are getting less than Rs. 50 a day. The minimum wage earned by the respondents is Rs. 15 per day. The maximum earned by these respondents is only Rs. 100. The average income earned is Rs 44.5and above 60 per cent.

Mode of Daily Wages Receiving

Usually in developed countries/areas the mode of payment of wages will be in the form of cash, where as in under developed particularly in rural areas the payment of wages vary from occupation to occupation. Hence the study also attempted to know the mode of payment of remuneration for their work table. The data reveals that Out of 262, 253 are (96.6 per cent) receiving cash and the remaining i.e., 3.4 receive in kind. The traditional practice of receiving the wage in kind still continues even in the modern times. However, the percentage of kind form remuneration is not high when compared with cash form of remuneration.

Table 13
Mode of Daily Wages Received

Kind	*Number*	*Percent*	*Valid Percent*
Cash	253	66.2	96.6
Kind	9	2.4	3.4
Total	262	68.6	100.0
No	120	31.4	
Grand Total	382	100.0	

Source: Computed

Child Labour in the Family

Child labor is one of the chronic problems of developing economies in the most of the poor countries. The Government of India abolished child labour by an Act and Children below 14 years are not permitted to work, since it hinders the growth of the child both physically and psychologically. But unfortunately in the rural areas especially in the agricultural sector children work and contribute to family income. In agricultural families children are considered as an asset rather than liability. Hence the existence of child labor in the families of respondents is examined and the results were given in Table.

Table 14
Investment on Fertilizers and Other Inputs

Invest-ment	*Number Fertilizer*	*Per-cent*	*Valid Percent*	*Number Other Exp.*	*Per-cent*	*Valid Percent*
>500	12	3.1	13.0	27	7.1	34.6
500-1000	13	3.4	14.1	12	3.1	15.4
1000-1500	4	1.0	4.3	7	1.8	9.0
1500-2000	13	3.4	14.1	6	1.6	7.7
2000-2500	7	1.8	7.6	1	.3	1.3
2500-3000	4	1.0	4.3	2	.5	2.6
3500-4000	1	.3	1.1	1	.3	1.3
4000-4500	2	.5	2.2	4	1.0	5.1
4500-5000	4	1.0	4.3	4	1.0	5.1
5000+	32	8.4	34.8	14	3.7	17.9
Total	92	24.1	100.0	78	20.4	100.0
No	290	75.9		304	79.6	
Grand Total	382	100.0		382	100.0	

Source: Computed

Out of 382 respondents, 304 (79.6 per cent) stated that there was no investment on other. Out of 78 respondent inputs who made investment on other, majority i.e., 27 (34.6 per cent) inputs invested Rs. 500 and another 12 (15.4 per cent) between Rs. 500-1000. Only 14 respondents invested more than Rs. 5000. The average investment on other was Rs. 5298 only. The minimum Rs 100 and the maximum is Rs 43000. The investment on fertilizers and other inputs are presented in diagram.

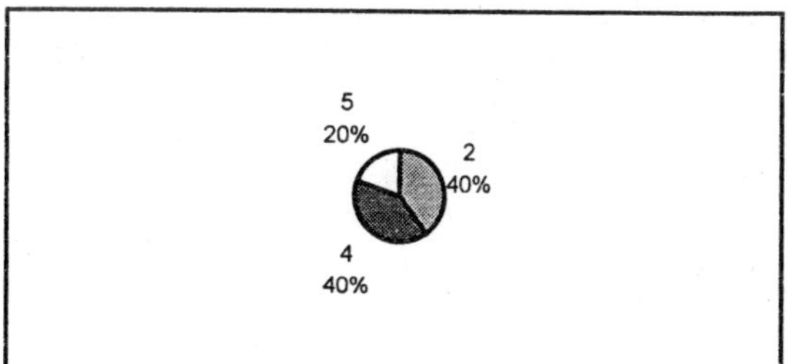

Diagram 13: Extent of Lease Land

The figures in the Table 14 are formed to know how many people are working on agricultural land. Out of 382 respondents, 222 respondents revealed that they are not working on any land. Out of remaining 160 respondents majority i.e. 87 (54.4 per cent) of the respondents work on own land, 68 work on others' land and 5 works on tenant land.

Government Antipoverty Schemes

An attempt is made to know whether the respondents are get any governmental assistance under any of the antipoverty programmes. Majority of the respondents i.e., 337 (88.2 per cent) revealed that they do not get any assistance. Only 45 (11.8 per cent) reveal that they are got the assistance from the government.

Table 15
Help of the Government Antipoverty Schemes

	Number	*Percent*	*Valid Percent*
Yes	45	11.8	11.8
No	337	88.2	88.2
Total	382	100.0	100.0

Source: Computed

Type of Antipoverty Scheme

With respect to the type of assistance that the respondents received, it is observed that all the benefited respondents in the study and cover either under DPAP are IAY out of 45 respondents receiving help majority receiving help trough Indira Ayas Yojana (IAY) and the balance through Drought Prone Area Programme (DPAP). Since most of the Scheduled Tribe people are economically poor, there is very need to provide more financial assistance to these people through various financial schemes.

Table 16
Type of Antipoverty Schemes

Name of the Programme	*Number*	*Percent*	*Valid Percent*
DPAP	16	4.2	35.6
IAY	29	7.6	64.4

Contd.

Name of the Programme	*Number*	*Percent*	*Valid Percent*
Total	45	11.8	100.0
No	337	88.2	
	382	100.0	

Occupation of the Spouse

The study also attempted to examine the occupation of the spouse. An analysis of Table 16 shows that only 169 (44.2 per cent) members work, out of them 78.7 per cent work as coolies followed by 4.7 per cent as watch man another 4.7 per cent work in the preparation of tadika bomboo curtains, 3.6 per cent are work as LIC agents and 1.8 per cent working in bank. Thus, most of the spouses work in low earning employments.

Table 17
Occupation of the Spouse

Occupation	*Number*	*Percent*	*Valid Percent*
LIC Agent	6	1.6	3.6
Bank	3	0.8	1.8
Teacher	7	1.8	4.2
Tadikala	8	2.1	4.7
Watch man	8	2.1	4.7
Business	3	0.8	1.8
Coolie	133	34.8	78.7
Agriculture	1	0.3	0.6
Total	169	44.2	100.0
No	213	55.8	
Grand Total	382	100.0	

Annual Income of the Respondent

Income is one of the important economic variables. The table reveals that majority of the respondents i.e., 119 (31.2 per cent) are earning annual income between Rs. 10,000 to 20,000, followed by 98 (25.7 per cent) earning below Rs. 10,000. Only 4 respondents are earning above Rs. 70,000. The average annual income of the respondents is Rs. Per annum.

Table 18
Annual Income of the Respondent

Annual income (Rs)	*Number*	*Percent*
Below 10000	98	25.7
20000-30000	119	31.2
30000-40000	29	7.6
40000-50000	61	16.0
50000-60000	18	4.7
60000-70000	39	10.2
70000-80000	14	3.7
80000+	4	1.0
Total	382	100.0

Annual Income of the Family

In every family not only the respondent but the other members of the family may also contribute to the family income. Out of the 382 respondents, majority i.e., 145 (38.0 per cent) respondent's family income is between Rs.50 to 60,000 per annum Table 19 Followed by 70 (18.3 per cent) respondents' families getting income between 20,000 and 30,000. 30 respondents family income is above Rs. 80,000.

Table 19
Annual Income of the Family

Annual Income from family (Rs.)	*Number*	*Percent*
Below 10000	52	13.6
10000-20000	13	3.4
20000-30000	3	.8
30000-40000	70	18.3
40000-50000	8	2.1
50000-60000	145	38.0
60000-70000	28	7.3
70000-80000	33	8.6
80000+	30	7.9
Total	382	100.0

Source: Computed

Annual Expenditure on Food, Habits and to work by the respondents

The analysis in the Table 20 depicts that, out of 382, majority of the respondents, (i.e.50.3 per cent) spent on food Rs.1000-

Table 20
Annual Expenditure on Food, Habits and to Work by the Respondents

Value (Rs.)	*No. Food*	*Per-cent*	*No. Habits*	*Per-cent*	*Valid Percent*	*Social Ceremonies*	*Per-cent*	*Valid Percent*
>1000	26	6.8	237	62.0	96.7	186		90.0
1000-5000	192	50.3	7	1.8	2.9	94		10.0
5000-10000	96	25.1	–	–	–	56	–	–
10000-15000	39	10.2	1	0.3	0.4	-32	–	–
15000-20000	18	4.7	–	–	–	-10	–	–
25000-30000	11	2.9	–	–	–	-4	–	–
Total	382	100.0	245	64.1	100.0	382		100.0
No	–	–	137	35.9	–		89.5	–
Grand Total	–	–	382	100.0	–	382	100.0	–

Source: Computed

5000 per annum, followed by 96 (25.1 per cent) spending between 5000-10000. Only 11 (2.9 per cent) spend on food between Rs 25000-30000. Hence it can be stated that the expenditure on food by the respondents is very low.

The study also attempted to solicitate information regarding the habits of the sample. Surprisingly 137 (35.9 per cent) do not spend on any thing on other habits such as drinking etc. Out of 245 respondents who have bad habits 237 spend less than Rs. 1000 on these. The average expenditure on habits is Rs. 911 only per annum's. It is observed that more than 40 per cent the respondents take liquor once in a week. About 20 per cent drink regularly, which is common among the tribals. With respect of the other habits such as smoking, chewing of tobacco is also existed among tribals. The tribals are not exempted from playing of cards . In our study 12 per cent are answered that they play cards. Very negligible percent go for bet games.

The Table 20 also examine the expenditure made buy the respondents towards social ceremonies. Out of 382 respondents, 186 respondents spend less than 1000 per year. Around 94 respondents spend less than 5000 rupees only. One the respondent answered that the social ceremonies are very important in the tribal life.

Maintenance Medical, Educational Expenditure

The below Table 21 shows that out of 382 respondents, 190 respondents do not incur family maintenance expenditure regularly. Out of 192 respondents, a majority 182 (94.8 per cent) expenditure spends on maintenance below Rs.1000 per annum, followed by 7 (3.6 per cent) spending in the range of Rs. 1000-5000. Only 3 (1.6 per cent) of the respondents spend in the range of Rs 10000-15000 on maintenance. So, the maintenance expenditure of the respondents is very low. The average maintenance expenditure is Rs. 1543 only.

Medical expenditure is another important one in general expenditure. Surprisingly 138 (36.1 per cent) do not have regular medical expenditure. Out of 244 respondents having medical expenditure, 222 respondents spend on medical

Table 21
Maintenance Medical, Educational Expenditure

Value (Rs.)	*Number Maintance*	*Per-cent*	*Valid Percent*	*Number Medical*	*Per-cent*	*Valid Percent*	*No. Education*	*Per-cent*	*Valid Percent*
>1000	182	47.5	94.8	222	58.1	91.0	139	36.4	82.7
1000-5000	7	1.8	3.6	19	5.0	7.8	23	6.0	13.7
5000-10000	–	–	–	–	–	–	3	0.8	1.8
10000-15000	3	0.8	1.6	–	–	–	–	–	–
15000-20000	–	–	–	–	–	–	–	–	–
25000-30000	–	–	–	3	0.8	1.2	3	0.8	1.8
30000+	–	–	–	–	–	–	–	–	–
Total	192	50.3	100.0	244	63.9	100.0	168	44.0	100.0
No	190	49.7	–	138	36.1	–	214	56.0	–
Grand Total	382	100.0	–	382	100.0	–	382	100.0	–

Source: Computed

expenditure less than Rs. 1000, only 3 respondents spend Rs. 25000-30000. The average medical expenditure is Rs. 2140 only.

Out of 382 respondents, 214 respondents do not have expenditure on education as most of the children studying either in government schools or do not have any child in their in their house. Out of 168 respondents having expenditure on education, 139 respondents spend less than Rs. 1000 on education; only 3 respondents spend in between Rs. 25000-30000 on education. The average expenditure on education is Rs. 3024 only.

Travel expenditure, clothing and other miscellaneous

The Table 22 given below , proves that out of 382 respondents, 134 respondents do not have expenditure on travel. Out of 248 respondents, a majority 242 (97.6 per cent) spend below Rs.1000 per annum on travel followed by 6 (2.4 per cent) spending in between Rs. 1000-5000. The average expenditure on travel is Rs. 1021 only.

Out of 382 respondents, 69 do not have expenditure on clothing The Nongovernmentsl organistions whciuihc are working for the development of tribals are distributing the clothes to the needy.The remaining 313 respondents spend on clothing. Out of them majority 275 (87.9 per cent) of the respondents spend less than Rs. 1000 on clothing followed by 17 (5.4 per cent) spending Rs. 1000-5000, and only 2 (0.6 per cent) of the respondents have expenditure on clothing in between 15000-20000. The average expenditure on clothing is Rs. 3091.

Out of 382 respondents, only 107 respondents have other expenditure. Out of them majority i.e., 101 (94.4 per cent) of the respondents have other expenditure upto Rs. 1000, followed by 5 (4.7 per cent) in between Rs. 1000-5000, and only 1 (0.9 per cent) respondent spends on other items in between 20000-25000.

Total Family Expenditure of the respondents

The analysis of Table 23 shows that out of 382 respondents, a majority i.e., 106 (27.7 per cent) of the respondents have total

Table 22
Travel Expenditure

Value (Rs)	*No. Travel*	*Per-cent*	*Valid Percent*	*No. Cloths*	*Per-cent*	*Valid Percent*	*Number Others*	*Per-cent*	*Valid Percent*
>1000	242	63.4	97.6	275	72.0	87.9	101	26.4	94.4
1000-5000	6	1.6	2.4	17	4.5	5.4	5	1.3	4.7
5000-10000	–	–	–	15	3.9	4.8	–	–	–
10000-15000	–	–	–	4	1.0	1.3	–	–	–
15000-20000	–	–	–	2	0.5	0.6	–	–	–
20000-25000	–	–	–	–	–	–	1	0.3	0.9
Total	248	64.9	100.0	313	81.9	100.0	107	28.0	100.0
No	134	35.1	–	69	18.1	–	275	72.0	–
Grand Total	382	100.0	–	382	100.0	–	382	100.0	–

family expenditure on food, traveling, clothing and social ceremonies is below Rs. 10,000 per annum, followed by 104 (27.21 per cent) of the respondents spending in between Rs. 10000-20000, and 61 (16.0 per cent) of the respondents have total expenditure above Rs. 30,000.

Table 23
Total Expenditure of the Respondents

Total Family Expenditure	*Member*	*Percent*	*Valid Percent*
Below 10000	106	27.7	27.7
10000-15000	104	27.2	27.2
15000-20000	47	12.3	12.3
20000-25000	40	10.5	10.5
25000-30000	24	6.3	6.3
30000+	61	16.0	16.0
Total	382	100.0	100.0

Source: Computed

Amount Taken from Others (Debt particulars)

An attempt is made to examine the amount of loan taken by the respondents. Out of 382 respondents, 259 (67.8 per cent)have not taken any loan. Only 123 respondents had taken loan. Out of them, majority i.e., 33 (53.7 per cent) of the respondents has borrowed loan between Rs. 5000-10,000, and another 27 (26.8 per cent) borrowed loan between Rs. 1000-5000. Altogether the respondents who had taken loan Rs 50,000 and above is only 21. The average amount of loan taken falls in the range Rs.1000–5000 which is considered to be very low. The observations are compiled in the below Table (24).

Table 24
Amount of Loan Taken from Others

(Rs.)	*Number*	*Percent*	*Cumulative Percent*
>1000	6	1.6	4.9
1000-5000	27	7.1	26.8
5000-10000	33	8.6	53.7
10000-15000	7	1.8	59.3
15000-20000	12	3.1	69.1

Contd.

(Rs.)	*Number*	*Percent*	*Cumulative Percent*
20000-25000	1	0.3	69.9
25000-30000	11	2.9	78.9
35000-40000	3	0.8	81.3
45000-50000	2	0.5	82.9
50000+	21	5.5	100.0
Total	123	32.2	
No	259	67.8	

Debt Period

The study also attempted the debt pattern of the tribals which mentioned in Table 25. In this the duration of the loan taken by the respondents is studied. Out of 123 respondents, majority i.e., 38 (30.9 per cent) have taken loan for a period of 3 years, followed by 32 (26.0 per cent) respondents taking loan for a period of 2 years, and 19 (15.4 per cent) respondents taking loan for 1 year. On the whole 72.4 per cent of the respondents have taken loan for the period of less than 3 years only. However, 23 (18.7 per cent) respondents had taken loan for 5 years. Hence, most of the loans are short-term loans only.

Table 25
Debt Period

	Number	*Percent*	*Valid Percent*
1	19	5.0	15.4
2	32	8.4	26.0
3	38	9.9	30.9
4	1	0.3	0.8
4	7	1.8	5.7
5	23	6.0	18.7
6	3	0.8	2.4
Total	123	32.2	100.0
No	259	67.8	
Grand Total	382	100.0	

Rate of interest for loan taken

An attempt is made to know the rate of interest that the tribals are paying for the loan they have taken. Out of 382, respondents 51 who had taken loans with only 8 percent. This is due to the providing of liberal loans to the agricultural sector. In the total 21, taken loan at the rate of 24 per cent of interest only, 11 respondents taken loan for 36 per cent and 1 respondent taken loan for even 48 per cent. 35 per cent of the respondents have taken loan for less than 18 per cent of interest. Perhaps the persons who had taken loan for high rate of interest hare taken from non-institutional agencies such as moneylenders, pawnbrokers etc.

Table 26
Rate of Interest

Rate of Interest (%)	*Member*	*Percent*
8	150	2.6
12	91	.3
18	117	1.8
24	11	5.5
36	12	2.9
48	1	.3
Grand Total	382	100.0

Amount Repaid

An attempt is also made to know the amount of the loan repaid by the respondents. Only 51 respondents repaid the loan, out of them majority 21 (41.2 per cent) repaid loan between Rs 1000–5000 and 8 respondents repaid between 15000-20000. The average amount of loan repaid by the respondents is Rs. 11988. An attempt is also made to know the amount of the loan outstanding by the respondents. In total, 119 respondents are having the loan outstanding. Out of them majority i.e., 40 (33.6 per cent) have outstanding loan between Rs. 5000-10000 and 10 respondents repaid between Rs 15000-20000.

Table 27
Amount Repaid

Amount (Rs.)	*Number Repaid*	*Percent*	*Valid Percent*	*Number Out-standing*	*Per-cent*	*Valid Percent*
>1000	4	1.0	7.8	5	1.3	4.2
1000-5000	21	5.5	41.2	30	7.9	25.2

Contd.

Amount (Rs.)	*Number Repaid*	*Percent*	*Valid Percent*	*Number Out-standing*	*Per-cent*	*Valid Percent*
5000-10000	7	1.8	13.7	40	10.5	33.6
10000-15000	4	1.0	7.8	9	2.4	7.6
15000-20000	8	2.1	15.7	10	2.6	8.4
25000-30000	3	0.8	5.9	1	0.3	0.8
35000-40000	3	0.8	5.9	7	1.8	5.9
40000-45000	1	0.3	2.0	–	–	–
45000-50000	–	–	–	17	4.5	14.3
Total	51	13.4	100.0	119	31.2	100.0
No	331	86.6	–	263	68.8	–
Grand Total	382	100.0	–	382	100.0	–

Reasons of Debt

An attempt is made to know the reasons for incurring debt. Out of 119 respondents who have taken loan majority i.e., 47 (40.2 per cent) taken loan for agricultural purposes another 22 (18.8 per cent) for family ceremonies, 19 (16.2 per cent) to meet of domestic expenditure.

Table 28
Reasons of Debt

	Number	*Percent*	*Valid Percent*	*Cumulative Percent*
Agriculture	47	12.3	40.2	40.2
Marriage	9	2.4	7.7	47.9
Ceremony	22	5.8	18.8	66.7
Education	8	2.1	6.8	73.5
Domestics	19	5.0	16.2	89.7
Old Loan clearing	7	1.8	3.4	93.2
Others	10	2.6	6.8	100.0
Total	123	31.2	100.0	

CONCLUSION

Majority of tribals in the country are still dependent on either satilled agriculture or shifting cultivation. The Tribal economy depends upon local and easily available resources. Because of the primitive Tribal Technology of cultivation Tribal lands are use productive. Hence there economy is still backward. In some parts of the country even today some tribes are depending upon forest productive for their lively hood. The

Government of India with an objective of Integrating Tribal Economy with the National Economy is implementing several developing programs. These programs are reviewed periodically to use their strength and weakness.

REFERENCES

Athreya. V. and Sheelarrani Chunkath (1996), "Literacy and Empowerment", Sage Publications, New Delhi.

Burman, B.K. (1985), "Transformation of Tribes and Analogues Social Formation", *Economic and Political Weekly*, Vol.XVII; No.27, pp.20-21.

Dangi K.L. and Intodia, S., (1991), "Occupational Aspiration of Tribal and Non-Tribal Educated Rural Youth", *Tribal Research Bulletin*, Vol.XXI, No.1, March.

Gautam, M.K.(1958), "The Asurs: Department of Anthropology", Lucknow University, Lucknow.

Gopala Rao, No., (1978), "Land Alienation-A Menace to Tribal Economy", *Tribe*, Vol.X, No.4.

Gupta (1986), "Functioning of the Integrated Tribal Development Project in Orissa", *Economic and Political Weekly*, Vol.XVIII.

Haimender, (1943), "C.V.F. Chenchus: Jungle Folk of Deccan", Mc Millan, London, p.87.

Hanumantha Rao. V.(Ed.) (1998), "Andhra Pradesh at 50: A Database Analysis", Hyderabad.

Krishna Reddy, B & Ramachandra Reddy (1991), "Introducing Direct Change in a Tribal Community", *Social Change* Vol.21(2), June, pp.25-31.

Krishna Sarma, (1978), "Fertility and Mortality in Kondas", *Man in India*, 58(1), pp.77-78.

Krishna, P.G. (1985), "Constitution and Tribal Welfare in Tribal Welfare", *Law and Practice*, Cochin University of Science and Technology, Cochin, pp.49-66.

Lakshmaiah, T., (1984), "Socio-Economic Development of Tribals", *Mainstream*, Vol.18, Dec.19, pp.21-22.

Lakshminarayana, (1990), "Health Condition in Tribal Areas of Maharashtra State", Tribal Research Bulletin, Vol.XII, No.11., Sept.p.3.

Mohan T.S., (1993), "Socio-Cultural Profile of Tribes of A.P.T.C.T. & T.I.", Tribal Welfare Development of Andhra Pradesh, Hyderabad, p.11.

Prakash Reddy, C. (1991), "HRD in Tribals", *Social Change*, June Vol. 2, No. 2, pp. 18-24.

Prasad. R.R. (1988), "Tribal Development in India Strategies Prgrammes", *Journal of Rural Development*, Vol. 7, January, No.1, pp.81-103.

Raghava Reddy G. and Subrahmanyam P. (2003), "Dynamics of Sustainable Rural Development", New Delhi, Serials Publications, New Delhi.

Saibaba. G. and Ranjendera Naidu, (1992), "Planning and Strategies of Tribal Development in Andhra Pradesh Administrative and Development Perspectives in Tribal Lands Capes" (ed.), Gupts, G.P. Arihant Publishers, Jaipur, pp.151-161.

Satish Reddy. K. and Mohan Reddy. (1991), "Absorption of Human Labour in Tribal Agriculture: A Study", Conference Volume of the Ninth Annual Conference of A.P. Economic Association, February 16-17.

Sharma Thakur, G.C. (1984), The Lalungs (Tiwas), in S.Karotemprell (ed.) "The Tribes of North-East India", Firma K.L.Mukhopadhyay Pvt. Ltd., Calcutta pp.138-56.

Sharma. B.D., (1998), "Integrated Tribal Development Projects" Course on Tribal Development, Hyderabad, pp.155-190.

Singh. K.S., (1978), "Transformation of Tribal System Integration Assimilation", *Economic and Political Weekly*, Vol. XVII, No. 34, pp. 1221-1232.

Sreenath, J. and S.H.Admad, (1989), All India Anthropomotric Survey: South Zone, Andhra Pradesh (Analysis of Data), Anthropological Survey of India, Calcutta.

Sudhakara Reddy, P.(1981), The Dispalced Yanadis of Sriharikota Island: A Study in Socio-Cultural Continuity and Change, Ph.D., S.V.Unviersity (Unpublished).

Vamala, (1991), "A Study of Scheduled Tribe Co-operative Finance Corporation (Conference Paper) Ninth Annual Conference of A.P. Economic Association, Feb.16-17, pp.54.

Varghese, N.V. (1994), "School Quality and Students Learning: A Study of Primary Schooling in Kerala". District Primary Education Program Baseline Study. National Institute of Educational Planning and Administration, New Delhi.

12

IMPLEMENTATION OF NREGS– A CASE STUDY OF THREE STATES IN INDIA

M. S. Narayana
K. Lalitha
N. Tyagaraju

The Government of India initiated the implementation of a revival package of the rural youth to generate employment opportunities, is the launching of National Rural Employment Act in Feb 2006. At the outset the act was implemented as a pilot plan in 130 districts, and later the scheme was extended to all districts by the end of April 2008. A budget allocation of Rs. 12,000 crore was also made in the budget of 2008–09. In the vote on account budget of 2009–10 a budget allocation of Rs. 30,100 crores was also made for the Act. The state Governments too made necessary legislations in this regard.

In this paper an attempt–is made to reviews the performance of the Act in two or three selected states in the country. The selection is made randomly on the basis of availability of information. They are:

(a) Tamil Nadu (b) Maharashtra (c) Orissa.

TAMIL NADU – A CASE OF NEGLECTED CHILD CARE

A social audit in Tamil Nadu finds that the National Rural Employment-Guarntee Act–has brought-about major changes in the lives of women. In Tamil Nadu, Women constitute an overwhelming proportion (more than 80%) of NREGAworkers. A survey was conducted during July 2007 covering 11 villages and 15 NREGA worksites located in two blocks of the villupuram district. The socio economic profile of women NREGA workers can be shown as under in Exhibit-I & II.

Case Study – I
Socio–Economic Back ground of Women NREGA Workers

Average Age	:	27 years
Average household size	:	4.5
Population who are illiterate	:	49%
Proportion who have completed middle school	:	5%
Proportion who belong to landless household	:	60%
Proportion who belong to S.C., B.C. N, M.B.C. communities	:	87%
Proportion who belong to agricultural labour Households	:	39%

Case Study – II
NREGA as an Employment Opportunity for Women

Proportion of respondents who said their household had no other source of income in the past few months.	:	41%
State that it was their own decision to work on NREGA	:	95%
Prefer wages in Celh	:	84%
Keep all or part of he wages they earn on NREGA	:	70%
Felt that NREGA is "very important" for the economic well–being of their households.	:	73 %

It is not surprising therefore that for some of those women, the NREGA was indispensable. The wages they earned as NREGA workers enabled them to accomplish a number of things–ranging from paying their debts or retrieving pawned gold spending on their children's health and education, or saving in chit funds, apart from meeting day - to - day expenses. There was a severe problems of water scarcity. The problem had been largely resolved as water was available from a pond constructed under NREGA when it was not in the pipe. The NREGA clearly states that in the event where there are at least five children under the age of six years at the work site. One of the female workers should be deputed to look after them and she should be paid the save wage as other NREGAworkers. However, in the survey it was found out that there were no child care facilities at the worksite are available. Most of the children who accompanied their mothers to the worksite were either left in the shade near by or kept hear the spot where the mother was working. To sum up, the provision of effective child care facilities at NREGAworksites in are important issue that calls for creative thinking and action. Tamil Nadu is well placed to take the lead in this field, given its earlier achievements in the domain of child care. Girls would not only be a step forward for Tamil Nadu but also and example for the whole country as a whole.

ORISSA – ILLUSIONS OF CHANGE

The National Rural Employment Guarantee Act as implemented by the Orissa Govt has resulted in grandiose claims of expenditure but very little to show the reality. The state has also been projected as the first state in implementation of NREGS, Showing a total expenditure of more than Rs. 700 crores, a fund utilization of 82.33 percent, surpassing all the major states in percentage of expenditure against available funds. The state claims to have issued job cards to 23.30 lakh households and provided employment to 11.19 lakh households. On an average, each household has been provided with 31 days of employment, while no household has comforted 100 days of employment, in all 19 districts selected for the scheme. However, there is shocking invisibility of these achievements on the ground. According to the report of Association for India's development (Aid) several discrepancies were observed in the muster rolls and attendance registers in one of the blocks in Orissa. The job cards were being kept in the Panchayats, and were not in the wage earners. A recent study conducted by Parshuram Ray of centre for Environment and Food Security Delhi also confirmed the irregularities.

These irregularities include.

1. Complete and correct job card entries are not available for any village.
2. 100 days of employment has not been provided to any of the villages.
3. In none of the villages workers were not allowed to check their muster rolls.

There is a complete disregard of any form of accountability and people's complaints. The Government of Orissa must rise to the occasion and take immediate steps to stop this most hypocritical and cruel joke on its poorest and most vulnerable communities.

MAHARASHTA – FAILURE TO TAKE OFF

In Feb 2006, Maharashtra Rural Employment Guarantee Scheme was made under the guide lives of NREGA. However, it appears that the scheme is performing poorly in Maharashtra and has not even spent half the amount allocated to the 12 districts selected in the first phase by the Central Rural Development Ministry. For ex : in chandrapur during 2005-06 and 2006-07, a total of Rs. 51.35 crore was allocated but only 8.04 crore was spent as on March 31, 2007. The data relating to the implementation of the scheme was provided by two organizations, Viz, Jawahar Adivasi Sera Viakas Samstha in Nandurbar and Jagrut Mahila Samaj in Chandrapur districts. In the second phase 14 districts were selected. The reason for the lag in the implementation of the scheme is outlined as under.

(i) The District Programme Council which is responsible for arranging help from live departments and getting it done was in the dark on the execution of the project.

(ii) Information sharing appears to be a major problem.

(iii) Discrepancies related to distribution of job cards were found. Out of 331 registered families in chandrapur district, only 69 families had received job cards.

(iv) Lack of Knowledge about the work procedure was the major phenomenon recorded every where relating to the implementation of NREGS.

(v) It appears that there is no enthusiasm among the political class as well as bureaucracy to accept the new scheme, which is more decentralized and likely to be more transparent and accountable to those who need work.

The government of Maharashtra should take imitative to educate the people in the new ethos and build their capacity to manage funds, build assets along inter and opportunity to create livelihood for themselves.

SUMMARY

Employment generation is one of the major priorities drawing the attention of the governments and economic planners all over the world. India is no exception. The approach to tackling unemployment problem varied from time to time. In the initial years of planning an attempt was made to define an independent employment strategy. In the five year plans, the generation of employment was viewed as a part of the process of development. The seventies and eighties saw the emergence of special schemes like NREP, RLEGPto provide wage employment through public works programmes and schemes to promote self employment and entrepreneuship to the unemployed and the poor. It may not be difficult to meet the formidable challenge of providing job opportunities to eight million people every year. For this, the growth rate of the economy has to be accelerated, special emphasis to be given to labour intensive sectors, improving labour skills and functioning of the labour market.

REFERENCES

M.L. Dbar (2008), Employment Scenario in India" Kurukshetra, Feb. Vol. 56, No. 4 pp. 39-40

Dey, N.J. Dreze, R. Khera (2006), "Employment Guarantee Act: A Prmer" National book Trust, New Delhi.

Dr. P.S. Nagarajan S. Gangadhram (2008), "Unemployment Scourge of Modern India" Feb, Vol. 28, No. 05, p. 34-35.

Milir Shah (2007) "Employment Guarantee, Civil Souicty and Indian Democracy" November, 10-16, Economic Political Weekly, Vol XLIT No.s 45-46, pp. 43-44.

Abhiroop Mukhopadhyay, Indira Rajaraman (2007), "Rural Unemployment 1999-2005. Who Gained, Who Lost" Economic & Political Weekly, Vol XLII No. 30, July 28-Aug-3, pp. 3121-3123

Lalit Mathur (2007), "Employment Guarantee, Progress sofar "Economic & Political Weekly Dec 29. Vol XLII No. 52, pp. 17-18.

KV Ramaswamy (2007), "Regional Dimension of Growth and Employment" Economic and Political Weekly, Dec 8-14 Vol. XLII No. 49, pp. 47-48.

Dr. Sanjay N. Aswale (2007), "Can We Create 50 Million Jobs Over the Temter Plan" Jan, Facts for you, Vol. 27 No. 4, pp. 39-41

Part – II

UNEMPLOYMENT SITUATION IN VARIOUS SECTORS

13

EMPLOYMENT AND POVERTY IN INFORMAL SECTOR AN ANALYSIS OF INTER STATE COMPARISONS

M. Sundara Rao
M. Sankara Reddi

The Indian National Sample Survey (NSS) included for the first time in 1999-2000 in its large-scale employment and unemployment survey, certain probing questions to usual status workers regarding some specific features of the enterprises in which they worked. The survey also collected, through an abridged work sheet, data on the consumer expenditure of the household to which the worker belonged. The survey was so planned and executed that it was possible to identify the members of the household who were employed as usual status workers in informal sector enterprises. The gender of the head of household as well as each member of the household was also recorded. In India, data on the consumer expenditure of household are used as proxy to income of household and form the basis of estimates of poverty. In view of this context, for the first time, the NSS could generate and disseminate in 2001 household level micro data, which could be used to undertake an analysis of links among "employment in informal sector", "poverty" and "gender". The principal focus of this paper is to explore these links in the Indian context by making use of the micro data at household level available from the 1999-2000 `employment and unemployment' survey.

The nature and type of work from which a household derives its major income is an important indicator of the activity pattern of its members. In the NSS every sample household is, therefore, categorized into 'household types', depending on the economic activity of the members of the household during the 365 days preceding the date of survey from which major income of the household is generated. Five household types are distinguished for the rural households, viz, Self-employed in agriculture; Self-employed in non-agriculture; Agricultural labour; Casual labour; others. For urban households, four categories of household types are distinguished, namely: Self-employed households; Regular wage/salaried households, Casual labour households, and others. During 1999-2000, members of about 33 percent of the rural households took recourse to self-employment in agriculture.

They constituted about 37 percent of the rural population. About 13 percent of the rural households derived their major income from self-employment in non-agriculture and 14 percent of rural population belonged to these households. About 32 percent of rural households were agricultural labour households accounting for 30 percent of rural population. Other labour households constituted 8 percent of rural households with about 8 percent of rural population in such households. The casual labour rural households formed 14 percent.

Nearly 34 percent of the urban households with 39 percent of urban population in those households had income mainly from self-employment. Among urban households, regular employment was the mainstay of 42 percent of households with 40 percent of urban population in such households. Casual labour households constituted 14 percent of urban households with 14 percent of urban population in such households. The urban casual labour households formed 10 percent with 6 percent of urban population in those households. In the present study we need certain additional definitions for identifying the type of households. We introduce a new definition of a "household sustaining on employment in informal sector" as a household having at least one usual principal status worker in informal sector and no usual principal status worker outside informal sector. A "household sustaining on self-employment in informal sector" is defined as a household sustaining on employment in informal sector and whose household type code is (a) self-employed in non-agriculture in rural areas and (b) self-employed in urban areas. A "household sustaining on regular salaried/wage employment in informal sector in urban India" is defined as a household sustaining on employment in informal sector and whose household type code is "regular salary/wage earning" in urban areas. A "household sustaining on casual wage employment in informal sector in urban India" is defined as a household sustaining on employment in informal sector and whose household type code is "casual labour" in urban areas. A "female headed household sustaining on employment in informal sector" is defined, as a household sustaining on employment in informal sector whose head is a female.

Making use of these additional definitions and the micro data at household level available from the 1999-2000 employment & unemployment survey of NSS, a set of tables, have been specially generated by the Indian National Sample Survey Organisation (NSSO) for the present study. Poverty is estimated officially in India on the basis of one measure, namely proportion of the population below an exogenously specified poverty line. For a household, monthly per capita consumer expenditure (MPCE) is its total consumer expenditure over a period of 30 days divided by the number of members in the household. A person's MPCE is understood as that of the household to which he or she belongs. The Indian Planning Commission, which officially estimates the incidence of poverty based on NSS household consumer expenditure survey data, has stated in its press note issued on 22 February,

2001 that in 1999-2000 the all-India poverty line corresponds to MPCE level of Rs. 327.56 in rural areas and Rs. 454.11 in urban areas. The proportion of the population below the specified poverty line (or head count ratio) is officially recognized as "poverty estimate", when the distribution of persons by MPCE is based on the NSS household Consumer Expenditure Survey (CES) data. Persons with consumption (MPCE) less than the poverty line are defined as `poor'. Persons with consumption less than three-fourth (75 percent) of the poverty line are defined as `very poor'. Persons with consumption less than the poverty line but not `very poor' are defined as `moderately poor'. Similar definitions are possible for households also. In 1999-2000, NSSO conducted a large scale CES, as usual with a detailed schedule wherein around 330 items of consumption expenditure are specified in detail over 15 pages to minimize recall lapse on the part of respondents. The distribution of persons by MPCE estimated from this CES of NSSO formed the basis for the official poverty estimates in 1999-2000.

As already mentioned earlier, in 1999-2000, NSSO also conducted a large scale employment and unemployment survey (EUES) wherein the schedule included an abridged one page worksheet in which 32 different groups of items of consumption were specified and household consumer expenditure data on each of these 32 item groups were collected. Considering the sizes of the schedules in the CES and EUES, it was thought that it would be very difficult to obtain information for both the schedules from the same household taking into account the fatigue of the respondent. Therefore, unlike in earlier CES and EUES of NSSO, the CES and EUES schedules in 1999-2000 were canvassed in separate sets of sample households. This is the reason why EUES schedule contained in 1999-2000 an abridged worksheet of one page to record household consumption expenditure of 32 different groups of items and it was considered adequate because MPCE of the household here was merely a classification variable for tabulation of employment characteristics and not the main subject of enquiry. However, the household reporting of consumer expenditure in an abridged schedule is known to be affected by a greater degree of recall lapse than in a detailed schedule and hence would tend to understate the total consumer expenditure in comparison with that based on a detailed schedule. This downward bias may be expected to shift the distribution of persons by MPCE based on EUES to the left of that based on CES in 1999-2000. In fact, published results of the 1999-2000 EUES and CES indicate that the cumulative distribution function of MPCE based on EUES lies uniformly above that based on CES at the all-India level both in rural and urban areas. This suggests that the poverty estimate (head count ratio) based on EUES distribution of persons by MPCE would be higher than that based on CES (which is the official estimate) and hence, would at best provide only an upper bound to the comparable official poverty estimate in 1999-2000.

In fact, the Indian Planning Commission, based on NSS 1999-2000 CES released at all-India level poverty estimates of 27.09 percent in rural areas and 23.62 percent in urban areas. Based on NSS 1999-2000 EUES, Sundaram and Tendulkar (2001) estimated at all India level poverty ratios of 36.45 percent in rural areas and 28.76 percent in urban areas. Using the household level micro data set of EUES and published CES results, Sundaram and Tendulkar (2001) derived a significant result. They found that if the understatement arising from the abridged worksheet used for consumption expenditure recording in EUES schedule is adjusted for in the distribution of persons by MPCE and the poverty estimates are made on the basis of such an adjusted distribution, then the adjusted poverty estimates derived from EUES are very close to the official poverty estimates based on CES both in rural and urban areas of India. This result provides us the requisite confidence that the adjusted distributions of persons by MPCE in rural as well as urban India derived from 1999-2000 EUES can be used as yardsticks (standards) for obtaining valid and reliable comparisons and conclusions on the links among poverty, employment in Informal Sector and gender.

INTER-STATE COMPARISONS

Results on incidence and intensity of poverty among persons in households sustaining on employment in informal sector non-agricultural enterprises have been obtained in rural and urban areas for 16 major States in India, namely (1) Andhra Pradesh, (2) Assam, (3) Bihar, (4) Gujarat, (5) Haryana, (6) Himachal Pradesh, (7) Karnataka, (8) Kerala, (9) Madhya Pradesh, (10) Maharashtra, (11) Orissa, (12) Punjab, (13) Rajasthan, (14) Tamil Nadu, (15) Uttar Pradesh, and (16) West Bengal. These results are presented in the following paragraphs, along with a comparison with the national level results.

Relevant inter-state comparisons of poverty ratios among members of different types of households during 1999-2000 are as follows: In comparison with the incidence of poverty in general households in rural areas at national level, the States of Andhra Pradesh, Gujarat, Haryana, Himachal Pradesh, Karnataka, Kerala, Maharashtra, Punjab, Rajasthan and Tamil Nadu recorded either lower or equal poverty incidence in general households in their respective rural areas. Same type of comparison also held good in respect of intensity of poverty in general households in rural areas. Households sustaining on employment in informal sector in rural areas of the States: Andhra Pradesh, Gujarat, Karnataka, Kerala, Madhya Pradesh, Maharashtra, Orissa, Punjab, Tamil Nadu and West Bengal experienced either lower or equal incidence of poverty as compared to the poverty incidence in general households in the rural areas of the respective states and these cases were success stories. In all these states except Madhya Pradesh the same type of comparison for the intensity of poverty was also true.

Households sustaining on self-employment in informal sector in rural areas of the States: Andhra Pradesh, Assam, Bihar, Gujarat, Haryana, Himachal Pradesh Karnataka, Kerala, Madhya Pradesh, Maharashtra, Orissa, Punjab, Rajasthan, Tamil Nadu and West Bengal recorded incidence of poverty which was less than or equal to the incidence of poverty in general households in the respective rural areas of the States and these were the success stories during 1999-2000. Same type of comparison was also valid in respect of the intensity of poverty in all these States except, Himachal Pradesh and Madhya Pradesh. Households sustaining on employment in informal sector with only one adult male worker in rural areas of the States: Andhra Pradesh, Bihar, Gujarat, Karnataka, Kerala, Madhya Pradesh, Maharashtra, Orissa, Punjab, Rajasthan, Tamil Nadu and West Bengal recorded both the incidence and intensity of poverty which were less than or equal to the corresponding poverty ratios in general households in the rural areas of the respective States and these were success stories. Andhra Pradesh had the distinction where in rural areas the incidence as well as intensity of poverty in households sustaining on employment in informal sector with only one adult female worker was lower than the corresponding poverty ratios in general households and this was a case of success story.

Households sustaining on employment in informal sector with only one adult male worker and one adult female worker in rural areas of the States: Karnataka, Kerala, Maharashtra and Tamil Nadu recorded either lower or equal incidence of poverty as compared to the poverty incidence in general households in the rural areas of the respective States. Same type of comparison was also valid in respect of the intensity of poverty in rural areas of Kerala and Maharashtra. These cases constituted success stories. Female headed households sustaining on employment in informal sector in rural areas of the States: Andhra Pradesh, Gujarat, Karnataka, Maharashtra and Tamil Nadu experienced incidence of poverty which was less than or equal to the poverty incidence in general households in rural areas of the respective States and these again were success stories.

Households sustaining on employment in informal sector with no adult female literate member in rural areas of the States: Karnataka, Kerala, Maharashtra, Orissa and Tamil Nadu were found to have incidence of poverty which was less than or equal to the poverty incidence in general households in rural areas of the respective States and these cases constituted success stories. In urban areas of the States: Assam, Gujarat, Haryana, Himachal Pradesh, Kerala, Punjab, Rajasthan, Tamil Nadu and West Bengal both the incidence and intensity of poverty were less than or equal to the corresponding poverty ratios in urban areas at national level during 1999 2000. Gujarat had the distinction where the poverty incidence in households sustaining on employment in informal sector in urban areas was slightly less than that in general households. In urban areas of the States: Andhra Pradesh, Gujarat, Haryana, Himachal Pradesh, Karnataka, Kerala, Madhya Pradesh, Orissa, Punjab, Rajasthan and Tamil Nadu households sustaining on self-employment in informal sector experienced poverty incidence which was either lower or equal to the incidence of poverty in general households in urban areas of the respective States and these constituted success stories. The same comparison held good for the intensity of poverty also in these States except in case of Himachal Pradesh and Punjab.

In the urban areas of the States: Andhra Pradesh, Gujarat, Haryana, Karnataka, Kerala, Madhya Pradesh and Tamil Nadu both the incidence and intensity of poverty in households sustaining on employment in informal sector with only one adult male worker were less than or equal to the corresponding poverty ratios in general households in urban areas of the respective States and these were success stories. In the urban areas of the States: Karnataka and Kerala, households sustaining on employment in informal sector with only one adult female worker had the incidence of poverty less than or equal to that in general households in urban areas of the respective States and these were examples of success stories. Similarly in the urban areas of the States: Gujarat, Kerala and Tamil Nadu, households sustaining on employment in informal sector with only one adult female worker experienced the intensity of poverty less than or equal to that in general households in urban areas of the respective States.

Gujarat had the distinction where both the incidence and intensity of poverty in female headed households sustaining on employment in informal sector in urban areas were less than or equal to the corresponding poverty ratios in the general households and this was a success story. In the urban areas of the States: Karnataka, Kerala, Madhya Pradesh, Maharashtra and West Bengal, households sustaining on regular wage/ salaried employment in informal sector had the incidence as well as intensity of poverty less than or equal to the corresponding poverty ratios in general households in urban areas of the respective States and these constituted success stories. Kerala had the distinction where in urban areas both the incidence and intensity of poverty in households sustaining on informal sector with no adult female literate member were less than or equal to the corresponding poverty ratios in the general households and this case was also a success story. In both the rural and urban areas, there were several types of households sustaining on employment in informal sector in a number of States with higher incidence and intensity of poverty than was the situation in general households and these were the groups of households engaged in informal sector economic activities and suffering from higher levels of poverty than in general households.

Inter-state variation in the incidence of poverty during 1999-2000 among members of different types of households, separately in rural and urban areas, wherein the ranges for incidence of poverty are taken as 0 to 10, 10 to 20, 20 to 30, 30 to 40, 40 to 50 and 50+ (50 and above). In the lowest range 0 to 10 for the incidence of poverty in rural areas, (a) general households in Haryana, Himachal Pradesh, Kerala and Punjab, (b) households sustaining on employment in informal sector in Andhra Pradesh, Gujarat, Himachal Pradesh, Karnataka, Kerala and Punjab, (c) households sustaining on self-employment in informal sector in Andhra Pradesh, Gujarat, Haryana, Himachal Pradesh, Karnataka, Kerala, Punjab and Rajasthan, (d) households sustaining on employment in informal sector with only one adult male worker in Andhra Pradesh, Gujarat, Haryana, Karnataka, Kerala, Punjab and Tamil Nadu, (e) households sustaining on employment in informal sector with only one adult female worker in Andhra Pradesh, (f) households sustaining on employment in informal sector with only one adult male and one adult female workers in Kerala and Maharashtra, (g) female headed households sustaining on employment in informal sector in Andhra Pradesh, Karnataka, and Gujarat, (h) households sustaining on employment in informal sector with no adult female literate member in Kerala and Punjab and (i) households sustaining on employment in informal sector with no adult literate member in Punjab, were represented during 1999-2000. These cases were the characterisations of the types of households in rural areas in specific States wherein the incidence of poverty (%) during 1999-2000 was in the lowest range 0 to 10.

In the highest range of 40 and above (40+) for the incidence of poverty in rural areas, (a) general households in Bihar and Orissa, (b) households sustaining on employment in informal sector in Assam and Bihar, (c) households sustaining on self-employment in informal sector in Bihar, (d) households sustaining on employment in informal sector with only one adult male worker in Assam and Bihar, (e) households sustaining on employment in informal sector with only one adult female worker in Assam, Bihar and West Bengal, (f) households sustaining on employment in informal sector with only one adult male and one adult female workers in Bihar, Uttar Pradesh, Madhya Pradesh and Orissa, (g) female headed households sustaining on employment in informal sector in Assam, West Bengal, Orissa and Bihar, (h) households sustaining on employment in informal sector with no adult female literate member in Bihar, Orissa and Assam and (i) households sustaining on employment in informal sector with no adult literate member in Madhya Pradesh, Orissa, Uttar Pradesh, West Bengal, Assam and Bihar, were observed during 1999-2000. These cases were the characterizations of the types of households in rural areas in specific States wherein the incidence of poverty (%) during 1999-2000 was in the highest range of 40+.

In the urban areas during 1999-2000, in the lowest range 0 to 10 for the incidence of poverty (%), (a) general households in the States: Assam, Haryana, Himachal Pradesh and Punjab, (b) households sustaining on employment in informal sector in Himachal Pradesh and Punjab, (c) households sustaining on self-employment in informal sector in Haryana, Himachal Pradesh and Punjab, (d) households sustaining on regular wage/salaried employment in informal sector in Punjab and West Bengal, (e) households sustaining on employment in informal sector with only one adult male worker in Assam, Haryana, Himachal Pradesh and Punjab, and (f) households sustaining on employment in informal sector with only one adult male and one adult female workers in Punjab, were represented. These cases were the characterizations of the types of households in urban areas in specific States where in the incidence of poverty (%) was in the lowest range 0 to 10.

In the highest range of 40 and above (40+) for the incidence of poverty (%) in urban areas, (a) general households in Orissa, (b) households sustaining on employment in informal sector in Bihar and Orissa, (c) households sustaining on self-employment in informal sector in Bihar and Orissa, (d) households sustaining on casual wage employment in informal sector in Andhra Pradesh, Karnataka, Madhya Pradesh, Maharashtra, Rajasthan and Uttar Pradesh, (e) households sustaining on employment in informal sector with only one adult male worker in Orissa, (f) households sustaining on employment in informal sector with only one adult female worker in Andhra Pradesh, Bihar and Madhya Pradesh, (g) households sustaining on employment in informal sector with only one adult male and one adult female workers in Madhya Pradesh, Maharashtra, Bihar and Orissa, (h) female headed households sustaining on employment in informal sector in Madhya Pradesh, Orissa, Rajasthan, Andhra Pradesh and Bihar, (i) households sustaining on employment in informal sector with no adult female literate member in Andhra Pradesh, Maharashtra, Uttar Pradesh, Bihar, Karnataka, Madhya Pradesh, and Orissa, and (j) households sustaining on employment in informal sector with no literate member in Tamil Nadu, West Bengal, Andhra Pradesh, Bihar, Karnataka, Madhya Pradesh, Maharashtra, Orissa, Rajasthan and Uttar Pradesh, were observed during 1999-2000. These cases were the characterizations of the types of households in urban areas in specific states wherein the incidence of poverty (%) was in the highest range of 40 and above.

CONCLUSION

The measures of employment used in the Indian NSS are based on time disposition of the labor force, and do not reflect the level of income or consumption of those who are counted as employed by these employment indicators. An analysis of those employed by the level of consumption expenditure helps to discern the extent of poverty among those who are employed. In the Indian situation, the incidence of poverty is much larger than the incidence of unemployment, leading to the observation that the 'poor are too poor to remain unemployed'. Another interesting observation is that poverty is related more to the nature of employment, such as self-employment, regular wage/salaried employment and casual wage employment, than the absolute rate of employment. That is why it is seen that the incidence of poverty is highest among agricultural labor in rural areas and casual labor in urban areas. Agricultural labor in rural areas is also casual workers. It is among this category of workers that non-availability of work from time to time (or high incidence of underemployment) would be a major cause of low income and high incidence of poverty. Poverty alleviation for this category of workers would naturally require creating work for them and this justifies largely the employment generation (poverty alleviation) programmes of the Government.

It has also been seen that self-employed workers in urban areas do somewhat better in terms of average earnings than the casual workers. It has been possible for a large proportion of workers to be self-employed in urban areas because of the existence of the informal sector. In view of this, our approach and policies towards the informal sector acquire significance. Though all the unemployed may not be poor, yet for the poor the only solution to poverty is employment with reasonable income. Such employment is not going to be generated on a large-scale in the formal sector in the country in the near future. That is why all efforts are needed to integrate the informal activities in the mainstream of economic activities, by providing space and facilities for such activities as well as making efforts to upgrade the productivity of workers in the informal sector through well designed programmes of skill up gradation. Literacy of workers plays an important role in the capability of the workers to absorb higher skills and thereby improve their earning capacities and lead to reduction in the incidence of poverty in the households sustaining on employment in informal sector. The inter-linkages among 'employment in informal sector, poverty and gender', as explored in this study are complex and need careful analytical scrutiny. The gender analysis of poverty should not be so much about whether women suffer from more poverty than men, but rather about how gender differentiates the social processes leading to poverty, and the escape routes out of destitution. An understanding of the casual processes leading to poverty has important policy implications: it raises important questions about whether it can be assumed, as is often done, that the kinds of policies and asset interventions that can strengthen the position of poor men are going to have much the same impact on poor women.

REFERENCE

Sundaram, K. and Tendulkar, Suresh, D. (2001), Recent Debates on Data Base for Measurement of Poverty in India: Some Fresh Evidence, Paper presented at the Workshop on Poverty Monitoring and Evaluation, jointly organised by the World Bank and Planning Commission, New Delhi, India, January 11-12, 2002.

14

AGRICULTURAL UNEMPLOYMENT IN INDIA: CAUSES AND REMEDIES

K. Siva Prasad
K. Kiran

In spite of more than five decades of planned development efforts, India is still facing the twin formidable problems of unemployment and poverty. Unemployment refers to a situation in which all the workers who are capable of working, and willing to work, do not get employment at a given wage rate. It amounts to a waste of the country's labour force. The nature of unemployment in an underdeveloped country like India is quite different from that of advanced countries. The problem of agricultural unemployment in India is particularly crucial due to a variety of factors. It arises primarily due to lack of capital as a complementary factor for labour. It is also due to lack of other complementary factors of production such as fertile land, entrepreneurship, management etc. The objective of this paper is to analyze the causes for unemployment in the agricultural sector in India with a view to offer appropriate policy measures.

The rapid growth of population in India has resulted not only in high density of population and also failed to absorb its huge and growing labour force. The galloping increase in the population of our country during last few decades has further aggravated the unemployment problem in the country. As adequate employment opportunities are not available in the non agricultural sector, the pressure of population on the land is high. As such around 57 percent of the labour force is still engaged in the agricultural sector. Land is thus overcrowded and a large part of labour force is unemployed resulting in mostly disguised and seasonal unemployment.

According to NSS data the current daily status of unemployment rate for the rural male workers was 5.64 per cent in1999-94 and 9.0 per cent in 2000. It reveals that agriculture unemployment has been increasing. The employment elasticity in agriculture was estimated to be 0.87 during the period 1983 to 1987-88, while it declined to 0.01 by 1999-2000. This has always been a great concern to the policy makers and they are continuously searching for some ways and means to solve it. More over, the share of agriculture in the gross domestic product had fallen to 24 per cent, while the share of industry remained somewhat constant at around 25 per cent, and the share of services has gone up to 51 per cent by 2001.The absorption of employment has also shifted in accordance with the sectoral shares in output. The share of industry in output went up and the share of agriculture came down. The employment shares too shifted with labour shifting from agriculture to industry and then on to services.

AGRICULTURAL CRISIS

The major cause for the collapse of employment as a whole is the *almost zero growth rate in agricultural employment* (0.02 per cent per year, by Current Daily Status, during 1993-94 to 1999-2000). However, agriculture is still the country's largest employer, accounting for 60.4 per cent of employment in 1993-94, and 56.7 per cent in 1999-2000. This is going to be less and less in the near future. The investment in agriculture registered a decline in the share of the capital formation in GDP from 2.2 per cent in the late 1990s to 1.7 per cent by 2004-05. As a result of the lower investments in agriculture coupled with higher input costs, the domestic crops have started facing sever competition from cheaper imports. Moreover as the state governments in the 1990s have cut short some of the rural infrastructure development and welfare programmes, the growth of *rural non-agricultural employment* in the 1990s has not been impressive. Thus, the agriculture sector, which happens to be a major employment-generating sector in the past, has almost stopped absorbing labour in the recent past.

The main reason for the freeze in agricultural employment is the proportion of land fewer houses holds among total rural households. It is observed that "The proportion of landless households among total rural households has risen from 35 per cent to 41 per cent between 1987-88 and 1999-2000".[1] Moreover the technological change witnessed in the Indian agricultural during the last few decades is resulting in negative impact on labour absorption. Mechanical innovations of labour saving nature will certainly displace the labour from work.

Hence, in spite of the rise in overall GDP growth rate in the 1990s when compared to the 1980s, the growth of employment has fallen from 2.7 per cent per annum to 1.07 per cent during the period 1993-94 to 1999-2000. The share of agriculture in total employment has come down from 61.67 per cent in 1993-94 to 54.19 per cent in 2004-05[2].

From this it may be inferred that in post-reform period, the polices pursued have failed to make agriculture an 'engine of growth', particularly in generating more employment. In short, the agricultural sector has failed to make any visible impact in mitigating the rural unemployment. The cheaper imports of agricultural products are also causing misery to farmers. The globalization of our agriculture gave scope for the evil designs of some corporate giants. The corporate sector by using capital intensive methods instead of labour intensive techniques is adding fuel to the fire. In light of the account given above, some remedial measures are offered bellow to mitigate the problems of agricultural unemployment in India.

Unemployment can be reduced to a large extent by raising the levels of investment in the agriculture. It should also be stated that without controlling the population, the unemployment will continue to exist in the Indian economy.

The government should enhance its investments in rural infrastructural facilities by penetrating into the nook and corner of each district, as India lives in its villages.

Massive investments are also needed to restore minor irrigation sources like tanks and wells. This calls for efficient management of available water resources in the country.

Concerted efforts should be made not only to expand but also to strengthen the tertiary sector, which has been exhibiting the potential to absorb the excess labour. The excess, and unproductive labour in the agriculture is to be shifted in to non-formal employment sectors like services in a planned manner.

In order to better utilize the stock of human capital, there is also the need for launching special programmes to improve the skills of the labour in the process of agricultural production.

Some more measures that require the immediate attention of the government include timely supply of inputs, easy and timely access to credit at lower rates of interest and agricultural extension services to farmers.

All these efforts go a long way in improving the situation of agricultural employment in the Indian economy. As pointed out by World Development Report "labour is main asset of the poor, making it more productive is the best way to reduce poverty"[3].

FOOTNOTES

1. The Real State of Indian's Economy March 2004(No S 36 & 37)
2. The Hindu, (editorial) Feb, 28, 2007.
3. W orld Development Report ; 2007, p. 2

15

TRENDS OF RURAL NON-FARM EMPLOYMENT IN INDIA: A SECONDARY DATA ANALYSIS

M. Koteswara Rao
P. Venu Gopal

INTRODUCTION

The discussion on rural development policy mostly focused on tenurial, institutional, technical, infrastructural and economic aspects of agricultural development. In India like other developing countries, labour absorption in agriculture and in urban and service sectors have not been enough to absorb the growing labour-force. Consequently, problems of poverty and unemployment and underemployment and out-migration have persisted in both rural and urban areas. Under these conditions the diversification of rural economy appears to be an important element of development strategy. Rural Non-Farm Sector (RNFS) plays a positive role in the removal of poverty, generation of employment and decentralization of urbanization. It is a significant source of income to small and landless farmers during the slack season. It also facilitates structural transformation. It is a source of employment and earnings and provides non-food goods and services to the rural population. Hence an attempt is made in this paper to analyse and examine the trends of RNFE in India with the help of various Census reports and various rounds of NSSO.

The results of some of the important studies that covered the trends in Rural Non-Farm Employment are also briefly highlighted and analysed in this paper. For example, Mahendra Dev[1] (1990) used the NSS data of 1972-73 and 1977-78. Vaidyanathan (1986)[2], Jeemol Unni (1991)[3] and Basant and Kumar (1989)[4] used both census and NSS data. The census data that they used are relate to one or more of the census years, 1961,1971, 1981 and 1991. On the other hand, the NSS data are related to 1972-73 (27th round), 1977-78 (32nd round), 1983 (38th round), 1987-88 (43rd round) and 1993-94 (50th round). Subsequently more recent data have become available both from the Census and NSS. The provisional figures of 2001 census and the estimates of 1999-2000 (55th round) of NSS are made available for analysis. The results of 2001 census and 1999-2000 NSS are emphasized in this paper. The results of our exercise will provide the changes that are taking place in the present economy. The main purpose in doing so is to test the stability of trends observed in the past with more recent data.

According to the Census of India, non-agricultural sector includes activities allied to agriculture such as animal husbandry, plantation, fishing and forestry etc., and other than crop production activities. But in NSS data, allied agricultural activities such as animal husbandry, plantation, fishing, forestry are not considered as non-agricultural sector. The present study relates to both the Census and NSS data. Along with agricultural work, non-agricultural work may often be undertaken in the same period. That is why in the rural areas other than agricultural work may often be undertaken as a secondary activity. In addition, number of non-agricultural occupations is undertaken at the same time by the same worker. In these circumstances, it is very difficult to determine the main occupation of a worker.

LEVEL OF RURAL NON-FARM EMPLOYMENT (RNFE)

The Census of India provides decennial data on the level and structure of the workforce. The Census data, is non dependable for judging the trends because of the changing concept of the 'worker'. However, for this purposes broad comparisons involving percentages in this data should be comparable over times.[5] In this Paper, the Census data pertaining to 1971, 1981, 1991 and 2001 (provisional) are examined.

The National Sample Survey Organisation (NSSO) conducted various rounds of quinquennial employment and unemployment surveys in 1972-73 (27th), 1977-78 (32nd), 1983 (38th), 1987-88 (43rd), 1993-94 (50th) and 1999-2000 (55th round). The data for the above said rounds are used. For the purposes of uniformity, the Indian States are divided into three groups such as states with high proportion of RNFE (above 25 per cent), medium proportion of RNFE (between 20-25 per cent) and low proportion of RNFE (less than 20 per cent).

Tables 1, 2 and 3 are prepared to present the data relating percentage of non-agricultural work force to the rural work force. The absolute amount of RNFE in rural areas are shown in parenthesis. It was striking in the census data that the percentage of non-agricultural employment had been rising at a faster rate between 1991 and 2001 as compared to the earlier decade. And, the NSS data show an increase in the percentage of RNFE over the period. However, when the rate of growth was examined, the 1980s showed a slowing down of rate of growth of RNFE.

Trends According to Census in RNFE

The trends were found uneven when the state wise results were examined. Out of the 15 States, as per census Gujarat, Haryana, Himachal Pradesh, Karnataka, Kerala, Orissa, Punjab, Tamil Nadu, Uttar Pradesh and West Bengal show an absolute rise in RNFE between 1981 and 1991. Andhra Pradesh, Bihar, Madhya Pradesh and Maharashtra and Rajasthan showed an absolute fall. However, consistent rise was found only in Gujarat, Haryana, Himachal Pradesh, Kerala, Orissa, Punjab, Uttar Pradesh and West Bengal. In other states viz., Bihar,

Table 1
Non-Agricultural Workers as a Percentage of Rural Work-Force: Census (1971-2001) and NSSO (1972-73 to 1999-2000): Total

	Census				*NSS*					
States	*1971*	*1981*	*1991*	*2001*	*1972-73*	*1977-78*	*1983*	*1987-88*	*1993-94*	*1999-2000*
All-India	17.69	19.02	19.80	26.70	14.50	16.70	18.60	21.84	21.6	23.7
Andhra Pradesh	20.87	19.60	19.20	24.84	16.5	17.60	22.80	22.35	20.80	21.20
Bihar	11.39	14.10	11.90	18.24	16.6	15.30	16.50	19.75	15.70	19.40
Gujarat	16.23	20.04	23.20	40.34	13.8	13.00	15.40	28.44	21.30	20.00
Haryana	23.02	24.52	25.20	52.01	18.7	18.30	22.30	21.11	28.1	31.6
Himachal Pradesh	20.42	24.00	25.50	26.28	–	12.20	12.90	17.82	19.35	25.55
Karnataka	20.21	19.72	20.30	26.47	13.5	15.20	15.80	18.03	18.10	17.90
Kerala	45.39	52.23	53.90	71.34	43.7	34.60	36.90	41.46	33.60	51.50
Madhya Pradesh	11.04	12.60	11.80	14.50	8.2	8.60	10.00	12.31	10.30	12.80
Maharashtra	14.34	17.00	16.90	19.92	14.8	14.20	14.30	17.10	17.40	17.30
Orissa	16.93	13.08	19.20	27.66	18.0	15.00	20.90	24.11	19.10	21.50
Punjab	21.55	23.75	24.40	26.28	24.5	18.50	17.50	23.73	25.30	27.50
Rajasthan	15.41	13.51	16.80	22.70	12.7	41.60	13.30	26.53	20.10	22.40
Tamil Nadu	21.61	21.45	22.40	30.05	21.6	22.00	25.40	29.62	69.5	31.70
Uttar Pradesh	12.91	13.68	15.50	22.29	17.2	17.30	18.00	17.66	20.00	23.90
West Bengal	21.94	26.22	29.90	41.60	26.9	24.40	26.40	28.11	36.70	37.00

Source: Census of India, 1971, 1981, 1991 and 2001 (provisional), Government of India.
NSSO, *Sarvekshana*, Nos. 1 & 2, 1977; Vol.V, Nos. 1 & 2, 1981,Table 29; Vol.VI, Nos. 1 & 2, 1982; Vol.VI. Nos. 3 & 4, 1983; Vol. VIII, Nos. 3 & 4, 1984, Table-6; Vol.IX, No.4, 1987, Table-1, 38th Round, 1983, No.341, Report on the Third Quinquennial Survey on Employment and Unemployment, All-India, Table-14, 43rd Round, 1987-88, *Sarvekshana*, Special Number, Report on the Fourth Quinquennial Survey on Employment and Unemployment, All-India, September 1990, data derived from Statement 36 (UPSS), pp.105-106.

Karnataka, Madhya Pradesh, Maharashtra, Rajasthan, Tamil Nadu, the trend was fluctuating. But in Andhra Pradesh, RNFE was found steadily declining. But between 1991 and 2001, all the States have showed tremendous rise in RNFE.

Trends According to NSS in RNFE

The comparison of the results of the census and NSS data is always useful. The share of total rural non-agricultural workers (male + female) increased substantially at the all-India level from 16.7 per cent in 1977-78 to 28.60 percent in 1999-2000. One important feature of the data of NSS is that all the 15 major states showed an increase in the share of rural non-agricultural workers between 1977-78 and 1999-2000. The NSS data showed that the share increased substantially for Andhra Pradesh also i.e., the state which experienced a decline in the share according to census data (between 1981-1991).

A comparison of the Census data with the NSS data state wise shows that the share of total rural non-agricultural workforce was larger than the share witnessed in 2001 census in many cases. Prominent among the states showing high rate of total rural non-agricultural workforce was Kerala, with 71.34 per cent (Census) and 51.5 per cent (NSS). The share of the total rural non-agricultural workforce was also very high in the state of West Bengal, 41.60 per cent according to census and 37.0 per cent according to NSS.

Based on the above analysis, it is noticed that for total rural non-agricultural workforce, the share is generally higher according to NSS than to census.

RNFE by Sex: Male

Having examined the share of total rural non-agricultural workforce we now deal with the share of the men and women in Table 2 and 3. As per the Table III.2, find, there was an increase is the share of male RNFE from 18.79 per cent in 1971 to 20.84 per cent in 1981 and to 22.1 per cent in 1991 and further, 47.84 per cent in 2001. The NSS data on the share of rural non-agricultural workforce increase from 19.5 to 28.61 during the same period found.

Table 2
Non-Agricultural Workers as a Percentage of Rural Work-frce: Census (1971-2001) and NSSO (1972-73 to 1999-2000): Male

	Census				*NSS*					
States	*1971*	*1981*	*1991*	*2001*	*1972-73*	*1977-78*	*1983*	*1987-88*	*1993-94*	*1999-2000*
All-India	18.79	20.84	22.10	47.84	16.70	19.50	22.40	25.50	26.00	28.60
Andhra Pradesh	24.40	23.46	23.60	46.06	21.40	19.70	25.60	25.90	24.40	25.60
Bihar	12.29	14.39	13.10	25.65	17.80	16.90	18.70	23.50	18.00	21.10
Gujarat	18.18	22.13	25.90	55.24	16.10	15.60	21.40	31.40	28.90	28.60
Haryana	23.02	25.37	26.70	54.78	19.90	22.50	27.80	29.10	39.10	40.40
Himachal Pradesh	26.62	31.04	33.30	46.56	18.90	22.60	22.90	31.30	34.20	46.20
Karnataka	20.50	21.06	22.90	50.86	14.80	16.80	18.40	20.40	21.20	21.50
Kerala	46.64	54.30	54.60	77.84	44.30	40.80	42.20	45.50	46.80	57.20
Madhya Pradesh	12.83	14.96	14.60	35.68	9.60	10.80	12.80	14.70	12.80	15.80
Maharashtra	18.18	22.92	24.00	56.57	17.60	19.60	30.40	24.20	24.70	26.20
Orissa	16.18	18.39	20.10	39.38	18.40	15.40	21.80	25.10	21.30	33.00
Punjab	21.02	23.07	23.60	58.09	20.60	22.20	22.50	21.30	31.80	36.30
Rajasthan	16.28	19.91	9.90	44.76	15.60	17.50	19.00	34.80	30.40	32.70
Tamil Nadu	23.45	25.23	26.30	58.23	24.60	26.10	31.10	34.80	36.80	31.80
Uttar Pradesh	13.52	14.11	16.30	36.90	18.10	19.80	21.30	21.10	23.70	28.20
West Bengal	21.17	25.34	27.20	56.65	22.40	22.30	26.90	27.80	35.30	33.60

Source: Census of India, 1971, 1981, 1991 and 2001 (provisional), Government of India.
NSSO, *Sarvekshana*, Nos. 1 & 2, 1977; Vol.V, Nos. 1 & 2, 1981,Table 29; Vol.VI, Nos. 1 & 2, 1982; Vol.VI. Nos. 3 & 4, 1983; Vol. VIII, Nos.3 & 4, 1984, Table-6; Vol.IX, No.4, 1987, Table-1, 38th Round, 1983, No.341, Report on the Third Quinquennial Survey on Employment and Unemployment, All-India, Table-14, 43rd Round, 1987-88, *Sarvekshana*, Special Number, Report on the Fourth Quinquennial Survey on Employment and Unemployment, All-India, September 1990, data derived from Statement 36 (UPSS), pp.105-106.

The share of male rural non-agricultural workforce varies very widely. It was 77.84 per cent according to the census (2001) in Kerala. While Kerala experienced the highest share, the lowest share in of Bihar with 25.65 per cent. The NSS data for 1999-2000 also showed that the share of the male rural non-agricultural workforce was the highest in Kerala at 57.2 per cent. But the lowest was in Madhya Pradesh at 15.8 per cent, while Bihar had 21.1 per cent share of the total RNFE. A comparison of the census 2001 and NSS 1999-2000 shows that the NSS data on the share of the workers is generally higher than that given by Census for most of the States.

RNFE by Sex: Female

The data on female rural non-agricultural workforce as a proportion of total female rural workers with in each State is presented in Table 3. One significant point to be noted from the table is that the share is varying widely across the states whether we consider the census data of 2001 or NSS data of 1999-2000. Interestingly, it is to be noted that the share of rural female non-agricultural work force is higher in 2001 than in 1971 in a large number of States. This is evident from census data. The rising share of female workers is also noticed when we compare NSS 1977-78 and 1999-2000. Most of these females may had been employed in the household industry, because the industry enables women to participate in rural non-agricultural workforce by working with in the household.

CHANGES IN RELATIVE POSITION OF STATES BY LOW, MEDIUM AND HIGH R.N.F.E. BY CENSUS AND NSS MEASURES: TOTALS

It is possible to group the states into high, medium and low proportion states in terms of rural non-farm employment. The states with over 25 per cent of rural non-agricultural workers are treated as high proportion states, the states having 20-25 per cent rural non-agricultural workers are labeled as medium proportion states and the states with less than 20 per cent rural non-farm workers are considered as low proportion states. This type of grouping the states into high, medium and low

Table 3

Non-Agricultural Workers as a Percentage of Rural Work-force: Census (1971-2001) and NSSO (1972-73 to 1999-2000): Female

	Census				*NSS*					
States	*1971*	*1981*	*1991*	*2001*	*1972-73*	*1977-78*	*1983*	*1987-88*	*1993-94*	*1999-2000*
All-India	12.96	12.73	13.10	28.07	10.30	11.90	12.30	15.30	113.80	14.60
Andhra Pradesh	12.96	12.27	12.20	23.87	13.80	14.60	18.70	17.90	16.30	15.70
Bihar	6.10	7.66	6.80	14.38	14.80	11.00	11.80	9.80	8.10	14.30
Gujarat	7.24	11.42	14.60	32.41	8.70	5.60	7.40	24.20	9.40	8.00
Haryana	23.06	14.89	13.70	34.82	15.60	9.50	9.70	7.20	6.80	7.90
Himachal Pradesh	5.12	5.91	7.60	10.97	1.60	1.80	2.40	3.60	4.50	4.90
Karnataka	19.17	16.60	14.80	31.63	10.90	12.50	11.80	14.50	15.40	12.20
Kerala	41.47	46.09	51.50	73.29	41.40	27.40	29.10	34.30	37.00	40.20
Madhya Pradesh	6.05	7.32	6.00	16.08	4.40	5.30	6.10	8.90	6.10	8.40
Maharashtra	5.94	6.70	6.50	23.28	6.60	7.80	7.10	8.60	8.80	6.10
Orissa	23.02	16.53	14.70	26.20	18.30	14.20	19.00	22.00	15.00	19.40
Punjab	67.15	17.69	37.90	69.07	37.00	10.00	7.40	8.40	7.30	9.40
Rajasthan	9.95	11.27	6.40	16.54	8.40	4.70	6.10	16.70	7.30	8.10
Tamil Nadu	15.47	13.43	15.50	35.84	15.60	16.40	18.20	32.90	21.50	24.10
Uttar Pradesh	7.86	9.55	10.40	24.46	15.00	10.90	10.30	8.70	10.00	12.50
West Bengal	30.56	33.46	34.30	54.16	43.10	31.30	24.90	29.20	41.00	45.90

Source: Census of India, 1971, 1981, 1991 and 2001 (provisional), Government of India.
NSSO, *Sarvekshana*, Nos. 1 & 2, 1977; Vol.V, Nos. 1 & 2, 1981,Table 29; Vol.VI, Nos. 1 & 2, 1982; Vol.VI. Nos. 3 & 4, 1983; Vol. VIII, Nos. 3 & 4, 1984, Table-6; Vol.IX, No.4, 1987, Table-1, 38th Round, 1983, No.341, Report on the Third Quinquennial Survey on Employment and Unemployment, All-India, Table-14, 43rd Round, 1987-88, *Sarvekshana*, Special Number, Report on the Fourth Quinquennial Survey on Employment and Unemployment, All-India, September 1990, data derived from Statement 36 (UPSS), pp.105-106.

categories is done for the years 1971, 1981, 1991 and 2001 for the census, and 1977-78, 1983, 1987-88, 1993-94 and 1999-2000 for the NSS.

The grouping of States according to the degree of rural non-farm employment is presented in Tables 4, 5 and 6. Table 4 presents the proportion of total rural non-agricultural workers in the rural workforce for three groups based on census (1971-2001) and NSS data (1977-78 to 1999-2000). According to Census, the States with high proportion of RNFE increased from one state in 1971 to nine states in 2001. Medium proportion of RNFE states are declining from seven states in 1971 to three states in 2001 and in case of low proportion states also there is a decline by four between 1971-2001. According to NSS data, the states with a high proportion of RNFE increased from one state in 1977-78 to five states in 1999-2000, medium proportion states also increased from two in 1977-78 to eight in 1999-2000. The low proportion of RNFE states, however, declined from twelve states in 1977-78 to one state in 1999-2000. The NSS data show a larger increase relative to the Census data.

Male

The grouping of states according to their shares of rural non-agricultures workers is considered. As before, we have grouped the states under high, medium and low proportion categories which are shown in Table 5. The classification is done using both the Census and NSS data. According to Census, the state with high proportion of RNFE (above 25 per cent) have increased from two states in 1971 to six states in 1991 By 2001 all the states crossed 25 percent share. The states with the medium proportion of RNFE declined from six states in 1971 to five states in 1991. The states with low proportion of RNFE also declined from seven states in 1971 to four states in 1991. NSS data show that the states with high proportion of RNFE increased between 1977-78 to 1999-2000 (i.e. two states in 1977-78 to eleven states in 1999-2000). During this period, the states with medium proportion of RNFE did not change in number. However, the composition of the states changed. The

Table 4
Classification of States by the Proportion of Rural Non-Agricultural Workers Based on Census and N.S.S. Data (TOTAL)

	Census				*NSSO*					
States with Proportion of RNFE	*1971*	*1981*	*1991*	*2001*	*1972-73*	*1977-78*	*1983*	*1987-88*	*1993-94*	*1999-2000*
High (above 25%)	HP(26.6)	H(25.4)	G(25.9)	P(46.1)	K(44.3)	K(40. 8)	WB(26.9)	AP(25.9)	K(47.0)	K(57.2)
	K(45.4)	HP(31.0)	HP(33.3)	B(25.6)		TN(26. 1)	K(42.2)	H(29.1)	H(38.9)	H(41.2)
		K(54.3)	TN(26.3)	G(55.2)			AP(25.6)	K(45.8)	TN(36.2)	TN(37.7)
		TN(25.2)	H(26.7)	H(54.8)			TN(31.1)	P(31.2)	WB(35.2)	P(36.2)
		WB(25.3)	K(34.6)	HP(46.6)			H(27.8)	TN(34.8)	P(31.9)	A(35.3)
			WB(29.2)	KA(50.9)				G(31.4)	R(30.3)	WB(33.5)
				K(77.8)				HP(31.3)	G(28.9)	R(32.7)
				MP(35.7)				O(25.1)		G(28.6)
				M(56.6)				R(34.8)		UP(28.2)
				O(39.4)				WB(27.8)		M(26.2)
				P(58.1)						AP(25.6)
				R(44.8)						
				TN(58.2)						
				UP(36.9)						
				WB(56.7)						
Average	36.60	32.20	32.67	49.56	44.30	33.45	30.72	32.70	35.49	34.77
Medium (between 20-25%)	AP(24.4)	AP(23.5)	P(23.6)		WB(22.1)	WB(22.3)	G(21.1)	UP(21.1)	M(24.8)	O(23.2)
	H(23.0)	G(22.4)	O(20.1)		TN(24.6)	P(22.2)	HP(22.9)	KA(20.4)	AP(24.5)	K(21.6)
	KA(20.5)	KA(21.1)	M(24.0)		P(20.6)	HP(22.6)	M(20.4)	B(23.5)	UP(23.7)	B(21.1)
	P(21.0)	M(22.9)	K(22.9)		AP(21.4)	H(22.5)	O(21.8)	M(24.2)	A(21.8)	MP(15.8)

Contd.

	Census				NSSO					
States with Proportion of RNFE	*1971*	*1981*	*1991*	*2001*	*1972-73*	*1977-78*	*1983*	*1987-88*	*1993-94*	*1999-2000*
	TN(23.5) WB(21.2)	P(23.1)	AP(23.6)				P(21.8) P(22.5) UP(21.3)		O(21.2) KA(21.1) B(18.0)	
Average	22.30	22.50	22.84		22.17	22.40	21.67	22.30	22.16	20.43
Low (below 20%)	B(12.3) G(18.2) MP(12.8) M(18.2) O(16.2) R(16.3) UP(21.2)	UP(14.1) R(19.9) B(14.4) O(18.4) MP(15.0)	UP(16.3) R(19.9) MP(14.6) B(13.1)		B(17.8) H(19.9) KA(14.8) M(17.6) R(15.6) G(16.1) HP(18.9) MP(9.6) O(18.4) UP(18.1)	B(16.9) KA(16.9) AP(19.7) M(19.6) R(17.5) G(15.6) MP(10.8) O(15.4) UP(19.8)	R(19.0) KA(18.4) MP(12.8) B(18.7)	MP(14.7)	MP(18.0)	
Average	16.50	16.40	15.97		16.68	16.90	17.22	14.7	18.0	

Source: Composed from Table III.1.

LEGEND:

AP :	Andhra Pradesh	K :	Kerala	TN :	Tamil Nadu
B :	Bihar	M :	Maharashtra	WB :	West Bengal
G :	Gujarat	MP :	Madhya Pradesh	UP :	Uttar Pradesh
H :	Haryana	O :	Orissa	HP :	Himachal Pradesh
P :	Punjab	KA :	Karnataka	R :	Rajasthan

states with low proportion of RNFE showed a decline. No state was there in 1999-2000 with low proportions, whereas there were nine states in 1977-78.

Female

The share of females in rural non-agricultural workers in the rural work force employing both the Census and NSS data is shown in Table 6. Both sets of data do not exhibit any significant change in the number of states shifting from low to high position. But the picture shown by NSS is slightly better than the Census. The number shifting low to medium position is larger by NSS criteria.

SUMMARY

This paper examines the changes in the levels of RNFE between 1971-2001 using census data and between 1972-73 and 1999-2000 using the NSS data. The results show that the percentage of non-agricultural workforce in the total rural work force increased over time. This conclusion holds whether we consider the decennial census data or the NSS data. It is notified from the census figures that the share of RNFE increased by considerable percentage points between 1971-2001. From the NSS data it is noticed that the share is increased by marginal percentage points. The shares of males and females in RNFE is calculated separately. A perusal of these shares show that the share of males increased by much a larger than the share of females. This fact is evident from Census and NSS data.

With regard to levels of RNFE at the state-level there are wide variations between Census and NSS. Measured by RNFE as in 2001, Kerala, Haryana, West Bengal, Gujarat, Haryana occupied the first four places. Madhya Pradesh, Bihar, Maharashtra and Uttar Pradesh occupied the last four places according to Census. By NSS, in 1999-2000, the first four places were occupied by Kerala, West Bengal, Tamil Nadu and Haryana and the last places are occupied by Madhya Pradesh, Maharashtra, Karnataka and Bihar. It is noticed that no agreement even in ranking between census and NSS data except in respect of Kerala which occupied the first rank by

Table 5

Classification of States by the Proportion of Rural Non-Agricultural Workers Based on Census and N.S.S. Data (Male)

States with Proportion of RNFE	*Census*							
	1971	*1981*	*1991*	*2001*	*1977-78*	*1983*	*1987-88*	*1993-94*
High	HP(26.6)	H (25.4)	G (25.9)	AP(46.1)	K (44.3)	K (40.8)	WB	AP (25.9)
(above 25%)	K (45.4)	HP(31.0)	HP(33.3)	B(25.6)		TN	(26.9)	H (29.1)
		K (54.3)	TN(26.3)	G(55.2)		(26.1)	K (42.2)	K (45.8)
		TN(25.2)	H (26.7)	H(54.8)			AP	P (31.2)
		WB(25.3)	K (34.6)	HP(46.6)			(25.6)	TN(34.8)
			WB(29.2)	KA(50.9)			TN	G (31.4)
				K(77.8)			(31.1)	HP(31.3)
				MP(35.7)			H (27.8)	O (25.1)
				M(56.6)				R (34.8)
				O(39.4)				WB(27.8)
				P(58.1)				
				R(44.8)				
				TN(58.2)				
				UP(36.9)				
				WB(56.7)				
Average	36.60	32.20	32.67	49.56	44.30	33.45	30.72	32.70
Medium	AP (24.4)	AP(23.5)	P(23.6)		WB	WB	G (21.1)	UP(21.1)
(between 20-25%)	H(23.0)	G(22.4)	O(20.1)		(22.1)	(22.3)	HP	KA(20.4)
	KA(20.5)	KA(21.1)	M(24.0)		TN	P (22.2)	(22.9)	B(23.5)
	P(21.0)	M(22.9)	K(22.9)		(24.6)	HP	M (20.4)	M(24.2)

Contd.

States with Proportion of RNFE	*Census*							
	1971	*1981*	*1991*	*2001*	*1977-78*	*1983*	*1987-88*	*1993-94*
	TN(23.5) WB(21.2)	P(23.1)	AP(23.6)		P (20.6) AP (21.4)	(22.6) H (22.5)	O (21.8) P (22.5) UP (21.3)	
Average	22.30	22.50	22.84		22.17	22.40	21.67	22.30
Low (below 20%)	B(12.3) G(18.2) MP(12.8) M(18.2) O(16.2) R(16..3) UP(21.2)	UP(14.1) R(19.9) B(14.4) O(18.4) MP(15.0)	UP(16.3) R(19.9) MP(14.6) B(13.1)		B(17.8) H(19.9) KA(14.8) M(17.6) R(15.6) G(16.1) HP(18.9) MP(9.6) O(18.4) UP(18.1)	B(16.9) KA(16.9) AP(19.7) M(19.6) R(17.5) G(15.6) MP(10.8) O(15.4) UP(19.8)	R(19.0) KA(18.4) MP(12.8) B(18.7)	MP(14.7)
Average	16.50	16.40	15.97		16.68	16.90	17.22	14.7

Source: Composed from Table III.2.

LEGEND:

AP	:	Andhra Pradesh	K	:	Kerala	TN	:	Tamil Nadu
B	:	Bihar	M	:	Maharashtra	WB	:	West Bengal
G	:	Gujarat	MP	:	Madhya Pradesh	UP	:	Uttar Pradesh
H	:	Haryana	O	:	Orissa	HP	:	Himachal Pradesh
P	:	Punjab	KA	:	Karnataka	R	:	Rajasthan

both the measures. The management is striking .Madhya Pradesh occupies the last place both in Census and NSS data. The general disagreement in ranking between Census and NSS (as in 2001, 1999-2000) can be seen both in respect of males and females.

The states are grouped on the basis of level of RNFE into high, medium and low categories. This is done for the 4 Census years between 1971, 1981, 1991 and 2001 and five NSS years 1977-78, 1983, 1987-88, 1993-94 and 1999-2000. According to the Census data, the states with 'high' level of RNFE increased from one state in 1971 to nine states in 2001. States with 'medium' level of RNFE declined from 7 to 3 during the period. NSS data show there was an increase in the number of states from one to five in the 'high' proportion category. There is also an increase in the 'medium' proportion category. The states with 'low' proportion of RNFE declined. Thus the NSS show a large increase relative to census.

The grouping of states into high, medium and low categories is done separately for males and females using both Census and NSS data. Considering the Census data on males it is noticed that the number of states in the 'high' proportion category increased from two to fifteen between 1971 and 2001. The states in the 'medium' category. Have not taken place in the favor and the states with 'low' category in 2001.

On the other hand, the NSS data on males show the states under high category increased from two to eleven between 1977-78 and 1999-2000. The states under 'low' category show a decline from nine to one by 1993-94. But no state is there in this category in 1999-2000. Considering the census data on females we do not find any significant shift in the number of states under the 'high' and 'low categories is not found. The NSS data on females show a slightly different picture. With a few states shifting from 'low' to 'medium' category. However, in brief, the state of RNFE as depicted by the NSS data is better than that shown by Census.

Table 6

Classification of States by the Proportion of Rural Non-Agricultural Workers Based on Census and N.S.S. Data (Female)

	Census				*NSSO*				
States with Proportion of RNFE	*1971*	*1981*	*1991*	*2001*	*1977-78*	*1983*	*1987-88*	*1993-94*	*1999-2000*
High (above 25%)	K (45.4)	WB(26.2) K (52.2)	WB(29.9) K(53.9) HP(25.5) H(25.2)	G (40.3) H (52.2) HP(20.5) K (71.3) O (27.7) P (26.3) TN(30.0) WB(41.6)	K (34.6)	WB(26.4) TN(25.4) K (36.9)	WB(28.1) R (26.5) G (28.4) TN(29.6) K (41.4)	K (43.8) WB(36.6) TN(29.7) H (28.2) P (25.4)	K (52.0) WB(36.3) A (32.2) H (32.2) TN (32.0)
Average	45.40	39.20	33.620	67.63	34.60	29.57	30.83	32.74	36.94
Medium (between 20-25%)	AP(20.9) H (23.0) TN(21.6) WB(21.9) HP(20.4) KA(20.2) P (21.6)	TN(21.4) P (23.3) HP(24.0) H (24.5) G (20.0)	G (23.2) P (24.4) KA(20.3) TN(22.4)	AP(24.8) R (22.7) UP(22.3)	WB(24.4) TN(22.0)	AP(22.8) H (22.3) O (20.9)	AP (22.3) H (21.1) O (24.1) P (23.7)	G (21.2) A (20.7) AP(20.8) R (20.1) UP(19.9) O (19.0) KA(18.7) M (17.5) B (15.6)	UP(23.9) R(22.3) O (21.9) AP(21.3) G (20.3) B (19.4) K (18.0) M (17.4)

Contd.

	Census				NSSO				
States with Proportion of RNFE	*1971*	*1981*	*1991*	*2001*	*1977-78*	*1983*	*1987-88*	*1993-94*	*1999-2000*
Average	21.40	22.70	22.57	23.27	23.20	22.00	22.82	19.27	20.56
Low (below 20%)	B (11.4)	UP(13.7)	UP(15.5)	B (18.2)	AP(17.6)	B (16.5)	B (19.7)	MP(10.1)	MP(12.9)
	G (16.2)	AP(19.6)	O (19.2)	MP(14.5)	G (13.0)	KA(15.8)	KA(18.0)		
	MP(11.0)	B (14.1)	MP(11.8)	M (19.9)	HP(12.2)	HP(12.9)	UP(17.6)		
	M (14.3)	KA(19.7)	AP(19.2)		MP (8.6)	M (14.3)	HP(17.8)		
	O (16.9)	MP(12.6)	R (16.8)		O (15.0)	MP(10.9)	MP(12.3)		
	R (15.4)	M (17.0)	M (16.9)		R (11.6)	R (13.3)	M (17.1)		
	UP(12.9)	O (18.1)	B (11.9)		B (15.3)	P (17.5)			
		R (18.5)			H (18.3)	UP(18.0)			
					KA(15.2)	O(15.4)			
					M (14.2)				
					P (18.5)				
					UP(17.3)				
Average	14.00	16.70	15.90	17.53	14.73	14.86	17.11	10.1	12.9

Source: Composed from Table III.3.

REFERENCES

1. Mahendradev, S. (1991), "Non-Agricultural Employment in Rural India: Evidence at a disaggregate Level", *Economic and Political Weekly*, Vol.25, No.28, July 14, pp.1526-36.

2. Vaidyanathan, A. (1986), "Labour Use in Rural India: A Study of Spatial and Temporal Variations", *Economic and Political Weekly*, Vol.21, No.52, Review of Agriculture, December 27, pp.A-130-146.

3. Unni, Jeemol (1999), "Regional Variation in Rural Non-Agricultural Employment; An Explanatory Analysis", *Economic and Political Weekly*, January 19, pp.109-122.

4. Basant, R. and Kumar, B.L. (1989), "Rural Non-Farm Employment in India: A Review of Available Evidence", *Social Scientist*, Jan-Feb., pp.13-71.

5. Murthy, C.S. and Durga, C. (1992), "Rural Non-agricultural Employment with Reference to Employment in Handloom Weaving in Andhra Pradesh", *Manpower Journal*, Vol. XXVIII, No.3, October-December, p.7.

6. Basant and Parthasarathi (1991), "Correlations of Inter-regional Variations in Rural Non-agricultural Employment in Gujarat", *Indian Journal of Labour Economics*, 35 (2), pp. 111-21.

7. Pravin Visaria (1995), "Rural Non-Farm Employment in India : Trends and Issues for Research", *Indian Journal of Agricultural Economics*, Vol.3, July-Sept., p. 398.

8. Papola T.S., (1992), "Rural Non-Farm Employment : An Assessment of Recent Trends", *The Indian Journal of Labour Economics*, Vol. 35, No.3, July-Sept, pp.238.

9. Chadha G.K. and A.N. Sharma (eds.) (1997), Growth, Employment and Poverty– Changes and Continuity in Rural India", Vikas Publishing House, New Delhi.

16

UNEMPLOYMENT INSURANCE–NEED OF THE HOUR

A. V. V. Siva Prasad
M. Srinivasa Narayana

INTRODUCTION

In economics, a person who is able and willing to work yet is unable to find a paying job is considered unemployed. Unemployment will have its impact on society and the economy in terms of various costs. The social costs of unemployment include severe financial hardship and poverty, debt, homelessness and housing stress, family tensions and breakdown, boredom, alienation, shame and stigma, increased social isolation, crime, erosion of confidence and self-esteem, the atrophying of work skills and ill-health. Most of these increase with the duration of unemployment. Unemployed people report that being unemployed is one of the worst things that can happen to them (White 1991). In addition, unemployment falls disproportionately on already disadvantaged groups in society. Understanding the forces that create unemployment, and then trying to mitigate their negative effects to the greatest extent possible, is a central issue in economics.

CAUSES OF UNEMPLOYMENT

There are differed views and opinions on the causes of unemployment in an economy. Keynesian economics views that unemployment results from insufficient effective demand for goods and service in the economy (cyclical unemployment). Others point to structural problems (inefficiencies) inherent in labor markets (structural unemployment). Classical or neoclassical economics tends to reject these explanations, and focuses more on rigidities imposed on the labour market from the outside, such as minimum wage laws, taxes, and other regulations that may discourage the hiring of workers (classical unemployment). Yet others see unemployment as largely due to voluntary choices by the unemployed (frictional unemployment). On the other extreme, Marxists see unemployment as a structural fact helping to preserve business profitability and capitalism (Marxian unemployment). The different perspectives may be right in different ways, contributing to the understanding of different types of unemployment.

UNEMPLOYMENT SCENARIO IN INDIA

The unemployment scenario in India has always been quite acute. With a huge population and slow growth of job opportunities, unemployment has been widespread in India. Large scale unemployment has led to several socio-economic problems like poverty, malnutrition, antisocial and criminal activities, drug and substance abuse, etc. The lack of proper unemployment insurance schemes has further aggravated this problem.

In the early 1990s, major economic reforms were undertaken in India. One of the major objectives of these economic reforms was to boost employment in the Indian economy. However, though the economic reforms were successful in raising productivity and attracting FDI (Foreign Direct Investment), the growth in job opportunities was not as high as had been expected.

SOME OF THE IMPORTANT ASPECTS RELATED TO THE UNEMPLOYMENT SCENARIO IN INDIA

The growth in labor force in India is much higher than the growth of jobs.

Table 1
Comparison of Population Growth Rate and Unemployment Growth Rates

Year	*Unemployment Rate (%)*	*Population Growth Rate (%)*	*Net Migration Rate /1,000 Population*
2002	8.8	1.51	-0.07
2003	8.8	1.47	-0.07
2004	9.5	1.44	-0.07
2005	9.2	1.4	-0.07
2006	8.9	1.38	-0.07
2007	7.8	1.606	-0.05
2008	7.2	1.578	-0.05

Unemployment rate: This entry contains the percent of the labor force that is without jobs.

Population growth rate: The average annual percent change in the population, resulting from a surplus (or deficit) of births over deaths and the balance of migrants entering and leaving a country.

Migration rate: This entry includes the figure for the difference between the number of persons entering and leaving a country during the year per 1,000 persons (based on midyear population). An excess of persons entering the country is referred to as net immigration (e.g., 3.56 migrants/1,000 population); an excess of persons leaving the country as net emigration (e.g., -9.26 migrants/1,000 population). The net migration rate indicates the contribution of migration to the overall level of population change. High levels of migration can cause problems such as increasing unemployment and potential ethnic strife (if people are coming in) or a reduction in the labor force, perhaps in certain key sectors (if people are leaving).)

- The unorganized sector in India accounts for 90% of the employment. The unorganized sector consists of agricultural workers in the rural areas and contract and sub-contract laborers in the urban areas.
- More than 90 per cent of the labour force is employed in the "unorganised sector", i.e. sectors which don't provide with the social security and other benefits of employment in the "organised sector."
- Self employment accounts for more than 60% of the employed population of India.
- Casual workers, who get jobs only at times and remain unpaid when they don't have work, constitute 30% of the workforce, while only 10% are regular employees. Merely two-fifth of this 10% is employed in the government sector.
- Around 70% of the labor force in India has education below primary level or is illiterate.
- There exists very high underemployment in various sectors of the labor force in India. Disguised unemployment also exists in various sectors of the Indian economy.
- Regional imbalances in the unemployment scenario in India are another important factor. This has led to inter-state labor migration in the Indian economy.
- India's labour force is growing at a rate of 2.5 per cent annually, but employment is growing at only 2.3 per cent. Thus, the country is faced with the challenge of not only absorbing new entrants to the job market (estimated at seven million people every year), but also clearing the backlog.
- Unorganised sector is made up of jobs in which the Minimum Wage Act is either not, or only marginally, implemented. The absence of unions in the unorganised sector does not provide any opportunity for collective bargaining.

Table 2
Sector-wise Absorption of Labour

Agriculture	62 per cent
Manufacturing & construction	16 per cent
Services	10 per cent
Sundry/miscellaneous jobs	12 per cent

Table 3
Unemployment–Age Structure

Age (years)	*Unemployment Rate*	*Males*	*Females*
0–14	31.5	189,238,487	172,168,306
15–64	63.3	374,157,581	352,868,003
65 and above	5.2	28,285,796 (2008 est.)	31,277,725

Table 4
Ratio of Youth Unemployment Rate to Adult Unemployment Rate

Year	*Both Sexes*	*Male*	*Female*
1994	3.7	4.1	3
2000	3.9	3.7	4.3
2004	3	3.1	2.8

Source: United Nations Statistics Division

Recent studies have revealed the fact that growth of unemployment in India at current rates can lead to devastating results. At this rate, India is expected to have a 30% unemployment rate by 2020. This would mean that there would be 21 crore jobless people in India. The decline in job creation in agriculture has been identified as one of the important reasons behind the increasing unemployment in India. To eradicate this problem, Government of India along with various state governments, developed and implemented various employment and social security schemes. The summary of these schemes are given in the following table.

FOCUS OF THE ARTICLE

From the above part of the article, it was clear that the unemployment problem in India is one of the serious issues which need to be tackled immediately. To mitigate this problem, Government of India has initiated several schemes right from the independence (see the schemes in the Table 5). Along with the central government initiatives, various state governments are also implementing several employment and social security schemes to eradicate the social evils that may arise with unemployment and poverty. The present article will now focus on one of the social security scheme named "Unemployment Insurance". These types of schemes are quite popular in most of the developed economies and now attracting the attention of other economies. The rest of the article will emphasizes on this scheme by throwing a light on the need of unemployment insurance, its application in India and the results of it.

Table 5
Various Employment and Social Security Schemes in India

- *Community Development Programme* - 1952 - Overall development of rural areas with people's participation.
- *Intensive Agriculture Development Programme* - 1960-61 - To provide loan, seeds, fertilizer, tools to the farmers.
- *Employment Guarantee Scheme of Maharashtra* - 1972-73 - To assist the economically weaker section of the rural society.
- *Twenty Point Programme* - 1975 - Poverty eradication and raising the standard of living.
- *Food for work Programme* - 1977-78 - Providing food grains to labour for the work of development.
- *National Rural Employment Programme* - 1980 - To provide profitable employment opportunities to the rural poor.
- *Development of women & children in Rural Areas* - 1982 - To provide suitable opportunities of self-employment to the women belonging to the rural families who are living below the poverty line.
- *Rural Landless Employment Guarantee Programme* - 1983 - For providing employment to landless farmers & labourers.
- *Self-employment of the Educated Unemployed Youth* - 1983-84 - To provide financial and technical assistance for self-employment.
- *Council for Advancement of People's Action & Rural Technology* - 1986 - To provide assistance for rural prosperity.
- *Self-Employment programme for the Urban poor* - 1986 - To provide self employment to urban poor through provision of subsidiary and bank credit.

- *Jawahar Rozgar Yojana* - 1989 - To provide employment to rural unemployed.
- *Nehru Rozgar Yojana* - 1989 - To provide employment to urban unemployed.
- *Scheme for Urban Micro Enterprises* - 1990 - To assist the urban poor for small enterprises.
- *Scheme for Urban Wage Employment* - 1990 - To provide wages employment after arranging the basic facilities for poor people in the urban areas where population is less than one lakh.
- *Scheme for Housing and Shelter Up-gradation* - 1990 - To provide employment by means of shelter up-gradation in the urban areas where population is between 1 to 20 lakhs.
- *Employment Assurance Scheme* - 1993 - To provide employment of at least 100 days in a year in villages.
- *Swaran Jayanti Shahri Rozgar Yojana* - 1997 - To provide gainful employment to urban unemployed and under employed poor through self employment or wage employment.
- *Swarna Jayanti Gram Swarozgar Yojana* - 1999 - For eliminating rural poverty and unemployment and promoting self employment.
- *Pradhan Mantri Gram Sadak Yojana* - 2000 - To line all villages with Pacca road.
- *Sampurna Gramin Rojgar Yojana* - 2001 - Providing employment & food security.
- *Jai Prakash Narain Rozgar Guarantee Yojana* - 2002-3 - Employment guarantee in most poor districts.
- *Rural Employment Guarantee Yojana* - 2005-6 - 100 days assured employment.
- *Rajiv Gandhi Shramik Kalyan Yojna* – 2005 - unemployment allowance for the employees covered under ESI scheme.

UNEMPLOYMENT INSURANCE

In economics unemployment compensation is termed 'unemployment insurance'. The closure of many industries and large scale retrenchment of workers leading to unemployment have rendered the working class without any social security cover. At present unemployment is one of the biggest challenges for the social security sector. As global competition increases, the burden of unemployment also develops on an unprecedented scale and strengthening the social safety net for such workers is imperative. National and International forum including the United Nations stress the need for social justice and safety net for the working population. According to the International Labour Office (ILO), seventy-five per cent of the 150 million people unemployed around the world lack any unemployment insurance protection. Austria, Belgium, Denmark, Finland, France, Germany, Iceland, Luxembourg, Netherlands, Norway, Portugal, Spain, Sweden and Switzerland provide the most generous unemployment protection systems while, Australia, Canada, Ireland, Japan, New Zealand, the United Kingdom and the United States belong to "medium-level type systems". Fewer of the unemployed in these countries receive benefits and the compensation that is provided is lower than those available in the first tier of countries.

Benefit payments (net wage replacement rates) range from 23% of wages in New Zealand to 58% in Canada and the United States, among these "medium-level" countries. In contrast, "top level" countries such as Finland and Spain provide 63% and 77% respectively of national average earnings in their unemployment insurance.

THE LACK OF UNEMPLOYMENT INSURANCE PROTECTION

Developed Countries

In the top 14 countries listed above, unemployment protection consists of various layers of benefits. The first and most important one consists of unemployment insurance benefits paid during the initial period following the loss of a job, with average net replacement rates of more than 60% of national average earnings. This rate is significantly higher than in those countries belonging to the next category.

Most countries with a high-level system have a second layer of unemployment benefits, usually called unemployment assistance. This layer covers workers who have exhausted their entitlements to unemployment insurance and provides them with a grace period before they come within the purview of less generous social assistance schemes.

Developing Countries

Workers who are fortunate enough to be covered by unemployment benefits are mainly concentrated in industrialized countries, but for those who work in the rural or urban informal sectors in developing countries-including 750 to 900 million underemployed workers-hardly any unemployment protection exists at all.

The ILO says that these groups of workers should be assisted through employment in labour-intensive infrastructure programmes - "feeder roads, land reclamation, minor dams, wells and irrigation systems, drainage and sewerage, schools and health centres". Employment provided under such programmes can be organized so that workers can obtain an employment guarantee for a number of days per year.

UNEMPLOYMENT COSTS

The existence of unemployment insurance discourages certain people from working; those who value the compensation over the amount gained if working will not seek employment. In economics unemployment refers to one that is seeking employment and cannot find it. If one does not wish to be employed (employed & unemployed), then they aren't even in the labour force, as they do not supply or wish to supply any labour. Excessive unemployment insurance (e.g. benefits in New Zealand) decreases the labour force and puts downward pressure on GDP growth by causing downward pressure on production levels.

Private Benefits/Costs vs. Public Benefits/Costs: The opportunity cost of being unemployed is the amount of money to be gained from being employed, pus the social aspects of employment and unemployment. If one values unemployment more than working, they will seek unemployment (i.e. quite or get fired) or continue to be unemployed. However, the fallacy in this reasoning is that this only concerns the individual's costs and benefits. The public costs and benefits are ignored when making an individual transaction, such as the downward pressure on GDP growth by creating a shortage (however subtle) of labour.

Downward Pressure on GDP: If one is employed, they provide income tax payments (government revenue), labour, and consumption for the economy. If one is unemployed they take unemployment insurance (government spending), decrease labour in the economy, and only provide consumption. Consumption would likely have been higher if the individual had sought employment, after all there are many negative connations with being unemployed, which would affect their decision on whether to seek employment or not.

NEED FOR UNEMPLOYMENT INSURANCE IN INDIA

With the initiation of economic reforms, Indian economy is undergoing unprecedented change. Integrating the Indian economy with that of the World's, the industry has been exposed to global competition. In order to remain buoyant most of the companies want to reduce costs by way of upgrading technology and reducing workforce. But under the Industrial Disputes Act, 1947 downsizing cannot be resorted to without Government permission. The Act is applicable to establishments employing one hundred workers or more. The experience shows that permission to close down have not been coming readily. As a result of compulsion of situation many such establishments have either introduced voluntary retirement schemes for downsizing or have closed down and vanished from the scene without paying compensation, dues etc. to workers.

The Second Labour Commission has reported that a large number of workers have lost their jobs as a result of VRS, retrenchment and closures both in the organised and unorganised sectors. The exact number is not known as no data on this has been compiled by any State Government.

COVER DURING UNEMPLOYMENT

The advocates of 'hire and fire' also want to bring about a fundamental change in the nature or perception of employment. They want employment to be on the basis of contracts for stipulated periods–a total departure from the current system in vogue in most kinds of employments.

Most of the developed countries where the majority of jobs are contracts have elaborate and effective system of social security. Even in China, to quote an instance, there are stringent laws on social security system that takes care of worker's income and requirements at least for two or three years of transition or unemployment. In India, we don't have such provisions. The Labour Ministry made a small beginning in this regard recently by launching Rajiv Gandhi Shramik Kalyan Yojana (RGSKY) for providing unemployment allowance to workers who are rendered unemployed involuntarily due to retrenchment/closure of factory etc. after fulfilling certain eligibility conditions.

Table 6
Highlights of Rajiv Gandhi Shramik Kalyan Yojana (RGSKY)

Eligibility Conditions: The loss of employment should be on account of closure of the factory or establishment, retrenchment or permanent invalidity arising out of non-employment injury.

(i) The insured person should have contributed under the ESI Scheme for a minimum period of five years prior to loss of employment.

(ii) The insured person should have been entitled for sickness benefit during the last four contribution periods immediately proceeding the date of unemployment.

(iii) Unemployment allowance shall cease to be payable from the date the insured person gets reemployed elsewhere.

Rate of Unemployment Allowance: The daily rate of unemployment allowance shall be the "standard benefit rate" as specified in the table of Standard Benefit Rates under Rule-54 of ESI (Central) Rules, 1950, corresponding to the average daily wage drawn by the said insured person during the last four completed contribution periods, immediately preceding the date of unemployment.

Duration of Unemployment Allowance: The maximum period for which an insured person shall be entitled to draw unemployment allowance during his entire insurable employment, is six months. The allowance can be availed in one spell or in different spells of not less than one month. The ESIC recently decided to increase the amount to six months' salary disbursed over a period of one year.

Medical care: During the period for which a person is entitled for unemployment allowance, he shall also be eligible for medical care for himself and his/her family from ESI Dispensaries, ESI panel clinics and ESI hospitals to which he/she was attached prior to the date of loss of employment based on a separate authorization by the Branch Manager making the cash allowance payment.

OUTCOMES OF RGSKY

Nearly three years after it was launched, the Rajiv Gandhi Shramik Kalyan Yojana, which promises affected workers half their pay for six months (now for one year), is yet to make its impression on the unemployed work force in India. The reason: Affected workers here find it impossible to get the "closure" certificate from their employer. With the Employees State Insurance Corp (ESIC), the Union government body that administers the scheme, unable to make any payment without this certificate, the jobless workers are unable to reap the benefits of the scheme.

Under the scheme, all workers covered by the ESIC who are laid off or rendered jobless by a factory closure are eligible to get half their pay for a maximum of six months, provided they can show that they lost their job because of a factory closure, or were retrenched or were declared permanently invalid because of a non-employment injury. Also, they must have been members of the ESIC for at least five years.

When launched in 2005, the scheme was expected to provide a much-needed social security cover to the eight million employees registered with the ESIC, which in turn had set aside Rs 300 crore for possible expenses under the scheme. But in the real picture is that it couldn't able to spend the allotted budget despite of increase in the rate of layoffs in India. It could be due to a total lack of awareness about the scheme and also, when a factory closes down, workers covered by the ESI have to file a benefit claim with the nearest ESIC branch office together with supporting documents, including a "closure certificate" from the company. Most companies refuse this certificate for obvious reasons, if a company declares itself as closed officially, it has to clear all statutory payments like provident fund and gratuity.

RECOMMENDATIONS

Despite of the efforts made by the Government of India to protect the involuntarily unemployed people, it couldn't make an impression among the work force in India. The author has identified some reasons for this situation. They are:

- restrictive eligibility criteria have resulted in low recipiency rates
- benefit levels are low
- the mechanism to automatically extend the scheme during periods of prolonged economic downturns is broken.

As a result of these and other factors, only negligible unemployed workers currently receive assistance under this scheme, and that assistance falls short of the original goal of replacing at least half of previous earnings. In addition, the system provides no assistance either to the self-employed or to those who become reemployed at lower wages.

In the light of the above findings, three broad reforms, each designed to help the unemployment insurance scheme to better meet the needs of a twenty-first century workforce. First, strengthening the central government role in this scheme by setting the standards that would require states to harmonize their eligibility criteria and benefit levels. These new standards would aim to raise average national benefit levels and average national recipiency rates. Second, a wage loss insurance program, as part of the Unemployment Insurance program, to provide an earnings supplement for those workers who become reemployed at a wage lower than the wage they earned at their previous job. Finally, allowing self-employed workers, to be covered under this scheme.

CONCLUSION

The existence of unemployment insurance does not eliminate the costs stemming from unemployment, though it may alleviate some of the costs by helping productive, skilled members of the workforce temporarily unemployed extend their job search period (according to "Job Search Theory") to match their skills to the right job, which maximises economic efficiency. However, the existence of an overly 'luxurious' compensation scheme may discourage skilled labour from retreating from the labour market, whilst defrauding the government by claiming they are unemployed in order to obtain social security payments. It may also discourage the unemployed from seeking employment, as the compensation gained is high enough to compensate for the lack of employment. The present scheme, that is under implementation in India need to be modified according to the changing economic conditions in the world and its ripples on the Indian economy. The coverage should be extended to non_ESIC members and should simplify the procedure of getting the benefits of it.

REFERENCES

Agarwal, R.N. and Goldar, B. (1995), Economic Reforms and Employment in India Projections for the Year 2001-02., in *Indian Journal of Labour Economics* (Delhi, Indian Society of Labour Economics), Vol.38, No.4, pp.577-95.

Akerlof, G. and Yellen, J. (1986), *Efficiency Wage Models of the Labour Market* (Cambridge, Cambridge University Press).

Banerjee, B. (1986), *Rural to Urban Migration and the Urban Labour Market: A Case Study of Delhi* (Bombay, Himalaya Publishing House).

Bhagwati, J. and Srinivasan, T.N. (1975), *Foreign Trade Regimes and Economic Development: India* (Delhi, Macmillan).

Bhalotra, Sonia R. 1995. *Four Essays on the Urban Labour Market in India*, D.Phil. thesis submitted to the University of Oxford.

—Centre for Monitoring of the Indian Economy (CMIE), Economic Intelligence Service. *Basic Statistics for the Indian Economy, All India* (Vol.1) and *States* (Vol.2), (Bombay), several issues.

—Government of India. *Indian Labour Statistics* (Delhi, Ministry of Labour), several issues.

Dixon, D (1992), *Unemployment: the Economic and Social Costs*, 2nd edn, Research for Action No. 1, Brotherhood of St Laurence, Melbourne.

—(2001), NSSO, *NSS Report No. 469. Employment and Unemployment Situation among Social Groups in India, 1999-2000*; National Sample Survey Organisation, September.

Ahluwalia, Montek S. (2000), "Economic Performance in States in Post-Reforms Period," *Economic and Political Weekly*, May 6: 1637-1648.

—(2005), ESI Samachar, December, News Journal of ESI Corporation.

C.P Chandra Sekhar (2006), Unemployed in a Thriving Economy, Frontline, volume 23, Issue 5.

Suchetana Haldar (2008), "State Yet to Get its First Jobless Worker Claimant of Centre's Shramik Kalyan Yojana".

AP : Andhra Pradesh

B : Bihar

G : Gujarat

H : Haryana

P : Punjab

K : Kerala

M : Maharashtra

MP : Madhya Pradesh

O : Orissa

KA : Karnataka

TN : Tamil Nadu

WB : West Bengal

UP : Uttar Pradesh

HP : Himachal Pradesh

R : Rajasthan

17

DROUGHTS AND THEIR IMPACT ON AGRICULTURE AND EMPLOYMENT OF ANANTAPUR DISTRICT, ANDHRA PRADESH

M. Sambasiva Rao
G. Venkata Ramana

INTRODUCTION

Drought is defined as lack of sufficient water to meet the requirements of a locality. Climatologically, agriculturally and economically the drought prone areas are marginal lands. They constitute a distinctive ecosystem which is sensitive and delicately balanced. They are subjected to ecological degradation. Drought represents an imbalance between the soil moisture and evapotranspiration in a region in which the latter is in excess. Drought is a natural hazard. The National Agricultural Commission defined drought as a condition when the rainfall is half or less than the half of the normal rainfall. The Indian Meteorological Department defined drought as a condition when the rainfall is less than 75 percent of the normal and severe drought when the rainfall is less than 50 percent of the normal. The National Agricultural Commission classified droughts into three types. The meteorological droughts occur where there is more than 25 percent decrease of rainfall from the normal over an area. The agricultural droughts occur when the soil moisture and rainfall are inadequate during the growing season to support normal crop growth. The hydrological droughts result when meteorological droughts prolong causing marked depletion of surface water and consequent drying up of surface water resources and steep fall of ground water levels on the basis of degree of intensity and duration the droughts can be classified into mild, moderate, severe and disastrous Thornthwaite (1947) has recognized three types of droughts on the basis of their periodicity and length of occurrence. They are permanent droughts, seasonal droughts and contingent droughts on the basis of time and occurrence droughts can be classified into early, mid and late. Based on periodicity and frequency the droughts can be classified into occasional and chronic.

STUDY AREA

Anantapur District is located in a chronic drought prone area in southwestern part of the Andhra Pradesh. The district geographically lies in between $13^0 40^1$ and $15^0 15^1$ North latitude and $76^0 50^1$ and $78^0 30^1$ East longitudes. The total area of the district is 19,125 km^2. There are three Revenue Divisions and 63 Mandals in the district. The average annual rainfall of the district is 558 mm. geologically the district is divided into Archeans and Proterozoic formations. The major part of the district is formed of Archean rocks consisting of unclassified granitic gneisses. The northeastern part of the district is formed of Proterozoic formations consisting shales, dolomite, limestone, steatite and serpentine.

OBJECTIVES

The main objectives of the study are:

1. To analyse occurrence of droughts and water balance of Anantapur District,
2. To study land use, irrigation and cropping pattern of Anantapur District,

3. To study the occupational structure and employment potential of Anantapur District and
4. To describe the impact of droughts on agriculture and employment of the Anantapur District.

METHODOLOGY

The monthly rainfall data over a period of hundred years has been collected for 13 stations from Indian Meteorological department, stations of the Anantapur District and are analyzed to study the occurrence of droughts, drought intensity and decadal variations in drought occurrence. The land use, irrigation and cropping pattern data at mandal level has been collected from chief planning office and are analyzed to study the distribution, intensity and combination. The occupational structure at mandal level of the Anantapur District has been collected from Chief Planning Office, Anantapur district and are analyzed to study the distribution of workers, non workers cultivators and agricultural labour. The water balance of the Anantapur District is brought out using Thornthwaite and Mathur (1955) water balance method. The water surplus and water deficit months are identified. Based on periodicity of occurrence of droughts, the effects on agriculture and employment potential of the Anantapur district is described.

DROUGHTS AND THEIR OCCURRENCE

The analysis of annual drought occurrence of Anantapur district reveals that the district experiences more number of droughts during the last hundred years (Table 1).

The drought occurence vary from a minimum of 47 drought years in Madakasira station to a maximum of 57 drought years in Tadipatri station. In Uruvakonda, Anantapur, Yadiki, Rayadurg, Kadiri, Penukonda, Dharamavaram, Hindupur and Bukkapatnam Stations the number of drought years vary from 50 to 55. In Kalyandurg and Gooty stations the number of drought years are 48 each. The average number of drought years in Anantapur District is 52. The occurrence of droughts is very high in northern, southeastern and southern parts of the district. In central and western parts of the district there is high occurrence of droughts.

The annual intensity of droughts vary from 47 per cent to 57 per cent. The intensity of droughts is very high in northern, southeastern and southern parts of the district and high in central and western parts of the district. From the analysis of droughts it is also found that in the district during the last hundred years there are more low droughts. However the severe and disastrous droughts are very low in the district. The decadal variations in the occurrence of droughts reveal that there are five to six drought years in each decade in the last hundred years. The trend analysis of occurrence of droughts donot shows much variation among the decades during the last hundred years. From the analysis of drought occurrence it may concluded that in all the stations of the Anantapur District the number of droughts vary from 5 to 6 in each decade and majority of them are low droughts.

Table 1
Drought Occurence and Intensity in Anantapur District Over a Period of Hundred Years

Name of the Mandal Years	*No. of Drought*	*Drought Intensity in Per cent*
Anantapur	55	55
Gooty	48	48
Bukkapatnam	52	52
Yadki	55	55
Dharamavaram	52	52
Rayadurg	50	50
Kadiri	53	53
Kalyandurg	48	48
Hindupur	51	51
Madakasira	47	47
Penukonda	54	54
Uravakonda	53	53
Tadipatri	57	57

LAND USE, IRRIGATION AND CROPPING PATTERN OF THE ANANTAPUR DISTRICT

The analysis of land use during 2005-2006 reveals that out of 1,912,500 hectares of land available in the district about 10.30

per cent is under forests, 9.2 per cent is barren land, 8.30 per cent is land under non agriculture use, 12 per cent is land under permanent pastures, 0.50 per cent is land under miscellaneous trees, 3.70 per cent is land under cultivable waste, 6.30 per cent is under other fallows, 7.4 per cent is under current fallows and 53.1 per cent of land is under net sown area. The distribution of land use categories reveals that forest cover is high in southeastern part of the district. The net sown area is widely spread in the Pedi plains of Anantapur District covering red sandy soils and black soil plains.

The total irrigated area of the Anantapur District is about 189,236 hectares of land. It accounts to 9.89 per cent of the total geographical area of the district. The remaining 90.11 per cent of the land has to depend on the rainfall of the district. The average annual rainfall of the district is 558 mm. The mean monthly rainfall received in the district reveals that the mean rainfall exceeds 100 mm in the month of September. During August and October months the mean rainfall varies from 60 mm to 80 mm. It ranges from 40mm to 60mm in May, June, July and November months. The mean rainfall varies from 20mm to 40mm in March and April months. It is less than 20mm in January, February and December months.

The canal irrigated area in the district is 75,888 hectares and accounts for 3.97% of the total area of the district. There are about 1694 tanks in the district with an ayacut area of about 59,056 hectares and amounts to 3.09% of the total geograhical area of the district. The well irrigated area of the district is about 54,292 hectares and accounts to 2.84% of the total area. The well irrigation could not spread on a large area due to hard rock granites terrain of the district where ground water resources are found only in weathered, fissured and faulted zones. Due to low irrigation potential, high occurrence of droughts, high water deficit and low recharge the water resources of the district have to be carefully conserved and optimally utilized.

The cropping pattern of the district reveals that there are ten major crops in the district. The total cropped area of the district during 2005-2006 is about 1,064,440 hectares which accounts for 55.65 per cent of the total geographical area of the district. The various crops cultivated are paddy, jowar, bajar, korra, pulses, cotton, ground nut, sunflower and mulberry. The predominant crop cultivated in the district is groundnut. The total area under ground nut cultivation is about 730,412 hectares and accounts to 68.62% of the total cropped area of the district. The ranking of other crops are sunflower (95,125 hectares 8.94%), paddy (82,279 hectares, 7.73%), pulses, (47,434 hectares 4.48%) jowar (41,431 hectares, 3.89%), korra (22,669 hectares, 2.13%), cotton (14,053 hectares, 1.32%), ragi (12,351 hectares, 1.16%), bajra (9,452 hectares, 0.89%), and mulberry (8,934 hectors, 0.84%). The yield of groundnut varies from 400 kgs to 800 kgs/hectares. The yield and production of major ground nut crop depends upon the total amount of rainfall received during crop period and number of rainy days. Due to 5 to 6 continuous droughts in a decade in the district during the last hundred years the groundnut productivity is very low.

WATER BALANCE OF THE ANANTAPUR DISTRICT

The total surface water resources of the district are about 10,671,750,000 m^3 of water. Out of this about 1,067, 175, 000m^3 (10%) is stored in reservoirs, surface tanks and ponds in the district. About 1,314,759,600 m^3 (12.32%) of surface water resources is recharged to ground water every year, 2,667,937,500 m^3 (25%) of water is lost in the form of surface run-off and 5,621,877,900m^3 of water is lost in the form of evaporation and evapotranspiration. The average annual potential evapotranspiration of the district is 1609mm and actual evapotranspiration is 756 mm. The average annual water deficit of the district is 853 mm. The annual recharge of the district is 69 mm. In view of high water deficit, low recharge and high water loss in the form of evaporation and evapotranspiration there is a need for conservation of available water resources in the district and run-off water. The run-off water should be stored in the surface tanks and underground tanks (quant) to minimize water losses in the form of evaporation.

POPULATION AND OCCUPATIONAL STRUCTURE OF THE ANANTAPUR DISTRICT

The total population Anantapur district during 1901 was 10, 25,322. It grew to 14, 83,591 in 1951 and 36, 40,478 in 2001. Over a period of hundred years the growth of population is 26, 15,156. If amount to 255% over a period of hundred years. There are about 15, 54,484 workers and 20, 85,994 non workers. In the agriculture sector there are about 5, 55,683 cultivators and 11, 80,825 are agriculture labour. Occupationally majority of the population of Anantapur district are cultivators and agricultural labors. There are no major industries in the district. However, there are about 900 small scale industries in the district which provides employment for about 10,000 people in the district. Recently the L &T and Pennar Cement factories are established in the Tadipatri of Anantapur District which employs about 8,000 workers. There are about 70 colleges, 100 junior colleges, and 250 secondary and 1000 primary schools in the Anantapur District which provides employment for about 13,000 people. The employment in service sector is about 15,000 in the district. Altogether about 45,000 people are found employed in the district. Every year about 1800 post graduates, 16000 graduates, 4500 graduates in education, 2000 technical graduates, 1000 polytechnic students, 200 medicos and 18000 tenth class students are passed out.

Due to poor economic conditions, low agricultural productivity, poor industrial and infrastructural development the employment opportunities in the district are very meager. Thc students should migrate to the near by metropolitan cities in search of employment. Therefore, the migration of cultivators, agricultural labours and educated youth is taking place at the rate of 25 percent per year to other parts of the state and nation.

IMPACT OF DROUGHTS ON AGRICULTURE AND EMPLOYMENT

1. The crop yields are very much lowered. The agricultural productivity is very low. The ground water levels have steeply fallen and many deep bores have dried up.

2. The debts of the farmers have increased due to continuous failure of crops.
3. Due to increase in debts the farmers committed suicides. About 300 suicides by farmers have been reported during this decade.
4. The nutritional value is very much reduced due to malnutrition.
5. The poverty is increasing year after year.
6. The people are forced to carryout antisocial activities due to poor conditions.
7. The youth are forced to join in factionalist and naxalitic activities.
8. There is increase in unemployment and increase in crimes and thefts in the district.
9. The women are forced to join in illegal trafficking and prostitution.
10. The cultivators, agricultural labour and educated youth are migrating to near by metropolitan cities.

REMEDIAL MEASURES

1. Despite spending enormous amounts under DPAP, DRDA, Desertification, Rural Guaranteed Employment and Food for Work programmes by the state and central governments the results achieved are neither substantial nor enduring but remained illusionary and momentary.
2. There is a need for conceptual and empirical studies on rainfall, variability of rainfall and nature of rainfall deficiency on weekly, monthly, seasonal and annual basis at micro unit level.
3. Systematic collection of data and information on aridity and moisture indices, weekly water balance, wilting points of major crops particularly ground water, vegetation, cropping pattern at village level have to be carried out.
4. There is a need for conservation and management of water resources.

5. To mitigate miseries of the people in drought prone areas a series of relief measures like remission of land revenue, providing free food, clothing and shelter, providing loans to agricultural labors, small farmers and marginal farmers, providing rural employment, supply of food, water and fodder at subsidized rates and taking famine relief works should be implemented at gross root level.
6. Buffer stocks of food grains have to be stored in ware houses.
7. There is a need supply food and fodder for animals.
8. An efficient public distribution system, crop insurance, credit facilities to unemployed youth and unemployment dole are a few measures to mitigate migration of youth to metropolitan cities.
9. The district authorities with the help of state and central governments should strengthen and upgrade resource base industries, improve quality of farm land, develop modern irrigation facilities stabilize the agricultural economy and develop rural, cottage and silk industries in the district.
10. Finally it is concluded that the rural upliftment of a chronic drought affected area should be taken up at village level to fulfill the dreams of the "Father of our nation" Mahatma Gandhi.

REFERENCES

Thornthwaite, C.W (1947), Climate and Moisture Conservation.

—Annals of Association of Amercian Geographers Vol. 37 No.3 pp. 87-100

Thornthwaite, C.W and Mathur J.R. (1955), The Water Balance Publications in Climatology, Laboratory of Climatology Centerton (NJ) Vol. 8 No. 1 pp. 104

18

ON LEVELS OF EMPLOYMENT IN SERVICE SECTOR

A. Venkateswara Rao
Shaik Ameer
S. Narasimha Reddy

Services sector is a complex area and very often one finds different definitions of services. The US Trade and Tariffes Act defines services as economic activities whose output are other than tangible goods. However, in reality, one finds goods in which services are stored.

Commonly accepted definition of services sector includes labour services, travel, transportation, part & shipping and other related services, insurance, banking and other financial services, construction and engineering design services, education, tourism, health care and miscellaneous and other private services.

OBJECTIVES

The main objectives of this paper are:

- To state the contribution of service sector to the GDP
- To review the importance of service sector

- To analyse the occupational distribution of working population in India with a greater emphasis on service sector.

For this purpose the information is collected from the secondary sources.

SERVICE SECTOR AND ITS CONTRIBUTION

The service sector contributes about half of the world GDP. The share of this sector in the GDP increases, generally, as an economy develops. The advanced economics are predominantly service economics in the sense that services produce, on an average 60 percent of the GDP and generate about 60 percent of the total employment. Services assume special importance for developing countries. Producer services provide an essential link among the economic agents that enables the interdependent functioning of the markets. Services like banking, communication, transportation, etc. provide infrastructure services to the entire economy. In the low income economics, services contribute more than one third of the GDP. The share of the services in India's GDP increased form 33 percent in 1950-51 to 54 percent in 2004-05. Obviously, the service sector generally grows faster than the economy as a whole.

It may be noted that the growth of international trade in services in the last two decades has been much faster than that of the trade in goods. The value of international trade include transportation, travel, communications, media, business services, engineering and construction, and banking and financial services. International trade in many services involves international factor mobility.

There is a common belief that developed countries have tremendous potential in the services sector and the developing countries are at the receiving end with very limited options to improve their position. The contribution of services sector Gross Domestic Product (GDP) of the developed counties is very high and often large than the contribution of the industries to the GDP. In many developing countries having large agricultural sector, the contribution to the GDP from agriculture has been declining and that from services sector has been increasing more prominently. In India, the distribution of GDP between agricultural, industrial and services sector is roughly spread between 24 percent, 23 percent and 53 percent respectively.

Table 1
Occupational Distribution of Working Population in India

Occupation	*1951*	*2001*
Primary sector	72.1	59.3
Secondary sector	10.6	18.2
Tertiary sector	17.3	22.5
Total	100	100

Indian economy has developed fastly, So there is a shift of labour force from primary (agricultural) sector to secondary and tertiary (non-agricultural) sectors.

It is clear from the above table that, over a period of five decades there have been shifts of work force from primary to secondary and tertiary sectors. In 2001, the primary, secondary and tertiary sectors respectively occupied nearly 60%, 18% and nearly 23% of the working, population.

Important changes in sectoral distribution of Gross Domestic Product (GDP)

The share of agricultural sector in India's national income has decreased over the years and shares of secondary and tertiary sectors have improved in the GDP.

Table 2
Composition of GDP

Occupation	*1950-51*	*2004-05*
Primary sector	56.1	23
Secondary sector	11.7	23.8
Tertiary sector	32.7	54.1
Total	100	100

In the year 2004-05 the GDP of primary, secondary and tertiary sectors is nearly 23%, 24% and 53% respectively. It also indicates form above two tables that primary sector occupies nearly 60% of population and GDP is only 23% While tertiary sector occupies 23% of population, it contributes 53% (more than half) of GDP.

INCREASED IMPORTANCE

It may not be coincidental that the decline in the share of manufacturing begins at around the time when liberalization gathered momentum. The shift form public investment to private investment increases the demand for services to mobilize private capital, especially through the capital market. The increase in the inflow of foreign capital to creates a demand for new financial services. The importance of services of helping the mobilization of capital is further enhanced by the increased capital intensity in industry. Liberalization also increases by the shift towards markets. Competitive markets increase the demand for a variety of services ranging form advertising to market research. And the widening of the market to cover new geographical areas increases the demand for transport and communication in services.

To quote Centre for Monitoring Indian Economy (CMIE), the increase in rural non-agricultural employment is both significant and distributed across a variety of activities. The phenomenon is seen nearly in all major states, through the pace of change varies. The increase in employment has been slow relative to the growth in output.

Of about 18.6 million additional job opportunities generated during the past reform period to nearly half (9.03 million) have been in agriculture and allied sector alone. The manufacturing sector, which should have played a lead role comes third in employment generation (3 million) next to trade and transport (services) sector.

The majority of the work force is unorganized in nature with 8% living in rural areas, 63% being engaged in agriculture, 85% being self-employed or employed on casual wages. Only 15% of the work force have regular salaries employment.

According to CMIE, only about 10% of the working population is employed in the organized sector. About 55% of the total employment in the organized sector is in the services sector and less than 30% is in the manufacturing sector.

Needless to repeat that services sector is playing an important role in providing employment in organized sector.

Growth in employment in the organized sector slowed down considerably from 2.7% per annum in the seventies to 1.6% per annum in the eighties. The slow down in the growth rate was in both the public as well as the private sectors.

FOCUS NEEDED

In India, services are looked at skeptically and it is claimed that they are no more than adjuncts to manufacturing. This conventional attitude will have to be changed. In the US, the share of manufacturing in GDP is around 23 percent of services more than 70 percent, and this in reflected in employment patterns too. There is a lesson in this for India. Future investment and job creation will not be driven mainly by manufacturing. Indeed manufacturing may yield relatively few jobs-many big companies can trip production without hiring a single new worker. However, a huge number of jobs will be created in service industries , which will also soak up the bulk of investment. According to one estimate, telecom along could soak up Rs. 150,000 core in next few years, and it is a service industry.

UNIVERSAL TRENDS

There are some universal trends in employment pattern which we can ill afford to ignore. Newer technologies need fewer people in manufacturing. On the other hand, more jobs will be created in services, sub-contracting and unorganized sector. Traditional trade demarcations may not have the same place in a modern economy. Flexibility in operations and knowledge– more than muscle – will be required of employees. There is no doubt that a large number of illiterate and semi-literate workers in our industry will face problems. There will be increase in the requirement of part time and temporary workers. Activities will get specialized and a larger number of specialized vendors and sub-contractors will constitute manufacturing net works. As location of industries will no longer be decided by the government and will be based on economic choice, employees will have to be prepared for relocation. Industry clusters will emerge and not all areas will get equal investment or equal job opportunities.

Indian industrialists will be very unwise to focus on manufacturing alone. And the government needs to shift its thinking to create institutional structures that encourage private investment in services and remove road blocks and delays. That will create far more jobs than public sector investment.

SUMMARY AND CONCLUSIONS

In response to the declining share of agriculture in national income, a shift in the occupation of the rural population away from agriculture and towards those sectors that are growing most rapidly will have to be encourages. Such an occupational shift from agriculture to services has already started. But the proportion of the work force in agriculture is still far greater than the portion of agriculture in the national income. Obviously greater attention is to be paid to managing the shift from an agriculture economy to one that is dominated by services. The growth of services, such as these related to tourism or transport, in the rural areas can be supported by families who find the return from agriculture inadequate. Steps would have to be taken to increase the potential of the rural population to benefit from the growth of services. The handicap of an inadequate awareness of technology would need to be overcome by not only increasing the availability of education in rural areas, but also ensuring that it covers the requirements of modern services. Effective instruments will also need to be created to pool rural capital so as to enable investment in high technology services, including linking up directly with global financial and communication networks. Such a transition may not be very smooth but certainly not impossible if proper steps are undertaken with vision for future.

REFERENCES

—*Directorate General of Employment*, Ministry of Labour Govt. of India.

—*Centre for Monitoring Indian Economy*, India's social sector.

—*Indian Economy*–Rudra Dutt & K.P.M. Sundaram

—(2004), *World Development Report.*

—(2005), *Yojana,* November.

—(2007), *Kurukshatra,* January.

19

MIGRATION AND POVERTY: POLICY ISSUES

B. V. Raghavendar
M. N. Swarna
B. S. Rao

INTRODUCTION

Migration can both cause and be caused by poverty. Similarly, poverty can be alleviated as well as exacerbated by population movement. Easy generalizations are impossible to make but it is likely that the relative impact of migration on poverty, and of poverty on migration, varies by level of development of the area under consideration. In some parts of the world and under certain conditions, poverty may be a root cause of migration, whereas in other parts, under different conditions, the poor will be among the last to move. Equally, in some areas, migration may be an avenue out of poverty while in others it contributes to an extension of poverty. The situation in Asia and the Pacific. The situation is made complex because both terms, "migration" and "poverty", are difficult semantically: both are intuitively obvious but, in practice, have proved notoriously difficult to define and to measure accurately analysis.

The main objective of this paper to analyze the interdependent poverty and migration. The migrants are belonging to the category of landless agricultural labourers, and very often from scheduled, backward or tribal castes. In few cases, those who have limited land didn't possess the needed resource to develop the same and a result, the barred land is left uncultivated for years. Therefore, they are, compelled to work as agricultural labourers in the land of big landlords or Zamindars of the same village or adjoining villages or other districts. Hence the female migrants are going to the other places for their livelihood.

POVERTY AS A ROOT OF MIGRATION

Migration is often seen simply as a flight from poverty: there are no opportunities available locally so people migrate in order to survive. Flight from a devastating famine would appear to be the classic example of this type of relationship, well illustrated by pictures in the media of emaciated people who have walked great distances to reach feeding stations run by various agencies and charities The survival migration of the poorest is likely to be mainly local, or regional at most, and primarily within State. In apparent contradiction to the logic of survival migration, the general finding of most studies of migration in non-disaster situations is that it is not the poorest who move but those with access to some resources, no matter how meager these might appear.

Migration always involves some costs of transportation and the abandonment of many of the few possessions the poor might have. The poorest of the poor cannot afford either risk or movement and the majority starves in situ. This discussion is not to deny that poverty is an important cause of migration but to suggest that there are other factors at work. Except in particular areas and at particular times, it is not absolute poverty as such that is significant in accounting for migration but whether people feel that they are poor.

MIGRATION AS THE RESULT OF POVERTY

Poverty as the root cause of migration and migration as the result of poverty might Suggest the same thing but there are significant differences. Migration as the result of poverty shifts the focus to the issue of feeling poor: relative rather than absolute deprivation. Migration, either of outsiders into a community, or of natives going outside their community, establishes linkages between origins and destinations. These linkages spread knowledge about conditions in a wider country that can transform communities from conditions of "subsistence affluence" to those of relative deprivation without any significant real change in the quantity of subsistence in the community Thus, migration creates the conditions that lead to people feeling themselves to be poor, which in turn leads to further migration as they move in order to satisfy new-found aspirations. This process is perhaps at the root of most migration, giving the impression that poverty is the driving force but in reality is the product of a desire to better oneself against new standards rather than the result of absolute deprivation. Migration is thus both the creator and the product of poverty.

MIGRATION AS A CAUSE OF POVERTY

The migration can lead directly to an increase in the number of absolute poor. The clearest way is through forced relocation without adequate planning and support. In many cases, the forced relocation is essentially the product of development, mainly through the creation of lakes and reservoirs that are the result of the construction of dams, although displacement for roads and urban expansion is also important. In India alone, some 20 million people are estimated to have been displaced over about 40 years, the majority of whom became impoverished. While in China over a similar period, well over 30 million were displaced.

POVERTY ALLEVIATED BY MIGRATION

The relationship between migration and poverty should in some way be negative. Either that migration was the result of deprivation or that migration should lead to the impoverishment of certain areas. That the movement of population can be a significant factor for the alleviation of poverty. The principal reason lies in the nature of the migration process itself. Migrants rarely move simply from A to B but their movement is a complex system of circulation between two, or among several, destinations. Also, migrants are rarely individuals operating in a social vacuum but are meshed into family, household and community networks. Migrants, rather than individual income maximizes, can be conceptualized as existing within a communal risk-minimizing strategy.

Migration can therefore be seen as a system linking origins and destinations in which flow not just people, but also money and goods. The incorporation of new destinations broadens the resource base of a household, perhaps allowing a more optimal deployment of labour as those underemployed during the slack part of the agricultural cycle can find work on plantation or in town. Gender differences can become important. In areas where males undertake most of the agricultural work, women can be released from rural households to access off-farm activities in town, and vice versa in areas where women dominate labour input into agriculture as in much of India. Like so many components of migration and poverty, remittances are notoriously difficult to measure accurately but these remittances decreasing the poverty in the origin.

However, it is important to recognize that migration can involve costs, economic and social, as well as benefits. The challenge to policy makers is to facilitate the types of movement that are most likely to lead to an alleviation of poverty while protecting migrants from abuse and exploitation. It is likely that the relationship between migration and poverty will be different in the dynamic states. yet the immediate challenge remains the need to incorporate an appreciation of the potentially positive role of migration in poverty reduction programmes.

The requirement to prepare a schedule for phasing out of subsidies, resulted in the Urguay Round, Agreement on Agriculture (UR AOA) signed in Marakesh on April 15, 1994 as a part of the overall agreement. However, the agreement entails the review of its progress before the end of 1999 which has been a major

SUGGESTIONS FOR DECREASE POVERTY AND MIGRATION

Long term perspective plans are drawn up for both agricultural and industrial development for generating employment opportunities.

- Provide more irrigation projects need to be taken up earliest.
- Provide good infrastructure facilities in the place of origin.
- Needed to sustainable water resource management.
- Most of the migrants are belonged to the category of landless or marginal farmers. Therefore, land reforms to be needed.
- Encourage to farmers for 'Joint farming enterprises' which would be beneficial to the group as a whole.
- Small scale industries could be established.
- The government should lease out some common property land for purpose of grazing to landless labourers, particularly for women.
- The permanent long term measures need to be taken for employment generation particularly landless labourers.
- Most importantly some rural industries need to be established.
- This may require appropriate pricing policies of inputs and outputs.

20

AGRICULTURE AND UNEMPLOYMENT IN INDIA

G. Uma

A large number of people are known to be unemployed in India. Unemployment in India is structural in nature because the productive capacity is inadequate to create sufficient number of jobs for all those who are able and willing to work. This type of unemployment is not a temporary but a chronic phenomenon. On the other hand, cyclical unemployment and frictional unemployment are the features of developed economics.

Most of the unemployed are from the rural sector of the economy. The basic causes of unemployment in India are the under developed economy, poor manpower planning, population explosion, inappropriate technology and inappropriate educational system. However, people in the work force who catch hold of whatever work comes their way, however low paid it may be and however short its duration are excluded from the estimate of unemployment under the usual status. This is also referred to as 'open unemployment'.

AGRICULTURE

Agriculture plays a vital role in the Indian economy. Over 70 percent of the rural households depend on agriculture as their principal means of livelihood. Agriculture, along with fisheries and forestry, accounts for one third of the nation's Gross Domestic Product (GDP) and is its single largest contributor.

India is mainly an agricultural country. Agriculture accounts for approximately 33 percent of India's GDP and employs nearly 62 percent of the population. Since independence in 1947, the share of agriculture in the GDP has declined in comparison to the growth of the industrial and service sectors. However, agriculture still provides the bulk of wage goods required by the non-agriculture sector as well as numerous raw materials for industry. Moreover, the direct share of agricultural and allied sectors in total exports is around 18 percent. When the direct share of agricultural products in total exports, such as cotton textiles and jute goods, is taken into account, the percentage is much higher.

The dependence on agricultural imports in the early 1960's convinced planners that India's growing population as well as concerns about national independence, security, and political stability, required self-sufficiency in food production. This perception led to a program of agricultural improvement called the green revolution, a public distribution system, and price supports for farmers. In the 1980's despite three years merge rainfall and a drought in the middle of the decade, India managed to get along with very few food imports because of the growth in food-grain production and the development of a large buffer stock against potential agricultural shortfalls. By the early 1990's India was self-sufficient in food grain production. Agricultural production has kept place with the food needs of the growing population as the result of increased yields in almost all crops, especially in cereals. Food grains and pulses accounted for two-thirds of agricultural production in the mid-1990. The growth in food grain production is a result of concentrated efforts to increase all the Green Revolution inputs needed for higher yields.

India has a big and diverse agriculture sector. It provides food and fiber to the country's large population and employs over 70 percent of the population. It contributes close to 30 percent of the GDP.

NATURE OF INDIA'S AGRICULTURE

At the time of independence, India's agriculture was in a state of backwardness. Productivity per hectare and per worker was extremely low. The techniques employed were age-old and traditional. Because of low productivity, agriculture merely provided 'Subsistence' to the farmers and had not become 'Commercialized'.

AGRICULTURAL GROWTH SINCE INDEPENDENCE IMPORTANCE OF AGRICULTURAL SECTOR

India is primarily an agricultural country. Nearly 75 percent of the population depends on agriculture. Approximately 27 percent of GDP comes from agriculture and allied sectors. Further agro-based industries depend on agriculture for their raw material. More than 21 percent of India's exports are agricultural products. The importance of agriculture to supply food to the populace cannot be exaggerated.

NEED FOR DEVELOPING THE AGRICULTURAL SECTOR

- Provide increasing supplies of food for the growing population.
- Produce more agricultural products for export to earn more foreign exchange.
- Reference disguised unemployed labour to other sector of the economy.
- Increase rural incomes and purchasing power; and
- Help in capital information.

MEASURES FOR IMPROVING AGRICULTURE AFTER INDEPENDENCE

The First year plan priority was given to agriculture. Although, the priority shifted in the second plan to industry, there was no decrease in the share of resource allocated under the different plans to agriculture and community development.

Outlays on agriculture and allied sectors by the government in different five year plans.

Plans	*Outlays on Agriculture Sector in Crores*	*Percentage to Total Plan Outlay*
First plan	290	14.8
Second plan	530	11.5
Third plan	1089	12.7
Annual plan	1167	17.3
Fourth plan	2353	14.9
Fifth plan	4644	11.8
Sixth plan	12,539	12.9
Seventh plan	27,552	15.30
Eight plan	22,467	12.6
Ninth plan	42,462	4.9
Tenth plan		

Major share of this has gone for infrastructure development in agriculture.

OUTPUT GROWTH

Since independence output has grow in increasing rate. The most heartening feature is that output growth has occurred more as a result of increasing productivity and less by way of increase in net sown area. Output growth occurred in all types of crop food grains, non-food grains and plantation crops.

APPRAISAL OF DEVELOPMENT IN AGRICULTURE SINCE INDEPENDENCE

The development of agriculture since independence can be well appreciated only if we understand the negligible or nil growth prior to independence. Researchers have estimated that agricultural output registered 0.2 to 0.25 percent rate of growth before independence. In contrast, in the post independence period, the growth rate per year was around 3 percent.

Agricultural development can be looked from other angles also. In spite of the rapid growth in population, per capita availability of food grain has not decreased.

NATIONAL AGRICULTURAL POLICY 2000

The government announced the National Agriculture Policy (NAP) on July 28, 2000 envisaging over 4 percent growth rate per annum in the next two decades. The NAP focuses on efficient use of resources and technology and increased private investment while emphasizing on price protection to farmers in the WTO region.

NATURE AND ESTIMATES OF UNEMPLOYMENT IN INDIA

The problem of unemployment in underdeveloped countries is basically different from that in developed countries. In developed countries, unemployment generally assumes two forms, Vic, the Keynesian involuntary unemployment and temporary frictional unemployment. The demand for labours is less and employment opportunities limited in underdeveloped countries on account of agricultural backwardness, underdevelopment of industries, and small size of the service sector. Hence, a large number of people who will be too happy to accept jobs at the prevailing wage rates get more. This unemployment though involuntary in its nature is certainly not what we call the Keynesian unemployment. Unemployment in underdeveloped countries is both open and disguised. India presently suffers mainly from structural unemployment which exists in open and disguised forms.

NATURE OF UNEMPLOYMENT

Most of the unemployment in India is definitely structural. During the 1961-2001 periods, population in this country had grown at an alarming rate of around 2.15 percent per annum and with it the number of people coming to the labour market in search of jobs had also increased rapidly, whereas employment opportunities. Hence, there has been an increase in the volume of unemployment from one plan period to another.

CLASSIFY UNEMPLOYMENT IN THE COUNTRY

- Urban unemployment
- Rural unemployment

Urban unemployment is mainly of two types:

- Industrial unemployment
- Educated unemployment

Rural unemployment is classified as two types:

- Open unemployment
- Disguised unemployment

USUAL STATUS UNEMPLOYMENT

Usual status unemployment in rural areas cannot be clearly distinguished from seasonal and disguised unemployment. It is this reason why people remaining unemployed for long periods are sometimes counted as seasonally or disguisedly unemployed. This error crops up particularly if the survey is carried out in the off-season when most people in villages do not have any productive work with them. However, the usual status unemployment in March 1994 has been estimated on the basis of 50th round of the NSS.

CAUSES OF UNEMPLOYMENT

The analysis of unemployment in India has made it evidently clear that most of the unemployment in this country is structural.

JOBLESS GROWTH

Economic growth is usually expected to generate employment. However, in India most of the time growth has been jobless. For 30 years from 1950-5, to 1'980-81 GDP growth rate was as low as 3.6 percent per annum. At this rate of economic growth many jobs could not be created GDP growth accelerated to 5.6 percent per annum in the 1980's and stayed at this level in the 1990's. At this higher rate of GDP growth one would normally expect that many new employment opportunities would be forth coming.

INCREASE IN LABOUR FORCE

Since independence, death rate has rapidly declined and the country has entered the second stage of demography transition.

INAPPROPRIATE TECHNOLOGY

In India, while capital is scarce factor, labour is available in abundant quantity, under these circumstances, if market forces operate freely and efficiently, the country would have labour-intensive techniques of production.

Economic Disparity between the Poor and Rich has been Rising

Farmers/cultivaters have been loosing their status in the society gradually employees are refered first in case of marriages of daughters of even farmers with sole idea that employees income is more secured in addition to their fringe benefits.

Government of india and state government brought many reforms through very good proposals, but had set backs at implementation stage leading to many problems rather than expected output.

Plan Out lining Agriculture and Allied Sectors

Plans	*Total Plan Outlay*	*Agriculture and Allied Sectors*	*%age of Agriculture and Allied Sector to Total*
1plan(1951-56)	2378	354	14.9
IIplan(1956-61)	4500	501	11.3
IIIplan(1961-66)	8577	1089	12.7
Anuall plans(1966-69)	6625	1107	16.7
IVplan(1969-74)	15779	2320	14.7
Vplan(1974-79)	39426	4865	12.3
Anual plan(1979-80)	12177	1997	16.4
VIplan91980-85)	97500	5695	5.8
VIIplan(1985-90)	180000	10525	5.9
Annual plan(1990-91)	58369	3405	5.8
Annual plan(1991-92)	64751	3851	6.0
VIIIplan(1992-97)	434100	22467	5.2
IXplan(1997-2002)	859200	42462	4.9
Xplan(2002-07)	398890	20668	5.2
XIplan(2007-11)	–	–	–

Source: Planning Commission

Institutional Structure of Rural Credit
(Reserve Bank of India)

Schedule Commercial Bank (95) Cooperatives		*NABARD Regional Rural Banks (196) Rural*
8882	metro branches 15	SCB-31
10990	urban branches	BCCB'S-367
15018	semi urban branches	PACSC-112309
32080	rural branches	LDB'S-20
66970	total branches	PLDB'S-730

SCB – State Cooperative Banks
DCCB's – District Central Cooperative Banks
PAC'S – primary agricultural
LDBS'S – Land Development Banks
PLDB'S – Primary Land Development Banks

The earlier survey on the same subject was the NSS 61st round quinquennial survey(2004-5) spread over 7999 villages and 4602 urban blocks covering 1,24,680 house holds(79,306in urban areas and 45,374in urban areas) and enumerating 6,02,833 persons. The main characteristics associated with employment, unemployment broadly comparable at the national level.

SOME OF THE IMPORTANT FINDINGS

Above 74 per cent of the households belonged to rural India and accounted for nearly 76 per cent of the total population.

According to the usual approach, the unemployment rate in the areas was around 2 per cent (for male nearly 3 per cent and for female nearly 2 per cent). In urban area the unemployment rate was 5 per cent and (for female nearly 8 per cent).

The unemployment rate obtain by any of the approaches, was higher for female than that for the males in the urban area but it was lower than that for males in the rural areas.

CONCLUSION

As India is an agrarian country, it has to improve agriculture and allied enterprisers in areas for development and prosperity. The prosperity depends on utilizing present available resources in the country. The development is a slow process. It has brought many changes during the past 50 years in rural areas.

21

TRENDS IN THE DEPENDENCE ON AGRICULTURE IN COASTAL ANDHRA

Bhavani Akkapeddi

Indian agriculture continues to occupy a dominant position as the single largest provider of employment. This is evident from the fact that 58.4% of the workers in India are dependent on it for their livelihood as per 2001 census (*AP Census 2001 Paper-3,* p.50). And it accounts for 22.2% of the Gross Domestic Product at 1993-94 prices in 2000-01(*National Accounts Statistics 2002,* p.17). Evidently the contribution of agricultural sector is far less than the proportionate share of the country's population engaged there. The situation is much worse for Andhra Pradesh. The contribution of the agricultural sector to state domestic product at 1993-94 prices was 17.15% in 2001-02 (*State Domestic Product of Andhra Pradesh, 1993-94 to 2001-02, 2002,* p.25). Where as 62.3% of the workers were engaged in agriculture, as cultivators and agricultural labours as per 2001 census (*AP Census 2001 Paper-3,* p.64). Share of agriculture in State Domestic Product on the one hand, and concentration of workers on the other due to high growth rates of population and inelastic supply of land, indicate low labour productivity and overcrowding in agriculture leading to unemployment, low wages and poverty, resulting in some undesired consequences[i].

Agricultural labourers are known to belong to the bottom strata of society. Substantial proportion of the rural population is primarily dependant on wage employment. In Andhra Pradesh in the year 1991, 27.76% of the workers were cultivators while 40.76% were agricultural labourers, and in total 68.52% of population depended on agriculture (*AP Census 1991 Paper-1*, pp.19-20 & 66-67). The cultivators among the total workers in Andhra Pradesh were 22.7% in 2001. Cultivators and agricultural labourers put together 62.3% of population directly depends on agriculture in Andhra Pradesh (*AP Census 2001 Paper-3*, pp.49-64). Though it is a very good sign that the dependence on agriculture decreased by around 6% between1991-2001, the continuous dependence of 62.3% of population on the inelastic resource, i.e., land is considered to be a very high proportion and it is above the Indian average. The major cause of concern is that the percentage of cultivators fell by around 5 percentage points while the percentage of agricultural labourers fell by around 1 between 1991 and 2001.

Changes in the size of work force are determined chiefly by population growth and their work participation rates. Changes in the work participation rates have had many economic and social implications. Given the productivity levels of workers, increased participation rates lead to increased income to the economy and vice versa. In terms of percentage of workers, Andhra Pradesh has always been ahead of the national average all through the period 1961 to 2001 (see Table-1). The higher participation rate may reveal larger opportunities of work in those areas or it may reflect the backwardness of the tract which forces more number of people to work, to feed the household. The later explanation seems to be appropriate to the circumstances in our country. Children who should have been at school may probably find it necessary to do some work as tending cattle or assisting the elders in agriculture or the women in the households who while performing their duties as housewives would probably find it necessary to work as agricultural labourers or help their husbands in other agricultural operations or work as Domestic servants and so on.

Table 1
Percentage of Workers to Total Population in India and Andhra Pradesh: 1961-2003

Year	*India*	*Andhra Pradesh*
1961	42.98	51.87
1971	32.93	41.39
1981	33.45	42.26
1991	34.1	42.77
2001	30.5	38.10

Source: Census of India, 2001, *paper-3, Andhra Pradesh*, p.29.

It will be observed that generally where the proportions of workers in agriculture are small, the proportion of non-workers is large. "*It would therefore, appear that in areas where the population depend largely on agriculture, there is a greater participation of all members of the household both women and children which thus reduces the proportion of non-workers consequently. ... The participation rates, therefore, are largely governed by the proportion of workers in agriculture*" (*AP Census 1961 Part I–A (iii)*, p.16). The high participation rates in Andhra Pradesh clearly reveal the heavy concentration of workers on land.

The work participation rates are generally high for Srikakulam, Visakhapatnam and Nellore (see Table-2). After the formation of Prakasam and Vizianagaram districts, they also continued to have high work participation rates. In each and every decade the work participation rate of north coastal Andhra, consisting of Srikakulam, Vizianagaram and Visakhapatnam was higher than South coastal Andhra consisting of East Godavari, West Godavari, Krishna, Guntur, Prakasam and, Nellore. To make a few general observations, the districts, which show the least proportion of workers in agriculture, have the highest proportion of non-workers as in East Godavari, West Godavari and Krishna (See Table-3). One would normally think that in agriculturally advanced delta districts as East Godavari, West Godavari and Krishna, the participation of workers in agriculture might have been large. But due to the prosperous agriculture of the tract, the cultivating families apparently can afford not to utilize the

Table 2
Proportion of Total Workers to Total Population 1961-2001

Year	*Sri*	*Vizia*	*Visakha*	*NCA*	*EG*	*WG*	*Kri*	*Gun*	*Pra*	*Nel*	*SCA*	*CA*
1961	57.1		52.93	55.02	46.9	47.7	46.9	50.1		52.5	48.8	50.6
1971	42.7	41.99	40.65	41.62	38.3	40.6	38.3	40.2	40.5	41.2	39.7	40.2
1981	49.1	48.49	43.49	46.63	40.6	43.3	43.1	47.4	48.7	46.4	44.6	45.1
1991	48.6	50.33	43.11	46.75	38.5	43.4	43.3	47.9	48.6	45.6	44.1	44.8
2001	47.5	52.25	41.84	46.21	39.6	44.2	44.1	49.1	50.3	45.5	45.1	45.4

Source: Census of India, 1961,Vol.II, Andhra Paradesh, Part-II – B (i), Economic Tables, Table B-I, pp.1-13.

Census of India, 1961,Vol.II, Andhra Paradesh, District Census Hand Book (Srikakulam- Statement III-2, p.XI, Visakhapatnam-Statement III-2, pp. A20-21, East Godavari – Statement IV-I, p.xxvi, West Godavari – Table AII, p.7, Krishna – Table A-II,p.10, Guntur – Statement III-2, p.xiii and Nellore – Table A-II, p.10).

Census of India, 1971, Series-2, Andhra Paradesh, Part II -B, Economic Tables.

AP Census DCHB 1981: (Srikakulam – pp.352-357, Vizianagarma – pp.294-299, Visakhapatnam – pp.2-7, East Godavari – pp.280-288, West Godavari – pp.216-221, Krishna – pp. 224–232, Guntur – pp. 210-218, Prakasam pp.252-257, Nellore – pp.266-271.).

AP Census DCHB 1981: (Srikakulam – pp. 166-171, Vizianagarma – pp. 150-155, Visakhapatnam – pp.56-61, East Godavari – pp.204-209, West Godavari – pp.140-145, Krishna – pp. 172-177, Guntur – pp. 148-153, Prakasam pp.154-159, Nellore – pp.160-165.).

AP Census 2001, Paper – 3, Tables 1 and 2, pp.234-580.

Notes: Sri:- Ganjam/Srikakulam; Vizia:- Vizianagaram; Visakha:- Visakhapatnam; NCA:- North Coastal Andhra; EG:- East Godavari; WG:- West Godavari; Kri:- Krishna, Gun:- Guntur; Pra:- Prakasam; Nel:- Nellore; SCA:- South Coastal Andhra; CA:- Coastal Andhra.

Table 3
Proportion of Total Agricultural Workers to Total Workers 1901-2001

Year	*Sri*	*Vizia*	*Visakha*	*NCA*	*EG*	*WG*	*Kri*	*Gun*	*Pra*	*Nel*	*SCA*	*CA*
1961	75.66		71.63	·73.74	60.48	68.31	65.35	63.65		68.25	64.89	67.62
1971	76.53	74.70	70.91	73.68	66.31	72.46	65.49	68.01	70.66	71.98	68.81	70.19
1981	66.97	66.98	56.15	62.87	60.39	67.84	59.70	65.02	68.37	65.28	64.19	63.83
1991	67.06	65.58	55.63	62.14	62.46	67.29	62.14	68.76	73.44	64.75	66.39	65.20
2001	68.44	68.46	53.52	62.45	62.24	69.40	59.15	67.10	68.48	62.56	64.83	64.17

Source: As in Table -2
Notes: As in Table -.2

services of all the members of the family. The rich cultivators of this tract might be sending out more of their children to schools, as they are not required to work on land. Similarly more number of women may be mere housewives without having to toil in the fields with the men-folk in these districts compared to their sisters in other less fortunate areas (*AP Census 1961 Part I- A (iii)*, pp.21-22). Districts vary very little in their agricultural character. The districts, which exhibit low percentage of agricultural workers to total workers is not in any way infertile or unsuited to agriculture (*Madras Census 1901*, p.192). It shows, higher the productivity of the land, higher will be the production and income per labourer, and hence, smaller number of workers are sufficient to earn for the entire household. With higher income their children need not attend to work and women can have an opportunity to enjoy leisure, which results in more number of non-workers to workers. The low productivity of less fertile and backward districts resulted in high work participation rates in those districts. From the above analysis it can be concluded that high work participation rates are always not a positive aspect.

To study the trends in work participation rates and dependence on agriculture, a village study was taken up. There is a benchmark study available from the Agro-Economic Centre, Madras University on the village, Jonnalagadda of Narasaraopet Mandal, Guntur district[ii]. The socio economic conditions including work participation, classification of workers by sectors, nature of work and wages were thoroughly studied in the year, 1958-59 in the survey published in 1963.

The village was a part of the upland area of the Guntur district till 1962 with out any irrigational facilities and now it is fully irrigated under Nagarjunasagar right canal.

NATURE OF WORK AND WORK PARTICIPATION RATES OF THE VILLAGE BETWEEN 1961 AND 2001 BY SEX

There were changes in the agricultural character of work by sex. Hence the study of male and female was taken up separately.

Male Workers

The male work participation rate decreased in the period 1961-2001 (see Table-4). Between 1971 and 1981, there was 1% increase in the work participation rate. This increase in this period may be because of the under enumeration of workers in 1971 census due to the definition change in the concept of work, between 1961 and 1971. Between 1981-1991 the work participation decreased significantly and between 1991-2001 it is almost the same or increased very marginally. The reason for decreasing work participation may be because of the increase in the enrolment ratios into schools and colleges. Another reason can be the educated youth might be waiting for a non-agricultural job based on their qualification. But because of lack of opportunities in non-agricultural sectors or other suitable jobs they might not be participating in any work.

Male Agricultural Workers

The proportion of male agricultural workers to total male workers increased continuously between 1961 and 1991 though at a decreasing rate. Between 1991 and 2001 the male agricultural workers to total male workers decreased by around 6%.

Male Agricultural Labourers

In Jonnalagadda, the proportion of male agricultural labourers as a proportion of agricultural workers is almost on an increase except a marginal and insignificant decrease between 1971 and 1981 and around 2% decrease between 1991 and 2001. In 1961 the proportion of agricultural labourers in the total agricultural workers was only 15.42% but by 1971 it increased to 47.76%. The sudden increase in the agricultural labourers to the agricultural workers may be attributed to the increase in demand for labour, caused by changed cropping pattern, which was the result of availability of irrigational facility through Nagarjunasagar Project. The anticipated Land ceiling Act discouraged large holdings. The increase in population and the disappearance of joint family system, giving place to nuclear families led to sub division, and fragmentation of the

Table 4

Male Workers in Jonnalagadda Village During the Period from 1961 to 2001

Year	*Male Population*	*Male Workers*	*Male Cultivators*	*Male Agricultural Labourers*	*Male Total Agricultural Workers*	*Proportion of Male Workers to Male Population*	*Proportion of Male Agricultural Workers to Male Workers*	*Proportion of Male Agricultural Labourers to Male Agricultural Workers*
1961	1274	840	395	72	467	65.93	55.60	15.42
1971	1606	1011	380	346	726	62.95	71.81	47.66
1981	1918	1229	542	481	1023	64.08	83.24	47.02
1991	2548	1490	502	756	1258	58.48	84.43	60.10
2001	2758	1617	518	742	1260	58.62	77.92	58.89

Source:Census of India, 1961, A.P. District Census Hand Book, Guntur district, pp.134-137
Census of India, 1971, A.P. District Census Hand Book, Guntur district pp.268-273.
Census of India, 1981, A.P. District Census Hand Book, Guntur district, pp.350-352.
Census of India, 1991, A.P. District Census Hand Book, Guntur district, pp.230-233.
Census of India, 2001, A.P. (CD) Guntur District, Office of the Director of Census Operations, Andhra Pradesh, Hyderabad.

land. These holdings, which are very small, do not provide sufficient income for the family's minimum needs of food clothing and shelter making the family dependent on agricultural labour. Between 1991 and 2001 the male workers in male population increased marginally. The male agricultural workers to male workers decreased by more than 6%. But the decrease in male agricultural labourers to male agricultural workers was less than 2%. This shows still majority of the male are dependent on agriculture as labourers. The decrease in dependency on agriculture between 1991 and 2001 may be because of the occupational shift of landless agricultural labourers, tenants and land owners to non agricultural sector into different occupations, like clerks, attendees, watch men manual works and trading in the town expecting better income.

Between 1961 and 2001, the male work participation decreased from 66% to 59%, male agricultural workers to total male workers increased from 56% to 78% and male agricultural labourers to male agricultural workers increased from 15% to 58%. These figures reflect the disappearance of non-agricultural occupations and increased dependency on agriculture. The constant size of land and increased dependency on that resulted in increased number of casual labourers.

Thorough enquiries were made to collect information about all the non-agricultural occupations being followed by the villagers of Jonnalagadda from different sections of the population of the village through the field survey conducted in February 2003 and it was compared with that of 1958. There were fairly good number of households in the year 1958 in Jonnalagadda, which were engaged in non-agricultural enterprises. Among the total number of households 38.39% were engaged in some non-agricultural enterprise or the other. Non-agricultural enterprises are the primary source of income for 28.87% of the households. Arts and crafts occupied an important place and essential services were of next importance among the non-farm enterprises. The total number of 81 arts and crafts households, belonged to 25 cobblers, 21 weavers, 13 potters, 10 basket makers, 5 carpenters, 3 goldsmiths, 3 tailors and 1 blacksmith. *Madigas* got converted into

Christianity but continued to follow cobblery, which was their hereditary and caste occupation. All the cobblers suffered due to under-employment and insufficient income with the increased tendency on the part of the villagers to go in for readymade footwear sold in the town. There were 21 households engaged in hereditary profession of weaving. For *Malas* converted into Christianity called *saale malas,* it was a hereditary occupation. The weavers purchased yarn from outsiders and weaved only coarse cloth. This cloth was of brownish in colour and only the very poor among the villagers wore it. Others used that as some sort of a rug to cover themselves when they go to bed. It was sold inside the village. Weavers also suffered from lack of good market resulting in under employment and insufficient income (*Survey 1963,* pp.94-96). There were 13 potter households with 17 workers. This was both a hereditary and caste occupation of *kummaras* of the village. The potters reported that there was no sufficient market due to the appearance of metallic vessels in the market. Basket making was another craft pursued by 11 workers belonging to 10 *erukula* households of the village. This was also a hereditary and caste occupation. These craft men produced articles like baskets and winnows, which were daily used in both household and agricultural works. Even these craft men complained of inadequate wages and under employment. There were 5 carpenters in the village. This was followed by *viswabrahmins* as hereditary and caste occupation and there was also a Muslim Carpenter. Carpenters were indispensable to the village. They made and repaired the agricultural implements like ploughs and carts besides playing their part in construction of buildings. There were 3 goldsmiths in the village. All of them were *viswabrahmins,* who followed it as their hereditary and caste occupation. Since their market was limited and readymade ornaments were available in the town, they were unable to have full time employment. 3 heads of households followed tailoring. 2 Muslims followed it as their caste occupation and there was a tailor from *chakali* caste. There was 1 blacksmith. There were 55 essential servants who provided the services of washing clothes and hair cutting, which were the caste occupations of *chakalis* and *mangalis* respectively. It was the custom in these parts to engage washer men who gathered the clothes of their customers daily in the morning and returned them in the evening after washing them in the nearby stream or *vagu* (*cited* pp. 96-106). There were many non-agricultural activities followed by the villagers but the importance of some of the occupations like cobblery, pottery, weaving, basket making, and gold smithy was decelerating and they were suffering from underemployment and they were suffering from lack of sufficient income.

Now there are only four persons who follow cobblery as their caste occupation and one is running a *chappal* sale shop, which brings readymade *chappals* for sale from the town. The young generation is not ready to take up this work as it is considered indecent. Now weaving is not done in the village. In addition to insufficient income the other reason is that, in 1958 the cotton produced was of the native variety. Now as high-breed cotton is cultivated, it is not suitable for weaving the cloth on these looms. As production and productivity of cotton increased, the farmers are selling the cotton to the millers. Hence, there is no more weaving in the village. Pot making also disappeared from the village. Some of the *Kummaras* for some time shifted to brick making. But as that was not profitable they discontinued brick making. Now there is no basket making and gold smithy. The relevance of black smithy and carpentry got reduced because of the disappearance of agricultural implements like wooden ploughs and carts. Only tailoring and essential services are being practiced in the village. Among the providers of essential services *Mangalis* are continuing their caste occupation, of course taking up other occupations and cultivation as supplementary. C*hakali* men are not continuing their caste occupation but *chakali* women took over it and the women of *chakali* caste do now washing clothes at the owners' houses. All these show that the men of all these castes mainly shifted to agriculture, either as owners of petty lands, tenants and/or agricultural labourers.

Female Work Participation Rates

The female work participation rate increased between 1961 and 2001 (see Table-5). There is a sharp fall in the work participation rate for females in 1971, which was because of the well-known fact of under enumeration of female workers in 1971 census. From then on it increased continuously till 1991.

There is both a positive association and a negative one too between female participation rates and the availability of irrigational facilities in Jonnalagadda. The increased incomes because of the improved irrigational facilities made women of the big landowners' families' non-workers and concentrate only on the domestic work. On the other hand, the increased demand for labour, especially female labour due to the changed cropping pattern towards paddy led to increased participation of women from the poorer households. All this depends on the financial position of the households.

Female Agricultural Workers

In Jonnalagadda the work participation of women mainly tends to remain confined to agriculture and cattle rearing. The women of *chakali* caste numbering around 30 and 40 also wash clothes in addition to agricultural work and cattle rearing. Few women of *yadava* and *kummari* caste sell curds in Narasaraopet. Women working in other than these occupations are almost non- existent.

In Jonnalagadda, the proportion of female agricultural workers to female workers is on an increase. In 1961 only around 52.3% of the workers were engaged in agricultural work. But, by 2001 the female workers engaged in agricultural work increased to 92.55%. The reasons can be as explained for males, the disappearance of arts and crafts like pot making, weaving and basket making. The increase is very high between 1991 and 2001. In the same period, there was a decrease of male workers from agricultural sector. Hence, as males are shifting to non-agricultural sector, females are taking active part in agricultural sector. It's the women by taking care of the family's subsistence needs allowing men to shift to other than agricultural sector and improve their incomes from diversified activities.

Table 5
Female Workers in Jonnalagadda Village During the Period 1961 to 2001

Year	*Female Population*	*Female Workers*	*Female Cultivators*	*Female Agricultural Labourers*	*Total Female Agricultural Workers*	*Proportion of Female Workers in Female Population*	*Proportion of Female Agricultural Workers in Female Workers*	*Proportion of Female Agricultural Labour in Agricultural Workers*
1961	1243	587	251	56	307	47.22	52.30	18.24
1971	1580	534	73	329	402	33.80	75.28	81.84
1981	1903	825	110	497	607	43.35	73.58	81.88
1991	2473	1233	216	743	959	49.86	77.78	77.48
2001	2692	1339	388	851	1239	49.73	92.53	68.68

Source: As in Table –4

Agricultural Labourers

The poverty of the household and its low capacity to absorb female labour on a family farm, led to a high incidence of female agricultural labourers. The incidence of women agricultural labourers in the female population is fairly high in the paddy growing, high productivity coastal districts of Andhra Pradesh. For Jonnalagadda, the proportion of female agricultural labourers in female agricultural workers increased from 18.24% in 1961 to 81.84% in 1971. Between 1971 and 1981 it was almost the same and decreased continuously between 1981-1991 and 1991-2001, and reached 68.67%. Because of the increased tenancy, female agricultural labourers in female agricultural workers are decreasing. Though decreased, still it is very high, as around 70% of them are working as agricultural labourers and it is very high compared to 1961. The substantial increase in female agricultural labourers is because of the increased population, improved irrigational facilities influencing cropping pattern and demand for female labour and disappearance of non-agricultural occupations in the village.

CONCLUSION

Increasing work participation rates cannot be taken as a positive factor in economic development without considering the other economic variables like wage rates and sectoral dependence. There is an increased dependence on agriculture, especially in the form of wage labourers both at the regional level and at the village level. This is the result of disappearance of non-farm employment at the village level. There is feminisation of agriculture over a period of time reflecting shifting of women to the low productive agricultural sector.

SUGGESSIONS

Heavy pressure on land results in low wages in agricultural sector and rural poverty. Diversification of workers from farm to non farm sector is very much necessary to improve wages and living conditions in rural areas. The Tata group's Titan outsourced bracelet making to rural areas, which reduced the cost of production for Titan and increased the wage and income levels of the rural population concerned. Another such effort by the Atlas Documentary Facilitators Company, a rural BPO, wholly owned by HDFC Bank recruited 550 odd employees at Tirupati, in Andhra Pradesh. The unique characteristic of all the workers at this BPO is their rural background. Among these employees, about 55% are women. They are first generation graduates and some the sole graduates from their villages. These were selected and given training by the government run Employment Generation Marketing Mission, which works in tandem with the Department of Rural Development. Some NGOs from Noida, Delhi and Tamilnadu have shown interest in replicating this model in their states (Business Line, Life, 6-2-2009, p.1). Opportunities for formal education and training for self employment are to be enhanced. Government can make the same strategy continued by other Corporate by giving some tax concessions or motivating them to take up Corporate Social Responsibility.

REFERENCES

—(1961), Census of India , Vol.II, Andhra Paradesh, Part-II – B (i), Economic Tables, Table B-I, pp.1-13.

—(1961), Census of India , Vol.II, Andhra Paradesh, District Census Hand Book (Srikakulam- Statement III-2, p.XI, Visakhapatnam- Statement III-2, pp. A20-21, East Godavari – Statement IV-I, p.xxvi, West Godavari – Table AII, p.7, Krishna – Table A-II,p.10, Guntur–Statement III-2, p.xiii and Nellore – Table A-II, p.10).

– -(1971), Census of India, Series-2, Andhra Paradesh, Part II -B, Economic Tables.

—(1981), AP Census DCHB : (Srikakulam – pp.352-357, Vizianagarma – pp.294-299, Visakhapatnam – pp.2-7, East Godavari – pp.280-288, West Godavari – pp.216-221, Krishna – pp. 224–232, Guntur – pp. 210-218, Prakasam pp.252-257, Nellore – pp.266-271).

—(1981), AP Census DCHB : (Srikakulam – pp. 166-171, Vizianagarma – pp. 150-155, Visakhapatnam – pp.56-61, East Godavari – pp.204-209, West Godavari – pp.140-145, Krishna – pp. 172-177, Guntur– pp. 148-153, Prakasam pp.154-159, Nellore – pp.160-165).

—(2001), AP Census, Paper – 3, Tables 1 and 2, pp.234-580.

—(1971), *Census of India, A.P. District Census Hand Book, Guntur district* pp.268-273. *Census of India, 1981, A.P. District Census Hand Book, Guntur district,* pp.350-352.

—(1991), *Census of India, A.P. District Census Hand Book, Guntur district, pp.230-233.*

—(1961), *Census of India, A.P. District Census Hand Book, Guntur district,* pp.134-137.

—(2001), Census of India, A.P. (CD) Guntur *District,* Office of the Director of Census Operations, Andhra Pradesh, Hyderabad.

—(1961), *AP Census Part I-A (iii): Census of India, 1961, Vol.II, Andhra Paradesh,* Part I–A (iii), *General Report.*

—(1991), *AP Census Paper I: Census of India, 1991, Series-2, Andhra Paradesh, Paper I, Provisional Population Totals.*

—(1901), Madras Census : Census of India, 1901, Madras, Imperial series, Vol.XV, Provincial series Part I, The Report on the Census.

—(2002), *National Accounts Statistics,* Central Statistical Organisation, Ministry of Statistics and Programme Implementation, Government of India.

—*State Domestic Product of Andhra Pradesh, 1993-94 to 2001-2002,* 2002, Directorate of Economics and Statistics, Government of Andhra Pradesh, Hyderabad.

—(1963), *Village Surveys, Agro Economic Research Centre, University of Madras, Jonnalagadda Village, Guntur District, A.P.*

22

AGRICULTURAL GROWTH, INCOME AND EMPLOYMENT IN RURAL AREA

N. T. K. Naik
Y. Maddileti

Interdependencies in the food and labour markets are important for the development process. A strategy combining promotion of agricultural growth, productive non-farm employment and high levels of social development would be needed for labour-intensive growth in rural areas. There should also be substantial investment in human resource development for enhancing people's earning capacity. The aim thus would be the generation of self-reliant employment.

Agriculture dominates change in India through its causal links with factor and product markets. It employs 57 percent of the labour force and contributes 2o percent of the gross domestic product. In the poorer states, its contribution to the domestic product is close to 40 percent. Low productivity in agriculture has led to the concentration of the poor in this sector. Due to the sheet size of the agricultural economy and the importance of its major products (cereals) in the diets of the poor, gains in agricultural productivity have significant potential impact on poverty. There is a widely held view that in a large country like India, the demand stimulus for industrialization would come mainly from agriculture with less social and economic costs.

Interdependencies in food and labour markets are important for the development process. An increase in the food supply would simultaneously result in an increase in the labour demand. The magnitude of the interdependence depends on the technique of production causing the raise in the food supply. The extent of interdependence between the forces of labour supply and out put elasticity and the income elasticity of demand for food. The important inter-dependency, which plays a crucial role in inducing indirect employment, is that between food and other sectors through demand linkages. Since food accounts for a major share in the budget of the poor and any reduction in the food price level a significant proportion of income for other items, a lower food price service sectors.

Both cost reducing as well as labour absorbing technical progress in agriculture and expansion of the non-farm sector are essential for development in a country like India. If rural non-farm and urban informal sectors grow at a sufficient rate, they can absorb the surplus labour and surplus food. If they grow at a lower rate, the terms of trade turn against agriculture, and consequently, agricultural incomes are depressed. In practice, price fall is moderated either by increasing buffer stocks or by expanding wage employment programmes. On the other hand, if agricultural production lags behind demand, it leads to an increase in food prices and thereby to an increase in nominal wage rates of industrial workers, which in combination with higher prices of agricultural raw materials, contributes to cost puts inflation. The performance of the non-agricultural sector is there, harmed by too high as well as tool low levels of agricultural prices, which is the razor's edge characteristic of agriculture (Alagah 1991).

The virtuous cycle between agriculture and non-agricultural enterprises plays a strategic role in providing employment opportunities in rural areas. In the ongoing globalization process, production and demand patterns undergo significant change. While better-off farmers produce high-value products for exports and for the affluent segment of the domestic market, the small farmers are likely to grow crops mainly to meet domestic food needs. Small and medium industries in the rural and semi-urban areas produce consumer goods to meet the needs of the lower strata of society.

India's agricultural growth reveals two distinct phases during the pre-reform period: pre-green revolution period and post-green revolution period. The first phase, from the beginning of planning to the mid-1960 was characterized by severe imbalances between the demand for food and its domestic supply. In the post green revolution period, from about the mid 1960s to the close of the 1980s, the country achieved near self-sufficiency in food and food security. The later phase warrants further sub grouping; the 1970s characterized by the emergence of intra and inter-regional and inter-crop imbalance in crop yields, and the eighties, when yields of crops like rice, oilseeds and pulses registered high growth, especially in the backward regions.

RURAL EMPLOYMENT TRENDS

Of the 1937 million people in the labour force in 1999-00, 388 million were employed and 9 million (2.2 percent) reported unemployed during the greater part of the year. The priory sector-agriculture, animal husbandry, fisheries and forestry – employed 238 million (60 percent) of the workforce, unorganized non-agricultural sector 133 million (33 percent) and organized sector 28 million (7 percent). Employment in the organized sector increased slowly from 24 million in 1983 to 28 million in 1999-00. Evidently, unless some spectacular changes occur, the organized sector's share in the absorption of additions to the labour force will remain small in the near future. As a result, a major will have to be absorbed in the unorganized non-agriculture sector as agriculture is already over crowded.

Though the usual principal status unemployment rate at 1.96 percent in 1999-01 is not a serious concern in rural India, current daily status unemployment rate at 7.21 percent is high. Unemployment among educated youth (15-29 years) has been high. The usual status unemployment (1999-00) among rural youth with secondary education and above is estimated at 12.5 percent in 1999-01 and those with technical education at 23 percent. What is of particularly serious concern in unemployment among educated females in rural areas, which is about three times more than that of their male counterparts, presumably due to limited chances open to them for migration to urban areas to secure employment.

Growing commercialization in the rural economy has influenced expansion of rural non-farm sector. Employment potential of the non-farm sector appears to be directly related to commercialization of agriculture. This is the normal pattern of development and in fact the process has been very slow in India.

Yield improvements and growth of the rural non-farm sector contributed to the diversification of employment opportunities. However, slow growth of the rural non-form sector failed to create sufficient jobs to employ the large surplus agricultural labour.

Irrigated agriculture has now reached the take-off stage where growth with good spread and coverage can be generated through normal market mechanisms and right policy mix. Since income improvement in these regions is likely to increase the demand for the products of animal husbandry, fruits, vegetable and processed foods, marketing and agro-processing should receive the attention of policy makers. Public spending in irrigated regions should be very selective, facilitative and confined to those critical areas which would supplement private initiative.

Poverty alleviation programmers should be beyond their present minimal concerns of providing protective 'safety nets'. There should be substantial investment in human resource development for enhancing people's inherent earning capacity. Along with this, there should be attempts to create more economic space for the poor by equipping them with assets and sills for livelihood outside agriculture. All this should contribute to the generation of self-reliant employment.

23

AGRICULTURE DEVELOPMENT: ISSUES IN INDIA

K. V. R. Srinivas
Srinivasa Charyulu
K. Hari Babu

The importance of agriculture in the economic development of any country, rich or poor, is borne out by the fact that it is the primary sector of the economy which provides the basic ingredients necessary for the existence of mankind and also provides most of the raw materials, which when transformed into finished products serve as basic necessities of the human race. In a preponderantly agrarian economy, agriculture play a most strategic role from several points of view. At a minimum, farm production must be increased rapidly enough to keep pace with population growth. However, in a speedy industrializing economy, this is not enough. Industrialization necessarily brings with it urbanization and a rapid expansion of the industrial labour force. This may then be expected to bring with it a rising per capita demand for food, based on higher urban incomes.

Therefore, the pace of advance in a wide range of consumer goods manufactures will be eventually affected by the pace of agricultural development. In addition, agriculture must generate export surpluses in order to earn the foreign exchange with which to finance the import of capital goods and certain kinds of industrial raw materials. However, agriculture is not only a supplier of goods for domestic and export needs but is also a supplier of production factors, such as capital and labour.

Ricardo had scientifically explained the ideas of Adam Smith, Ricardo considers agriculture the most important sector of the economy. The difficulty of providing food for an expanding population serves as the focal point for his entire analysis. The centralization serves as the focal point for his entire analysis. The central problem for classical economists was the analysis of the overall movement of the economy through time involving changes in population, capital accumulation and technical progress. According to Adam Smith, the objective of economic analysis was the understanding of the nature and the causes of wealth of nations. But to David Ricardo, the principal problem of political economy was to determine the "laws which regulate of distribution of commodities among the classes of society. It was through the laws which regulate distributive shares the he was trying to build up a simple macro-economic model of economic development.

IMPORTANCE OF AGRICULTURAL

A group of thinkers (Barker, Wilson, Barsodi and Humphries etc.,) have commonly held the orthodox view that agriculture is par excellence the fundamental industry. They support this contention with the explanation that agriculture being the producer of basic food for the human being is the basis of existence of human race. Besides, it produces raw materials to many industries and also is important constituent of trade. Hence it is foundation of manufacture as well as commerce.

Adam Smith in his Wealth of Nations took vigorous exception to the physiocrats notion that agriculture is the only productive activity ; but still he ranked agriculture as highest in wealth creating powers.

T.R. Malthus's first essay on population, which appeared in 1798, gave very pronounced emphasis to agriculture. The face of capitalist economy, according to Ricardo, is purely dependent upon the yield rate in agricultural sector.

ROLE OF AGRICULTURE IN INDIA

A flourishing agricultural sector is far more important for the development of Indian economy, since farming is less a business than a tradition in India. Even at this semi-industrialization stage, about 80 per cent of its population still lives in the rural areas and directly or indirectly depends on agriculture for its livelihood. The mere existence of about 65 cores of persons, which are further multiplying at a rate of 2.5 per cent per annum, depends on a developed agricultural sector. Further, most of our traditional industries on whose products depend our bulk of foreign trade and foreign earnings draw their raw material from this very sector. It is the surplus generated by this sector that would help Indian economy to reach the "Golden stage" since total savings fund is made up of savings from industrial sector and savings from agricultural sector.

SHARE OF AGRICULTURE IN NATIONAL INCOME

Share of agriculture in national income is a crucial indicator of the role that agriculture plays in economic development of a country. As the country rides on the wheels of progress, the relative contribution of agriculture in national income declines with the country becoming more and more prosperous. The expanding non-agricultural sector diverts surplus manpower from agriculture to industry and the improvements in agriculture enable a smaller number of people to produce for a larger population. With advanced agricultural technology, agricultural products are produced even for exports. To the extent, therefore, the share of agriculture in national income declines, it marks a better level of economic advancement. On the other hand, agriculture is the single larger contributor to national income. Therefore, progressive agricultural sector means a higher level of national income and consequently a higher level of economic development.

EMPLOYMENT POSITION IN AGRICULTURE

Agriculture has a greater role in economic development in the less developed countries as it provides livelihood to a vast majority of people living in the country. This figure is not significant in terms of percentages only, but more so in terms of absolute numbers. The agricultural sector provides livelihood to about three-fourths of the Indian Population, that is, seven out of every ten persons in India depend on agriculture. At the turn of the century, 71.5 per cent of the total labour force was engaged in agriculture and this situation has not changed up till now. According to 1971 census, 72 per cent of the working force was still engaged in the primary sector. This indicates that in spite of rapid industrialization in the country, primary, sector is still the main sector providing employment opportunities for the majority of the workers and has, thus, acted as the big shock-absorber. This fact reflects the importance of agriculture and lesser development of other sectors of the economy.

India agriculture is of considerable importance in so far as it can offer enormous scope of alternative employment. Past experience shows that the development of large industries has not helped significantly in absorbing unemployed labour force. It has been estimated that since 1971, the labour force has increased by about 35 million. Of these about 25 million have been absorbed in agricultural and 9 million in non-agricultural activities. Thus agricultural sector has absorbed bulk of additional labour force, though many must have got low intensity employment and consequently low incomes. Agro-industries and agro-processing industries hold a great promise for employment in our country. Forestry, fishery and animal husbandry can also be developed on a large scale and considerable employment can be generated for the rural youth.

AGRICULTURE AND INDUSTRIAL DEVELOPMENT

The role of agriculture in industrial development can hardly be overlooked. In fact all growth models for surplus labour countries have underlined the importance of agriculture for developing the industrial sector in the initial stages.

Agriculture supplies manpower and raw materials to industries and provides a wide market for industrial products. In India, most of our leading industries depend on agriculture for their raw materials. Cotton and jute textiles in textiles industries, sugar, vanaspati, and plantation industries depend on agriculture directly. There are a number of other industries whose dependence on agriculture is indirect.

ROLE OF AGRICULTURE IN THE FIELD OF INTERNATIONAL TRADE

Indian agriculture has been a net earner of valuable foreign exchange for the country. Agricultural goods like, tea, sugar, oil seeds, tobacco, spices, etc. constitute the main item of exports of India. Agricultural exports constitute a major portion of India's exports and accounted for 42 per cent of the exports in 1977-78. This percentage will increase considerable if export of jute manufactures and cotton textiles, whose 65 per cent of production cost is accounted for by raw jute and raw cotton are included in the agricultural exports. This has great significance for India's economic development because increased exports help the country to pay for the increased imports of oil, machinery and raw materials.

DETERMINANTS OF AGRICULTURE

Land is the basis of agriculture. Virtually all types of production depend on land, in general, and all agriculture production depends on it, in particular. Besides being the resource for crop, fodder, and forest production, it also provides space for building cities, roads, airports, health resorts, schools, industries and so on. So far as the role of land in agriculture is concerned, serves as the source of food and fiber production, pastures and grazing lands and forests.

TECHNOLOGY IMPACT ON AGRICULTURE

Technology plays a pivotal role in any production enterprise. The nature of technology determines the magnitude of success in raising higher yields from any production effort. Technology is still more crucial in agriculture because of the fact that the basic resource in agricultural production viz., land is limited in supply. The efficiency of a given technology shall, therefore, determine, in general, the efficiency of farm enterprise. In any business enterprise, the level of productivity may be raised without increasing the unit cost or the current level of output may be maintained at a lower unit cost. If a new technology succeeds in it, it results in increased economic progress. It is ultimately an increase in ends relative to means that leads to economic progress. Given, that means are limited in supply and ends to be realized are varied, it is only through technology that a society can aim at increasing the economic progress.

AGRI-DEVELOPMENT THROUGH INNOVATION

New farm technology is not an abrupt development. Changes have been occurring in farm t4echnology on continuous basis. Since firm technology consists of a number of components, changes have occurred component wise in a gradual manner. By development path of new farm technology, we are referring to the process of change in a chronological order. The world farm technology is held have undergone change in the following chronology.

Changes in farm machine technology.

Changes in animal production technology.

Changes in plant production technology.

Changes in land use technology.

Changes in food and fiber processing technology.

CONCLUSIONS

Developing countries like India and some another countries face additional problems owing to limited applicability of new farm technology. Some pockets have become extremely affluent while majority of farmers have lagged far behind. Creation of islands of prosperity amidst an ocean of misery leads to social economic and regional tensions. Even among the adopters, rich farmers could afford to adopt it much earlier for they had the capacity to invest and to bear risks compared to others and succeeded in mopping off the initial gains and further consolidating their strong-hold. Going into the implications of new farm technology may not be required in the present context but the fact remains that while on one side more advances have to be made on the agricultural front, on the other side the issues arising out of the new farm technology have also to be given a serious thought lest we miss the race in the bid to win to son.

24

UNEMPLOYMENT, LABOUR MOBILITY AND MIGRATION–POLICY PRESCRIPTIONS

Swapna. V

This paper examines a few issues concerning the performance of agriculture and Unemployment in agricultural sector, state of Indian labor mobility and migration.

The importance of agriculture in India is very obvious. Agriculture continues to be the main employer in India. It provides employment opportunities for over 60 crore women and men.

This has great significance as a viable alternative source of livelihood and employment is not available for vast amount of the population in the near future.

In India due to the agrarian sector, with seasonal operations and availability for work have been the criteria for measuring employment. As per the result of the national sample survey conducted in 1999–2000, the total work force employed in informal or unorganized sector in 93 percent.

Employment for agricultural is seasonal, where during the peak season workers can get up to 20 days of employment in a month, but this may well be zero during the slack season.

WORKFORCE AND LABOUR FORCE

The workers participation rate of the rural segment is higher compared to urban as shown in the below table. The labour force or active population is made up of the employed and the unemployed populations. The employed population consists of persons who are working while the unemployed population consists of persons who are *not working* but who are *looking for work* and are *available for work.*

India's labour force is growing at a rate of 2.5 per cent annually, but employment is growing at only 2.3 per cent. Thus, the country is facing with the challenge of not only absorbing new entrants to the job market (estimated at seven million people every year), but also clearing the backlog.

Table 1

Trends in Labour Force Participation Rates

Per Thousand of Population

		Male		*Female*	
Age Group	*Period*	*Rural*	*Urban*	*Rural*	*Urban*
15-29	1977-78	879	746	515	257
	1987-88	824	710	478	211
	1993-94	804	684	455	204
30-44	1977-78	990	990	619	324
	1987-88	988	987	603	301
	1993-94	990	986	600	300
45-59	1977-78	963	940	538	291
	1987-88	964	933	538	275
	1993-94	968	937	543	283
60+	1977-78	667	517	221	130
	1987-88	670	482	220	123
	1993-94	699	443	241	114
All (15+)	1977-78	904	831	517	269
	1987-88	879	810	496	239
	1993-94	877	811	491	238

Majority of the work force, not only in rural areas but also in urban areas does not possess any identifiable skill in urban areas which is only 19.6 male and 11.2 female. In rural areas about 10 percent males and 6.3 percent of female persons possess skills.

In rural India from the proportion of males usually employed, about 66 percent of the males were engaged in agricultural activities in 2004. The corresponding proportional males engaged in agricultural activities was 78 percent in 1983, 71 percent in 2000.

Sixty per cent of India's workforce is self-employed, many of whom remain very poor. Nearly 30 per cent are casual workers (i.e. they work only when they are able to get jobs and remain unpaid for the rest of the days). Only about 10 per cent are regular employees, of which two-fifths are employed by the public sector.

More than 90 per cent of the labour force is employed in the "Unorganised sector", i.e. sectors which do not provide with the social security and other benefits of employment in the "organised sector."

In the rural areas, agricultural workers form the bulk of the unorganised sector. In urban India, contract and sub-contract as well as migratory agricultural labourers make up most of the unorganised labour force.

The addition to the labour force during the Plan period is estimated to be 53 millions on the "usual status" concept. The acceleration in the economy's growth rate to 7 per cent per annum, with special emphasis on the agriculture sector, is expected to help in creating 54 million work opportunities over the period. This would lead to a reduction in the open unemployment rate from 1.9 per cent in 1996-97 to 1.47 per cent in the Plan's terminal year, that is, by about a million persons–from 7.5 million to 6.63 million.

Underemployment in various segments of the labour force is quite high.

For instance, though open unemployment was only 2 per cent in 1993-94, the incidence of under-employment and unemployment taken together was as much as 10 per cent that year. This, in spite of the fact that the incidence of underemployment was reduced substantially in the decade ending 1993-94.

According to the Planning Commission, the States which face the prospect of increased unemployment in the post-Ninth

Plan period (2002- 2007) are Bihar, Rajasthan, Uttar Pradesh, Kerala and Punjab.

Sector-wise Absorption of Labour

Agriculture	62 per cent
Manufacturing & construction	16 per cent
Services	10 per cent
Sundry/miscellaneous jobs	12 per cent

Unemployment is a pressing problem for millions of India. But the most seriously affected are the unorganized sector workers. This sector is characterized by the temporary seasonal and changing the nature of unemployment after resulting in long periods of unemployment failures of crops, irregular incomes.

High levels of unemployment in urban areas could be explained by a larger proportion of unorganized sector.

MIGRATION AND MOBILITY

Workers moving from slow growing to rapidly expanding sectors and there is evidence to show that this does in fact happen. Also, dislike the agricultural work to obtain cash and worsening of economic situation were most frequent cited reasons for migration.

An agricultural labourer, drought–prone area as an excavation worker in a project and dry land farming communities seeking seasonal work in neighboring wet cultivation areas leads to migration.

Reasons	*Agriculture Labour*	*Other Rural Labour*
Not sufficient work in the villages	60	34
Skilled work only outside village	11	16
Expectation higher income	08	17
Group affinity	20	31
Social Factors		12
Indebtedness	51	40
All	150	150

Mobility means shift ability of individuals between jobs occupations or locations in response to the incentives. Mobility may be horizontal as between similar jobs and occupations, a vertical such as the upward mobility of workers from casual labour generation.

SOCIO ECONOMIC CONDITIONS OF MIGRANT LABOURER

Housing Conditions

They have no primary facilities like both rooms and toilets. Majority of regular casual workers live in houses with tiled and asbestos roofs. The average size of a house for six people is 18ft. by a 9 ft. with a varying number of rooms. Access to both rooms and other facilities is yet another indicator of the quality of life. In the Indian social context the lack of access to these facilities is much more distressing for female workers than for male.

Health

Daily casual and contract workers without any insurance especially for those who live alone, sick ness can be disastrous, often prompting people to go back to their villages. The disease pattern shows a high incidence of dysentery , skin infections, diseases of teeth and bone related.

EMPLOYMENT GENERATION PROGRAM

Anti-poverty strategy comprises of a wide range of poverty alleviation and employment generation programmes, many of which have been in operation for several years and have been strengthened to generate more employment, create productive assets, impart technical and

EMPLOYMENT GENERATION IN INDIA

7% of the total employed are in the organised sector i.e., unorganised sector dominates in the employment scenario. Additional employment generation in the organised sector is not significant i.e., scope for additional wage employment in the organised sector continued to be less. Significant employment generation took place in the tertiary sector particularly in services industries. Substantial employment growth was observed in the small and unorganised sector, i.e., in small and tiny enterprises. Self-employment and casual labour continued to play a pivotal role in rehabilitation of the unemployed.

A special group in the Planning Commission was constituted under the Chairmanship of Dr. S.P.Gupta, Member, Planning Commission to suggest strategies and programmes in the Tenth Plan for creating gainful employment opportunities for one crore people per year during each year of the Tenth Plan. The special group has also submitted its report in May 2002.

The special group has also suggested restructuring in the following sectors in favor of labour intensive activity for generating additional gainful job opportunities for the Tenth Plan.

(a) Agriculture & allied sectors.

(b) Greening the country through Agro Forestry

(c) Energy Plantation for Biomass power Generation.

(d) Rural Sectors and Small and medium enterprises (SMEs).

(e) Education and Literacy.

(f) Employment through ICT Development.

(g) Health, Family and Child Welfare.

CONCLUSION

The labour demand is not adequate to provide sufficient work to the existing rural labour force in the villages. There is thus, shortage of employment opportunities and uncertainty of work. This situation has promoted some workers to shift occupation and some to shift places. Hence to escape the scarcity conditions people have migrated far and near for work of any kind and anywhere for their survival in the off season. However a planned strategy of rural nonform sector can prevent the rural migration.

PREVENTIVE MEASURES

Accelerating the rate of growth of GDP, with a particular emphasis on sectors likely to ensure the spread of income to the lower income segments of the labour force.

Pursuing suitable policies for education and skill development, which would upgrade the quality of the labour force. and make it capable of supporting a growth process, which generates high quality jobs?

Implementing focused special programmes for creating additional employment of enhancing income generation from existing activities

Ensuring that the policy and legal environment governing the labour market encourages labour absorption, especially in the organized sector.

REFERENCES

—(2006), The Indian Journal of Labour Economics—Volume 49, Number 3, October – December.

—(2006), The Indian Journal of Labour Economics—Volume 49, Number 4, October – December.

—Economic Structure of Indian Agriculture——A.N.Sharma, Himalaya Publishers

—Issues in Agriculture and Forestry——Vasant Desai, Himalaya Publishers

—(2007), Migration of Labour from Rural Areas — Kurukshetra, June.

—Indian Economy —— Datt and Sunderam.

—Unemployment Scenario in India —— Internet

—India's Perspective —— Internet.

25

WOMEN LABOUR MIGRATION: AN EMPIRICAL INVESTIGATION IN KARIMNAGAR TOWN

Lal B. Suresh
Sujatha
Kavitha

INTRODUCTION

Internal migration is an important factor, which affects the economic development of developing countries like India. In India, although literature on internal migration in general is abundant, little attention was given in the sociological research to the causes and nature of female migration in India and the impact of migration on women (Mazumdar, 1990; Singhal, 1995). Research works on female migrants in other countries have made it clear that there is special need for field research and new methods of investigation. Much of what we know today of female migration in India is derived from census statistics. Census based studies traditionally view women migrating as wives and daughters of the breadwinners. This presents a biased picture of female migration in India as being dominated by low status of women moving to the major metropolises/towns where they become one of the primary examples of the social and economic marginality section of society. Even within towns/metropolises, the reference framework has many times been a segment of the city population usually slum dwellers.

Mobility a term widely used in migration studies includes all kinds of territorial movements both temporary and permanent. However, the term migration is used more restrictively referring to a relatively permanent change of residence. Operationally studies on migration are usually based on temporal, locational, and directional Ontario. When one talk about direction, distinction has to be made between in-migration and out migration which again refer to internal migration because external migration or migration to other countries or into the country is emigration and immigration?

In the post Independent India, women who have been entering salaried remunerative occupations and professions are increasing substantially. Women are working in almost all type of jobs such as technical, professional, non-professional and non-technical in both private and public sectors, residing in rural and urban areas with or without their kith and kin. So, the traditional role of housewife has gradually changed into working women and house wife (Reddy, 1986; Anand, 2003). Women constitute an integral part of the socio-economic life and they actively participate in socio-economic development of the nation. Sometimes, the need for supplementing the family income has been considered as the chief motivating factor encouraging women for aspiring jobs (Mittal, 1994).

CONCEPTUALIZING MIGRATION

A voluminous literature is available explaining migration that mirrors the discipline and ideological underpinnings of the research. Although sociologist like Lee (1966) conceptualized migration as the play of negative and positive forces that respectively pushes a migrant from the place of origin to migrate and pulls him to the place of destination, neoclassical constructs dominated the explanations. Locating migration decisions at the household level and arguing that such decisions are based on opportunities and constraints that the household face, the neoclassical theorists propagated human capital theory (Sjaastad: 1962; Todaro: 1969, 1980). This construct argued that inclination to migrate is determined by difference in income between source and destination of migration, and may result in equating expected income. Given their skills, decisions about where to live are based on where individuals can optimize the present value of their discounted stream of expected future earning.

WOMEN AT WORK PLACE

The migrant women's occupational status is low compared to natives. Also, urban life brings with it a variety of unfavorable conditions such as problems of housing, urban congestion, and the high cost of living (Clausen, 2002). In most of the cases the girls occupy the middle or lower middle ranks of the office hierarchy, where the pressure to prove their worth is constantly present causing a great deal of tension and mental fatigue (Chauhan, 1986). Despite the poorly paid jobs, they may be able to work more hours and earn more money per hour than before migration. Their income levels may not be as high as had been expected; many of these women can improve their level of living (Findley and Williams, 1991). Migrant women have very little protection against eve teasing and for this reason many of them are forced to live a life of seclusion in their new places of residence. Some times working women have to face exploitation including sexual exploitation from their boss or other colleagues in the office/working places. If she permits them to exploit, it generally creates tensions and conflicts within herself in the form of guilt complex, and apart from this, her home life and interaction with colleagues get affected who look down upon her. If on the other hand if she resists, and if the person happens to be boss, she might loose job or her promotional avenues are liable to become dim and working life painful (Reddy, 1986). The process of preserving image, avoiding exploitation and at the same time keeping the channels of upward mobility open are found very tedious and nerve-racking by most of the girls (Chauhan, 1986).

METHODOLOGY

The present study is a modest attempt to study the different aspects of migrant women and to find out the impact of migration on them in terms of working conditions. Wages and earnings, their living conditions and problems at work place. A sample of hundred women labour households pursuing different types of occupation were selected for survey in Karimnagar town of Andhra Pradesh.

OBJECTIVES

1. To study the socio-economic background of the women migrants
2. To identity the socio-economic factors responsible for migration
3. To examine the changes in employment, wages and other living condition of the women after migration
4. To make recommendations on the bases of field study findings

The movement of population from rural to urban areas depends on the extent of the demand for labour in the urban areas which intern is determined by so many factors like the level of industrialization in urban areas, the development of other sectors like services, trade and commerce, the level of wages in the above sectors and the increase of disguised unemployment of the economy.

RESULTS AND DISCURSION

The age composition of the sample respondents as shown in the Table-1 reveals that a majority of the respondent belong to the younger age group of 15to30 years i.e 66 out of the 100 accounting for 66 percent. Further 15 out 100 belong to the age group of 30 to 40 years. The number of very young and very old respondents is relatively small.

Table-2 presents the data relating to the lost residence of the sample respondents. Out of 100 sample women migrant 50 i.e, 50 per cent are from the rural areas of the Nalgonda district, other women migrant came from the kammam district and 30 percent migrant from karimnagar district itself.

Table 1
Age Composition of Sample Respondents

Range	*No. of Samples*	%
Below 15 years	09	09
15 to 30 years	66	66
30 to 40 years	15	15
Above 45 years	10	10
Total	100	100

Table 2
Last Residence of Sample Respondents

Range	*No. of Samples*	%
Karimnagar	30	30
Nalgonda	50	50
Khammam	20	20
Total	100	100

The literacy composition of the sample respondents as shown in the Table-3 reveals that 80 out of 100 sample migrants are illiterates i.e, 80 per cent Nearly 70 per cent of them i.e, 70 out 100 are married as indicated in table-4.

Table 3
Educational Composition of Sample Respondents

Education Status	*No. of Samples*	%
Literate	20	20
Illiterate	80	80
Total	100	100

Table 4
Marital Status of Sample Respondents

Marital Status	*No. of Samples*	%
Married	70	70
Unmarried	30	30
Total	100	100

Majority of these migrants' primary occupation is agricultural labour at the place of origin and they are primary engaged in non-agricultural labour work, especially in construction activities at the place of destination.

Information regarding the present occupation pursued by the woman sample respondents is given in Table-5. Majority of the sample respondents have taken to house construction work i.e, almost 75 per cent of the sample respondents. Next comes the servant in the houses as one of the important occupation of the respondents.

Table 5
Present Occupation Composition of Sample Respondents

Occupation	*No. of Samples*	%
House Construction work	75	75
Servent in the house	25	25
Total	100	100

Table 6
Family Type of Sample Respondents

Type	*No. of Samples*	%
Nucleus	32	32
Joint	68	68
Total	100	100

Table 7
Reasons for Permanent Migration of Sample Respondents

Reasons	*No. of Samples*	%
Economic	05	05
Big size of family	30	30
Continuous drought	50	50
Employment	12	12
Social	03	03
Total	100	100

Table 8
Changes in Quality of Life of Sample Respondents After Migration

Responces	*No. of Samples*	%
Yes	95	95
No	05	05
Total	100	100

Table-6 we have presented the family size of the respondents. Nearly 68 per cent of the migrants come from joint families and 32 per cent come from nucleus families. The respondents were asked to explain the reasons for their permanent migration. The responses are tabulated and presented in Table-7. Nearly 50 per cent of the respondents told that it is continuous drought which induced them to migrate. Their higher family size, employment and other economic factor were also mentioned as other important reasons for their migration by another 50 per cent of the respondents. The women labour migrants who were selected for the sample study were asked a question as to whether there is a qualitative change in their general living conditions for which nearly 95 per cent of them responded positively and only the remaining 5 per cent said "on change" in their general living conditions.

Table 9
Awarness About Family Planning of Sample Respondents

Responces	*No. of Samples*	%
Yes	65	65
No	35	35
Total	100	100

Table-9 present data relating to the awareness of the respondents about family planning. 65 per cent of the respondents were aware of the family planning. Nearly 90 per cent of the women migrants are facing the problem of physical exploitation at work place and remaining 10 per cent said that no.

Table 10
Physical Explantation at Work Place

Responces	*No. of Samples*	%
Yes	90	90
No	10	10
Total	100	100

Further, caste composition of the migrants indicates that out of the total migrants, 60 per cent belong to Backward Caste and 25 per cent scheduled Caste. The percentage of Scheduled Tribe migrants is 15 per cent.

Table 11
Debt Details of Sample Respondents

Responces	*No. of Samples*	%
Yes	70	70
No	30	30
Total	100	100

MIGRATION IMPACT AT RURAL AND URBAN AREAS

Migrants are facing different problems at their native place and at place of residing. They are withdrawing child from school, started doing degrading jobs, old family members sent out, increased land mortgage, reduction in food consumption, depletion in mulch animals, increased debt, increased intensity of migration, unpaid hospital bills, fodder availability reduced and short term land transitions. Increase of slums, increase of health problems due to leaving in slums, increase of pollution, low-wages, increase of crimes and suicides, reduce in nutritional food consumption, and increase of trafficking and accidents and in secured life.

Following are the summarized results of the empirical study conducted in Karimnagar town/city.

1. The socio-economic background of the sample respondents shows that a majority of the migrants belong to younger groups and illiterates.
2. Out of the 100 sample migrants 50 percent are from the rural areas of the Nalgonda District. Other women migrants came from the Karimnagar District itself.
3. More then 98 percent of migrants migrated to the Karimnagar town permanently.
4. Nearly 70 percent are married.
5. Majority of the sample women respondents have taken to house constructions, followed by servant in the houses as one of the important occupation.
6. Continuous drought is identified as one of the important reasons for migrations

7. Bigger family size, employment and other economic factors were able to mentioned as other important reasons for their migration
8. Nearly 95 percent of sample migrants respondents positively and only the remaining 5 percent said 'no change' in their general living conditions.
9. It is also observed that there is slight improvement in their economic status at their native place.
10. Nearly 65 percent of the respondents were aware of the family planning and only about 30 percent of them underwent family planning operation.
11. The survey reveals that nearly 70 percent of the sample migrants are still having debts. Majority respondents are carrying debts in the range of Rs.50,000 to 100,000. These debts are on account of agricultural inputs investment and marriage of their daughters.
12. Majority women migrants are facing the problem of physical exploitation/ harassments at work place.

SUGGESTIONS

Based on the above findings the following suggestions are offered to address the problem of female labour migration.

Firstly, as it is revealed by the empirical study, the inability of the rural agriculture sector to absorb the rural labour, especially women labour, they are migrating to the nearly urban centers where they get employment causing population pressure in cities/town and resulting in frictions between migrants and natives. It is hence imperative that appropriate policy measures are to be undertaken to augment the agricultural sector and provide alternative non-agricultural employment opportunities in the rural sector.

Secondly, basic amenities like food, shelter, health and educational facilities are to be provided on adequate scale both in rural and urban areas

Thirdly, since lack of development of the non–household manufacturing sector in the rural areas is an important contributing factor in rural-urban women migration, development of industrialization process in rural areas is a necessity. Also lack of irrigation facilities acts as a significant push factor for rural out-migration. To abate the unbalanced flow of rural population to urban areas, high priority must be given to development of irrigation facilities in rural areas.

Finally, the economic coercion and exploitation of the women labour must be arrested with appropriate agrarian reform policies to prevent excessive rural–urban migration. The present study revealed that about one forth of the migrant women from rural areas of the same district is not satisfied with their present job/work. But still, due to severe unemployment in the society they have to migrate to other places/ towns for searching jobs/ work. Therefore, appropriate policies for education as well as employment should be implemented by the State Government of Andhra Pradesh to reduce the unemployment problem among rural unemployed.

REFERENCES

Anand, N. (2003), Working Women: Issues and Problems, Yojana, Vol. 47, No.3, pp.11-14.

Chauhan, I. (1986), The Dilemma of Workingwomen's Hostellers, B.R. Publishing Cooperation, Delhi.

Clausin, A. (2002), Female Labour Migration to Bangkok: Transforming Rural-Urban Interaction and Social Networks through Globalisation, Asia Pacific Population Journal, Vol.17, No.3.

Das, Biswaroop (1994), Socio-Economic Study of Slums in Surat City, Centre for Social Studies, Surat

Desai, AR, & Pillai, SD (1990), Slums and Urbanization, Popular Publication, Bombay.

Findley, S and Williams, L. (1991), Women Who Go and Women Who Stay-Reflections of Family Migration Processes in a Changing World, Women Employment Programme Research, Working Paper No. 176, UNFPA.

Lal B Suresh (1995), Rural-Urban Migration of Tribal Labour: A case Study in Warangal District, Unplished M.Phil Dissertation, KU.

Lal B Suresh & Hussain SA, (2005), Socio-Economic Environment of Daily Labour Market in Andhra Pradesh: A Case Study of Karimnagar Town, Kakatiya Business Review, Warangal.

Lal B. Suresh, Vasavi & Anitha (2006), Socio-Economic Conditions of Women Ragpickers in Karimnagar Town, AP Economic Association Conference on 26th November.

Mittal, M. (1994), Educated Unemployed Women in India, Anmol Publications Pvt.Ltd, New Delhi.

Reddy, C, R. (1986), Changing Status of Educated Working Women-A Case Study, B.R Publishing Corporation, Delhi.

Saxena, DP, (1977), Rural to Urban Migration in India, Popular Prakasham, Bombay.

Sengupta, C. (2000), Urban Poverty and Vulnerability in India: Nature, Dynamics and Trends, Oxford India, N.D

Singhal, S. (1995), Development of Education, Occupation and Employment of Women in India, Mittal Publications, Delhi.

Todaro,.Philip (1969), Internal Migration in Developing Countries, Geneva: ILO.

Todaro Philip (2002), Impact of Women's Employment on Family and Marriage: A Survey of Literature, Social Change, Vol.32, Nos.1&2.

UNO, Publications, Methods of Measuring Internal Migration Manual-VI.

26

INDIAN AGRICULTURE POLICY AND PERFORMANCE–EMPLOYMENT GENERATION

P. Y. Sastry
V. Jaya

20TH CENTURY AGRICULTURE SCENARIO

Since Independence, India has preferred the "sustenance growth policy." Policy planners have quantified major chunk of planning funds to agricultural infrastructure, like irrigation projects, command area development, with hefty input and output subsidies. The grand "green revolution" has brought sea change in the rural areas. It has created huge Govt. sponsored agriculture markets and interactions of markets with farmers have churned huge agricultural wealth, in terms of food grain production, like wheat and paddy. Agricultural subsidy charts and performance results became political handouts gradually and political parties have carved out niche areas and preferred agricultural constituents to contest elections on brand equity "Agricultural bias". The market cost of' water projects and transfer price mechanism' has resulted in negative growth in agriculture and contribution of very paltry amount to GDP growth. The rent seeking behavior of progressive farmers and subsidy outlay have made agriculture business more profitable than staying behind the plough.

Agricultural production at village level became more unorganized and ad hoc. Basket of fruits of green revolution has been hijacked by higher profile farmers. This has resulted in birth of militancy outfits and social tensions at village level.

There is huge migration of labor from rural areas to urban areas- rural push and urban pull" became fixed feeling and there is huge development of under employment in agriculture. Added to this the core farming community at village level gone to high value ventures, hoteling, contracting and other 'quick kill' profit enterprises thereby the capital resources starving agriculture infra structural facilities still dwindled.

Due to division of land holdings and fragmented house hold land holdings became 'so micro' that it resulted in negative growth of agriculture. Statistic reveal the at cost benefit analyses speaks of the fact that it costs Rs. 50,000/-per hector to provide water, which is turned as "blue gold" in modern contest.

The social scenario at village level became hard nut to crack and become complicated due to non breaking of cast occupation correlation.

The critical term land reforms is directly associated with agrarian structure of India which includes institutional frame work, distribution of land ownership, farm of land tenure and pattern of agricultural employment. If we say that Indian agrarian structure is not conductive to high agricultural production, it means that all above indications are not well placed according to desired state of affaires. The distribution of land ownership is quite a complicated phenomenon. It refers to property rights, private or public or cooperative owner ship. The nexus between the ownership of land and other means of production, output, income and social economic power became unconcerned and unaddressed in policy matrix. Thus employment generation in agricultural sector became thin and feather weight. The VI five year plan (1981-85) has mentioned the objectives of land reforms as follows;-

1. Abolition of intermediary tenancies.
2. Tenancy reforms comprising regulating of rent, security tenure and confinement of ownership rights on tenants.
3 Ceiling of land holdings and distribution of surplus lands.
4. Consolidation of holdings and completion of updating of land records.

None of the above reforms became a starter. Thus the land reforms appear to have two main objectives. Firstly to remove such impediments to quick start agricultural production and secondly to eliminate exploitative elements from the agricultural society. Wrapped and distorted development in agriculture is the worst hit when it recorded .07 rural employments in 1990.

21st CENTURY AGRICULTURE AND POLICY CHANGES

21st century is witnessing sea changes in agricultural policy and agriculture is included in W.T.O. discipline. The major policy change in agriculture is movement of agriculture from subsistence to commercial activity. The new concept of global village became buzz word. The marketing of goods and services world wide rationalization of world natural resources is the key objective of W.T.O. The era of mass production came to an end. The diversification of high value agricultural and allied activities are inevitable for the process and food industry of rural India. The modernization of agriculture requires huge capitalization of billion dollars and technical requirement. Hence private partnership route to building huge infrastructure become inevitable path. 21st century agriculture is employment centric and village economy will be come vibrant and progressive creating employment for around 70% of rural population.

Indian agriculture is coming free of the traditional markets, with the space of credit to farmers' involvement of corporate sector and further commodity exchanges. Indian agriculture is once again on the threshold of vast chance that could transform the nature of the agricultural operations in the decade. The change should be of no comparison to that of "Green Revolution" of 1970. The suitable change of technology break thru should be for seed quality and other important modernization.

The capital formation now in agriculture should be augmented through foreign direct investment. Marketing regulation should be changed from food grains to fruits and vegetables, if the actual rate should rise 4%. The restructure of agriculture should be given priority in spite of political divergent views. Corporate participation should strike balance with free market production and high value advance. Commission agents and rent rules should be removed.

The small holding and ineffective cooperative system of farming miserably failed. The consolidation of land holdings in corporate sector will utilize the available rural human capital into productive asset by providing employment through out the year cycle with diversification of crop pattern as per demand and supply in the world market.

PART – III

MEASUREMENT AND REMEDIES OF UNEMPLOYMENT

27

EMPLOYMENT POLICY IN A LABOUR SURPLUS ECONOMY

N. Sudhakara Rao
R. Nagi Reddy

INTRODUCTION

In most parts of world the level of unemployment and under employment remains high and India is no exception. Population explosion, growth of labour force, under-employment, illiteracy, unskilled persons, globalization of world economy are some of the concerns before us. The level and quality of skills of a nation are becoming critical factors in taking advantage of the opportunities thrown open by the rapid technological changes and more open economy. Rapid globalization and fast-paced technological progress also pose new challenges. The increased competition and economic change that result from the combined forces of global economic integration and technological advance can cause instability and difficulties in maintaining the employability of large segments of a country's labour force. At the same time, the new economic forces provide, new opportunities for economic growth and expansion of employment. A country's economic performance depends critically on access to and the adoption of new technology and improving the skills of labour force.

Employment– Unemployment is a hotly debated subject among academicians, government circles as this is viewed as one of the important indexes of ultimate success or otherwise of public policies. This aspect is of great concern for the public at large because standard of living, disposable income, savings, education, health and overall psyche of the people is determined by current levels of employment and unemployment.

Generation of gainful employment both skilled and unskilled has been one of the important target areas vigorously pursued under the planning process both by central/state governments. The gap between the job seekers and avenues of employment remained an unbridgeable gap.

The whole population of a country can be divided into economically active and inactive population. The economically active population is sometimes[1] regarded as the labour force or the working population in the age group 15-60 years. The activity rate of population is the proportion which is economically active. A part of the labour force may remain under employed which is below the full employment level. Under employment is a conspicuous problem in developing countries particularly in the agricultural sector. It may be open or hidden. It is caused by many factors such as dualism high-man land ratio, lack of alternative openings, high rate of growth of population, fixed supply of land and so on. In developing countries the activity rate is low, where as in developed countries the activity rate is quite high.

EMPLOYMENT AND UNEMPLOYMENT SCENARIO

The global employment and unemployment situation according to the World Employment Report 1998-99 shows that out of an estimated 6 billion population in the year 1997 around 3 billion was in the labour force. 160 million persons have been estimated to be fully unemployed. 25 to 30 percent of the employed labour force is under employed. A large number of young people in the age group of 15 and 24 (around

60 million in 1997) are continuously in search of work. Unemployed.

Basically India's unemployment is structural nature. The rate of increase in job opportunities is below the rate of increase in labour force. Structural unemployment is chronic in nature and can be removed by changing the socio-economic structure through economic development. The five year plans have failed to achieve the objectives of full employment and failed to absorb the net addition to labour force and have added to growing back log of unemployment. Employment objectives and growth objectives are not mutually consistent, in the developing economies.

Table1
Estimates of Population, Labour Force, Employment and Unemployment

(in million)

	1983	*1988*	*1994*	*1999-2000*
Estimated population	718.21	790.00	895.05	1004.10
			(2.12)	(1.93)
Labour Force	308.64	333.49	391.94	406.05
			(2.05)	(1.03)
Employed	302.75	324.29	374.45	397.00
			(2.04)	(0.98)
Unemployed	5.89	9.2	7.49	9.05
			(—)	(—)
Unemployment rate (as percentage of labour force)	1.91	2.76	1.96	2.23
			(—)	(—)
Employment in organized sector	24.01	25.71	27.37	28.11
			(1.20)	(0.53)
Employment in unorganized sector	278.74	298.58	347.08	368.89
			(—)	(—)
GDP Growth	7.7	3.8	5.9	6.4

Note:

1. Employment, Unemployment, Unemployment rate and Labour force are on usual status basis and based on estimates given in various rounds of NSSO
2. Population estimates are as per protection made by expert Committee on Population projection.
3. Organized sector employment are on the basis of data collected by DET & T.
4. GDP growth rates from Central Statistical Organization.

As per the results of the National Sample Survey conducted in 1999-2000, total work force as on 1.1.2000, as per Usual Status approach (considering both principal and subsidiary activities) was of the order of 406 million. About 7 per cent of the total work force is employed in the formal or organised sector (all public sector establishments and all non-agricultural establishments in private sector with 10 or more workers) while remaining 93 per cent work in the informal or unorganised sector. An overwhelming proportion of the increase in the labour force will have to be adjusted in the unorganised sector. About 369 million workers are placed today in unorganised/ informal sector in India; agriculture workers account for the majority of this work force.

The rate of growth of employment declined sharply from 2.04 per cent per year in the period 1983-94 to only 0.9 per cent per year in the period 19994 to 2000. There was sharp deceleration in the growth of labour force from 2.05 per cent during the same year. Growth rate of employment is less than the growth rate of the labour force indicating an increase in the unemployment rate. The open unemployment which is of the order of 9 million is not significant compared to the size of the population in the country. Though, open unemployment is only 2.23 per cent (9 million), the percentage of the population below the poverty line is as high as 26.1 per cent.

Organised sector employment is not growing and its share is only 7 per cent of the total employment. There was decline in self-employment whereas regular salaried and casual employment showed an increasing trend during 1993-94 to 1999-2000. There was substantial increase in the average daily wage earnings in the rural areas. 7 per cent of the total employed are in the organised sector i.e., unorganised sector dominates in the employment scenario. Additional employment generation in the organised sector is not significant i.e., scope for additional wage employment in the organised sector continued to be less. Significant employment generation took place in the tertiary sector particularly in services industries. Substantial employment growth was observed in the small and unorganised sector, i.e., in small and tiny enterprises. Self-employment and casual labour continued to play a pivotal role in rehabilitation of the unemployed.

Little Growth in the organised sector employment has been noticed in the private sector. Public sector has shown a negative growth. Share of public sector in the overall organised sector employment being around 3/4th the increase in private sector employment cannot change the organised sector scenario. Organised sector employment has not improved in spite of various policy incentives through plan exercises, globalization and economic liberalization. Growth of informal sector has been primarily on account of necessity. Market being too much competitive in view of globalization and economic liberalization, marketing of product by small enterprise may be difficult.

Over two-fifths of the population (43 per cent) in rural areas–and more than one-third (36 per cent) in urban areas–were in the employed category as per their usual status. The worker population ratio (WPR) according to the usual status (principal and subsidiary status taken together) differed between males and females in both rural and urban areas. In rural areas, the rates were 55 and 31 per cent for males and females, respectively. In urban areas, the corresponding rates are 55 and 14 per cent, respectively. Both for males and females, the unemployment rates were appreciably higher in urban areas than in the rural areas. In rural India, according to the usual status, about 68 per cent of the male workers and 84 per cent of the female workers were engaged in agricultural activities. In urban India, about 60 per cent of the male workers and about 46 per cent of the female workers were engaged in the tertiary sector activities as per the usual status? The proportion of usually employed who reported themselves as not employed as per current weekly status was higher for females than for males. For females, it was 24 per cent in the rural areas and 20 per cent in the urban areas.

Beginning from the first round (1950-51) of the National Sample Survey (NSS), data on household consumer expenditure were collected in every round up to the 28th

(1973-74). After the 26th round of the survey "quinquennial" surveys on consumer expenditure and employment were conducted in the 27th, 32nd, 38th, 43rd, 50th and 55th rounds of NSS, at roughly 5-year intervals. The approaches are: (i) *usual status* approach with a reference period of 365 days preceding the date of the interview; and (ii) *current weekly status* approach with a reference period of 7 days preceding the date of the interview. The activities pursued by a person are grouped into three broad categories: (i) working or employed, (ii) seeking or available for work, i.e., unemployed, and (iii) not in labour force.

The unemployment rate went up between 1993-94 to 2004. On the basis of current daily status (unemployed on an average in the reference week), during the reference period, unemployment rate for males increased from 5.6 per cent to 9.0 per cent in rural areas, and from 6.7 per cent to 8.1 per cent in urban areas. Similarly, unemployment rate for females increased from 5.6 per cent in 1993-94 to 9.3 per cent in 2004 in rural areas and from 10.5 per cent to 11.7 per cent in urban areas. Furthermore, unemployment rates on the basis of current daily status were much higher than those on the basis of usual status (unemployed on an average in the reference year) implying a high degree of intermittent unemployment. This could be mainly because of the absence of regular employment for many workers. Urban unemployment rates (current daily status) were higher than rural unemployment rates for both males and females in 1993-94. However, in 2004, a rural unemployment rate for males was higher than that of urban males. Unemployment rates varied sharply across States. States, where wages are higher than in neighboring ones because of strong bargains or social security provisions, such as high minimum wage, had high incidence of unemployment, in general.

The results of the 60th round NSSO Survey on Employment and Unemployment situation conducted during January–June 2004 shows that the unemployment rate, based on the current daily status, in 2004, for males at 9.0 per cent (up from 5.6 per cent in 1993-94) in rural areas and at 8.1 per cent (up from 6.7

per cent in 1993-94) in urban areas. The corresponding figures for females were 9.3 per cent (up from 5.6 per cent) in rural areas and 11.7 per cent (up from 10.5 per cent) in urban areas. The survey results show how the annual growth rate of employment, which had declined from 2.1 per cent during 1983-1994 to 1.6 per cent during 1993-2000, went up to 2.5 per cent during 1999-2005. . While employment has grown faster than before, with the demographic dynamics and higher labour force participation, rate of unemployment (as measured by 'usual principal statuses) also went up marginally from 2.8 per cent to 3.1 per cent during 1999-2000 to 2004-05. Slowing down of the growth of agriculture could be one of the main reasons for the growth in the unemployment rate. There is an overall rise in rural unemployment, in terms of both total and partial failure to find work during the reference week, between the 55th (1999-2000) and 61st (2004-05) round employment surveys of the National Sample Survey. This is the worrisome marginal decline in employment in the organised sector between 1994 and 2004, according to the Annual Survey of Industry data.

As per estimates of the National Sample Survey Organisation, there were about 90 lakh people totally unemployed in 1999-2000, out of which about 55 lakh were educated with secondary and higher education levels. Compared to the size of the population, these numbers appear small. What is serious is the large number of employed persons working with low levels of productivity and income. Out of an estimated 397 million employed, about 122 million are poor, i.e. living below the poverty line. The main reasons for such a situation include inadequate growth of the economy, power productivity and labour force being in adequately skilled and growth rate of labour force being higher than the growth rate of employment etc.

Scheduled tribes face the highest incremental unemployment, which remains un-changed into the 61st round. This is an important pointer to the required regional configuration of workfare programmes like the National Rural Employment Guarantee Scheme, and for the spread of rural schools.[2]

As per NSS 61 round during Jan-June 2004 (Usual Status basis)]. Total Labour Force 5.8 Crore, total Employment 44.7 Crore, Total Number of open unemployment, 1.06 Crore Employment in organized sector, 2.64 Crore, Employment in Unorganized Sector, 42.10 Crore, No. of job seekers with Employment Exchanges 4.03 Crore, (as on 31.12.2005), 71 per cent of the job seekers registered with the Employment Exchanges are less than 29 years of age during 2003. Educated (X Standard and above) job seekers constitute about 75 per cent of the total job seekers registered with the employment exchanges during 2003. Most of the job seekers (about 80 per cent) in employment exchange are without any professional skill.

According to the usual principal and subsidiary statuses taken together (called 'all' usual status), nearly 44 (37) percent of the rural (urban) persons were in the labour force. The corresponding percentages for males (females) were 55 (32) in rural areas and 56 (16) in urban areas. In the usually employed ('all' workers) category, 57 per cent among males and nearly 62 per cent among females were self-employed. The corresponding proportions in urban India were 44 per cent for males and 45 per cent for females. In the rural areas, about 66 per cent of usually employed males and 84 per cent of usually employed females were engaged in the agricultural sector. In urban India, the tertiary sector engaged 59 per cent of male workers while secondary sector accounted for 35 per cent of the usually employed males. For females, the corresponding proportions were lower at 53 and 31 per cent.

DETERMINANTS

There are many determinants of economically active population in a country. These determinants are mainly social and economic i.e size of population, age structure, the health of the population, the skill and education.

From time to time economists have formulated models for the determination of wage and employment. The classical economists postulated that there is always full employment. According to them only voluntary and frictional unemployment exists. The general employment is impossible in the long run. If there is a tendency towards unemployment it can be corrected by wage-price flexibility. During the period of unemployment the wage level would be reduced and more labour would be demanded so that unemployment can be eliminated. This is also substantiated by Says' Law of Market i.e supply creates own demand. During the Great Depression of 1930's the classical theory of employment proved to be unworkable. During this period there arose unemployment and over-all dispersion in the market which reduces not only employment but also income and output. To explain this one theory which is micro based was provided by Joan Robinson of England. Another version of it was provided by Edward H. Chamberlain of the US. They felt unemployment was mainly due to market failures and called for Government intervention for increasing income, output and employment.

Later J.M. Keyens (1936) in his famous book General Theory of Employment, Interest explained that there is nothing which will guarantee automatic full employment and unemployment exists due to a gap in aggregate production function. It can be eliminated only by increasing aggregate income. If there is unemployment or under employment there must be an increase in the aggregate total demand through which direct increase in Government expenditure is needed. But this model is not fully applicable to the Third World Countries and works out only for the free market capitalistic economy, where there are no institutional or structural rigidities. In many developing countries the main obstacles for higher employment is not the lack of demand but lack of supply of complimentary factors. They have different types of rigidities and inelasticities in developing economies. Shortage of capital, storage of raw materials, shortages of high quality manpower, shortages of intermediate products and so on. Credit markets and transport and communication also play a crucial role. High dependency on capital and equipments for foreign exchange and also technology is another cause. They are handicapped by shortage of resources. Under these circumstances an increase in aggregate demand will lead to inflation. Unemployment is caused not lack of aggregate demand but lack of complementary resources and deficit finances which is inflationary.

In the developing countries by following the Keynesian model of employment, attempts were made to increase employment by increasing the rate of capital formation and GNP. The theoretical tool used was the Harrod–Domar model. In this model economic growth is the result of the rate of saving the resultant physical capital accumulation on the one hand and capital output ratio another. Employment creation always lagged behind rate of growth of output leading a conflict between employment and output. In many developing countries output growth and employment growth do not increase in the same proportion. They are conflict in nature. In many cases output growth has failed to generate corresponding growth in employment. The Harrod-Domar model shows that higher capital labour ratios will generate more saving, more profit and the higher rate of growth. According to neo classical model of growth, the optimal savings rate which leads to maximum output growth can be generated only by capital intensive technique of production. The substitution of more capital for labour is bound to display labour and create unemployment. The introduction of machinery may be labour saving in character. More substitution of capital for labour is not desirable for a labour surplus economy such as India. In these countries more and more labour intensive method of production has to be introduced for maximization of employment creation. In recent years people argue in favor of employment growth objective, because this is capable of reducing poverty by increasing income. The strategy which accelerates employment can also accelerate economic progress[3]. In order to achieve the objectives of income growth and employment growth at the same time, a complementary policy of removing factor price distortions and promoting labour intensive technology will be essential[4]. In many developing countries capital intensive modern method of production is applied in firms and factories while labourers remain idle and unemployed.

The actual impact of the removal of factor price distortion on employment will depend on the degree to which labour can be substituted for capital in the production process in the Leduc's.

POLICY MEASURES

If we want to raise overall output and employment in the economy, the most effective means would be to raise the productivity of agriculture, since it represents a 'slack' in the economy. The key to employment planning in India can, therefore, be seen to lie in raising the productivity of the agricultural sector. Within agriculture, it is the sizeable but low productivity dry land segment which arguably represents a huge untapped potential for growth. The potential of dry lands can be tapped if we concentrate our investment in these areas on labour-intensive works which raise productivity through the process of environmental regeneration this could also go a long way towards making the overall growth path of the Indian economy both employment-oriented and sustainable in the long-run.

The approaches to tackling the task of unemployment have varied from time to time. In the initial years of planning reliance was placed primarily on the expectations of a rapid industrial development and control of population. These expectations did not materialize and it was observed that the rate of growth of employment was generally much lower than the GDP rate of growth of the economy. Seasons of severe drought and failure of monsoons exposed large sections of population to extensive deprivations. Successive plans, strategies, policies and programmes were, therefore, re-designed to bring about a special focus on employment generation as a specific objective. The seventies and eighties saw the emergence of special schemes like NREP, RLEGP to provide wage employment through public works programmes and schemes to promote self-employment and entrepreneurship through provision of assets, skills and other support to the unemployed and the poor. While employment levels expanded steadily during the seventies and eighties, the rate of growth of employment continued to lag behind that of the labour force. Unemployment among the educated showed a rising trend. Another feature of the employment situation is the sizeable proportion of the employed working at low levels of the productivity and income. The eighties exposed the weakness in the then ongoing strategies of expanding public sector irrespective of competition.

A large number of small and marginal farmers, operating very small, low-productivity holdings that cannot meet their livelihood needs, are forced to enter the labour market. So the productivity-enhancing and labour intensive works would make a three-fold contribution to employment generation: (*a*) by providing short-run ('revolving') employment; (*b*) by increasing the productive capacity of the economy, which would create demand for labour in the next round ('sedimented employment'); (*c*) by raising the ability of the land to sustain the household, which would reduce the dependence of these farmers on wage labour, thereby improving prospects of other workers in the labour market.

Planning in India focused at realizing a high rate of growth of output in the long term. The planning process made no attempt to define an independent employment strategy; the focus on economic growth was viewed as essential for improving the employment situation. Thus, in the Five Year Plans, the generation of employment was viewed as part of the process of development and not as a goal in conflict with, or to be pursued independently of economic development.

Appropriate Employment Strategy

The appropriate comprehensive employment strategy that can be followed by a labour surplus economy such as India is as follows:

1. It is necessary to expand labour intensive industries especially small scale industries and cottage industries. There is need to find out the appropriate labour intensive method of production. Public works programmes which are cost effective and which require low investment should be preferred.

2. There is a need to eliminate the factor price distortion by curtailing the growth rate of urban wages and also by eliminating the various types of capital subsidies.
3. It is necessary to create proper balance between the urban and rural sectors. Development of agricultural sector is necessary for the purpose of creation of additional employment opportunities and also to prevent unnecessary migration from rural sector to the urban areas.
4. It is necessary to control the haphazard growth of our education system particularly the higher education. This will help to reduce unemployment among the educated persons.
5. The industrial sector can create more jobs by fully utilizing the installed capacity, by changing the product mix, by giving more emphasis on the labour intensive method of production and by involving more suitable intermediate technology. The intermediate technology can be more appropriate for the developing countries such as India
6. The service sector has to observe the growing labour force in developing countries and it is more suitable for additional employment creation since it requires less of capital and more labour intensive and skill requirement is moderate[5].

Skill Development Programmes

Skills and knowledge are the driving forces of economic growth and social development of any country. The economy becomes more productive, innovative and competitive through the existence of more skilled human potential. The level of employment, its composition and the growth in employment opportunities are the critical indicator of the process of development in any economy. Increasing pace of globalization and technological changes provide both challenges and growing opportunities for economic expansion and job creation. In taking advantage of these opportunities as well as in minimizing the social costs and dislocation, which the transition to a more open economy entails, the level and quality of skills that a nation possess are becoming critical factors. Countries with higher and better levels of skills adjust more effectively to the challenges and opportunities of globalization.

Directorate General of Employment and Training (DGE and T) in Ministry of Labour is an apex organization for development and coordination of the vocational training including Women's Vocational Training to the employable youth in the country and to provide skill manpower to the industry besides providing Employment Services.

Anti-poverty strategy comprises of a wide range of poverty alleviation and employment generation programmes, many of which have been in operation for several years and have been strengthened to generate more employment, create productive assets, impart technical and entrepreneurial skills and raise the income level of the poor. Under these schemes, both wage employment and self-employment are provided to the people below the poverty line. In 1998-99, various poverty alleviation and employment generation programmes are grouped under two broad categories of Self-Employment Schemes and Wage Employment Schemes.

Timely Investment in skill development and training at enhanced level. Enhancement of education and skill level of workers Responsive training system. Need for effective partnership of all stake holders.

RECENT POLICY RECOMMENDATIONS

Considering the problems of employment and unemployment situation in the country Planning Commission set up a Task Force under the chairmanship of Dr. M.S. Ahluwalia to go into the details of the employment generation taking place in the economy and suggest measures for creation of 100 million jobs (10 million per year) in a period of 10 years.

The Task Force has recommended intervention in five major areas as under:

1. Accelerating the rate of growth of GDP, with a particular emphasis on sectors likely to ensure the

spread of income to the lower income segments of the labour force.

2. Pursuing appropriate sectoral policies in individual sector, which are particularly important for employment generation. These sector level policies must be broadly consistent with the overall objective of accelerating GDP growth.
3. Implementing focused special programmes for creating additional employment of enhancing income generation from existing activities aimed at helping vulnerable groups that may not be sufficiently benefited by the more general growth promoting policies. Pursuing suitable policies for education and skill development, which would upgrade the quality of the labour force and make it capable of supporting a growth process which generates high quality jobs.
4. Ensuring that the policy and legal environment governing the labour market encourages labour absorption, especially in the organized sector.

REFERENCES

Raj Krishna "Unemployment in India", Economic and Political Weekly, 3 March 1973, reprinted in V. Krishna (ed.), Raj Krishna; Selected Writings, Oxford University Press, New Delhi, 1995.

A. Vaidyanathan, 'Employment in India, 1977-78 to 1999-2000; Characteristics and Trends', Journal of Indian School of Political Economy, April–June 2001, Table 19.

S. Mahendra Dev and Ajit K. Ranade, 'Employment Guarantee Scheme and Employment Security', in S. Mahendra Dev, Piyush Antony and V. Gayathri (eds), Social and Economic Security in India, Institute for Human Development, New Delhi, 2003; and S. Mahendra Dev, 'Rural Public Works', in K. Seeta Prabhu and R. Sudarshan (eds), Reforming India's Social Sector–Poverty, Nutrition, Health and Education, UNDP, New Delhi, 2003.

FOOTNOTES

1. J.J. Clark (1972), Population Geography, Pergamon Press.
2. *Abhiroop Mukhopadhyay , Indira Rajaraman, Rural Unemployment 1999-2005: Who Gained, Who Lost?* Issue : VOL 42 No. 30 July 28 - August 03, 2007

3. P. Streeten and F. Stewart, (1971) , "Conflicts between Output and Employment Objectives in Developing Countries", Oxford Economic Papers, July, PP. 145-168
4. M.P. Todaro, (1981), Economic Development in the Third World, Long man, New York, P. 219
5. E.O. Edwards (ed), (1974), Employment in Developing Nations, New York, pp. 1-46

28

ISSUES RELATING TO MEASUREMENT OF UNEMPLOYMENT

M. Sundara Rao
M. Sankara Reddy

The unemployed are those who are looking to work or are willing to work but cannot find it at the going wage. This notion of unemployment is motivated by the neoclassical conception of the labour market where wages clear the market and the failure to get work is voluntary. Deviations from this ideal are measured by the above definition of involuntary unemployment. Other definitions have also been used. The influential two sector development models (Lewis, 1954, Rannis and Fei, 1964) theorized non neoclassical labour markets in the sectors dominated by subsistence family enterprise (such as agriculture). As output was shared among the family members, the family enterprise aimed to produce as much as possible without regard to the marginal productivity of labour. This led to the concepts of 'labour surplus' and 'disguised unemployment' both of which referred to people who were employed with low productivity in the subsistence sector and could therefore be transferred to the modern high productivity sector without output loss in the subsistence sector. The early literature on unemployment in India attempted to measure such unemployment through measures that were defined with respect to low productivity or low incomes. However, they suffered from inconsistencies and were hard to implement operationally as well (Krishna, 1976). Unemployment is measured through labour force surveys which elicit the activity' status of the respondent for a given reference period. First, the respondent is identified as not working. Second, for those not working, the typical question is of the form: are you available for work, and have you made some effort to find work during the last *x* days. Those who answer in the affirmative are the unemployed while those who answer in the negative are the people who have opted out of the labour force. The labour force is the negative are the people who have opted out of the labour force. The labour force is the to four weeks to a year. Such an approach works well when the activity status is invariant within the reference period, i.e., either the person is employed, unemployed or out of the labour force. But what if an individual is unemployed for part of the reference period and is either employed or out of the labour force for the remainder?

DIFFERENT MEASURES OF UNEMPLOYMENT

In India, employment-unemployment surveys are conducted by the National Sample Survey (NSS) Organization. Beginning with the 27th round in 1972/73, labour force surveys have been conducted every five years using standardized concepts and procedures based on the recommendations of the Committee of Experts (Planning Commission, 1970). The usual status unemployment measure is defined with respect to a reference period of a year. The multiple activity status issue, which is more acute longer the reference period, is resolved on the basis of majority time. This criterion is used first to classify a person as either belonging to the labour force (i.e., employed or unemployed) or not belonging to the labour force. If the person belongs to the labour force, then whether the person is to be classified as employed or unemployed is decided once again on majority time. The survey also uses a reference period of a week to compute a 'weekly' status unemployment measure. Here a person is regarded as employed if she or he worked for at least one hour during the reference week. It follows that a person is unemployed if she or he did not work for even one hour during the reference week and sought work or was available for work during the reference week.

Clearly, the usual status measure reflects only long unemployment spells. For instance, a male in the working age group would be unemployed on the usual status measure only if the unemployed spell during the year is longer than the employed period. While, the weekly status measure captures short unemployment periods, it ignores unemployment for less than a week. A third approach is to abandon the effort to assign every individual a unique activity status over the reference period. The NSS employment survey elicits an individual's time disposition during each day of the reference week. A day is split into two half-units and an individual is assigned a unique activity status for that period. This information can be used to compute person days of unemployment in the economy. As households are surveyed uniformly throughout the year, the aggregates derived from weekly data are representative of annual aggregates. The daily status rate of unemployment is the proportion of labour force that is unemployed. Individuals with regular wage employment constitute only 14% of the work force. More than half of the work force is self-employed (53%), the great majority of them in agriculture and about one-third are casual wage workers (Pappola, 2006). Furthermore, over 80% of female workers in unorganized manufacturing work out of their homes mostly in sub-contracting relationships where the intermediary supplies raw material and buys back their output (Unni and Rani, 2005). For most of the labour force, therefore, work is seasonal, short-term and without tenure. Consequently, an individual's activity status can vary even within as short of a reference period as a week. The daily status unemployment rate would therefore seem the appropriate one for capturing their unemployment and the related data is presented in the following Table 1.

Table 1
Multiple Activities in the Rural Sector and Percentage of Individuals who had Some Unemployment

Period of Unemployment	*Rural*	*Rural Labor Households*
< = ½ Week	50	55
< = Full Week	67	73
> = Full Week	33	27

The Table shows a clear and stable ordering among these unemployment rates . Between 2004-2005 and 2005-2006, daily status unemployment rates are the highest (between 6-8%), usual status rates are lowest (3-4%) and weekly rates are in between (4-5%). The data imply that while few are unemployed all through the year, unemployment spells are not uncommon. As the daily status measure is the only one that is immune to multiple activity status, it is widely agreed to be the most accurate measure of unemployment (Planning Commission, 2001; 2002). For instance in the rural sector, among those who reported some unemployment during the reference week, 67% reported a spell of less than a whole week and 50% a spell of less than ½ a week (Table 1). Among rural labor households, 73% of those who experience some unemployment report spell of less than a whole week and 55% report spell of less than ½ a week. None of these would be counted as unemployed even under the weekly status. Therefore, from the point of view of designing poverty alleviation programs that target the unemployed, the daily status measure would seem to provide the best estimate of unemployment, since it is the poor who are likely to experience short spells of unemployment rather than the non poor who can afford to stay unemployed longer. The rest of this article will restrict its attention to daily status rates. Table 2 presents the All India Unemployment Rate 2003–2006.

The data presented in the above Table also broken down by gender and by location (rural/urban). Two robust facts emerge from the tabulation. Unemployment rates in the urban sector are higher than in the rural sector. While urban rates are in the range 8-9.5%, rural rates are about one percentage point lower fluctuating in the range 7-8%. The second feature is that female unemployment rates are markedly higher than that for males in urban areas while they match that for males in the rural sector. Urban female unemployment rates have ranged between 9.5-11% as compared to the 7-9% range for males. In the rural sector, while the unemployment rate for women in 1983 was higher than that of males by more than one percentage point, the rates became similar in later years.

Table 2
All India Unemployment Rates 2003–2006 (%)

	2003-2004		*2004-2005*		*2005-2006*	
Gender	*Rural*	*Urban*	*Rural*	*Urban*	*Rural*	*Urban*
Male	7.09	7.45	5.64	6.72	7.51	9.22
Female	7.03	9.42	5.55	10.52	8.98	11.01
All	7.08	7.79	5.61	7.43	7.93	9.53

While there is not much variation in the unemployment rate across sectors in 2003-2004, there is considerable variation across states. Gujarat, Haryana, Karnataka, Madhya Pradesh, Punjab, Rajasthan and Uttar Pradesh have unemployment rates much lower than the national average, ranging 4% to 6%. Andhra Pradesh, Assam, Bihar, Maharastra and Orissa have unemployment that is close to the national average. Finally, Kerala, Tamilnadu and West Bengal have rates far in excess of the national average with unemployment in Kerala being greater than 20%. These high unemployment rates pose a challenge to the understanding of labour markets. Why do wages not fall in the face of such unemployment. A generic explanation is the efficiency wage theory according to which wages higher than market clearing levels can be sustained if they elicit more effort from the employed. Other explanations have been offered in terms of societal norms and the workings of particular institutions such as trade unions and government laws on minimum wages. The latter set of factors would seem to be relevant for employment in the organised sector. But what about the labour force that does not have these protection and will they have low unemployment rates. It is often asserted that the poor cannot afford to remain unemployed. This is not borne out by the data, however. Table 3 presents the daily status unemployment rates in 2003-2004 for poor households and for labour households.

Table 3
Unemployment Among the Poor 2003–2006

Unemployment Among the Poor	*Rural*	*Urban*
Poor Households	9.19	9.38
Labour Households	11.74	11.61

From the Table it can be noticed that poor households are those with monthly per capita expenditures less than the official poverty line. Labour households are those that obtain their major source of income from agricultural labour and other manual work in rural areas and from casual labour activities in urban areas. There is a large overlap between the poor and labour households. While 55% of poor households are rural labour households, only about 39% of rural labor households are poor. However, if we look at the average consumption expenditure of rural labour households, 75% have expenditures which are less than 1.5 times the rural poverty line and 90% have per capita expenditures less than twice the poverty line. The figures are similar for casual labour households in the urban sector. Table 3 shows significant unemployment among poor and labour households with rates approaching 12% for labour households in both urban and rural areas. These rates are higher than for the overall population (in Table 2). As the NSS surveys households throughout the year, we can also compute the distribution of the unemployment rate across different quarters for rural and casual labour households (Table 4).

The data presented in the above Table shows that, there is no particular seasonal pattern in the urban sector, while rural unemployment displays clear seasonality. The unemployment rate at 15% is highest in the monsoon months from July to September when not much work can be done in the fields. The data relating to unemployment across 15 major states during the period 2003-06 are presented in the following Table 5.

Table 4
Seasonality in Unemployment 2003–2006

Seasonality of Unemployment	*Rural Labour Households*	*Urban Casual Labour Households*
July–September	14.95	12.10
October–December	10.10	10.70
January–March	10.64	10.79
April–June	11.20	13.02

Table 5
Unemployment Across 15 Major States 2003–2006

Seasonality of Unemployment	*Rural Labour Households*	*Urban Casual Labour Households*
Andhra Pradesh	12.81	11.88
Assam	5.20	6.25
Bihar	9.09	8.58
Gujarat	8.76	7.05
Haryana	11.79	5.99
Karnataka	7.63	8.12
Kerala	26.30	25.74
Madhya Pradesh	6.39	8.52
Maharashtra	10.27	11.46
Orissa	8.34	5.18
Punjab	5.66	5.38
Rajasthan	4.99	5.63
Tamilnadu	18.90	20.28
Uttar Pradesh	8.58	7.91
West Bengal	24.94	12.02

It is indicated through the above Table that agriculture driven seasonality is part of the explanation for high unemployment rates among rural labour households, it cannot be the complete story as the unemployment in the busy kharif period (October to December) is as high as 10%. The overall all India picture masks significant inter-state variation in the incidence of unemployment among labour households. Kerala, Tamil Nadu and West Bengal are striking for unemployment rates of 20% and more. Bivariate associations (not reported here) do not suggest any systematic relationship between real wages and the level of unemployment. A satisfactory theory of labour markets in India will have to reckon with persistent short-term unemployment among the poor.

REFERENCES

Krishna, Raj (1976), "Rural Unemployment–A Survey of Concepts and Estimates for India", Centre of Development Studies, Trivandrum, Reprinted in Raj Krishna: Selected Writings, Ed. V. Krishna (1995): Oxford University Press, Delhi.

Lewis, W. Arthur (1954), "Economic Development with Unlimited Supplies of Labor." Manchester School of Economic and Social Studies 22: 139-91.

Pappola, T. S. (2006), "Employment Trends in India", this volume Planning Commission (1970), Report of the Committee of Experts on Unemployment Estimates, New Delhi: Government of India.

Planning Commission (2001), Report of the Task Force on Employment Opportunities, New Delhi: Government of India.

Planning Commission (2002), Report of the Special Group on Targeting Ten Million Employment Opportunities per year over the Tenth Plan Period, New Delhi: Government of India.

29

WHAT'S DRIVING MIGRATION

M. Lakshmi Narasaiah

The scale and diversity pf today's migrations are beyond any previous experience. Rapid urban growth and environmental degradation in rural areas have led to internal migration affecting hundreds of millions of people. Migration is now seen as a priority issue equal in political weight to other major global challenges such as the environment, population growth and economic imbalances between regions.

Families and households form the basis for economic growth, social development and personal fulfillment. Decisions, by individual women and men on marriage, family, a place to live, shape the destinies of communities and nations. National policies and international conditions provide the context for individual decision-making. Effective development policies, including population, reproduction health and family planning policies, address this reality.

Data on national and global population trends set the agenda for national policy. An important element of population programmes is gathering data that will allow policy-making responsive to the realities of daily life, and to the needs and aspirations of individuals. The dominant feature of global demographics Is still growth. Age distribution is a growing concern, as the numbers of young and elderly people, grow, relative to the working- age population. The world is growing steadily more urban. From being a sign of strength and dynamism in the national economy, the rate and scale of urban growth has become increasingly a cause for concern. The influx of migrants to the biggest cities may be weakening both urban and rural sectors.

International migration is small in extent compared with internal movements' but has a disproportionate impact. Both internal and International migration are driven by population growth, and any inequities between countries. Migration is one of the choices which shape people's lives and the destiny of nations. But it can also be a symptom of inequity and underdevelopment. Migrants are by definition the most vulnerable members of a host community. Their living and working conditions should be protected. Open and frank exchange of information and views between host and sending countries Is needed more than ever. The aim of the international community should be to protect the right to move, but to ensure that movement is voluntary and that it stimulates rather than holds back personal and national development. "The point of departure should be the human right to live and work where one pleases, so long as it does not infringe on other people's rights to do the same".

THE URBAN TRANSFORMATION

The rural sector is declining in Importance and its contribution to national economics. It is increasingly part of a unified economy based on the city. Contact with the urban areas is easier than ever and is encouraged by rural development,

Temporary and circular migration is giving way to more permanent settlement. The largest Cities are under increasing difficulties in improving or even maintaining living conditions. Nevertheless, migration continues, driven by a variety offered both positive and negative. The choice to move can be part of a strategy for survival or personal development ; but it is often enforced by external conditions.

The urban transformation is irreversible, but the rural, sectors must also be strengthened to balance the developing economy. Attention to gender issues will be crucial in ensuring a successful transition. The forces driving internal and international migration have much in common. Demographic pressures are contributing to both. As the pressures encouraging migration increase, the options for migrants become more limited. This collision is contributing to the atmosphere of crisis surrounding both urban and international migration.

COSTS AND BENEFITS

Migration is the result of Individual or family decisions. But it is also part of social- process. In economic terms, migration Is as much a global phenomenon as trade in commodities or manufactured goods. It is part of a. broader pattern, and evidence of changing economic, social and cultural relationships,

But migration may be evidence of a different kind of relationship: the combination of poverty, rapid population growth and environmental damage is a powerful destabilizing factor driving urban growth and eventually International migration. On the recipient side. Migration has usually been seen as evidence of a thriving economy: today's Industrial Mates were built In part by migrant labour, skills and investment. In today's increasingly uncertain conditions, migration may be seen as a threat to the security and well-being of the local workforce and society at large.

The only effective means to reduce migration pressures over the long term are to slow population growth; to stimulate economic growth and job creation at home, and promote the development of the individual and the family as the basic economic and social unit.

A QUESTION OF GENDER

It is often assumed that most migrants are men, In reality, women make up nearly half of the international migrant population. Gender differences in social and economic roles affect migration decision making, household strategy, and the sex composition of labour migration. Attention to the gender dimension of migratory movements ought to be an important component in population and development planning.

Women frequently take the initiative in migration decisions, which may reflect limited opportunity in rural areas. Low status limits women's choices at home and may increase pressure to migrate, but it may also affect life in the host community. Opportunities may be limited by lack of education or skills, or by customer limitation on women's freedom of action outside the family or ethnic group. Paid employment for migrant women is usually in the lowest wage. least secure, and lowest status Jobs, mostly in housework, child care and trade.

Most educated women end up In the same low-status, low-wage production and service jobs as unskilled female migrants. Men, too, experience downward mobility, but the contrast yes the decline In women's employment status is far greater. Despite these disadvantages women migrants have become significant economic actors. Their status may be improved by migration, but the advantages are not clear-cut. Women's status as migrants Is affected by their vulnerability, and by their lack of reproductive freedom. To ensure improved status they will need both legal protection and essential services, including reproductive health services.

REFUGEES

Refugees in the 1990s are overwhelmingly In Asia, Africa and Latin America. Their numbers are large, about 17 million, and growing rapidly. A further 3.5 to 4 million were thought to be in "refugee-like situations", though estimates are probably extremely conservative, and an estimated 23 million people Internally displaced.

It is important to recognize the common roots of refugee and other forms of mass movement of populations. At the same time, despite the difficulty of distinguishing between political and socio-economic causes of migration, there i3 a clear need to distinguish between refugees and other groups of migrants.

Participation in international efforts of burden-sharing would ensure that most refugee problems would be dealt with in their regions of origin.

CONCLUSIONS AND POLICIES

Migration highlights linkages and interdependencies within countries, with many implications for development agendas, including population programmes and development assistance. Policies to regulate or moderate international migration have concentrated largely on urban growth. They have been only intermittently effective. The most successful have concentrated on stimulating rural development and the growth of alternative urban centers,

Migration is also a personal or family decision, which is affected by external conditions such as poverty or environmental degradation, improving conditions of personal and family life can make a crucial difference in the decision to migrate, reducing dependence on migration as a strategy. Because migration is the result of personal and family decisions, it can be influenced by policies that improve the quality of life.

This offers that opportunity for policies emphasizing individual development, among them education, health (including reproductive health) and family planning. Such policies are particularly relevant to the Strategies must take into account gender differences in social and economic life and the differentia! effects of policies.

Migration decisions are about family security and long-term-life-chances, rather than simply the maximization of income. They are ultimately strategies designed to look after the individual's and the house-hold's needs, safeguard their security, and respond to their aspirations. If the goal is to reduce migration pressures through development it will be essential to increase the capacity but reduce the need to migrate. Long-term external support will be required to make such policies a reality, particularly in areas of rapid population growth and potential mass outward flows. Highly coordinated allocation of development assistance can help establish priorities and focus attention on basic needs. The challenge to both international donors and co-operating governments is to direct programme spending to the areas where it can be most effective.

30

RURAL PRIMARY SECTOR IS THE WAY TO REDUCE UNEMPLOYMENT IN INDIA

Chandraiah Miriyala
Suryanarayana Neduri

The massive poverty in most of the densely populated underdevelopment countries of the World has often been identified with the presence of massive unemployment and underemployment. In most cases agriculture predominates as an economic activity. As such, a study of the problem of unemployment in agriculture is of crucial importance.

Growth in forms of GNP has been remarkable in most of these countries over the decades. National income did in fact, grow by historical standards, exceptionally quickly much more quickly than they did in the now developed counties of a comparable stage of their development. Growth, however, has occurred mainly in the relatively small modern sectors of the economics while the traditional sectors, especial agriculture, fend to stagnate. Growth has benefited mainly those who are already relatively well-off while the vast majorities–the agriculture working force–suffer from abject poverty, unemployment. It is true that the above problems cannot be solved without rapid economic development but it is also true that GNP alone has proved to be an inadequate indicator of social progress. The major reason for the acute poverty of the vast majority is that they cannot find suitable work or can find work that yields only an extremely low income. By far, the most important single instrument in the policy basket for ensuring wide spread and equitable sharing in the fruit of economic growth must be an effective employment policy.

"The benefits of more employment where many people are in need of work are clear enough. Leaving aside the question of effects on output and growth more employment not only (i) can make for a more equitable distribution of income but in addition (ii) can satisfy the human needs for useful and creative activity (iii) can provide more people with opportunities for acquiring skills and the habit of work and thus participating in the tasks as well as the benefits of economic development, and (iv) for all reasons can contribute to a reduction of political and social tensions."

Employment therefore, has to take pride of place along side growth forgets as a major objective of economic and social development. This has resulted in an increasing interest in the problem of unemployment especially in Agriculture.

Over the last quarter of a century, a large number of growth models have been formalized on the assumption of surplus labour in traditional sectors and the savings potential inherent in it. Ragnar Nurkse, Arthur Lewis, Fei and Ranis in their illumination theses showed how the surplus labour in subsistence agriculture can help generating and accelerating economic development. This makes the study of unemployment in Agriculture more significant especially for countries looking for rapid economic development with few non- human resources but flooded with a vast sea of unutilized man power.

UNEMPLOYMENT AND UNDEREMPLOYMENT– RELEVANT CONCEPT

Emphasizing the need for a study is one thing and study itself is another. In the former, we had vertically no difficulty but we go deep into the study, we face innumerable difficulties. The first and for most being the problem of defining the relevant concepts. Proudly speaking the concepts of "unemployment" and "underemployment" have been built on a number of build–brocks concepts like 'labour force' 'man power' 'work force' 'participation rate' 'activity rutes' and a variety other almost synonymous concepts used in various estimates.

'Labour force' includes all persons classified economically active i.e., those who actually supply effort for the production of goods and services.

The term 'man power 'is same times used to refer to the potential labour force which would include both physically and mentally efficient persons.

'Working force' refers only to the employed labour force.

The terms participation rate and activity rate are synonymous. They refer to the ratio of persons in the labour force to the population.

Most of these concepts have been measured in various ways, in various estimates of unemployment and underemployment.

Unemployment has been defined as involuntary idleness due to lack of work. Unemployment refers to person belonging to the labour force, not doing any work during a specified period but seeking work. Underemployment can be considered an intermediate phase between employment and unemployment.

In the Agricultural sector the employment pattern is significantly influenced by the seasonality of prediction process. Seasonality arises from the problem of inelasticity of the time pattern of primary production. Few persons remain unemployment for a long time, whereas a most of cultivations remain unemployed at particular periods of the agricultural season.

Two important things emerged from the above discussion. In the agricultural sector, no sharp line of distinction can be drawn specifically between unemployment and underemployment.

Secondly, underemployment as it is manifested in various forms like low income, low productivity and lower utilization of available time.

MULTIPLE DIMENSIONS OF UNEMPLOYMENT AND UNDEREMPLOYMENT

Employment has many dimensions employment refers to the utilization of time which a labourer has at his disposal. It gives an income to the employed and yields an output and gives a person the realization of being engaged in something worth while. Four aspects of employment thus emerge:

1. Time aspect
2. Income aspect
3. Production aspect and
4. Recognition aspect. The same aspects can be applicable to unemployment also

Time aspect

Employment traditionally refers to time employed. Time unutilized is a great lists and this never be regained. It is unemployment. Every member of the labour force offers his time for creative employment on the basis of his wage, leisure preference and configuration. Depending on the demand conditions for labour, he gets employed for the whole day or remains under–employed with part time works or may remain totally unemployed as well.

Similarly, a person fully employed according to labour time utilization standard may at but consider himself under-employed but he cannot consider 'unemployed '. Thus, time aspect captures partially, the recognition aspect as well.

Income aspect

Employment generates income. When a labourer aspects employment he utilizes his labour time for wages, it being the primary consideration in taking up employment.

Keynes thought of paying wages for digging holes and filling them up in a situation of unemployment.

Production aspect

Most people do not work for the sake of working but, for the sake the fruit of their labour. Employment is commonly judged by "the fruit of action". Employment has to be productive and unemployment has no product. Productivity is the vital aspect for self-employment persons also. An individual was time employed, income employed, and production. These applicable to unemployment also.

Recognition Aspect

Employment can be a factor in self esteem and indeed in esteem by others.

In peasant economics most of the self-employed formers hardly recognize themselves to be unemployed. They may be working only for short hours, their income may be extremely poor and their productivity may be abnormally low, and this is to be said on the level of agricultural unemployment.

SURPLUS MANPOWER–ECONOMIC DEVELOPMENT

Over–crowded agriculture continues to be principal feature of an under–developed economy and the problem of surplus manpower in agriculture in under-developed world has been a matter of concern for economists is since long.

In the context of Indian agriculture this problem has been duly discussed and analyzed by a number of economists particularly during forties and fifties.

Studies of various aspects of surplus manpower in agriculture including quantifications of its volume have been attempted by different economists.

The main objective of this paper is to analyze the concept of surplus manpower in agriculture of Indian economy.

Economic development in any country depends on natural and human resources. Economic growth with out natural resources may be possible to same extent but economic growth without human resources is even unthinkable. Population acts as both means and ends of economic development. In the past economic development and rapid population growth have usually gone together. World population has grown faster since the industrial revolution than ever before.

The problems related to excessive pressure of population in agriculture and their solutions have been widely discussed in the wake of growth interest of economists in development aspects of the third world. With the emergence of Gunnar Myrdal's 'Asian Drama' or 'An enquiry into the Nature and causes of poverty of Nations or Schulty's 'Transforming Traditional Agriculture' or even before that economics of development was given an additional dimension dealing out rightly with developmental question in economics of third world with unlimited labour supply economists like Arthur Lewis and Ragnar Nurkse directly discussed the various implications of excessive population in developing agriculture and tried to come out with possibilities of its solution both with in and outside agriculture.

Since the forties of 20th century, the theory of surplus manpower in agriculture has been playing a very controversial role. The fragments of theory that have appeared under the label "unlimited supply of Labour", "Fixed Factor proportions", in agriculture "Dualism" "Seasonal Labour Surplus" and "under–employment" in general, could not settle the Controversy.

Surplus labour may be defined as having components of open and hidden unemployment and under employment of which disguised unemployment forms only apart. Or guised unemployment may or not be removable, but surplus labour is always removable. The main feature of surplus labour is that its generally confined to those who are "self employed"

In Agriculture sector, the number of surplus agricultural workers for the whole year may be insignificant bur surplus labour time is enormous.

The concept of surplus labour has been interpreted from a new angle by Shakuntala Mehra taking into consideration the question of labour requirement at the peak time of agricultural operations. In fact, appropriate concept of surplus labour refers to that workforce as surplus which with unchanged techniques and organisation of form structure can be siphoned off without adversely affecting agricultural output.

Another concept which is very close to the concept of both surplus labour and disguised unemployment is that of under employment. Indicating the relation between disguised unemployment and under-employment B.N. Ghosh explains it is perfectly rational to consider under-employment to be disguised in agriculture when the marginal productivity of labour is low but positive and the worker is working below the norm.

So far, surplus is concerned; it includes disguised unemployment and under-employment–open and hidden unemployment in agriculture sector.

CONCLUSION

Some of the findings that were high lighted in different studies are as follows: Firstly it was observed that the labour force participation rate was declined in the 1990 in rural areas.

Secondly, the proportion of male workers in the rural primary sector (Agriculture) has been declining over the part 25years. By contrast, female workers in rural area being more dependent on the agriculture sector.

Thirdly a preponderant proportion of agricultural workers was uneducated, more it amongst females than males.

REFERENCES

J. Mouly and E.Losta (1974), "Employment Policies in Developing Countries–A Comparative Analysis" Report of International Labour Organization, p.10

—(1964), International Labour: Employment and Economic Growth, p.12 Organization

A. K. Sen (1975), Employment, Technology and Development, Oxford University Press Note, p.8

Muhammad Masum: Unemployment and Underemployment in Agriculture, B. R. Publishing Corporation, New Delhi.

P.C. Varma: Surplus Manpower in Agriculture and Employment Policy, Deep and Deep Publishing, New Delhi.

Errol D. Soza (2002), "Impact of Economic Reforms on Rural Employment" Indian Journal of Agricultural Economics Vol.57, No.1, January-March, p.36

Puran Singh: National Rural Employment Guarantee Schema: A Task Ahead.

31

INTEGRATED TRIBAL DEVELOPMENT PROGRAMMES AND ERADICATION OF UNEMPLOYMENT: A NOTE

S. Ramachandran

INTRODUCTION

Authors have brought to focus that the implementation of the different development programmes in tribal areas have been increasing their income and employment which in turn have changed their life style.[1] Some evidences, which obtain from authors show, that considerable progress in tribal areas, has been achieved in the implementation of various programmes with the special programmes benefiting the tribals[2]. For example, Devan pointed out that with the advancement of communication and transport system and the implmentation of welfare programmes by the government, drastic changes have been brought about in the lives of Wynad tribals[3]. In the same the study of Katoch opined that the inception of new development programmes, including the 20 point programme changed the Gujjars tribal's fortune in Dhaulakaun of Sirmur District[4].

Many authors have attempted to assess the impact of special development programmes in tribal areas. Some studies have established that the TDA have produced favourable impact on employment, income and asset formation of the beneficiary families.[5] Ajit Singh emphasized the people's understanding and participation in the programme to ensure its success, which involves social process being set in motion.[6]

Gupta and Gupta show that development plans in tribal areas in Madhya Pradesh could prevent female labour migration of tribal population to other areas of the state and to the other states.[7] Satya Raju stated that though the government has provided facilities and amenities for the development and advancement of scheduled tribes in Andhra Pradesh, they are still lagging behind in many respects and living under darkness with their age old customs and traditions.[8]

Pratap in his study of Tribal Situation in Andhra Pradesh, says that the integrated approach of the Community Development Programme has not come up to the expectations as it resulted in diffusion of human effort and finance.[9] Still there are varied and alternative views that persist with regard to functioning and the impact of various development programmes. In this context, the present study is taken up to make a close probe into the impact of the Integrated Tribal Development Programmes on employment generation among the tribals of Tamilnadu.

METHODOLOGY

According to 2001 census, the tribal population in Tamil Nadu is 6.51 lakhs i.e., 1.04 Percent of the total population of the state. The areas where the population of scheduled tribes exceeds 50 Percent of the total population is divided into nine ITDPs. Among the ITDPs the Kalrayan hills of Villupuram district has been selected for the purpose of the study. For long even after the independence, this area had remained fully isolated from the democratic processes of the country. Surprisingly, the old jagirdary continued to rule, for all practical purposes until 1976, when the Government, entered the scence during the declaration of the national emergency. It has been stratified into three groups in the first stage for the purpose of the study i.e. the hamlets located adjacent to plain villages constitute the first group, whereas those situated in the top hill areas, with approachable road facilities form the second group. Last, those hamlets which are away from the approachable road and the Block head quarters are categorized as the third group. To select the hamlets from these areas the names of the hamlets were compiled from the revenue records, and four hamlets were randomly selected from each group for the purpose of the study. To assess the level of benefits of the respondents, the households were classified into five categories based on their land holding such as landless, marginal, small, medium and large. Then the data were collected through structure questionnaire.

RESULTS AND FINDINGS

Average Household Additional Employment Generation

The average household additional employment generated by the ITDPs, has been reckoned in terms of hours spent for tending the animals and to use for their cultivation. Among the three groups, average additional household employment generation is higher (1411.16 hours) in the case of first group hamlets than the other groups. The same trend is noticed as among the different categories. It depends upon the level of success of the different kinds of animal husbandry schemes, particularly milch animal scheme.[10] In the first group hamlets, it varies among the different categories. It depends upon the level of implementation and level of success of the milch animal scheme, which has a high employment potential in this area. In the case of second group hamlets, it is higher in the case of large farm households (954.29 hours) than that of other categories. The reason noticed is just the same as found in the case of first group hamlets. Average household additional employment hours of the third group hamlets are higher in the marginal farm households (440 hours) than for other categories. It varies among the different categories. It mainly depends upon the level of implementation and level of success of the sericulture scheme.[11]

Table 1
Average Household Employment Generation (In Hours)

	I Group			*II Group*			*III Group*		
Employment Hours Household Categories	*No. of House-holds*	*Total Employment Generation*	*Average Household Empt. Generation*	*No. of House-holds*	*Total Empt. Generation*	*Average Household Empt. Generation*	*No. of House-holds*	*Total Empt. Generation*	*Average House-hold Empt. Generation*
Landless	10	17840	1784	–	–	–	–	–	–
Marginal	14	15480	1105.71	7	2020	417.14	4	1760	440
Small	25	40680	1627.20	17	9080	534.12	27	9492	351.56
Medium	18	20560	1142.20	24	9880	411.67	26	8920	343.08
Large	19	26800	1410.53	28	26720	954.29	26	10920	420
Total	86	121360	1411.16	76	48600	639.47	83	31092	374.60

Source: computed

A Note on Unsuccessful of the Schemes

It is regrettable to note that the worst kind of exploitation originates from the implementation of the scheme by the Government officials. It is found that in some hamlets, houses have already been constructed under different programmes, and the construction work of some other hamlets are under progress. Mostly the house construction contracts have been undertaken by the officials in the name of their relatives or their friends. In some hamlets it is noticed that the contract has been unofficially transferred to some third person on sub contract at a lower sum than the actual sanction. It is reported that in a few hamlets the village administrative officers demanded Rs.100 from each tribal for the house allotment. It is found that in the interior hamlets houses have been constructed by blue metal with clay and also by using inferior quality of other materials like wood, etc. Hence in a few places, houses collapsed even during construction. A few housing contractors defended such failure referring to the poor finance allotment which was not enough for construct pucca houses. Hence they used clay for cement and other materials of inferior quality. It seems such houses were provided with tiled roof, not suitable for the climate of the area and hence most of them remained unused. The people felt that the housing programme, benefited the officials more rather than the people. For the provision of protected drinking water they have constructed overhead tanks in some of the hamlets. Due to lack of maintenance, some of them have been put to disuse. So they are using canal water for their domestic consumption. Non tribal labourers from the plain areas are used for all construction works and the tribal labourers are not engaged for these works. Hence they do not benefit from these programmes.

Regarding horticulture department the tribals admitted that they gave seedlings of several categories. But they provided them during summer. The people, being totally ignorant of the new plants, could not be successful with them. Further the officials too did not make many efforts to teach the people. Hence most of the plants died. In general, an

Appendices

Table 2
Average Household Employment Generated By Milch Animal Scheme (In Hours)

Employment Hours Household Categories	I Group					II Group					III Group				
	No. of Household	*Total Empt. Hours*	*Average Household Empt. Hours*	*No. of Cases Success*	*No. of Cases Failures*	*No. of Household*	*Total Empt. Hours*	*Average Household Empt. Hours*	*No. of Cases Success*	*No. of Cases Failures*	*No. of Households*	*Total Empt. Hours*	*Average Household Empt. Hours*	*No. of Cases Success*	*No. of Cases Failures*
Landless6	17520 (100)	2920	6	– (100)	–	–	–	–	–	–	–	–	–		
Marginal	2 (100)	5840	2920	2 (100)	–	1 (100)	2920	2920	1 (100)	–	1 (100)	–	–	–	1 (100)
Small	14 (100)	37960	2711.43	13 (92.86)	1 (7.14)	1 (100)	2920	2920	1 (100)	–	1 (100)	–	–	–	1 (100)
Medium	6 (100)	17520	2920	6 (100)	–	2 (100)	5840	2920	2 (100)	–	–	–	–	–	–
Large	7 (100)	22040	3148.57	7 (100)	–	10 (100)	23680	2368	9 (90)	1 (10)	1 (100)	2920	2920	1 (100)	–
Total	35 (100)	100880	2882.29	34 (97.14)	1 (2.86)	14 (100)	35360	2525.71	13 (92.86)	1 (7.14)	–	2920	973.33	1 (33.33)	2 (66.67)

Source: computed. Figures in the parentheses denote percentage to the total.

Table 3
Average Household Employment Generated by Plough Bullock Scheme (In Hours)

	I Group					*II Group*					*III Grpul*				
Employ-ment hours House-hold Categories	*No. of House-hold*	*Total Empt. Hours*	*Average House-hold Empt. Hours*	*No. of Cases Suc-cess*	*No. of Cases Fail-ures*	*No. of House-holds*	*Total Empt. Hours*	*Average House-hold Empt. Hours*	*No. of Cases Suc-cess*	*No. of Cases Fail-ures*	*No. of House-holds*	*Total Empt. Hours*	*Average House-hold Empt. Hours*	*No. of Cases Suc-cess*	*No. of Cases Fail-ures*
Landless	3	320		106.67	1	2	–	–	–	–	–	–	–	–	–
	(100)				(33.33)	(66.67)	–	–							
Marginal	6	880	146.67	3	3	3	–	–	–	3	–	–	–	–	–
	(100)			(50)	(50)	(100)				(100)					
Small	8	2560	320	6	2	10	320	32	1	9	9	480	53.33	2	7
	(100)			(75)	(25)	(100)			(10)	(90)	(100)			(22.22)	(77.78)
Medium	11	3040	276.36	5	6	17	1120	65.88	4	13	11	1120	101.82	3	8
	(100)			(45.45)	(54.55)				(23.53)	(76.47)				(27.27)	(72.73)
Large	13	4160	320	8	5	13	3040	233.85	8	5	18	640	35.36	2	16
				(61.54)	(38.46)				(61.54)	(38.46)				(11.11)	(83.89)
Total	41	10960	267 32	23	18	43	4480	104.19	13	30	38	2240	58.95	7	31
				(56.10)	(43.90)				(30.23)	(69.77)				(18.42)	(81.58)

Source: computed. Figures in the parentheses denote percentage to the total.

objective appraisal of the performance of this programme shows that the investment made in this scheme so far, seems to have gone a waste. The scheme is implemented mostly in the road side hamlets and still most of the interior villagers do not know about the horticulture scheme.

But sericulture seems to register a better performance than other schemes. However, it is a fresh scheme for them and owing to their prolonged isolation they do not know cocoon rearing. After a long and earnest efforts of officials now it is under progress in some hamlets like Ararnpoondi. In general top hill hamlets have a favorable climate for cocoon rearing. If the Government attempts to implement the programme in all those hamlets, imparting prior training to the people it would be able to generate more income and employment there than what is possible in plain areas. It is heartening to note that the officials pay frequent visits to the interior hamlets by foot path through jungles and also they stay for a few days in a week if necessary and monitor the progress.

In view of the investment aspects and level of implementation, animal husbandry scheme assumes importance. But the malpractices are rampant and deep-rooted that the officials and middlemen benefit more than the tribals themselves. The latter are vulnerable to the joint exploitation of various departments like veterinary department, LAMPS, etc. Because of the inner dispute between the officials of the above two departments it is reported that many applications are still pending the disposal. If a tribal wants to apply for a loan against any scheme, he needs a village administrative officer's certificate which would be issued only on money considerations. After the sanction, the animals had to be purchased through the veterinary department and LAMPS officials. When it is reported that the officials took nearly from 20 to 40 per cent of the total investment with the help of middlemen. Generally it is reported that the allotment for purchasing milch animals is Rs.5000, but the officials bought animals at a much lower price say Rs.3000. The tribals could not exercise their option with regard to the choice of animals. If they insisted upon it, they had even to face physical threat

Table 4
Average Household Employment Generated by Sheep Rearing Scheme (In Hours)

	I Group					*II Group*					*III Grpul*				
Employment hours Household Categories	*No. of Household*	*Total Empt. Hours*	*Average Household Empt. Hours*	*No. of Cases Success*	*No. of Cases Failures*	*No. of Households*	*Total Empt. Hours*	*Average Household Empt. Hours*	*No. of Cases Success*	*No. of Cases Failures*	*No. of Households*	*Total Empt. Hours*	*Average Household Empt. Hours*	*No. of Cases Success*	*No. of Cases Failures*
Landless	1	–	–	–	1	–	–	–	–	–	–	–	–	–	–
	(100)				(100)	–	–	–	–	–	–	–	–	–	–
Marginal	8	8760	1095	3	5	3	–	–	–	3					
	(100)			(37.50)	(62.50)	(100)				(100)					
Small	3	–	–	–	3	6	5840	973.33	2	4	3	3352	1117.33	2	1
	(100)				(100)	(100)			(33.33)	(66.67)	(100)			(66.67)	(33.33)
Medium	1	–	–	–	1	5	2920	584	1	4	7	6160	880	3	4
	(100)				(100)	(100)			(20)	(80)	(100)			(42.86)	(57.14)
Large	–	–	–	–	–	5	–	–	–	5	7	3720	531.43	2	5
						(100)				(100)	(100)			(28.57)	(71.43)
Total	13	8760	673.85	3	10	19	8760	461.05	3	16	17	13232	778.35	7	10
				(23.08)	(76.92)	(100)			(15.79)	(84.21)	(100)			(41.18)	(58.82)

by the officials and middlemen. Further, the old buffaloes provided to them, would not survive long in the top hill climate, new to them. In the interior hamlets, people still entertain certain peculiar views such as milking is a sin. In some hamlets there are no purchasing centers, to enable the tribals sell their milk. The plough bullock and sheep rearing schemes too have the same lapses as the previous scheme. Hence, neither the schemes create assets nor do they generate income and employment to any significant level. The present researcher could record certain cases in which some sheep's expired on the way coming from shindig (local market) and the remaining sheep's were sold at cheap rate by the beneficiaries. Further the plough bullock provided to them too were either very old animals or very young calves, which did not survive long for one reason or the other.

CONCLUSION

From the analysis it is found that the average household employment generation is higher in the first group hamlets than for the other groups. However, the performance registered by the various household categories has not been uniform, the variation arising form the level of success and the extent of investment made through different schemes. Further, it is found that among the different kinds of programmes, milch animal scheme creates greater employment hours than the other schemes in the case of the first and second group hamlets. Likewise in the case of the third group hamlets among all the schemes, sericulture scheme generates additional employment but it is not at the expected level however, being a new venture in this area in which people are involved only a part time basis. So it could be suggested that if they undertook this as a full time work, it would generate, still additional employment From the foregoing results one can conclude that the milch animal scheme is suitable for the first and second groups. For the agricultural purposes plough bullock scheme may be implemented for all the three groups, but it is worthwhile only in the first group. People express their view that instead of sheep rearing, goat rearing may be helpful to them better to

Table 5
Average Household Employment Generated by Sheep Rearing Scheme (In Hours)

Employment hours Household Categories	I Group					II Group					III Grpul				
	No. of Household	Total Empt. Hours	Average Household Empt. Hours	No. of Cases Success	No. of Cases Failures	No. of Households	Total Empt. Hours	Average Household Empt. Hours	No. of Cases Success	No. of Cases Failures	No. of Households	Total Empt. Hours	Average Household Empt. Hours	No. of Cases Success	No. of Cases Failures
Landless	–	–	–	–	–	–	–	–	–	–	–	–	–	–	–
Marginal	–	–	–	–	–	–	–	–	–	–	3 (100)	1760	586.67	3 (100)	–
Small	–	–	–	–	–	–	–	–	–	–	14 (100)	4960	354.29	11 (78.57)	3 (21.43)
Medium	–	–	–	–	–	–	–	–	–	–	7 (100)	1440	205.71	3 (42.86)	4 (57.14)
Large	–	–	–	–	–	–	–	–	–	–	3 (100)	1600	533.33	3 (100)	–
Total	–	–	–	–	–	–	–	–	–	–	27 (100)	9760	361.48	20 (74.07)	7 (25.93)

Source: computed. Figures in the parentheses denote percentage to the total.

generate additional income and employment. Soil conservation scheme will help to generate additional income and employment for all the three groups. As per the views of the officials and people about the progress of sericulture scheme, it is found to be helpful in the third group, and hence it is suggested being non–appropriate than other schemes in this area. From the above, one is inclined to suggest that all corruption and malpractices witnessed of the various levels of implementation authorities and middlemen must be eliminated. Further, it may be suggested that the respondent should be trained before introducing them to the schemes. Further attempts, should be made to instill practical awareness among the respondents regarding the benefit of the schemes, methods and maintenance of properties.

REFERENCES

1. Sinha and Prasad have found that the programmes have resulted increasing a positive impact on generating employment and increasing earnings of the poorest section of the society. See, S.P.Sinha and Jagadish Prasad, "Special Programmes for weaker sections: An Evaluation–A Case Study in Musahari Block, District Muzaparpur, Bihar," *Indian Journal of agricultural Economics*, 35:4, Bombay: (Oct. – Dec., 1980).

2. A spokesman of the Publication Division suggests that considerable progress in tribal areas has been achieved in the implementation of programmes benefiting the tribals during the past years. Additional areas were brought under minor irrigation and soil conservation. More tribal villages have been electrified. The horticultural programme has received attention. The involvement of scheduled tribe children in various stage of education has gone up. Moreover till the end of December, 1979 about 2400 large sized multi purpose co-operatives were established in the tribal sub–plan areas these societies in the tribal sub plan areas. These societies purchase surplus agricultural and forest produce, sell essential consumer commodities at reasonable price and lend consumption and production credit. See, The Director, Publications Division, "Tribal Development Programmes," *Economic and Political Weekly*, 30:12, New Delhi: (March 16, 1982); The same view is stressed by Pachauri as regards the direct (Individuals) benefits derived by them from

Governments, Panchayat Raj Administration, the number of respondents together with frequently are recorded. Social amenities are provided to certain respondent households more than four times. As regards economic benefits most of the respondents are not benefited more than three times. In the case of schemes like improved implements, irrigation wells and milch cattle more than 50 percent of the respondents are benefited under high yielding varieties scheme, health and education schemes, See, S.K. Pachauri, *Dynamics of Rural Development in Tribal Areas: A study of Srikakulam District, Andhra Pradesh,* New Delhi : concept publishing company, (1984).

3. P.K. Devan, "Impact of Various Development Programmes on Tribals of Wynad," Kurukshetra, 36:4, New Delhi: (Jan., 1988)
4. S.C. Katoch, "Tribal Beneficiaries of 20 Point Programme," Kurukshetra, 34:4, New Delhi: (Jan. 1986).
5. Hanumant Yadav and C.S. Mishra, "Impact of Tribal Development Programmes on Employment, Income and Asset Formation in Bastar District of Madhya Pradesh, "Indian Journal of Agricultural Economics, 35:4. Bombay, (Oct.-Dec.,"T9-8~0 | ; Pattanaik have found out that there are about 30,000 tribal families in the project area Parlakhemundi, out of which at least 10,000 families have so far been substantially benefitted through the schemes sponsored by this TDA. See, T.K. Pattanaik, "Good Progress in Parlakhamundi," Kurukshetra, 23:1, New Delhi: (Oct., 1974; Hanumant Yadav study in TDA Dantewada thehsils shows that though the income and assets of beneficiaries family increased in comparison to the non beneficiaries by the increase could not be treated as remarkable, See, Hanumant Yadav, "Impact of Farm Subsidies on Tribal Development," Kurukshetra, 29:13, New Delhi: (April 1,1981). Singh's study revealed that the introduction of the high capital-intensive projects in the tribal region have considerably changed the socio-economic situation in the tribal villages and geo-ecological balance in this area of Bihar. See, Ghanshyam Narain Singh, '"Design of Development for the Tribal Region of Bihar," in D.M. Nanjundappa and R.K. Sinha, (eds) *Backward Area Development* Problems & Prospects, (New Delhi: Sterling Publishers Private Limited, 1982) "Gunasekaran and Ramasamy found that the Integrated Tribal Development Programme made a profound impact on the life of Malayalis in Kolli Hills. See, R. Gunasekaran and G. Ramasamy, "Social Changes Among Tribals–A Study," *Kurukshetra,* 36:4, New Delhi: (Jan., 1988).

6. K. Ajit Singh, *Tribal Development in India*, (Delhi: Amar Prakashan, 1984).
7. Ram Pratap Gupta and P.C. Gupta, "Development of Tribal People," *The Economic Times*, 3:170, Bangalore: (March 27, 1988).
8. R. Satya Raju, "Role of Government in Scheduled Tribes Development," *Kurukshetra*, 34:4, New Delhi: (Jan., 1986).
9. D.R. Pratap, "Tribal Situation in Andhra Pradesh," in K. Suresh Singh (ed.) *The Tribal Situation in India*, (Shimla: Indian Institute of Advanced Study, 1986).
10. See, Appendix Tables 2,3,4
11. See, appendix Table 5.

32

SPECIAL ECONOMIC ZONES IN INDIA

T. M. Rajendra Prasad
D. Purushotham Naidu

Special Economic Zones (SEZs) have played a pivotal role in the economic growth of several countries and have been a key to paradigm shift undertaken by various countries from the planned economy to the market economy. As part of its continuing commitment to liberalization, the Government of India, since the last decade, adopted a multi pronged approach to promotion of foreign investment in India. As a result, in the recent budget as well as in the new Exam Policy (2002–2007), the Government has given special importance to the Special Economic Zones in the country,

WHAT ARE SEZS?

SEZs are specifically demarcating zones where units operate under a set of rules and regulations different from those applicable to other units in the country. They are-effected to give a big push to exports, employment and investment in the SEZs. The emphasis is on enhancing exports and creating an environment for attracting foreign direct investment by offering tax sops. While units in the one zone have to be foreign exchange earners, they are not subjected to any pre-determined value addition or minimum export performance requirements, ft is a specifically delineated duty - free enclave and shall be deemed to be foreign territory for the purposes of trade operations, duties and tariffs, usually is to increase foreign investments.

It is claimed that SEZs will build infrastructure and enhance employment generation. Likewise, the infrastructure deficit must be made up and maintained in good order. To this end, SEZs are being promoted to develop the necessary infrastructure and foster industrialization, exports and concomitant urbanization and services. Some 181 SEZs have been promoted by Commerce Ministry and the Prime Minister has forecast an investment of the order of Rs. 14,15,000 crore by 2012 on this programme. Any private, public, joint sector or State Government or its agencies can set up SEZs. Foreign companies too, are eligible.

Performance of the SEZ units will be monitored by Unit Approval Committee comprising Development Commissioner, customs and a representative of the state government on an annual basis.

SEZ units will be eligible for 100 per cent tax exemption for the first 5 years, 50 per cent for the next 5 years, 50 per cent of the ploughed back profits for the next five years. Further, 100 per cent income tax exemption for 10 years in a block period of 15 years for SEZ developers.

FACILITIES FOR SEZ DEVELOPERS?

Developers may import/promote goods without payment of duty for the development, operation and maintenance of SEZs. They will also have the freedom to allocate developed plots to approved SEZ units on a purely commercial basis. They will also have the full authority to provide services like, water, electricity, security, restaurants recreation centre etc., on commercial lines. Moreover, they will be exempted from paying service tax. Company that develops infrastructure an other facilities on land earmarked as SEZs besides a legislative framework for setting up offshore banking units. In addition to this, company that sets up units also takes advantage of the tax waivers and other incentives. India is at last moving into a bigger leag'ie. New laws allow for zones on virgin sites that range upwards from a minimum of 10 hectares (24 acres) for business such as software and biotechnology to 1,000 hectares for multi-sector zones that might involve more than one developer and would include residential areas, hospitals, shopping centres and other amenities.

Land will often by provided by State Governments at concessionary rates and both developers and operating units can receive tax breaks for up to 15 years, provided they are export oriented.

LABOUR LAWS APPLICABLE

Labour laws applicable in the respective states will also be applicable in SEZ units. There is no special dispension of SEZ units. India has 8 working SEZs. all converted from erstwhile Export - Processing Zones (EPZs). They are located in Kandia and Surat (Gujarat), Cochin (Kerala). Santa Cruz (Mumbai - Maharastra). Fatta (WB), Chennal (TN), Vishakapatnam (AP) and Noida (UP). The most massive SEZ spread however, is in Maharastra, AP, Karnataka, TN, Haryana, Punjab, Rajasthan, and West Bengal. The total land to come under these 181 SEZs is staggering 1,53,716 hectares.

BENEFITS OF SEZS?

- SEZs will build infrastructure.
- Enhance employment generation.
- Boost industrial investment and exports, while persuading the private sector to build social infrastructure that states cannot afford.

To enhance foreign direct investment and provide an internationally competitive and hassle free environment for exports.

The idea was to promote exports from the country and realizing the need that level playing field must be made available to the domestic enterprises and manufacturers to be competitive globally.

- Since the passage of the bill, the government has received over 380 proposals. The list of bidders read like a who's who of corporate India Reliance, Infosys, Wipro. Tatas-Foreign based companies' et al and even public sector giants like ONGC. The Government hopes that SEZs will bring in billions of dollars in investments and create over a million new jobs.
- While the proponents of the SEZs, across the world talk of higher exports, greater industrial productivity and increasing job opportunities.

EMERGING ISSUES

Village after village Is being appropriated. In every village, there is 25 to 30 per cent labour. Where will they go? There is no rehabilitation for them. The current promotion of SEZs is unjust and would act as a trigger for massive social unrest, which may even take the form of armed struggles.

The point is that this promotion is completely skewed. The Finance Minister has expressed reservations that it would cause a revenue lost of Rs 1,00,000 crore. The Reserve Bank of India has questioned the tax concessions being granted to 8EZ projects and the big Pope of globalization and liberalization, the International Monitory Fund (IF) has also raised it voice against the way things are being advanced.

Farmers across the country are agitating against the virtual confiscation of their land. Is it that the SEZs have come to stay and farmers and farm labor have to go?

This has created a situation where the government is acting as the music man of corporate powers to usurp the land of farmers. The government virtually forcing the farmers to subsidize industry.

Large tracts of land are being taken over, in many cases forcibly and I violation of the SUEZ Act, by government agencies for private promoters.

SEZs pave the way for private capital to make huge profits at the expense the small property owner and the state.

It favors private capital and' honors profit making independent of how it ensured.

- So long as the SEZ developer can find the clientele, huge untaxed profits are guaranteed.
- If export zones fail to attract clients. what happens to the land acquired through the state?
- SEZs enjoy the status of "Public Utility Services" which will reduce the scope for collective bargaining.
- SEZs could aggravate the uneven pattern of development by pulling out resources from less developed states.
- The greatest concern expressed even by some eminent World bank Economists and International Labour Activities that these islands virtually insulated from most economic and labour taws, their exploitation is increasing.
- With the SEZ rules saying that only 25 per cent of the total land needs to be used for the purpose, for which it is approved, say for IT, gems and jewellery. whatever the remaining land is bound to become the islands of high-flying mansions and office complexes and condominiums. The scent of a huge real estate scam is in the making under the benevolent gaze of the governments. both central and state i.e., the emergence of real estate racketeers class.

POLICY PERSPECTIVES:

To start wit, if the entire initiative is based on market economy, let it be ruled and guided by the actual operative mechanisms of market economy. That is, let it operate as it should. Let the SUEZ developers negotiate with the farmers directly and arrive at a mutually agreeable compensation. Development is, of course, required. But if you say that to promote development the- batik rights of lakes and lakes or people have to be denied, if you say that the interests of corporate have to be advanced at the cost of farmers, and that is not acceptable. That is, no appropriation using the governments might.

Let there be a clear affirmation that fertile land or land with double crop would not be given to SEZs. And most importantly, let the farmers and their families get not only jobs in the prospective SUEZ firms but also a proprietary stake In them. Let there be an inductive approach and not an exclusive one. There should be a six-month moratorium on the implementation of policy. In this period, there should be a national referendum on it and finally the government should come out with detailed guidelines on how the Act can be implemented. Our suggestion is that their should be a regulatory authority for framing the guideline and monitoring the implementation. The authority should include representatives of farmers' organizations and social activists because the virtual confiscation of agricultural land without paying adequate compensation is a central feature of the *SEX promotion.*

Agricultural land should not be handed over to corporate houses for industries or SEZ projects since this will jeopardize the food security system in the country.

The possibility of the policy being misused by real estate racketeers who had no interest in the development of either industry or infrastructure. It is not the corporatisation of agricultural land but the diversion of agricultural land that is the issue. The premise Is that food security is paramount, but at the same time agriculture Is not showing the kind of buoyancy it should show.

There is shared responsibility for the state and central governments. Given the awareness that has come about on the farmer's issue, the governments as well as the corporate players need to take measures that enhance their credibility. Further, it is in the industry's own Interests to secure the participation of land-owners, whether through ensuring jobs or making them

SHAREHOLDERS

- The single most important benefit from the SEZ would be stimulating investment in labour intensive manufacturing. If that is not happening, we should review the policy. If It is merely going to promote IT investment, it is noting great as IT would have developed in any case, because we already have a competitive edge.

- !f the SEZs being in big investment In textile, leather, agro-processing, light engineering or consumer-oriented engineering, then that would be worthwhile. The Nokia SEZ in Sriperumbudur (near Chennai) is a good example of this kind of labour intensive initiative.
- Proper homework ought to be done before hand Including building a broad consensus among those concerned and putting in place a proper rehabilitation policy for those affected and displaced by the proposed legislation.
- Only barren wasteland, and if necessary, single crop agriculture land should be acquired. But this is being observed more in breach than in practice.
- Our tract record in rehabilitation and resettlement (R & R) is deplorable, to put it mildly. The country needs to change the way it handles R & R. the project implementing agency (PIA) must set up a special purpose vehicle

(SPV) TO HANDLE R & R ISSUES

- A regulatory framework Is planned to ensure equity, appropriate compensation and resettlement of those displaced. R & R must move away from the futility of "land for land" to re-housing and stakeholder participation for those displaced, with training for new employment opportunities created by or around the new facilities or industries being created.
- Engagement of civil society will reduce the possibility of corruption. Use of information technology can reduce the possibility further by bringing in more transparency.

CONCLUSION

One would do better that the change never comes without its costs. SEZs cannot be panacea Tor the country's ills. But they represent a new -strategy that has worked well elsewhere to stimulate growth; not at the cost of farming or the poor but as part of an integrated programmed in which human resource development and poverty alleviation remain core values. Projected rural hubs and retail trading with linkages to rural supply and national marketing chains must be harnessed for garibi hatao. Planners must take land and water as limiting factors. States should be taken on board and necessary incentives offered to them to plan around natural constraints.

All said and done there can be no dispute of the fact that SEZ can play a positive role in boosting country's overall economic growth. SEZ offers massive potential to trigger a large flow of foreign direct investment in infrastructure and productive capacity leading to creation of new employment opportunities. Sincere efforts must be made to ensure that legitimate interests of all stakeholders are fully protected and no section of society especially those who part with land for setting up SEZ are exploited.

REFERENCES

Pankaj. K. Choudhary (2006), 'Special Economic Zones-Do SEZs, Drain Revenue or Draw FDI, Yojana, October, pp. 7-8.

Ardhana Aggarwal (2005), 'SEZs and Growth' Civil Services Chronocle, October.

G. Verghese (2006), 'SEZ Acquisitions' Economic and Political Weekly, May 22, pp. 2136-2140.

Ramakrishan Upadhya (2007), 'SEZ: Squeeze Ease of Zap it out? Yojana, December, pp. 8-10.

Saumitra Mohan (2005), 'Special Economic Zones', Yojana, May.

Suresh Prabhu (2007), 'Lessons from Singur', Times of India, January 20, 2007.

33

ROLE OF SEZS IN EMPLOYMENT GENERATION AND ITS EFFECT ON LABOUR WELFARE.–A STUDY

B. Lilly Grace Eunice

INTRODUCTION

Globalisation is perceived as a dynamic and open-ended process which helps in integrating the economy of a country with the world economy and in turn influences the economic, social, cultural, political, legal and technological environment of the nation. Consequently globalization has its own impact on employment.

An SEZ is a trade capacity development tool, with the goal to promote rapid economic growth by using tax and business incentives to attract foreign investment and technology. Today, there are approximately 3,000 SEZs operating in 120 countries, which account for over US$ 600 billion in exports and about 50 million jobs. By offering privileged terms, SEZs attract investment and foreign exchange, spur employment and boost the development of improved technologies and infrastructure. (ILO, 2003.)

OBJECTIVE

The present paper *aims* at examining *the employment effects of SEZs and its impact on labour welfare.* Before dealing with the employment effect and labour welfare this paper also gives brief account of SEZ Policy in India.

METHODOLOGY

The paper is based on secondary data and information collected from documents like Economic Survey, articles published in various journals and news papers. Basically this paper is a descriptive and analytical work.

SEZ POLICY IN INDIA

The SEZ policy was first introduced in India in April 2000, as a part of the Export-Import ("EXIM") policy of India. Considering the need to enhance foreign investment and promote exports from the country and realizing the need that level playing field must be made available to the domestic enterprises and manufacturers to be competitive globally.

The policy provides for setting up of SEZ's in the public, private, joint sector or by State Governments. It is also being envisaged that some of the existing Export Processing Zones would be converted into Special Economic Zones. Accordingly, the Government has converted Export Processing Zones located at Kandla and Surat (Gujarat), Cochin (Kerala), Santa Cruz (Mumbai-Maharashtra), Falta (West Bengal), Madras (Tamil Nadu), Visakhapatnam (Andhra Pradesh) and Noida (Uttar Pradesh) into a Special Economic Zones. In addition, 7 new SEZs have become operational in 2004/2005 which is given as under:

To provide a stable economic environment for the promotion of Export-import of goods in a quick, efficient and hassle-free manner, Government of India enacted the SEZ Act, which received the assent of the President of India on June 23, 2005. The SEZ Act and the SEZ Rules, 2006 ("SEZ Rules") were notified on February 10, 2006. The SEZ Act is expected to give a big thrust to exports and consequently to the foreign direct investment ("FDI") inflows into India, and is considered to be

Table 1

Name of the SEZ	*Name of the developer*	*Type*	*Year of Commencement of Operation*	*Area in Acres*	*Investment on Infrastructure*
Manikanchan SEZ (West Bengal)	West Bengal Industrial Corporation	Gems & Jewellery	2004	5	Rs.25 crores (approx)
Jaipur SEZ (Rajasthan)	Rajasthan State Industrial Development Corporation	Gems & Jewellery	2004	110	Rs.26 crores (approx)
Indore SEZ (Madhya Pradesh)	M.P. State Industrial Development Corporation	Multi-product	2004	2600 (1st phase in 132 acres)	Rs.100 crores
Salt Lake Electronic City (Kolkata)	M/s. Wipro Ltd.	Software development & IT enabled services	2005	16	Rs.125 crores
Mahindra City, Chennai (Tamil Nadu)	M/s, Mahindra Industrial Park Ltd.	IT, hardware and bio-informatics	2005	665.68	Rs.100 crores
Mahindra City, Chennai, (Tamil Nadu)	M/s, Mahindra Industrial park Ltd.	Apparel and fashion accessories	2005	86.71	Rs.100 crores
Jodhpur (Rajasthan)	RIICO.	Handicrafts	2005	180.94	Rs.30 crores

one of the finest pieces of legislation that may well represent the future of the industrial development strategy in India. The new law is aimed at encouraging public-private partnership to develop world-class infrastructure and attract private investment (domestic and foreign), boosting economic growth, exports and employment.

The Special Economic Zone Act 2005 came into force with effect from 10th February 2006, with SEZs Rules legally vetted and approved for notification. The SEZs Rules, inter-alia, provide for drastic simplification of procedures and for single window clearance on matters relating to central as well as state governments. Investment of the order of Rs.100, 000 crores over the next 3 years with an employment potential of over 5 lakh is expected from the new SEZs apart from indirect employment during the construction period of the SEZs. Heavy investments are expected in sectors like IT, Pharma, Bio-technology, Textiles, Petro-chemicals, Auto-components, etc. The SEZ Rules provides the simplification of procedures for development, operation, and maintenance of the Special Economic Zones and for setting up and conducting business in SEZs.

Table 2
Exports from the Functioning Sezs During the Previous Years are as Under

Year	*Export*	*Growth Rate (over previous year)*
2003-04	13,854	39%
2004-05	18,314	32%
2005-06	22 840	25%
2006-07	34,615	52%
2007-08	66,638	92%

http://www.theindiastreet.com/2008/06/exports-in-sezs-grown-by-92.html

Shri Kamal Nath, Union Minister for Commerce & Industry, has stated that the Special Economic Zones (SEZs) and Export Oriented Units (EOUs) have significantly contributed towards employment generation and encouraged manufacturing activity in the country. Speaking at the Export Awards function organized by the Export Promotion Council for EOUs & SEZs (EPCES) Shri Nath informed that during the period 2003-04 to 2007-08, exports from SEZs and EOUs have increased from Rs.42,641 crore to Rs.221,066 crore, a growth of 418% in four years.

The Minister mentioned that SEZ success has been possible due to a participative and interactive approach between the government and industry. "In the last three years, incremental investment of more than Rs.90, 000 crore have taken place in the SEZs. During this period, SEZs have provided incremental direct employment to over 2, 27,000 people. Exports from SEZs have gone up from Rs.22, 840 crore in 2005-06 to Rs.66, 638 crore in 2007-08. By the end of December 2008, Indian exports from the SEZs stood at Rs.70,000 crore, crossing last years exports from SEZs" (Government of India, 2009).

SEZS IN ANDHRA PRADESH

Andhra Pradesh is one of the major states in India positively responding to the SEZ policy. An estimated 4.5 lakh employment opportunities have been proposed to be created through the 48 Special Economic Zones (SEZs) coming up in Andhra Pradesh by October 2006 (www.newkerala.com). The total number of approved SEZs in Andhra Pradesh as on October 3rd 2007 was 66. The total number of SEZs in India is 395. The percentage of SEZs of the Andhra Pradesh in the country amounts to 16.70 (C.P.Chandrasekar, Jayathi Ghosh, 2007). The Centre has approved 48 SEZs of which IT/ITES - 27 SEZs, pharma 6, multi product 4, footwear 3, and one each for biotech, apparel, building products, services sector, paper, textile, gems and jewellery and semiconductors. Some of the SEZs are highly employment potential-gems and jewellery (50,000 jobs), footwear and leather (30,000 jobs) and apparels (60,000 jobs). While 11 SEZs are to be developed by the State government, remaining are to be established by the private players.

The state is encouraging such SEZs keeping in view the high employment potential. By establishing these SEZs, 1, 40,000 jobs would be created among lower middle class, weaker sections particularly SCs, STs, BCs and minorities.

These are long term projects and when become fully functional, it would create about 50,000 jobs in the manufacturing sector (C.P.Chandrasekar, Jayathi Ghosh, 2007). If the SEZs are established in the backward areas, they will be helpful in reducing regional inequalities in the State. For this purpose, the State

Government may link up the SEZs to the Growth Centres. The Government of India approved the Growth Centres by providing the required infrastructure facilities with a view to attract industries in the backward areas. The essential cost of Rs.30 crores for each growth centre is to be shared by the Centre and States in the ratio 2:1(Govt. of A.P. 2006-07). The Central Government sanctioned 4 Growth Centres in the State –Bobbili, Ongole, Hindupur and Jadcherla–So the SEZs can be established at the growth Centres and in other backward areas, so that the existing regional inequalities in per capita income, due to additional employment and business opportunities may be reduced.

One of the important problems in establishing SEZs in Andhra Pradesh and elsewhere in India is the acquisition of land. If the SEZs are established in the already developed areas, not only the land would be much costilier but also not readily available. Some times acquisition of fertile land in the developed areas would be more difficult and opposed by the farmers compared to the land in a backward area. Acquisition of fertile lands in a large scale may lead to shortages in the availability of food and vegetables. Moreover, the individual farmer's loss of income due to the foregone land would be much less than the compensation he receives and the income he gets due to gainful employment in the SEZs. Therefore, it is necessary to establish the SEZs either by the government or private players in the districts of North Coastal Andhra, North Telangana and in Rayalaseema districts of Andhra Pradesh.

EMPLOYMENT EFFECTS OF SEZ

The employment effect of SEZs operates through three channels:

(i) SEZs generate Direct Employment for skilled and unskilled labour.

(ii) They also generate Indirect Employment and

(iii) They generate Employment for Women workers.

It is believed that employment creation generates incomes, creates non-pecuniary benefits improves the quality of life of labour and enhances their productivity.

Direct Employment Generation

Due to the availability of labour at low wages, developing countries generally attract investment into simple processing labour intensive industries. This increases demand for unskilled labour within the zone. Shift towards higher value added activities as SEZs grow might increase demand for skilled labourers also.

SEZs also generate employment for unskilled labour by creating demand for physical infrastructure within the zone. This stimulates local construction industry giving employment to unskilled labour.

Sivalingam (1994) reports that in cities surrounding the Malaysian SEZs, there is even labour shortage in this industry. Demand for utilities such as water, electricity, communications and administration also rises.

Finally there has been increasing demand for various support services such as hotels and restaurants, and transport, which is expected to have a substantial impact on employment generation.

Indirect Employment Generation

The indirect effect is manifested as ancillary employment opportunities generated by SEZ. These include transport, communications, automobiles, civil aviation, shipping, tourism, hospitality, packaging banking and insurance. Employment opportunities are thus generated for both skilled and unskilled labour.

Employment for Women

Evidence suggests that women's share to total employment in SEZs is substantially higher than both the economy as a whole as well as the manufacturing sector outside the SEZs (Kusago

& Tzannatos, 1998). Women workers are considered more disciplined and hard working. It is found that employers prefer female workers to male workers in the belief that manual dexterity, greater discipline and patience make women more suitable for the unskilled and semi-skilled activities carried out in the zones. Besides, they are less likely to exert pressure for high wages and better working conditions.

Majority of working women are young, single and come from rural backgrounds. But for SEZs they might not have been absorbed into formal employment at all and hence SEZ employment can be said to afford then an independent source of income that would otherwise have been denied. SEZs are thus expected to contribute substantially to the employment of women (Madani, 1999).

REVIEW OF LITERATURE

One group of studies argues that EPZs can be instrumental in promoting Human Development. (ILO/UNCTC 1998, Basile & Germidis 1984, Willmore 1995). Another group of studies (ILO 1998, ICFTU2004, PRIA 200, Hossain 2001, Majumdar 2001, and Kemal 2001) shows that zones are target oriented workplaces where virtually all indicators of sustainable Human Development, including labour standards, labour laws, human rights, health and safety nets and the environment are ignored. Review of existing studies, however, suggests that a comprehensive analysis of EPZs labour related effects in scarce.

WHETHER SEZS ARE LABOUR INTENSIVE?

Out of the 404 formal approvals given till date, 137 approvals are for sector specific and multi product SEZs for manufacture of Textiles & Apparels, Leather Footwear, Automobile components, Engineering etc. this would involve labour intensive manufacturing. The employment projected in the 172 SEZs notified so far is over *21, 42,089* additional jobs. SEZs are thus going to lead to creation of employment for large number of unemployed rural youth. Nokia and Electronics hardware SEZs in Sriperumbudur are already providing employment to 7932 and 2069 persons, majority of which are women. Hyderabad Gems SEZ for Jewellery manufacturing in Hyderabad has already employed 1200 women majority of who are from landless families, after providing training to them. They have a projected direct employment for about 30,000 persons.

Apache SEZ being set up in Andhra Pradesh will employ 20, 000 persons to manufacture 10,00,000 pairs of shoes every month. Current employment in Apache SEZ is 3549 persons. Brandix Apparels, a Sri Lankan FDI project would provide employment to 60,000 workers over a period of 3 years. Even in the services sector, 12.5 million sq meters space is expected in the IT/ITES SEZs which as per the NASSCOM standards translates into 12.5 lakh jobs. It is, therefore, expected that establishment of SEZs would lead to fast growth of labour intensive manufacturing and services in the country (Ministry of Commerce, 2007.

SEZs act as engines for export led economic growth in India. "Internationally, free zones have been 'publicly' funded. However, in India, fiscal constraints are coming in the way of public funding for SEZs. The government has been encouraging participation of private players by offering regulatory and fiscal incentives in setting up SEZs," (Utkarsh Palnitkar, 2006).

IMPACT OF SEZS ON LABOUR WELFARE

However, it can not be assumed that employment in SEZs enhances Human Development, which depends on wages and working conditions. It is generally claimed that in order to attract investment, in particular FDI, governments of host countries eliminate labour standards, consequently promoting labour exploitation and depletions of human capital.

There are restrictions on the right to join a trade union, bans on collective bargaining and the right to strike. Employees often pay scant regard to labour laws, employment regulations and health and safety norms at work. These issues are critical in determining employment effects of zones on living standards, poverty reduction and human development.

There are several reports of exploitation of women in SEZs. The vast majority of workers in SEZ firms are young women aged 16-25 years. (Kreye et.al.1987) it is found that women are paid less than men for similar jobs (Jahan, 2003, Bhattacharya & Rehman 1999) and are subject to sexual harassment and violence.

SEZS A SUCCESS IN INDIA

Describing the success of the SEZs in India, Mr Gopal Krishna Pillai, Secretary of Commerce, Ministry of Commerce and Industry, India said that the response from Indian SEZs has been tremendous. The Government has already formally approved 404 SEZs, of which 172 have been notified. About 60 of these have already generated direct employment of about 52,000 and indirect employment of 1,00,000. With growth likely to be exponential, these numbers could shoot up to 150,000 by March 2008 and to 600,000 by the end of 2009. It is expected that the foreign direct investment in SEZs increases 3-4 folds within the next year (G.K.Pillai, 2007).

CONCLUSION

SEZs found to be most important channel to generate employment opportunities in India. Even though their contribution to national employment has been rather limited they have contributed significantly to employment generation at the regional level. If fresh investments are attracted to SEZs, with the SEZ Act, which generates huge employment potential in the economy.

The experience so far proves that zones are particularly beneficial to female employment in formal sector, thereby increasing their employability as well as improving their position in the household.

Indian zones have the potential for generating direct and indirect effects in promoting employment. It is unfortunate that the public opinion has turned highly unfavourable to the SEZ Policy, which reveals the government's inability to implement the policy effectively. Hence it is crucial to develop a clear and comprehensive strategy to deal with subsidiary issues that emerge and it must create confidence among public that its operations are for their benefit only.

India's SEZs appear small compared to the massive Chinese counterparts for a host of reasons. Partly, it is because China has divided each region into an SEZ and granted preferential treatment to foreign ventures that have enabled high-cost industrialised countries to use it as an attractive outsourcing platform for manufacturing activities. While India has, of late, emerged as the preferred destination for back-office business process outsourcing in IT and software industry, it is way behind China as an emerging outsourcing platform for manufacturing activities.

With regard to the labour welfare government needs to ensure the implementation of labour standards, conditions of work, and health and safety standards and the creation of support infrastructure for education and training of labour. It is also important to promote management labour councils in SEZ units as an effective means of developing sound labour relations in SEZs.

The productivity of labour forces in developing countries has failed to improve due to uncompetitive conditions and lack of required skills. Hence SEZs can be used as a policy instrument in upgrading skills and building human capital.

REFERENCES

Basile, A. & D. Germidis (1994), *Investing in Export Processing Zones*, OECD, Paris.

Bhattacharya, D and Mustafizur Rahman (1999), "Female Employment under Export Propelled Industrialisation: Prospects for Internalising Global Opportunities in the Apparel Sector in Bangladesh", Occasional Paper, 10, the United Nations Research Institute for Social Development (UNRISD); Geneva.

C.P.Chandrasekhar and Jayati Ghosh (2007), 'Recent Employment trends in India and China: An unfortunate convergence?' Paper presented at ICSSR–IHD-CASS Seminar on Labour markets in India and china: Experiences and emerging perspectives 28-30 March, New Delhi.

C.P.Chandrasekhar, Jayati Ghosh (2007), SEZs in India: The Record so far, Business Daily from The Hindu Group of Publications, Tuesday, Nov.27.

—Government of India, Ministry of Commerce and Industry, 2009. (http://commerce.nic.in/pressrelease/pressrelease_detail.asp?id=2377).

Hossain, I (2001), 'Export Processing Zones in Bangladesh and Industrial Relations' in A.S.Oberoi, A.Sivananthiran and C.S.Venkatramana, et.al (ed) *Labour issues in Export Processing Zones: Role of Social Dialogue*, South Asian Multidisciplinary Team and Indian Industrial Relations Association, ILO, New Delhi.

ICFTU (2004), 'Behind the Brand Names'http://www.icftu.org/www/pdf/sezsreportE.pdf.

ILO (1998), 'Labour and Social Issues Relating to Processing Zones', Technical Background Paper for *the International Tripartite Meeting of Export Processing Zone –operating Countries* in Geneva, from 28 September to 2 October 1998, ILO, Geneva.

ILO/UNCTC (1988), *Economic and Social Effects of Multinational Enterprises in Export Proceesing Zones*, ILO, Geneva.

Jahan,S.(2003): Reorienting Development: Towards an Engendered Employment Strategy, Paper presented at the *Gender Poverty Summit* Organised by the NCAER and Women's Political Watch in New Delhi on 9-11 November 2003.

Kreye, Otto, Jurgen Heinrichs and Floker Frobel (1987), 'Export Processing Zones in Developing Countries: Results of a New Survey', Multinatinal Enterprises Programme No.43, ILO, Geneva.

Kemal, A.D (2001), 'Freedom of Association and Promotion of Social Dialogue in SEZs in Pakisthan', in A.S.Oberoi, A.Sivananthiran and C.S.Venkatramana, et.al (ed) *Labour Issues in Export Processing Zones: Role of Social Dialogue*, South Asian Multidisciplinary Team and Indian Industrial Relations Association, ILO, New Delhi.

Kusago, T., and Z.Tzannatos (1998), 'Export Processing Zones: A Review in Need of Update', World Bank Discussion Paper No.9802, World Bank, Washington,DC, January.

Madani, D., (1999), 'A Review of the Role and Impact of Export Processing Zones', World Bank Policy Research Paper, No.2238, World Bank, Washington, DC.

Majumdar, I., (2001), 'SEZs and their Workers in India: A Study of the Noida Processing Zone', in A.S.Oberoi, A.Sivananthiran and C.S.Venkatramana, et.al (ed) *Labour Issues in Export Processing Zones: Role of Social Dialogue*, South Asian Multidisciplinary Team and Indian Industrial Relations Association, ILO, New Delhi.

—Ministry of Commerce and Industry, Wednesday, December 27, 2007.

Pillai, G.K. (2007), 'Describing the Success of the SEZs in India', Ministry of Commerce and Industry, New Delhi, India, December 03, 2007

PRIA (2000), 'Export Processing Zone in India and the Status of Labour', Available at *http://www.pria.org.*

Sivalingam, G.(1994), The Economic and Social Impact of Export Processing Zones : The Case of Malaysia, *Multinational Enterprises Programme*, No.66, ILO, Geneva.

—(2006-07), Socio-Economic Survey, GOAP, Planning Department, Hyderabad.

Utkarsh Palnitkar (2006), 'Shaping SEZs', Partner, Transaction Advisory Services, Ernst &Young.

Willmore, Lorry (1995), 'Export Processing Zones in the Dominican Republic: A Comment on Kaplinskly', *World Development*, 23(3):529-35. http: / / www.newkerala.com/

34

EMPLOYMENT GENERATION THROUGH ENTREPRENEURSHIP

G. Paidi Raju

In broad sense a state of unemployment appears when a labour does not obtain employment opportunity despite his willingness to work on existing wage rate. India is a developing economy where the nature of unemployment is entirely different from that of developed nations. The Indian economy is going through a paradox of growth and unemployment. The only solution to tackle this paradox is to inculcate the spirit of entrepreneurship among the educated youth. Entrepreneurship brings prosperity both to the entrepreneur and to the nation.

There are various determinates of unemployment in our economy, such as population explosion, economic backgrounds, inadequate structural base of economy, wrong priorities in industrialization during Indian planning, adoption of modern technology in all sectors in economy, decreasing rate of investment in agricultural and industrial sectors, increasing rate of urbanization, unhealthy education policy of the government, political instability, corruption, etc.

NATURE OF EMPLOYMENT AND UNEMPLOYMENT IN INDIA–62ND ROUND OF NSSO

Subsequent to the 61st round in 2004-05 which was a quinqennial round, NSSO conducted an All India Survey (62nd Round) of moderately large sample size on the situation of employment and unemployment in India during the period July 2005 to June 2006 as part of the annual series of rounds. The main findings of this survey are as follows-

Overall unemployment rate for rural are as according to usual status approach was around 2 per cent (3 per cent for male and 2 per cent for females). Urban rates were higher than the rural rates except for the CDS approach in which unemployment rates for rural and urban areas were almost equal (nearly 8 per cent). The unemployment rate, obtained by any of the approaches, was higher for females than that for males in the urban areas, but it was lower than that for males in the rural areas.

The reversal of the declining trend in employment growth-from an annual 2.1 per cent in the ten year ending in 1993-94 to 1.6 per cent in the five years ending in 1999-2000 to 2.5 per cent in the five years ending in 2004-05 is an encouraging development. Nevertheless, there is need for faster employment growth for not only absorbing the addition to the labour force, particularly with the ongoing demographic changes, but reducing the unemployment rate. The share of agriculture in total employment has come down from 61.67 per cent in 1993-94 to 58.54 per cent in 1999-2000, and further to 52 per cent in 2004-05. While the manufacturing sector's share increased marginally during this period, trade, hotel and restaurant sector contributed significantly higher to the overall employment than in earlier years. The other important sectors whose shares in employment have increased are transport, storage and communications apart from financial, insurance, real estate, business and community, social and personal services.

EMPLOYMENT GENERATION: 11TH PLAN VIEW POINT

The Eleventh Plan envisages rapid growth in employment opportunities while ensuring improvement in the quality of employment. It recognizes the need to increase the share of regular employees in total employment and a corresponding reduction in casual employment. The employment generation strategy of the Eleventh plan is also predicated on the reduction of underemployment and the movement of surplus labour in agriculture sector to higher wage and more gainful employment in non-agriculture sector. Agriculture sector is projected to generate no increase in employment during the Eleventh Plan period. Employment in manufacturing is expected to grow at 4 per cent while construction and transport and communication are expected to grow at 8.2 per cent and 7.6 per cent respectively. The projected increase in total labour force during the Eleventh Plan is 45 million. As against this, 58 million employment opportunities would be created in the Eleventh Plan. This would be greater than the projected increase in labour force leading to a reduction in the unemployment rate to below 5 per cent.

ENTREPRENEURSHIP

The term entrepreneur is derived from the French word "entreprendre" denoting to undertake". It was first used by Cantillon to designate the traders who buy wares of a country and sell them again through wholesale or retail at uncertain prices. Entrepreneurship means the function of seeking investment and production process, raising capital, hiring labour, arranging supply of raw materials, finding site, introducing new techniques and commodities, discovering new sources of raw materials and selecting top managers for day-to-day operation of the enterprise. Thus the term entrepreneurship refers to the qualities that are required to innovate and start a new enterprise; accept the challenge and bear the risk. Entrepreneurship may involve creating many job opportunities.

Women and Entrepreneurship

"Woman entrepreneur according to Government of India is an entrepreneur who runs an enterprise owned and controlled by her and having minimum financial interest up to 51 per cent of the capital and giving at least 51 per cent of the employment to women". Thus, woman entrepreneur is one who initiate, organize and operate a business enterprise. In developing countries like India such innovators are found less in number when compared with advanced countries.

Commercialization and modernization of the economy gradually eliminated many of the avenues of employment to women in agriculture and industries and thus enabled them to find ways of supplementing their family income. As a result of this, a section of urban women have emerged as potential entrepreneurs. This development is of significant importance in the society. It is since the last decade that the women have started emerging on the business scene and some of them have achieved remarkable success too. Some of the successful women entrepreneurs in India are Smt. Vimala Pitre–manufacturer of surgical equipment, Smt. Manik Vanrekar of Leather crafts, Smt. Radhanika Pradhan of Plastic industries and Smt. Gogate for Drugs etc.

Reasons for Women Entrepreneurship

One must accept the fact that entrepreneurship is not related to sex of an individual. Women can be as successful entrepreneurs as men. The entry of women in business is only a recent development in the orthodox, traditional, social and cultural environment of our society. Our society has not allowed women to think independently in the past. But in the last decade, economic compulsions have led more and more young girls to take-up employment and potential source of women entrepreneurship has emerged. The following are some of the reasons for emerging women entrepreneurship;

(a) Not finding a job
(b) Unable to work in her house.
(c) New challenges and opportunities for self-fulfillment.

(d) Proving their innovative skills.

(e) Need for additional income.

The above reasons clearly indicate that economic compulsions, family responsibilities and desire to enjoy social status compel the women to take up enterprises.

In India women constitute 48.2 percent (49.6 crores a per 2001 census) of the total population. Women are the focus of all development. Any sustainable change towards progress needs involvement of women. Development of entrepreneurship among women has become an important aspect of the over all economic development of women. Many organizations both at the central and state levels have come up to cater to the needs of potential women entrepreneurs. Financial institutions, commercial banks and non-government organizations are playing an important role in promoting entrepreneurship among women.

Self-Employment Concept

In view of the increasing modernization, mechanization and computerization, employment opportunities in traditional and organized sectors have diminished considerably. There is bright scope for self-employment in the services sector due to a large demand by the public for a wide variety of services. The government is motivating the educated unemployed youth who have registered their names in employment exchanges to form homogenous groups based on their complementary skills and training. Such groups could then register themselves as cooperative societies, and start their own business or occupation. Unemployment and underemployment have forced these people to take up self-employment either individually or through self-help groups. The unemployment and under-employment rates are very high in the world and India is no exception to it. Unemployment leads to poverty, hence should be checked and curbed immediately. The creation of employment opportunities through self-employment schemes is to be achieved by providing a package of financial assistance in the form of bank credit and subsidy provided by the Government. These schemes are basically meant for weaker sections of the society who, because of low level of education and lack of skills, cannot compete for jobs with other. Some of the Government schemes envisage provision of training appropriate to the activity sought to be undertaken by the prospective beneficiary. A large number of persons are expected to avail of the benefit of self-employment schemes to generate income. These schemes for providing self-employment are:

1. Sampoorna Gramin Rozgar Yojana
2. Swarnajayanthi Gram Swarozgar Yojana (SGSY)
3. Jawahar Gram Samridhi Yojana
4. Employment Assurance Scheme
5. National Social Assistance Programme

ESSENTIAL FOR SELF-EMPLOYMENT

1. Land and building
2. Machinery and instruments
3. Raw materials
4. Electricity
5. Trained Human Resources
6. Capital.

EMPLOYMENT AND ENTREPRENEURSHIP OPPORTUNITY PROGRAMMES

The various types of employment and development programmes are being introduced by the central & state governments to improve the employment and entrepreneurship opportunities. The programmes are :

- Development of Women and Children in Rural Area (DWCRA)
- Jawahar Rozgar Yozana (JRY)
- Training for Rural Youth and Self-Employment (TRYSEM)
- Indira Mahila Yojana (IMY)
- Rashtriya Mahilakhosh (RMK)

- National Rural Employment Programme (NREP)
- Rural Landless Employment Guarantee Programme (RLEGP)
- Employment Guarantee Scheme (New EGS)
- Integrated Rural Development Programme (IRDP)
- Kisan Nurseries
- Three Patta Scheme
- Differential Rate of Interest Scheme (DRI)
- The Norwegian Agency for International Development (NORAD) Aid to Local Projects for Women
- Entrepreneurship Through Poverty Alleviation Programmes
- Swarnajayanthi Grams Swaraozgar Yojana (SGSY)
- Rural Employment Generation Programme (REGP)
- Prime Minister's Rozgar Yojana (PMRY)
- Urban Self-Employment Programme (USEP)

SOME IMPORTANT EMPLOYMENT GENERATING PROGRAMMES

Many of the employment generating programs are being implemented by both central and state government to bring the people out of the ambit of poverty. NREGS, SGRY, SGSY are some of the programs being implemented to reduce unemployment in rural areas. Programs like Swarna Jayanti Shahri Rozgar Yojna are implemented to remove unemployment in urban areas.

NREGS: National Rural Employment Guarantee Act was passed in September 2005. Under the Act, 100 days of employment are guaranteed to one able bodied person from each rural households. The scheme was implemented in 530 districts covering almost entire country. However, from April 2008 the remaining districts are also covered under the scheme. For financial year 2007-08, 2.75 crore households demanded rural employment. Under the scheme, 2.72 crores household were provided with employment generating 96.03 crores person days in that year. The fund allocated in 2007-08 was Rs. 16059.94 crores.

SGRY: Sampoorna Grameen Rozgar Yojana was formulated by merging Jawahar Gram Samridhi Yojna and Employment Assurance Scheme in September 2001 however in 2008 the scheme was made a part of NREGS. The programme was formulated with a view to provide wage employment. Along with it other objectives like providing food security, improving social and rural infrastructure were also combined. Under the scheme priority was given to weaker and vulnerable sections of social fabrics.

SGSY (Swarnajayanti Gram Swarozgar Yojna): The scheme was started in 1999 after restructuring Integrated Rural Development Programs and its allied programs like training of rural youth for self employment (TRYSEM), development of women and children in rural areas (DWCRA), supply of toolkits in rural areas (SITRA), Ganga Kalyan yojna and Million Wells scheme. The scheme aimed at encouraging the rural population for self employment by providing them with income generating. Assets, bank credit and government subsidy. It is funded by centre and state government on 75:25 ratio. Until, December 2007 it helped in formulating 27,41081 Self Help groups (SHGs) and assisted 93,32,572 gram swarojgaris. Under the scheme 35,19,927 individual swarojgaris benefited till 2007.

Apart from these pilot schemes some other organization are also involved in enhancing skills and encouraging self-employment among rural youths. Other institutions like DRDA and CAPART are also involved in providing such facilities so as to increase employment in rural areas. Also it help in organization and setting up for small scale or cottage industry production.

SJSRY (Swarna Jayanti Shehri Rojgar Yojana): It was implemented in December 1997. The Urban Self Employment Programme and Urban Wage Employment Programmes are two special component of SJSRY. It aims at assisting urban poor to set up micro enterprise and get trained for skilled works.

MEASURES TO DEVELOP RURAL ENTREPRENEURSHIP

1. Develop the entrepreneurship qualities in rural people.
2. Increase the number of branches of institutions like financial institutions, promotional institutions, training institutions and voluntary organizations in rural areas and strength their performance in creating and developing rural entrepreneurship.
3. Reduce the constraints in economic, social religious, cultural and psychological factors in the growth the rural entrepreneurship.
4. Increase the supply of technical guidance, financial and marketing support and infrastructure facilities like water, fuel, housing, primary health care, child care centers and transport etc., in rural areas.
5. Establish effective research studies, research and technological innovations in the development of rural entrepreneurship.
6. Develop the literacy promotion rate and eradicate the not useful, ineffective rural culture.
7. Oppose the negative social factors like caste, community, religion, joint family system which are hurdle for the development of rural entrepreneurship.
8. Promote liberal credit facilities and increase the supply of raw material in rural areas.
9. Creation of awareness among bureaucrats for rendering assistance to entrepreneurs.
10. Identify the correct, eligible and efficient entrepreneurs and provide proper assistance from various rural programmes.
11. Grant complete tax exemption and avoid the harassment from tax collectors.
12. Provide marketing help and abolish licensing system etc.
13. Encourage women entrepreneurs who are taking active participation in various rural activities.
14. The government should provide subsidy like fertilizer subsidy, subsidy on agriculture inputs, power subsidy etc.,

to encourage the new entrepreneurs, uplift the people who are living below the poverty line and motivate the unemployed youth to take up venture, Subsidy is a boom to the rural people to improve their economic condition and rural entrepreneurship.

Similarly, under the Prime Minister's Rozgar Yojana (PMRY) implemented in both rural and urban areas, self-employment opportunities are made available to educated unemployment youth. This is a credit-linked subsidy scheme and is implemented through the District Industries Centers of the States and Union Territories, with the loans being provided by banks.

ENTREPRENEURSHIP IN TINY, SMALL AND MEDIUM INDUSTRIES

Small Scale Industries form a significant part of Indian economy. The Government of Andhra Pradesh has selected many of the growth engines, eg., IT Constitution and Pharmaceuticals for focused development. The Small Scale Industries sector will then be a major focus in the strategy to create rapid growth in the State.

Small Enterprise creation in an economy leads to proper utilization of the available resources and promotes employment, thereby achieving good economic growth and raises the general income levels. Hence the concept of entrepreneurship development holds great relevance in the progress of the economy.

WOMEN-SELF-EMPLOYMENT IN THE SERVICE SECTOR

1. Identification and organization of innovative and high income generating activities suitable for women.
2. Development of entrepreneurial abilities of women by organizing special types of training.
3. Encouraging women to take up part-time jobs while being in the house itself, to earn additional income to support the family.
4. Effective planning at the micro-level.

5. Adequate representation of women experts in the case of women related development planning.
6. Central and state governments to place more emphasis on untouched areas in the service sector to involve women.
7. Government can establish a separate mechanism at the center, state and district levels to look after women's employment and their problems.
8. Development of infrastructure facilities and supportive services like land, building, transport and also to look after the children.
9. Encouraging women through formal and non-formal education to involve themselves in the service sector.
10. Organizing women laborers in the service sector through women's associations, cooperative societies or Mahila Mandals, etc.
11. Establishment of supervisory bodies to monitor the implementation of Constitutional provisions related to women.
12. Steps to make women aware of technical and financial assistance available to women entrepreneurs, and to encourage them through concessions and incentives to enter into the service sector.
13. Government should encourage research and development in the service sector to find out high income generating activities for women.
14. Wide publicity to training programmes in the service sector.
15. Creating awareness among educated and uneducated youth about the availability of facilities and concessions for entrepreneurs.

MOTIVATING STRATEGIES FOR ENTREPRENEURSHIP DEVELOPMENT

A self-employed person while employing himself also provides employment to others. Entrepreneurship education and training can help a great deal in leading enterprising students towards self-employed careers. It is possible to develop entrepreneurship through planned efforts. The colleges can arrange some programmes to motivate the students to become entrepreneurship in future by

- Introducing of Entrepreneurship as a subject in their courses.
- Arranging guest lectures by successful entrepreneurship in their fields.
- Organizing entrepreneurial awareness camps
- Conducting self-employed programmes
- Organizing workshops/Seminars on entrepreneurship development
- Organizing exhibition of model enterprises.
- Showing a documentary film by giving all necessary information like financial resources, Govt. Incentives and Schemes etc., to start a new venture.

These above programmes pave the way to motivating the student to become an entrepreneur which creates employment in future.

The government has put emphasis on employment generation. The planning commission has setup a task force on employment opportunities to examine the employment and unemployment situation in the country and suggest strategies of employment generation for 100 million people over the next 10 years. Besides, efforts are also being made to accelerate the process of entrepreneurship development, particularly at the small scale and micro level. Entrepreneurship is one of the options available to rural population, which can serve the dual purpose of checking migration and providing self-employment to rural people. So the entrepreneurship development in rural and urban people including women is necessary to increase the production, employment and proper distribution of wealth and optimum utilization of resources.

Entrepreneurial Development in India

There are several institutions engaged in conducting entrepreneurship development programmes in India.

Government of India at an early stage realized the importance of promoting new ventures particularly small scale industries as a means of employment generation. Small Industries Development Organisation was setup at the apex level to provide technical inputs and guidance to small industries. Khadi and Village Industries Commission was established to promote village industries. In 1984, Government of India setup National Institute for Entrepreneurship and Small Business Development (NIESBUD) and apex organization for promotion of entrepreneurship and small business. At the same time IDBI and other financial institutions setup Entrepreneurial Development Institute of India (EDI). With the same objectives NIESBUD and EDI have been conducting research in entrepreneurship development programmes and imparting training to entrepreneurs. These Institutes did a pioneering work in selection and training of entrepreneurs and brought number of publications. Entrepreneurial development in Gujarath has been conducted for a long time, and sophisticated selection techniques and training methodology have been developed. The programme has integrated identification and training of potential entrepreneurs, identification of viable industrial projects and development of managerial capabilities. Other organizations like State Bank of India, Entrepreneurial Motivation Training Centre in Northern-Eastern Region, Small Industries Extension Training Institute etc., are imparting training tc entrepreneurs in India. But there is a need for an apex organization to co-ordinate training programme of various organizations in the country.

Experience in India showed that various training programmes of these institutions are aimed at training people to take up self-employment and or to get gainful employment. This does not really help the entrepreneurial development among the youth. We need more practical training programme which must be in tune with the Indian economic environment and should be in regional languages. Presently, there is a need to develop genuine entrepreneurs for the industrial development. Institutions both at state level as well as national level are established and promoted to provide assistance in areas such as selection of projects, financial assistance, technical guidance, training and market information. The names of some of the important institutions operating at the state level to assist the entrepreneurs are given below:

(a) Small Industries Service Institute (SISI)
(b) District Industrial Centre (DIC)
(c) State Finance Corporation (SFC)
(d) Technical Consultancy Organisation (TCO)
(e) State Small Industries Corporation (SSIC)
(f) State Industries Corporations (SIC)
(g) Commercial Banks
(h) State Industries Promotion Corporation.

At the national level, the following institutions are helping the entrepreneurs;

(a) Small Industries Development corporation (SIDC)
(b) Industrial Finance Corporation of India (IFCI)
(c) Industrial Development Bank of India (IDBI)
(d) Industrial Credit and Investment Corporation of India (ICICI)
(e) Minerals and Metals Trading Corporation (MMTC)
(f) National Small Scale Industrial Development Corporation (NSSIDC)
(g) Khadi and Village Industries Centre (KVIC)
(h) National Bank of Agriculture and Rural Development (NABARD)
(i) Small Industries Development Bank of India (SIDBI)
(j) Unit Trust of India (UTI)
(k) Life Insurance Corporation of India (LIC)
(l) National Institute of Small Industry Extension Training (NISIET)

The state and central level promotional agencies have announced a series of fiscal and non-fiscal incentives, concessions and facilities for attracting new entrepreneurs to setup tiny, small, medium and ancillary industries in their regions. This has helped in promoting balanced entrepreneurship development and to remove the regional imbalances and unemployment.

In the current scenario of globalization and liberalization our young graduates and professionals should discard their prejudices against business and take a fresh look at entrepreneurship as a dynamic and challenging opportunity. The education system should highlight the importance of entrepreneurship and inspire the students to undertake entrepreneurial ventures when they come out of their institutions.

Entrepreneurs help in generating employment directly and indirectly. Entrepreneur becomes self-employed and becomes self-sufficient and lead a honorable life. They do not depend on the government jobs or private jobs and directly employ themselves by starting their own enterprise. Indirectly, they also provide jobs to many unemployed by setting up large and small scale industries. Thus, entrepreneurs play an important role to reduce the unemployment problem in the country and paves the way for economic development.

REFERENCES

Arul Kamaraj J.M (2005), "Motivation for Entrepreneurial Opportunities", Sedme, Muralidaran K. Vol.32, No.3, September, p.p. 51-54.

Gadage R.S.(2006) "Unemployment in India: A Study", Southern Economist, September 15, p.p. 7-8.

Mary Jessica V. (2005), "Role of Nationalized Banks in Promoting Self-Help Sireesha N. Groups for Self-Employment", Sedme, Vol.32, No.3, September, p.p. 35-37.

Narasimha Reddy P. (2006), "A Study on Success Rate of Entrepreneurship in Tiny, Naga Srinivasa P.R. Small and Medium Industries of Hyderbad", Sedme, Surya Prakash Goud K. Vol.33, No.3, September, p.p. 39-40.

Laxmana B. Patel M.M.(1995), "Role of Entrepreneurship in Agricultural Development", Kurukshetra, Vol.XLIII, No.12, September, p.p. 41-43.

Pulak Mishra (2003), "Developing Entrepreneurship in India", Yojana, Ramakantha Prusty 18 December, p.p. 15-18.

Rajavel N. (2005), "A Study on Entrepreneurial Awareness Among the Educated Unemployed Youths", Sedme, Vol.32, No.4, December, p.p. 51-61.

Ramana A.V. (1999), "Entrepreneurship and Economic Development", Kurukshetra, Vol.48, No.2, November, p.p.8-9.

Shankaraiah. A. Rudra SaibabaRamana Rao Pongugoti (2002), Entrepreneurship Development, Kalyani Publishers, Ludhiyana, p.p. 60-63.

35

NATIONAL RURAL EMPLOYMENT GUARANTEE SCHEME: IT'S IMPACT IN RURAL AREAS

P. Mercy Kumari
K. Mahendra Kumar
B. S. Rao

INTRODUCTION

The National Employment Act, 2005, which confers legal right to employment on the rural citizens, is landmark in the history of independent India. It seeks "to provide for enhancement of livelihood security of the households in rural areas of the country (except J&K) by providing at least one hundred days of guaranteed employment in every financial year of every household whose adult members volunteer to do the unskilled work with the schemes made under the Act." Initially starting from 200 most backward district of the country, it will be extended to the whole country within a period of five years.

The launch of this ambitious scheme at the Center has been guided by the success of the Maharashtra Employment Guarantee Scheme (MEGS), which is implemented for over last 30 years in Maharashtra, without decline in the demand for ; unskilled wage work. The experience gained in implementation of different wage employment programmes like National Rural Employment Programme (NREP, 1980), Rural Landless Employment Guarantee Programme (RLEGP, 1983), Jawahar Rozgar Yojana *JRY, 1989), Employment Assurance Scheme (EAS, 1993), Jawahar Gram Samridhi Yojana (1999), Sampooran Grameen Rozgar Yojana (2001) and National Food for Work Programme (NFFWP, 2004). During the past more than two decades, have also been taken into account while formulating the Act.

MAIN FEATURES

The onus of implementation of the scheme lies with the states as the states have been given the responsibility to prepare, finalize and approve the schemes 'self of projects' (annual action plans) which ensue 100 days guaranteed manual unskilled employment to every rural household who is willing to work. The plan prepared in this manner will be given wide publicity through local newspapers for awareness generation among masses. The main features of the scheme are as under:

1. *Registration of Employment seekers:* The registration of employment seekers will be done at the Gram Panchayat level along with their full particulars. The registration will be done after proper enquiry for a period of at least five years. A job card will be issued with photograph. The employment seekers will submit the applications to the Sarpanch of the Gram Panchayat or the Programme Officer at the block level.
2. *Availability of Employment Opportunities:* Minimum 100 days employment will be provided to all adult members of a registered family taken together in a financial year, who are willing to do unskilled manual work in such a manner that 1/3 opportunities are available to women. However, there is no upper ceiling on the number of employment days. The Programme officer at the block level will be responsible for making available the manual work within 15 days of the application. The job seeker will

have to work together for not less than a fortnight meaning thereby that he/she will continuously work for at least 15 days at a given point of time. An advance application can also be made for the employment. The intimation for offering employment shall be given in writing and through public notice.

3. *Minimum requirement for starting a new work:* If the job seekers cannot be absorbed on the ongoing work, minimum 50 applicants are required for starting a new work. There has to be perfect liaison between Gram Panchayat and Programme Officer for success of the scheme.
4. *Provision of wage:* At the national level, average minimum wage rate will be Rs.60/- per man-day though it has been left to the state governments to fix wages as per the prevailing minimum wage rates in the state, which shall be equal to working of seven hours normally. The disbursement of wage shall be made weekly but not later than a fortnight. In case the work site is beyond 5 km radius, the applicant will be entitled to 10 per cent extra wages on account of traveling allowance.
5. *Wage Material Ratio:* The cost of material component of works including wage to skilled and semi-skilled workers will be restricted to 40 per cent of the total project cost.
6. *Contractors and Machines:* The contractors are not allowed to be engaged in implementation of the NREGS projects. As far as practicable, the task under the scheme shall be performed manually and not be machines.
7. *Institutional Mechanism:* The state administration from the central level down to the village level as well as Panchayat Raj institutions have been entrusted with joint responsibility to implement the scheme as under:
   (a) *Central Employment Guarantee Council:* At the central level, a Central Employment Guarantee

Council (CEGC) will be constituted to deal with the matters concerning dissemination of information, implementation, supervision, monitoring and grievance redierssal. The CEGC will consist of members from different fields like senior officials of central ministries, planning commission, state governments, including 15 non-officials comprising 02 chairpersons of the ZP by rotation, 1/3 women and not less that 1/3 SCs/STs/OBCs/minorities.

(b) *State Employment Guarantee Council:* At the state level, a State Employment Guarantee Council (SEGC) shall will be constituted, which will comprise of members nominated by the state governments consisting of upto15 non-officials nominated from the PRIs, organization of workers and disadvantaged groups including 1/3 women, and 1/3 SCs/STs/OBCs/minorities. The SEGC, besides advising the state government on matters concerning the implementation of the scheme, monitoring, supervision, dissemination of information, shall determine the prepared works and will place the prepared annual report before the state legislature.

(c) *District Project Coordinator (DPC) at the District Level:* District Project Coordinator (i.e., CEO Zilla Panchayat or Collector) will be responsible for implementation of NREGS at the district level, who will further assist the District Panchayat in discharging its functions, i.e., consolidation of block plans for inclusion in the shelf of projects to be approved by ZP, according necessary sanctions and administrative clearance, coordinate the Programme Officers, reviewing, monitoring and supervision of PO's conduct periodic inspections of the works in progress, redressal of grievances and preparing budget for the next year.

(d) *Programme Officer at the Block Level:* Programme Officer at the Block Level under the overall direction, control and supervision of the District Project Coordinator, will assist the panchayat Samiti in discharge of its functions under the NREGS, who shall be responsible for matching the demand for employment and employment opportunities arising from projects, consolidating project proposals under the jurisdiction of Panchayat Samiti prepared by Gram Panchayats and received from Intermediate Panchayat, monitoring, sanctioning, ensuring payments of unemployment allowance, prompt and fair payment of wages, ensuring regular social audits and grievances redress. The powers to scrutinize and sanction of works has been given to the Programme Officer. The Programme Officers shall aloot at least 50 per cent works in terms of its cost under NREGS a Gram Panchayat. He will supply muster rolls and a list of available employment opportunities to the GP.PO shall be responsible for ensuring provision of unskilled manual work in accordance with the provision of the scheme within 15 days of receipt of the application or from the date he seeks work in case of advance application.

8. *Role of Panchayati Raj Institutions (PRIs):* The Panchayati Raj Institutions (PRIs) i.e., Gram Panchayati at the village level, Panchayat Samitis at the block level and Zilla Parishad (ZP) have been assigned a pivotal role in successful planning and implementation of NREGS.

(a) *Gram Panchayat:* The Gram Panchayat with involvement and recommendations of the people (Gram Sabha), shall be responsible for identification of projects in their jurisdiction and will prepare development plan and maintain a 'shelf of projects', decide the priority of works and recommend it to the programme officer for scrutiny and approval, prior to the commencement of the year. They will also be responsible for execution and supervision, conducting regular social audit and maintenance of the records pertaining to works and employment. The Gram Panchayats have been further entrusted with the responsibility to register the employment seekers, maintain details of registered households and supply the same to PO. It shall also received applications for job and will allocate employment opportunities among the applicants and intimate the applicants in writing through letters and public notices displayed at the office of Gram Panchayat, Intermediate Panchayat, Zilla Panchayat, shall maintain registers, vouchers and other documents related to the scheme.

(b) *Intermediate Panchayat:* The block level shelf of projects (plan) will be approved and finalized by the Panchayat Samitis. The PS will forward it to the ZP, supervise and monitor the projects taken up at the Gram Panchayat and block level.

(c) *District Panchayat:* The district panchayat shall approve the block plans (shelf of projects) under the scheme, supervise and monitor the projects at block and district levels.

9. *Funding of NREGS:* The funding of NREGS will be shared between both the Central and State Governments. The Central Government will establish National Rural Employment guarantee Fund (NREGF) at the Central level and meet the cost of components such as i) 100 per cent wage expenditure of unskilled manual work, ii) 75 per cent material cost and payments made and semi-skilled workers, and iii) part administrative expenses. In the same fashion, the States will create State rural Employment Guarantee Fund (SREGE) for implementation of the scheme and shall meet the cost of i) unemployment allowance if any, ii) 25 percent of expenditure on material and

payments made to the skilled and semi-skilled workers and iii) part administrative expenses.

10. *Unemployment allowance:* The applicant shall be entitled to get unemployment allowance if the authorities fail to provide job within fifteen days of demand for job, which will be equal to ¼ of the wages for the first 30 days and thereafter for the remaining period @ 50 per cent of the wages which should not exceed 100 days, wages. The wage payments have to be made on weekly basis.

DEFICIENCIES AND SUGGESTIONS

1. Any programme or scheme, which has universal applicability with wider implications should be seen in broader perspective such as acceptance and consensus at the national, regional, district block and village levels. Therefore, wide public consultation should have been made before formulating a scheme of the importance of NREGS, which is targeted at the villagers, who are the key stakeholders and partners in its success. The states are mainly responsible to implement the scheme. But they were never taken into confidence while formulating the act-whether the states have the requisite infrastructure and mechanism to implement the NREGS successfully, given the experience of the earlier schemes; whether, they are in a position to contribute 10 per cent cost of NREGS?
2. The scope of the scheme is limited which needs to be widened. Besides bringing all the arable, non-arable, private, community, Panchayat, forest, institutional and Government lands, all the existing water bodies, common property resources which help in creating employment opportunities, sectors like animal husbandry, food processing, cottage, handicrafts, schooling, health care, child care, housing and sanitation etc also need to be brought under the ambit of the scheme.
3. To have a grater impact, the ongoing SGRY, NFFWP, and Area Development Programmes like DPAP/DDP/IWDP

should be integrated into the NREGS as the objectives and the works taken up under these programmes are similar in nature. There should be further synergization of programmes like Bharat Nirman, RSVY and other rural development programmes.

4. The role of Gram Panchayat and Programme officer for providing employment needs to be clearly demarcated. The applicant will submit the request for employment to the GP, but the PO will arrange the employment. This gap will allow responsibility-shifting. The Panchayats employment; the PO should play only facilitation role.
5. 100 days offer of employment to a family in one financial year is in no way sufficient to sustain a family leave aside helping them cross the poverty line Moreover the scheme universal applicability. There should have been some weightage for BPL/landless families in job opportunities. The BPL/landless families should be offered at least 200 days of work as against 100 days for others.
6. The experience of earlier schemes shows that 60:40 wage material ratio is unrealistic and was never adhered to Except for afforestation and plantation, none of the work given in Schedule 1 (1) of the Act is labour-intensive. Technically also, the cost of unskilled labour is never as high as 60%. Moreover, the material cost is always higher than 40 per cent. How can a scheme based on false notions and assumptions succeed? Fudging of muster rolls takes place under such circumstances and the scheme looses focus.
7. More than 50 per cent of the states could not release the 25 per cent matching share of the grants under the SGRY. If the same happens to NREGS, can we ensure guaranteed employment to the people?
8. The scheme is to be implemented both by the government machinery and Panchayati Raj Institutions. The past experience of such synergisation has not been encouraging. Coordination between the PO and the Sarpanch and the employment seekers has been very difficult to come by.

Therefore, the scheme should be implemented through the PRIs only. The District Panchayat, Intermediate Panchayat and Gram Panchayat should be made responsible to implement the scheme. The technical wing of Panchayati Raj does not have the requisite technical manpower to supervise each an every work. Therefore Technical Support Groups (TSG) on the Kerala pattern, with the help of unemployed technical graduates and retired technocrats, should be created to support the panchayats in planning, estimation of costs, measurements of works done.

CONCLUSION

The success of NREGS depends on the acceptability of the people, which further rests on the level of awareness among various stakeholders and the d4esire among them to implement it. Therefore the government should launch an intensive awareness programme through different media and make the masses aware of he objectives and provisions of the scheme. The government should appoint public information officers at the central and state levels specifically for the purpose of NREGS. Print media, small media like, folk, street theatre, group radio, doordarshan/video, or internet etc can play a catalytic role in changing the mindset/behaviour of the people. For success of the scheme, it is also imperative that a village level micro plan is prepared and the works taken up under the NREGS form part of the village area plan. Lastly, PRIs should be made solely responsible for the implementation of the NREGS, successfully.

36

THE HUNDRED DAYS BASKET

S. Indrasen

A social audit of the functioning of the National Rural Employment Guarantee scheme in Villupuram district in Tamil Nadu revealed that despite many problems it enhances transparency and offers a lifeline to the rural poor.

In the rural hinterlands of Tamil Nadu, particularly in the poorer districts where chronic poverty and deprivation is not uncommon, a revolution of sorts seems to be happening. Under the National Rural Employment Guarantee Act (NREGA), which came into force in February last year, close to 70 per cent of the households in Villupuram district have job cards which show an average of 25 days of employment since April this year. What is more, an astonishing 82 per cent of the women in Villupuram district have found employment under the NREGA earning Rs. 80 a day as opposed to the largely arbitrary and discriminatory wages that they earned previously. By ensuring guaranteed wage employment for 100 willing to work, the NREGA is the first legislation that compels the state to provide a social safety net for the poorest people of issues of hunger and rural distress that afflict large parts of India.

Although Villupuram was chosen as one of the 200 districts for the initial phase of the scheme, the programme did not take off until recently. A surge in employment has occurred over the last few months indicating that there was an unprecedented response from the local population as soon they became aware of the scheme. A large-scale social audit was conducted in Villupuram district recently by an informal coalition of Non-Governmental Organization (NGOs) activists, women's rights organizations, and Dalit rights groups called the 'NREGA Watch Tamil Nadu', to access the impact of the programme on the people. This audit was part of the twice-yearly audit mandated by the NREGA act and conducted by the gram sabhas. Unlike other audits, a social audit is a participatory process that involves both people and the government in verifying outcomes and thus helps to strengthen transparency and accountability at all levels. In Villupuram,

The social audit began with the gram sabha. Twenty-five gram panchayats in five blocks were considered, and the audit was followed by a district level public hearing at Villupuram. It was convened by the local administration; state officials as well as the members of the Central Employment Guarantee Council Aruna Roy, Annie Raja, and Jean Dreze participated. These members also made filed visits. Jean Dreze observed however that everything that they saw in Villupuram only "strengthened our hopes for it. What ever the problems, the programme does provide hobs and wages for the poor and deprived... In terms of outcomes it is a positive picture, although in terms of processes and procedures, there are many issued that need to be addressed..."

Key among the positive findings of the audit was the fact that the daily minimum wage of Rs. 80 was being paid to everyone and that too within a week. Contractors and machines seem to have disappeared at the NREGA work sites and the over 80 per cent participation of women in the scheme indicates that it has become the mainstay for the women of the district, many of whom were working for Rs. 30 to Rs. 40 a day previously. Soumya Kidambi of the Mazdoor Kisan Shakti Sangathan (MKSS), who participated in the audit narrates how nitially when the women heard about the scheme they rushed to work sites with whatever vessels and utensils they had to carry head loads at the site. As soon as they had some money to spare from their early wages, the first thing that most of them bought was a basket for greater convenience at work. The local shops then started selling this basket, which is now colloquially referred to as "the hundred days basket." This symbolizes the empowerment and growing economic strength of women in the area. The mobilization of women is dramatically visible in the district; this in turn has the potential to positively impact on the economic conditions of the hitherto poor and marginalized rural communities.

There are however many areas of concern. The social audit found that across many villages, there was very little awareness of the entitlements of workers under the scheme such as the concept of work on demand, unemployment allowance, and the availability of work site facilities. Annie Raja however pointed out that awareness levels of entitlements jumped by about 80 per cent *after* the social audit. Discrepancies in the maintenance of job cards and muster rolls were also evident in many panchayats, the NREGA Council members observed. One audit participant said that the names of people who had gone to other districts to work were also found in some of the muster rolls. However there was not much evidence of any large-scale fudging, the audit noted. Among the more serious concerns was that employment is "rationed" in many gram panchayats and work is also "rotated" between different cast groups live in different wards, employment segregated by caste. As Aruna Roy pointed out, this contravenes the very intent of the Act which is meant to foster class solidarity and not intensify divisions.

The state administration has contended that "rationing" is the "democratic" way of giving work. This is incorrect, according to S. Kannayian of the Human Rights Law Network (HRLN). "The state is bound to give work on demand and this is a fundamental principle of the NREGA," he said adding that rationing will disappear if there is a change from supply to demand driven employment. The need to identify a shelf of work which will end rationing was also stressed in the social audit. If a wide range of work could be identified in the NREGA including the development of Dalit and Adivasi land sit would also enhance asset creation in poor communities, said Mr. Kannayian. The need to enlarge the scope of NREGA work to include other community and development projects was emphasized by many participants.

During the district level hearing in Villupuram, many of officials involved in local administration pointed out that there were problems such as the lack of productivity and problems with the measurement of work. Jean Dreze said that while productivity needs to be improved, it should not in any way undermine the Rs. 80 minimum wage which must be paid. The problem of work site measurement and a revised schedule of rates based on the nature of the work, the type of soil and other factors needs to be urgently re-examined. "There seems to be measurement illiteracy at all levels," said Mr. Kannayian. "A fresh time and motion study needs to be done with the people who are participating in the NREGA with complete transparency so that a fair and reasonable schedule of rates can be arrived at," he said. The lack of adequately trained staff at the local levels to administer the scheme transparently is also a serious drawback.

Other issues of concern include the absence of adequate work site facilities such as the lack of water and child care arrangements at the work sites. Where water was being provided, money was often being deducted from the wages. As for child care facilities, in a statement that was widely reported in the press, the administration initially suggested that with the existence of multiple balwadis and anganwadis in the State, there is no need for crèche facilities at the work site. When it was clarified that work site crèches are mandatory in the Act, the government revised its view and agreed to look into the matter. A survey of 104 NREGA participants by the students of Stella Maris College, Chennai, found that around 65 per cent of them were unaware that there should be a child care facility at the work site. Nearly half of the women said that they left their children at home and about 19 per cent brought them to the work site. These women said that they were often harassed by the supervisors and their co-workers. In many cases as the survey revealed, very young children often left at home unsupervised, and shockingly, there were a few cases where babies as young as 5 and 10 months were left alone at home unattended. Women with older children however did not report such difficulties as many of them were being sent to balwadis or schools.

In spite of a variety of challenging issues, the NREGA is still a big success especially when compared to other rural programmes. The government of Tamil Nadu has also not shown any intransigence in responding to the issues raised by the social audit. State officials have accepted that while the positive findings reflect the core strengths of the programme, there are many procedural problems that need to be urgently addressed. The Act itself if properly implemented in consonance with the Right to Information Act can enhance accountability and transparency in democratic governance and become a strong lifeline for the rural poor in India.

37

FACTORS SUSTAIN UNEMPLOYMENT–MEASURES TO MITIGATE IT

S. H. K. R. Prasad
D. Rajasekhar
N. Srihari
N. L. Swapna

INTRODUCTION

The term unemployment is very complex. The economists have used this term in various senses. According to William Beveridge, the unemployment indicates the absence of full employment and the full employment means having always more vacant jobs than unemployment, not slightly fewer jobs. It means that jobs are at fair wages, of such a kind, and so located that unemployed men can reasonably be expected to take them by consequence that the normal gap between leaning job and finding another will be very short. Mr. Fairchild defines the term 'unemployment' as "it is a forced and involuntary from remunerative work on the part of number of the normative working number of normative working forces during normal working time, at normal wages and under normal conditions."

THE TYPES OF UNEMPLOYMENT

The classical economists were of the view that the unemployment could be caused due to the demand of supply of labour. They enumerated two types of unemployment– frictional and voluntary. Frictional unemployment denotes mal-adjustment in the conditions of demand and supply of labour. The voluntary unemployment refers to the refusal to worker to accept a nominal wage in order to live. Considering the above two notions it can be said that unemployment does not exist under conditions of equilibrium.

However, this view has been refuted by Mr. J.M. Keynes. He opines that mere engagement in some productive occupation does not mean absence of unemployment. It is due to the fact that people may do inferior jobs inspite of their ability to do better jobs.

THE CAUSES OF UNEMPLOYMENT

The unemployment is caused due to external as well as internal factors.

- *The External Causes:* The external or objective causes of unemployment refer to economic conditions. This may result in out of cyclical fluctuations, industrial changes, seasonal economic activities and casual labour system.
- *The Internal Causes:* The internal or subjective causes of unemployment refer to physical, mental and moral deficiencies of the laboures responsible for their unemployment. It is important to note that the social and economic structure of the country is largely responsible for unemployment.

EVILS OF UNEMPLOYMENT

The evils of unemployment are many. Its evil effects may be summarized as follows:

- *Effects On Efficiency:* Unemployment adversely affects the efficiency of worker on account of low standard of living, the spirit of worker is greatly reduced.

- *Effects On Health:* The health of worker is greatly affected by unemployment. The unemployed people can't have sufficient money to spend on medicines and other amenities if needed.
- *Effects On Mental Ability:* The unemployment considerably increases the mental agony of workers.
- *Effects On The Standard Of Living:* The standard of living is also affected. It falls down.
- *Effects On Consistency And Responsibility:* The unemployed men cannot be responsible. They are always busy in looking after suitable jobs. They do not find suitable time to do a job in time.
- *Effects On National Income:* The national income is also affected by unemployment. The national divided is reduced and this leads to several hazards.
- *Wastage Of Labour:* During unemployment period a labour which is very important factor of production is wasted. Labourers keep on consuming without any addition to national product.
- *Instability:* Unemployment people are more attracted towards disturbances like demonstrations, strikes, processions. It has become the common phenomenon to undergo strikes to demand employment.
- *Exploitation Of Labour:* In unemployment conditions, supply of labour dominates the demand. More labourers become ready to work on less wage which results in their emploitation. The lack of the bargaining power, because of poverty and abundance of labour force.

SUGGESTIONS TO ERADICATE THE PROBLEM OF UNEMPLOYMENT IN INDIA

It is realized fact that unemployment affects our society and manifests itself in shape of crime, inefficiency, moral hazards etc. A good number of suggestions have been given for complete eradication of the problem. They may be summarized as follows:

- *Control Over Increase In Population:* In our country, the population is increasing in geometrical proportion. Therefore, the government of India have been trying its best to achieve the desired and through family planning and other devices.
- *Control Over Higher Education:* It now felt that the unemployment amongst educated people is because of fact that the door higher learning is open to all. The persons who don't get employment what to continue their study even through they don't perform well. The higher education should be given to those only who have aptitude and capabilities for that.
- *Change In The Education System:* The present system of education is not suited to our country. Gone are the days of British's who wanted to trained Indians for clerkship. Our education system should be recognized that it may not be able to produce clerks only but may produce persons who have a due respect for labour. Further more, the education should be employment oriented.
- *Emphasis On Indian Agriculture:* In India, the problem of unemployment is not only in urban sector but in rural sector as well. It has been suggested that the Indian agriculture should be reoriented. Method of cultivation should undergo some radical changes. Beside emphasis should be put on cottage industries.
- *Rapid Industrialization:* Rapid industrialization may solve the problem in many ways. It will provide employment opportunities to skilled workers. It will entail upon the industrial in efficiency also.
- *Extension Of Social Service:* The employment opportunities may be provided to a good number of people with the government launches upon social service programmes.
- *High Rates Of Investments And Savings:* By increasing domestic investment and savings, the problem of unemployment can be remedied to some extent.

- *Increasing The Number Of Employment Exchanges:* Employment exchanges provide informations regarding employment opportunities it is, therefore, necessary that a good number of employment exchanges should be opened.
- *Change In Social Structure:* Change in Social structure is also essential for eradication of unemployment. The people should not be bound by the traditional concept of cast system rather the should inculcate the sense of respect for physical labour.
- *H.M.L. Schemes:* The hard manual labour schemes should be implemented at large scale in rural areas. Recently the government of India give sanctioned a number H.M.L. schemes for different parts of our country.

By following, the above mentioned suggestions in a systematic planned manner no doubt in reducing unemployment.

REFERENCES

Karnati Lingaiah and T. Satyanarayana (1990), "Indian Economy", Stepling Publishers Pvt. Ltd., Noida, India.

Andrew J Osward (1991) "Surveys in Economics", Black well Oxford UK and Cambridge USA.

Dr. Nand Kishore Sharma (1993), "Managerial Economics ", RBSA Publishers S.M.S Highway, Jaipur, India.

Ramachandra. A and Ramana Murthy.V.V, (2003), "Business Economics". Tata Mc Graw – Hill Publishing Company Ltd., New Delhi.

LIEBENSTEIN (1957), "Economic Backwardness and Economic Growth", Wiley, New York.

38

PROVIDING LIVELIHOOD SECURITY: EXPERIMENT THROUGH NATIONAL RURAL EMPLOYMENT GUARANTEE SCHEME

P. Madhavi

INTRODUCTION

Government of India has initiated a programme, which aims at providing income security to (nose who do not have employment for atleast 100 days in a year. It recognizes peoples right to work, through the NREG Act, 2005. If implemented effectively, the Act operationalises the concept of right to work enshrined in the Constitution under the Directive Principles of State Policy (Part IV, Article 41). "The draft that was circulated attracted diverse opinions ranging from ridiculing it as a populist measure to hailing* it as the greatest ever initiative towards poverty alleviation and empowerment of the poor" T.S. Papola, 2005). Initially the intention was to provide legal guarantee for at least 100 days of employment, to one able bodied person from rural and urban, poor and middle class households. When the Act was finally passed in September 2005, it covers specified rural areas. Earlier programmers aiming at providing employment have been more in the nature of dole (opcit, Mihirshah , 2005, assuming a top down character). This one is different. As stated earlier, it not only recognizes peoples right to work, but also requires that they demand work- There is a possibility that people ane more vigilant and become involved in the process. Intact the very success of the scheme will depend on how eager, vigilant and aware people are. It also means that Grama panchayats realize their responsibility in this regard.

The Act aims at enhancing livelihood security for poor households in rural areas of the country, by providing at least 100 days of guaranteed wage employment, in every financial year to every house hold whose adult members volunteer to do unskilled manual work. The Act assures legal guarantee for at least 100 days through employment in asset creating public works programme at the minimum wage. No minimum wage is mentioned in the act. States are free to provide wages as per state laws. However, till further notice wages paid under the. scheme should not be less than Rs- 60/- per day.

Important features of the Act are:-

(i) One adult member from each house hold should make application to do unskilled, manual work.

(ii) Responsibility to provide work lies with the Gram Panchayat, although, monitoring and funding agencies are at the district that and state level.

(iii) If Grama panachayat is not in a position to provide employment within 15 days of q application being made. It has to pay unemployment allowance. Grama panchayat is required to identify projects in the Grampanchayat area as per recommendations of the Gram Sabha. This requires periodic convening of Grama Sabhas and Ward Sabhas. On their recommendation Gram Sabhas are expected to prepare development plans and maintain a shelf of possible works to be taken up under the scheme and when demand for work arises.

(iv) Programme officers, who are appointed by* the State Govt, are required to approve the projects, on a priority basis and sanction them.

(v) Grampanchayat shall allocate employment opportunities among the applicants and ask them to report to work.

(vi) Those who accept and take up work, are entitled to wages not less than the minimum wages applicable in the state, u/s. 3 of the Minimum Wages Act, 1948 for Agricultural labourers. Until a notification is made in this regard wage paid should not be less than Rs. 60/-

NREG SCHEME–FIELD STUDY AT NALGONDA DISTRICT

The most profound of schemes can get diluted, when it comes to implementation. Although, the Act in Just about two years old, it operates in the existing administrative setup. To study the effectiveness of the implementation of the scheme, Nalgonda Dist, in the Telangana region is chosen. Some-part of the studied is in the areas which are irrigated under the Nagarjuna Sagar canal and the remaining parts have no irrigation facility and are drought prone.

PROFILE OF NALGONDA DISTRICT

The profile is from the point of view of the NREGA. The District is notified under the Act, for the purpose of implementation.

No. of Mandals	:	59
No. of Grampanchayats	:	1184
No. of Job cards issued	:	5,29,634
No. of adults registered	:	12,58,637
No. of families	:	1,78,430
No. of persons	:	2,61,511
No. of works approved	:	25,907
Value of the works	:	Rs. 2,06,27,000
No. of works taken up	:	10,797
Value of the work	:	Rs. 85,32,000
No- of works completed 3	:	56
Value of the Work	:	Rs. 2,31,000
No. of household benefiting under the programme	:	1,78,430

No- of persons	:	2.61,571
Men	:	1.26.057
Women	:	1,40,864
No. of Man days work	:	29,78.315
No. of households which received 100 days of work	:	1.575

(Adapted from the Report submitted under the APREGS covered by the NREGA 2005.)

The report may appear impressive, although some short comings are obvious. The micro level facts are more revealing. The present study covers around 10 mandals majority of which come from the command area and are irrigated by Nagarjuna Sagar Canal. The remaining i.e. Devarakonda mandal, Chandampet mandal and P.A. Pally mandal however is not irrigated by the canal. They are drought prone areas. There is heavy migration from this area to Hyderabad, Ranga Reddy and Guntur Districts, The.study seeks to:-

(a) Comment on the effectiveness of implementation of the Act and problem associated with it.

(b) Usefulness of the Scheme in providing employment in regions with water resources and irrigated agriculture and regions without it.

Effectiveness in the Implementation of the Scheme and Problems Associations with it

The researchers conducted field survey and had interaction with Mandal development officers, Grama Sarpanch, Programme officers, village assistants appointed under the Act. Except for MDOs and Grama Sarpanch, rest are positions exclusively created under the Act. The effectiveness of implementation of the Scheme requires commitment of people at all levels particularly MOO downwards. A huge hierarchical structure in created, which, in itself creates"problems for implementation. This will be clear when we look at the powerlessness of the Gram Sarpanch who is expected to play a very important role in the Scheme.

Gram Sarpanch is the most critical element in the NREG Scheme

The Act provides for the Gram Panchayat as an institution, and Gram Sarp'ancn as the individual who have to make the scheme possible. The duties of Gram Panchayat as per Chapter IV of the Act are:-

1. Identification of projects in the Gram Panchayat area to be taken up under ^, the Scheme, on the recommendation of Grama Sabha.
2. Taking up projects under the scheme sanctioned by the programme officer. t
3. Prepare development plans for the area and maintain a shelf of possible works to be taken up as and when demand for work arises.
4. Identify priority of works to be taken up each year.
5. To deal .with problems arising in identification of works, payment of wages and implementation of the Scheme.
6. Monitor the execution of works within the Gram Panchayat.
7. Conduct regular social audit of all the projects taken up-
8. Make available all documents including muster rolls, bills, vouchers. measurement books for the purpose of conducting social audit.

If one examines the extent to which grampanchayats have actually the powers to do all the above, and even when they do have the powers, are they sufficiently committed to use them properly, we have some surprises coming.

The survey revealed that Grampanchayats do not have powers of identifying the works to be taken up. In all the mandals covered, only two types of works were under taken.

(i) Desilting of lakes and construction of bunds
(ii) Planting Acacia , sweet lime trees in privately owned lands.

Gram sarpanches told the researcher that they would want to take up construction and maintenance of roads in the villages, drainage work, construction and maintenance of school buildings, village health centers, community halls etc. In fact the procedure recommended to identify the works i.e. involving the villagers in the Gram Sabhas, is also not being adopted any where. Demand for bunds for the takes and tanks is an obvious choice. Where as plantation, work in private land holdings, has no particular long term relevance except a little commercial value when the trees grow up through the sale of timber. According to the Act, works to be taken up under the scheme have to be identified by organizing Gram sabhas and Ward sabhas. This is rarely done. Gram sabhas are often organized during the day time when only very old and very young are available. Those who can and will take up the jobs are not present. Further, people are not yet used to either making applications asking for work, nor participating in these decisions. They consider it the responsibility of the government to provide tnem work- Ironically, it is the farmers who are making demands on the sarpanch for employing workers on his land, for construction of bunds, planation work, cleaning and wells situated in their fields etc. In other wards, work is being provided as and when it is available but not when the workers actually needs it. The sarpanches with whom the researcher had discussion, i.e.Venkatapuram, Badaaiapurm. Damancheria, feel that the norms are very rigid.

It is difficult to show works on a continuous basis due to this. Their role appears to be restrictred to identifying works and making allotment. They have no freedom in using funds. There is no allocation of funds under the scheme. Works are identified according to the norms, allotted, and work undertaken in measured based on which payment is made. Thus there is no motivation or commitment on part of the Sarpanch in implementing the scheme. In fact they do not even play a role as active as the field assistants are the technical assistants.

It was observed that field assistants were both inexperienced and over burdened. They directly deal with the workers organise them in to groups, identify the sites, monitor the work, measure the work, check job cards, prepare muster rolls, deal with the workers dissatisfaction, answer their queries etc. Intact much of the day to day issues of effectiveness of the scheme depends on the village assistants. In the Devarakonda Mandal and Chandampeta mandal fraud by the field assistants reported. The MDO of the region is said to have expelled some of the field assistants against whom charges of fraud were proved.

The EGS is envisaged to be recognizing a persons right to demand paid work for livelihood. There is rarely any scope for people to demand work- The study revealed highly contradicting situations. In the command area of Miryalaguda Mandal, there are hardly any takers for work at given level of wages paid under the scheme. Except of a couple of summer months, they have enough work available. Farmers are vying with each other to influence the labour to work for them. The scheme has actually improved their bargaining, capacity. For a good days work. a worker can earn as much as Rs. 100 (due to ceiling, but more if permitted). Work on field pays them only Rs. 30/- Rs. 60/~ for an 8 hour day hard labour. Workers are found to be refusing to work in the field they used to work earlier, unless they Were paid better. Work under the scheme is referred to as governmental work and other work as non-governmental work. Where the villagers are aware of the work, and are more conscious of their rights, like in the command area, the wage levels have improved. However, in the non-command area, where the scheme has more fundamental implications of reducing migration if not arresting it, totally the situation is more complicated. The number of works identified are every few. There are number of instances where job cards were issued but no work provided for more than 6 months. Even when work was provided, it was hardly for 3-4 days and not beyond that. In some cases Job cards were not delivered to the villagers, and they are not sure what entries were made. Need for paid work at a decent wage in these areas (Devarakonda, Chandanampet and P.A. Palli mandate covered in the study) is &o high that. when an announcement is made the work is available under the EGS, hundreds from nearby villages turn up. Since none can be refused, all of them are offered work. In such cases, wages work out to be very less, say at the Rest. 20/- - Rs. 30/- per day, which is far below the minimum wage or even the expected wage by the villagers,

Another complaint that is heard, both in the command and non-command areas, which is also acknowledged by the officers incharge of the scheme, is the abnormal delay in payment of wages for work done. It is any where from one month to six months. More than non- availability of work, delay in the payment is the reason for the villagers in not being interested in the work. To quote the villagers in the Chandampet Mandal" We will work only if wages are paid immediately and as and when they arise. We get paid immediately when we work in towns end cities like Miryalaguda. Hyderabad & Guntur on construction sites and as hamalis. We go for work when we need money and don not go when we don't need money" What they mean is that, they should be provided with work when they need it and not made to work by compulsion. When they work, wages should be paid immediately. This is the only way to prevent migration. As of now, villagers from the non-command areas continue to migrate to urban areas in search of work. They even felt that if regular work was provided, wages paid immediately, they would be willing to stay back even if wages were tow.

Although person in charge of implementing the scheme attribute delays to the disinterested employees of the Postal Department, the. villagers believe that the field assistants and technical assistants do not maintain or submit records properly. It is true to say th»t wages are. not paid in cash, but are paid through, pay orders payable at post-offices or sub-post offices. Neither of them exist ir» some of the remote villages. There are sub-post officers for a cluster of villages- Some of these villages are not even connected by regular transport facilities. In some cases there is delay in opening accounts. The MDO appeared helpless as the subject comes under the Centra! Government. Apparently by the employees have no incentive to open and operate these accounts which they consider as over burden of work. Villagers complained about names being written wrongly, frauds in claiming the bills and the work undertaken under the schemes are of poor qualty. That the claims about allotment of work and its completion by the MDO's office was also misleading. The researcher is inclined to agree with the last aspect, because in the process of cross checking, it was observed that, which the MDOs office showed that nearly 50 days of work to those who needed it, villagers said that they worke*for less than 10 days for the whole year. Work not even continuous.

Another issue that appears to be contentious is that the type of work taken up under the scheme, requires team work. Work is offered only when groups of workers are available and willing to work. tt individuals have a need for work, no work is offered- This causes hardship. Even the official report prepared for the distinct (Nalgonda) shows that, where the No. of households demanding work under the Scheme are 1,76,430, only 1575,were provided with 100 days of work during the year. The report no where shows the average no. of days of work shown. The report shows that the average wage paid under the scheme in the district for the year is Rs. 88.7. There is wide variation within the region. Actual wage ranges between Rs. 30/– RS.100/.

Under the Act, Grama Sabhas have the power and the responsibility to conduct social audit of the implementation, periodically. No where in the region studied, have grama sabhas have they taken it up. In the Miryalaguda region. NGO's and others like the Loksatta party have conducted in some villages in the mandal- They have commented on delays in payment of wages, but have not commented upon nature of the work, and frauds in submitting the bills, quantity and quality of work. or the inability of the Grampanchayat to identify required number of works.

Thus the proactive role that Grama sabhas are required to play in the critical aspects of the EGS, they are not playing. The public continue to be at the receiving/or not receiving end, thereby, at the mercy of the district administration. Conceptually the NREGs is good. It can easily get diluted in its implementation without having any impact on the lives or live hoods of the rural people, for whom it meant. It is tile responsibility of all those alt concerned to prevent this.

REFERENCES

Mihirshaffi (2005), Economic and Political Weekly, EPW. Feb 12-18- Vol XL No.7.

Papola T.S. (2005), Employment Guarantee. A Universal Programme in Feasible" Economic and Political Weekly, Feb 12-18 Vol XL No.7.

39

SOCIAL AND ECONOMIC ASPECTS OF UNEMPLOYMENT AND REMEDIES

C. Singa Reddy

Can we segregate economics from society? Previously it was social status, But now it is economic, previously the relations were social. Now they are economic. The society counts you in monitory terms. In a way the society encourages you to earn more and more, persons forget means of earning and earn through all means. But some persons fail to earn. They don't find job opportunities. Not only the educated but also the illiterate fail to find worse. As there is no work their comes fell And in some cases there won't be only income. Some of the unemployed youth are becoming house husbands. You can estimate the respect of such house husbands.

Some persons may become thieves or they may indulge in anti-social activities, some demand dowry for future maintenance. And some may demand some more amount after marriage. The unemployed are becoming a burden for the society. You may find involvement of the unemployed in naxalism. Some are seeing for political employment for one post or other in politics- As marriage is a social aspect or a social compulsion, parents force their children for marriage. The unemployed youth/non-earning members also marry.

Resultantly they be get children, some of such parents may become prostitutes. The children of such parents fail to receive proper guidance and education.

I have seen some husbands who live on the earnings of their wives. Their earn something by stilling. These husbands spend a large position of such earning on purchase of alcohol or in playing cards. Most of the unemployed-are becoming sieves for one had habit or other. No doubt, education is the potential instrument. But education that we import now cannot solve economic problems. Then there should come a change in the system of education. If by education we mean writing and reading. What is the use of teaching some lessons from third standard to the P.G. Level. Of course the length of the some topic varies.

Education should not make un-productive educated persons, but productive educated. Many or all educational commissions demanded worse oriented or productive oriented education. The student who posses Ph.D may fail to earn some or any amount. But the student who posses VIII class will / may earn something if he is trained in mechanism or manufacturing items like dolls. I have met one of my students who is running a mechanism shop of his own- In his words, he learnt the mechanism while studying Intermediate. And now he is happy, in another case I saw a boy who posses VII class repairing gas sieves- So, education should be productive oriented. Some of the educated may join hands within the destructive forces. By the time she/he completes X class should be in a position to produce something or repair something.

I have mentioned the unemployed also be get children. The Government should that it will not give any aid financial assistance for those who deliver who deliver more than one. Otherwise that type of baby strength will be social and economic burden. They may pose a threat to the society, What happens if the Government posses a low that those who will be in a position to earn will only be eligible for marriage? Nothing, other than better. Otherwise even the persons who fail to earn or produce will produce children. Instead of pro unemployment scholarships/salaries better of the authorities pay attention on providing training facilities which enable the unemployed youth whether educated or uneducated to produce or repair. The Government is spend of huge amount on education. Resultant of may educated youth are coming as unemployed. But after VII, X class such spending may be stopped. Only the should be free education after certain level and the remaining, persons should be' trained in productive or mechanical worse. I mean to say provide free education only to the meritorious and force others to undergo training in one trend or other to produce or repair. The parents who are interested in the education of their children who are weak will be are their ex productive. The students who do not under go the training provided by the Government may learn the work of their parents. But after degree or P.G. they will not do the hard work of their parents. So the should be taken care of at the early stage from VIII/X Class.

40

EMPLOYMENT OPPORTUNITIES GENERATED THROUGH SEZS

M. Syamala

INTRODUCTION

SEZS are demarcated zones where units operate under a set of rules and regulations which differ from those applicable to other units in the country. They are present to give a big push to the trade, employment and investment in the country. It is claimed that SEZs would build infrastructure and enhance employment opportunities. SEZs play a pivotal role in the economic development of many countries.

This paper is an attempt is see the advantages and disadvantages of special economic zones. The losses and benefits that are gained from these zones are analyzed in the coming paras.

WHAT ARE SEZS?

SEZs are the Special Economic Zones which are proposed to be specially delineated duty free enclaves for the purpose of trade operations, duty and tariffs. SEZs are specially demarcated zones where units operate under a set of rules and regulations different from those applicable to other units in the country. SEZs help and become a means to develop urbanization in the country. These zones would be self contained and integrated having their own infrastructure and support services.

The very existences of SEZs are highly debatable. The Union Government after prolonged deliberations has notified SEZ Rules in February, 2006. The Union Government has cleared as many as 110 SEZs. SEZs are expected to offer high quality infrastructure facilities and support services, besides allowing for the duty free import of capital goods and raw materials. Further facilities like fiscal incentives, banking facilities and other procedures are offered. Setting of SEZs is also treated as an infrastructure development activity and offer same incentives.

Any private, public, joint sector or state Government or its agencies or Foreign Companies can set up an SEZ. 100 percent FDI is permitted for all investments in SEZs, except. SEZ units are required to be positive net foreign exchange earners and are not subjected to any minimum value addition norms or export obligations. Goods flow into the SEZ area from the Domestic Tariff Area (DAT) will be treated as exports and goods coming from the SEZ area into the DTA are treated as imports. For sector specific SEZS there is no restriction of minimum area.

Currently, a number of SEZ projects are coming up in the country. The government has sanctioned about 17 SEZs to be set up in the private sector or the joint sector. Of these, the projects at Positra (Gujarat), Vishakhapatnam (Andhra Pradesh), Indore (Madhya Pradesh) and Navi Mumbai (Maharashtra) are in advanced stages of planning and development, while the others are preparing to get off the ground.

INCENTIVES AND BENEFITS

Besides providing infrastructure and access to a large well-trained and skilled work force, the SEZ policy also provides enterprises and developers with a favourable and attractive framework of incentives. They are-

1. 100 percent income tax exemption for a block of five years and an additional 50 % tax exemption for 2 years thereafter.
2. 100% FDI in the manufacturing sector permitted through automatic route, barring a few sectors.
3. External commercial borrowing by SEZ units up to US $ 500 million in a year without any maturity restrictions through recognized banking channels.
4. Facility to retain 100% foreign exchange receipts in Exchange Earner's Foreign Currency Account.
5. 100% FDI permitted to SEZ franchisee in providing basic telephone services in SEZs.
6. No cap on foreign investment for small scale sector reserved items.
7. Exemption is given from industrial licensing requirements for items reserved for the SSI sector.
8. No import license required.
9. Exemption from customs duties on import of capital goods, raw material, consumables etc.
10. Exemption from Central Excise Duties on procurement of capital goods, raw materials etc from the domestic market.
11. Facility to realize and repatriate export proceeds within 12 months.
12. Job work on behalf of domestic exporters for direct export allowed.

INCENTIVES GIVEN TO THE DEVELOPERS

There are various incentives which are been provided to the developers of SEZs. Some of them are listed below–

1. Exemption from duties on import/procurement of goods for the development operation and maintenance of SEZ.
2. Income tax exemption for a period of 10 years in 15 years.

3. Exemption from service tax.
4. FDI to develop townships with in SEZs with residential, educational, health care and recreational facilities permitted on a case-to-case basis.

PROCESS OF ACQUIRING LAND FOR DEVELOPING SEZS

One has to follow some defined guide line while acquiring land for SEZS. The land Acquisition Act of 1894 provides for payment of compensation at market value and also a pay of 30 percent of market value of compensate for the compulsory nature of acquisition. The value of the land is determined on basis of the Archaic Act as on the date of issue of notification for acquisition of the land. The National Policy for Resettlement and Rehabilitation of Project Affected Families – 2003 is in force since February 2004. This is a small hope for the land lenders/ losers. The benefits that they can acquire are-

If an agricultural land is acquired for setting SEZ then an equal amount of agricultural land should be provided along with the stamp duty and financial assistance for developing the land.

Some percentage can be claimed in the SEZ area after it is developed.

In additional to the normal compensation for the land, the land owners can have rights of owing a part of the developed land in SEZ. This could be nearly 10 percent in industrial projects and 20 percent in the infrastructure projects.

The precautions which should be taken which acquiring land for SEZs are–

(a) The land should be a waste land which is vast in its length and width.
(b) It can also be that land which has just single crop in a year.
(c) Multiple crop land should never be acquired at any cost.
(d) The land locked in closed units can be included after paying the stakeholders.

(e) Land should be well connected when acquired for developing a SEZ.

(f) The SEZ land should not be located in too close proximity of urban center as it may pressures the urban centers.

(g) The topography should be convent for trading.

Some of the analyst view that if agriculture land is acquired for developing SEZ then in near future we may have to face food security problems. But some other analyze that acquisition of agricultural land may not really reduce the farm land or create any kind of food security problem at an alarming quantity. It is believed and understood by them that it can just decline the share of agriculture contribution to GDP and that would increase the industrial development and it is concluded that the ultimate result will be that there will be shifts in the occupational structure in the country. If we harbour ambition for a rapid economic growth and power in the global market we really cannot effort to remain largely agrarian.

SOME SUCCESSFUL CASES OF SEZS IN INDIA

Government of India has already given an in-principle approval for setting up an SEZ in Andhra Pradesh near the port of *Visakhapatnam* on the east cost of India. Two sites have been identified in the Atchuthapuram; these sites are adjacent to each other. While one site is towards Atchuthapuram, the other is towards Rambilli. The site is located 55 kms south of Visakhapatnam airport and 50 kms from the port. NH-5 is about 5 kms away and the Chennai Howrah main rail line is 20 kms away.

Advantages– This belt is closely located near sea belt. There is as much as 9,200 acres already been identified for SEZ development and that can also be easily acquired. The belt provides various advantages like-

1. There is are major habitation near by
2. There is no agricultural activity in the near by areas.
3. land for future development is available

4. 40% of the land is saline with no vegetation and rest is under single crop.
5. There are no industries in the surrounding areas.
6. Natural sea fronting and port proximity is very advantageous
7. Site infrastructure is very encouraging
8. No environmentally sensitive area is proximity
9. Time and cost of acquiring the land is very less
10. Large number of women and men get direct and indirect employment.

Other area is Santa Cruz Electronics Export Processing Zone *(SEEPZ) Mumbai*. It was established in 1973-74. Considering the high potential and free from pollution, the Government of India decided to permit manufacture and export of items from SEEPZ during 1987-88. The zone provides basic infrastructure such as constructed factory premises is well built, communication facilities etc. The SEEPZ centre also provides public utilities such as post office, public telex, banks including ATM. A new SEZ scheme has been introduced in the Export and Import Policy from 01-042000, with a view to provide an internationally competitive and good environment for export production.

Advantages– There are many advantages in the site some of them are listed below-

1. It reaps almost all the advantages which are listed above in the case of Visakhapatnam SEZ
2. No license required for import
3. 100% tax exemption for 5 year and 50 % exemption for 2 years thereby.
4. facilities to set up overseas banking units
5. employment opportunities for men and women
6. No cap on foreign investment of SSI reserved items.
7. job work on behalf of domestic exports for direct exports is allowed

8. developed plots and ready to use build up space is available
9. No separate documentation required for customs and exim policy.
10. And many more such advantages can be reaped.

EMPLOYMENT OPPORTUNITIES PROVIDED BY VARIOUS SEZS IN INDIA

Some of the Export Promote zones have been converted to SEZ and they too provide employment opportunities. The tables which are given below show as what is the level of employment observation by SEZs in various years. Table 1 shows the employment in government/state government/ private SEZs established prior to SEZ Act as on 31-3-2008. Accordingly nearly 2 lakhs people are employed in the central government SEZs in 1122 units. Nearly 45 thousand people are employed in the state government and private SEZs in 403 units. So a total of nearly2.4 lakhs are employed in 1525 units. Table 2 shows the government SEZs which are converted from EPZs. This table shows employment opportunities directly to both women and men. Table 3 shows the state/private SEZs employment opportunities directly and indirectly provided to various people prior to SEZ Act, 2005.

Table 1
Employment in Govt. /State Govt. /Private SEZs Established Prior to SEZ Act as on 31-03-2008

	Employment	*No. of Units*
Central government SEZs	193474 persons	1122
State Govt./Private SEZs established prior to SEZ Act	44768 persons	403
Total	238242 persons	1525

Table 2
Government SEZs (EPZS Converted as SEZs)

	Direct Employment		
Zone	*Men*	*Women*	*Total*
Kandla SEZ	9873	9129	19002

Contd.

Table 3
State/Private SEZs Prior to SEZ Act, 2005

Name of the Zone	*Indirect Employment*		*Direct Employment*			
				Current Direct Employment		
	Proposed Employment	*Current Employment*	*Proposed Direct Employment*	*Men*	*Women*	*Total*
Surat SEZ	8500	8200	10000	5580	3720	9300
Manikanchan SEZ	2500	–	–	1715	14	1729
Jaipur SEZ	100	75	2500	2403	38	2441
Indore SEZ	0	763	10000	4762	76	4838
Jodhpur SEZ	5000	967	2500	265	0	265
Salt lake electronic city WIPRO	6000	–	–	–	–	3948
Mahindra City SEZ (IT)	20550	8793	17360	4018	2135	6153
Mahindra City SEZ (Auto ancillary)	475	2566	530	428	23	451
Mahindra City SEZ (textile)	0	633	0	225	619	844
Nokia	0	596	20000	5920	7703	13623
Moradabad SEZ	500	105	5000	60	0	60
Surat Apparel Park	0	0	25000	810	306	1116
Total	43125	21997	42890	19396	6625	44768

	Direct Employment		
Zone	*Men*	*Women*	*Total*
SEEPZ SEZ	58747	26356	85103
Noida SEZ	27080	5920	33000
MEPZ SEZ	12706	16489	29195
Cochin SEZ	6336	5038	11374
Falta SEZ	5612	5988	11600
Vishakpatnam SEZ	2342	1859	4200
Total	122696	70778	193474

POLICIES OF THE GOVERNMENT

Government of India has come up with a policy and incentive framework to address the needs of the principal stakeholders in a SEZ. The key stakeholders have been defined as Developers and operators, locating industries, residents of the zone. The government aims to provide incentives to these stakeholders realizing fully that the success of SEZs would depend on an enabling policy frame work that balances interests of each of these stakeholders. In addition, the Government of A.P is examining additional incentives and benefits that can be extended to all the stakeholders, especially developers and operators. Some of these include–

- A state infrastructure Developed Enabling Act
- An Area Development Act to delegate single window approvals and clearance powers for zone administration
- Additional enabling provision in the state contract labour act.

CRITICISMS

There are various criticisms regarding land acquisition and developing SEZs. Some of them are listed below-

1. The incentive offered are excessive and inequitable
2. They entail revenue losses
3. The incentives that are provided to the developers are largely same.
4. The government should change the policy and legal environment to promote economic activity, instead if

creating islands or areas which are free from regulatory obstacles

5. Acquisition of land to set SEZ is been done in violent manner in some parts of the country.

CONCLUSION

SEZ is means to achieve growth and employment in the country. It helps in the development of industries. For this government should formulate and R&D policy in such a way that it can help the growth of SEZs and development of industries in the country which can solve the problem of unemployment to some extent. India has many advantages in setting suitable SEZs in various parts of the country. So, interest should be taken by both public and private individuals to develop the country. May be land available for us is not as vast as SEZs which are developed in China. But we can utilize the limited land in such a way that we could reap optimum returns and maximum advantages in providing employment to many. maximum advantage in providing employment to many

REFERENCE

—(2005), Yojana, May–Article–"Special Economic Zones", by Saumitra Mohan.

—(2006), Economic and Political Weekly.

—(2006), Yojana–October.

—www.pria.org

—www.sez/India/in

—www.icftu.org

41

UNEMPLOYMENT INSURANCE– NEED OF THE HOUR

A. V. V. Siva Prasad
M. Srinivasa Narayana

INTRODUCTION

In economics, a person who is able and willing to work yet is unable to find a paying job is considered unemployed. Unemployment will have its impact on society and the economy in terms of various costs. The social costs of unemployment include severe financial hardship and poverty, debt, homelessness and housing stress, family tensions and breakdown, boredom, alienation, shame and stigma, increased social isolation, crime, erosion of confidence and self-esteem, the atrophying of work skills and ill-health. Most of these increase with the duration of unemployment. Unemployed people report that being unemployed is one of the worst things that can happen to them (White 1991). In addition, unemployment falls disproportionately on already disadvantaged groups in society. Understanding the forces that create unemployment, and then trying to mitigate their negative effects to the greatest extent possible, is a central issue in economics.

CAUSES OF UNEMPLOYMENT

There are differed views and opinions on the causes of unemployment in an economy. Keynesian economics views that unemployment results from insufficient effective demand for goods and service in the economy (cyclical unemployment). Others point to structural problems (inefficiencies) inherent in labor markets (structural unemployment). Classical or neoclassical economics tends to reject these explanations, and focuses more on rigidities imposed on the labour market from the outside, such as minimum wage laws, taxes, and other regulations that may discourage the hiring of workers (classical unemployment). Yet others see unemployment as largely due to voluntary choices by the unemployed (frictional unemployment). On the other extreme, Marxists see unemployment as a structural fact helping to preserve business profitability and capitalism (Marxian unemployment). The different perspectives may be right in different ways, contributing to the understanding of different types of unemployment.

UNEMPLOYMENT SCENARIO IN INDIA

The unemployment scenario in India has always been quite acute. With a huge population and slow growth of job opportunities, unemployment has been widespread in India. Large scale unemployment has led to several socio-economic problems like poverty, malnutrition, antisocial and criminal activities, drug and substance abuse, etc. The lack of proper unemployment insurance schemes has further aggravated this problem.

In the early 1990s, major economic reforms were undertaken in India. One of the major objectives of these economic reforms was to boost employment in the Indian economy. However, though the economic reforms were successful in raising productivity and attracting FDI (Foreign Direct Investment), the growth in job opportunities was not as high as had been expected.

SOME OF THE IMPORTANT ASPECTS RELATED TO THE UNEMPLOY-MENT SCENARIO IN INDIA:

The growth in labor force in India is much higher than the growth of jobs.

Table 1
Comparison of Population Growth Rate and Unemployment Growth Rates

Year	*Unemployment Rate (%)*	*Population Growth Rate (%)*	*Net Migration Rate /1,000 Population*
2002	8.8	1.51	-0.07
2003	8.8	1.47	-0.07
2004	9.5	1.44	-0.07
2005	9.2	1.4	-0.07
2006	8.9	1.38	-0.07
2007	7.8	1.606	-0.05
2008	7.2	1.578	-0.05

Unemployment rate: This entry contains the percent of the labor force that is without jobs.

Population growth rate: The average annual percent change in the population, resulting from a surplus (or deficit) of births over deaths and the balance of migrants entering and leaving a country.

Migration rate: This entry includes the figure for the difference between the number of persons entering and leaving a country during the year per 1,000 persons (based on midyear population). An excess of persons entering the country is referred to as net immigration (e.g., 3.56 migrants/1,000 population); an excess of persons leaving the country as net emigration (e.g.,-9.26 migrants/1,000 population). The net migration rate indicates the contribution of migration to the overall level of population change. High levels of migration can cause problems such as increasing unemployment and potential ethnic strife (if people are coming in) or a reduction in the labor force, perhaps in certain key sectors (if people are leaving).

- The unorganized sector in India accounts for 90% of the employment. The unorganized sector consists of agricultural workers in the rural areas and contract and sub-contract laborers in the urban areas.
- More than 90 per cent of the labour force is employed in the "unorganised sector", i.e. sectors which don't provide with the social security and other benefits of employment in the "organised sector."
- Self employment accounts for more than 60% of the employed population of India.
- Casual workers, who get jobs only at times and remain unpaid when they don't have work, constitute 30% of the workforce, while only 10% are regular employees. Merely two-fifth of this 10% is employed in the government sector.
- Around 70% of the labor force in India has education below primary level or is illiterate.
- There exists very high underemployment in various sectors of the labor force in India. Disguised unemployment also exists in various sectors of the Indian economy.
- Regional imbalances in the unemployment scenario in India are another important factor. This has led to inter-state labor migration in the Indian economy.
- India's labour force is growing at a rate of 2.5 per cent annually, but employment is growing at only 2.3 per cent. Thus, the country is faced with the challenge of not only absorbing new entrants to the job market (estimated at seven million people every year), but also clearing the backlog.
- Unorganised sector is made up of jobs in which the Minimum Wage Act is either not, or only marginally, implemented. The absence of unions in the unorganised sector does not provide any opportunity for collective bargaining.

Table 2
Sector-wise Absorption of Labour

Agriculture	62 per cent
Manufacturing & construction	16 per cent
Services	10 per cent
Sundry/miscellaneous jobs	12 per cent

Table 3
Unemployment–Age Structure

Age (years)	*Unemploy-ment Rate*	*Males*	*Females*
0 – 14	31.5	189,238,487	172,168,306
15 – 64	63.3	374,157,581	352,868,003
65 and above	5.2	28,285,796	31,277,725

(2008 est.)

Table 4
Ratio of Youth Unemployment Rate to Adult Unemployment Rate

Year	*Both Sexes*	*Male*	*Female*
1994	3.7	4.1	3
2000	3.9	3.7	4.3
2004	3	3.1	2.8

Source: United Nations Statistics Division

Recent studies have revealed the fact that growth of unemployment in India at current rates can lead to devastating results. At this rate, India is expected to have a 30% unemployment rate by 2020. This would mean that there would be 21 crore jobless people in India. The decline in job creation in agriculture has been identified as one of the important reasons behind the increasing unemployment in India. To eradicate this problem, Government of India along with various state governments, developed and implemented various employment and social security schemes. The summary of these schemes are given in the following table.

Table 5
Various Employment and Social Security Schemes in India

- *Community Development Programme*- 1952- Overall development of rural areas with people's participation.
- *Intensive Agriculture Development Programme*- 1960-61 - To provide loan, seeds, fertilizer, tools to the farmers.
- *Employment Guarantee Scheme of Maharashtra*- 1972-73- To assist the economically weaker section of the rural society.
- *Twenty Point Programme*- 1975- Poverty eradication and raising the standard of living.
- *Food for work Programme*- 1977-78- Providing food grains to labour for the work of development.
- *National Rural Employment Programme*- 1980- To provide profitable employment opportunities to the rural poor.
- *Development of women & children in Rural Areas*- 1982- To provide suitable opportunities of self-employment to the women belonging to the rural families who are living below the poverty line.
- *Rural Landless Employment Guarantee Programme*- 1983- For providing employment to landless farmers & labourers.
- *Self-employment of the Educated Unemployed Youth*- 1983-84- To provide financial and technical assistance for self-employment.
- *Council for Advancement of People's Action & Rural Technology*- 1986- To provide assistance for rural prosperity.
- *Self-Employment programme for the Urban poor*- 1986- To provide self employment to urban poor through provision of subsidiary and bank credit.
- *Jawahar Rozgar Yojana*- 1989- To provide employment to rural unemployed.
- *Nehru Rozgar Yojana*- 1989- To provide employment to urban unemployed.
- *Scheme for Urban Micro Enterprises*- 1990 - To assist the urban poor for small enterprises.
- *Scheme for Urban Wage Employment*- 1990 - To provide wages employment after arranging the basic facilities for poor people in the urban areas where population is less than one lakh.
- *Scheme for Housing and Shelter Up-gradation*- 1990- To provide employment by means of shelter up-gradation in the urban areas where population is between 1 to 20 lakhs.
- *Employment Assurance Scheme*- 1993- To provide employment of at least 100 days in a year in villages.
- *Swaran Jayanti Shahri Rozgar Yojana*- 1997- To provide gainful employment to urban unemployed and under employed poor through self employment or wage employment.
- *Swarna Jayanti Gram Swarozgar Yojana*- 1999- For eliminating rural poverty and unemployment and promoting self employment.
- *Pradhan Mantri Gram Sadak Yojana*- 2000- To line all villages with Pacca road.

- *Sampurna Gramin Rojgar Yojana*- 2001- Providing employment & food security.
- *Jai Prakash Narain Rozgar Guarantee Yojana* - 2002-3 - Employment guarantee in most poor districts.
- *Rural Employment Guarantee Yojana*- 2005-6- 100 days assured employment.
- *Rajiv Gandhi Shramik Kalyan Yojna*– 2005- unemployment allowance for the employees covered under ESI scheme.

FOCUS OF THE ARTICLE:

From the above part of the article, it was clear that the unemployment problem in India is one of the serious issues which need to be tackled immediately. To mitigate this problem, Government of India has initiated several schemes right from the independence (see the schemes in the table 5). Along with the central government initiatives, various state governments are also implementing several employment and social security schemes to eradicate the social evils that may arise with unemployment and poverty. The present article will now focus on one of the social security scheme named "Unemployment Insurance". These types of schemes are quite popular in most of the developed economies and now attracting the attention of other economies. The rest of the article will emphasizes on this scheme by throwing a light on the need of unemployment insurance, its application in India and the results of it.

UNEMPLOYMENT INSURANCE

In economics unemployment compensation is termed 'unemployment insurance'. The closure of many industries and large scale retrenchment of workers leading to unemployment have rendered the working class without any social security cover. At present unemployment is one of the biggest challenges for the social security sector. As global competition increases, the burden of unemployment also develops on an unprecedented scale and strengthening the social safety net for such workers is imperative. National and International forum including the United Nations stress the need for social justice and safety net for the working population. According to the International Labour Office (ILO), seventy-five per cent of the 150 million people unemployed around the world lack any unemployment insurance protection. Austria, Belgium, Denmark, Finland, France, Germany, Iceland, Luxembourg, Netherlands, Norway, Portugal, Spain, Sweden and Switzerland provide the most generous unemployment protection systems while, Australia, Canada, Ireland, Japan, New Zealand, the United Kingdom and the United States belong to "medium-level type systems". Fewer of the unemployed in these countries receive benefits and the compensation that is provided is lower than those available in the first tier of countries.

Benefit payments (net wage replacement rates) range from 23% of wages in New Zealand to 58% in Canada and the United States, among these "medium-level" countries. In contrast, "top level" countries such as Finland and Spain provide 63% and 77% respectively of national average earnings in their unemployment insurance.

THE LACK OF UNEMPLOYMENT INSURANCE PROTECTION

Developed Countries

In the top 14 countries listed above, unemployment protection consists of various layers of benefits. The first and most important one consists of unemployment insurance benefits paid during the initial period following the loss of a job, with average net replacement rates of more than 60% of national average earnings. This rate is significantly higher than in those countries belonging to the next category.

Most countries with a high-level system have a second layer of unemployment benefits, usually called unemployment assistance. This layer covers workers who have exhausted their entitlements to unemployment insurance and provides them with a grace period before they come within the purview of less generous social assistance schemes.

Developing Countries

Workers who are fortunate enough to be covered by unemployment benefits are mainly concentrated in industrialized countries, but for those who work in the rural or urban informal sectors in developing countries-including 750 to 900 million underemployed workers-hardly any unemployment protection exists at all.

The ILO says that these groups of workers should be assisted through employment in labour-intensive infrastructure programmes- "feeder roads, land reclamation, minor dams, wells and irrigation systems, drainage and sewerage, schools and health centres". Employment provided under such programmes can be organized so that workers can obtain an employment guarantee for a number of days per year.

UNEMPLOYMENT COSTS

The existence of unemployment insurance discourages certain people from working; those who value the compensation over the amount gained if working will not seek employment. In economics unemployment refers to one that is seeking employment and cannot find it. If one does not wish to be employed (employed & unemployed), then they aren't even in the labour force, as they do not supply or wish to supply any labour. Excessive unemployment insurance (e.g. benefits in New Zealand) decreases the labour force and puts downward pressure on GDP growth by causing downward pressure on production levels.

Private Benefits/Costs vs. Public Benefits/Costs: The opportunity cost of being unemployed is the amount of money to be gained from being employed, pus the social aspects of employment and unemployment. If one values unemployment more than working, they will seek unemployment (i.e. quite or get fired) or continue to be unemployed. However, the fallacy in this reasoning is that this only concerns the individual's costs and benefits. The public costs and benefits are ignored when making an individual transaction, such as the downward pressure on GDP growth by creating a shortage (however subtle) of labour.

Downward Pressure on GDP: If one is employed, they provide income tax payments (government revenue), labour, and consumption for the economy. If one is unemployed they take unemployment insurance (government spending), decrease labour in the economy, and only provide consumption. Consumption would likely have been higher if the individual had sought employment, after all there are many negative connations with being unemployed, which would affect their decision on whether to seek employment or not.

NEED FOR UNEMPLOYMENT INSURANCE IN INDIA

With the initiation of economic reforms, Indian economy is undergoing unprecedented change. Integrating the Indian economy with that of the World's, the industry has been exposed to global competition. In order to remain buoyant most of the companies want to reduce costs by way of upgrading technology and reducing workforce. But under the Industrial Disputes Act, 1947 downsizing cannot be resorted to without Government permission. The Act is applicable to establishments employing one hundred workers or more. The experience shows that permission to close down have not been coming readily. As a result of compulsion of situation many such establishments have either introduced voluntary retirement schemes for downsizing or have closed down and vanished from the scene without paying compensation, dues etc. to workers.

The Second Labour Commission has reported that a large number of workers have lost their jobs as a result of VRS, retrenchment and closures both in the organised and unorganised sectors. The exact number is not known as no data on this has been compiled by any State Government.

COVER DURING UNEMPLOYMENT

The advocates of 'hire and fire' also want to bring about a fundamental change in the nature or perception of employment. They want employment to be on the basis of contracts for stipulated periods–a total departure from the current system in vogue in most kinds of employments.

Most of the developed countries where the majority of jobs are contracts have elaborate and effective system of social security. Even in China, to quote an instance, there are stringent laws on social security system that takes care of worker's income and requirements at least for two or three years of transition or unemployment. In India, we don't have such provisions. The Labour Ministry made a small beginning in this regard recently by launching Rajiv Gandhi Shramik Kalyan Yojana (RGSKY) for providing unemployment allowance to workers who are rendered unemployed involuntarily due to retrenchment/closure of factory etc. after fulfilling certain eligibility conditions.

Table 6
Highlights of Rajiv Gandhi Shramik Kalyan Yojana (RGSKY)

Eligibility Conditions: The loss of employment should be on account of closure of the factory or establishment, retrenchment or permanent invalidity arising out of non-employment injury.

(i) The insured person should have contributed under the ESI Scheme for a minimum period of five years prior to loss of employment.

(ii) The insured person should have been entitled for sickness benefit during the last four contribution periods immediately proceeding the date of unemployment.

(iii) Unemployment allowance shall cease to be payable from the date the insured person gets reemployed elsewhere.

Rate of Unemployment Allowance: The daily rate of unemployment allowance shall be the "standard benefit rate" as specified in the table of Standard Benefit Rates under Rule-54 of ESI (Central) Rules, 1950, corresponding to the average daily wage drawn by the said insured person during the last four completed contribution periods, immediately preceding the date of unemployment.

Duration of Unemployment Allowance: The maximum period for which an insured person shall be entitled to draw unemployment allowance during his entire insurable employment, is six months. The allowance can be availed in one spell or in different spells of not less than one month. The ESIC recently decided to increase the amount to six months' salary disbursed over a period of one year.

Medical care: During the period for which a person is entitled for unemployment allowance, he shall also be eligible for medical care for himself and his/her family from ESI Dispensaries, ESI panel clinics and ESI hospitals to which he/she was attached prior to the date of loss of employment based on a separate authorization by the Branch Manager making the cash allowance payment.

OUTCOMES OF RGSKY

Nearly three years after it was launched, the Rajiv Gandhi Shramik Kalyan Yojana, which promises affected workers half their pay for six months (now for one year), is yet to make its impression on the unemployed work force in India. The reason: Affected workers here find it impossible to get the "closure" certificate from their employer. With the Employees State Insurance Corp (ESIC), the Union government body that administers the scheme, unable to make any payment without this certificate, the jobless workers are unable to reap the benefits of the scheme.

Under the scheme, all workers covered by the ESIC who are laid off or rendered jobless by a factory closure are eligible to get half their pay for a maximum of six months, provided they can show that they lost their job because of a factory closure, or were retrenched or were declared permanently invalid because of a non-employment injury. Also, they must have been members of the ESIC for at least five years.

When launched in 2005, the scheme was expected to provide a much-needed social security cover to the eight million employees registered with the ESIC, which in turn had set aside Rs 300 crore for possible expenses under the scheme. But in the real picture is that it couldn't able to spend the allotted budget despite of increase in the rate of layoffs in India. It could be due to a total lack of awareness about the scheme and also, when a factory closes down, workers covered by the ESI have to file a benefit claim with the nearest ESIC branch office together with supporting documents, including a "closure certificate" from the company. Most companies refuse this certificate for obvious reasons–if a company declares itself as closed officially, it has to clear all statutory payments like provident fund and gratuity.

RECOMMENDATIONS:

Despite of the efforts made by the Government of India to protect the involuntarily unemployed people, it couldn't make an impression among the work force in India. The author has identified some reasons for this situation. They are:

- restrictive eligibility criteria have resulted in low recipiency rates
- benefit levels are low
- the mechanism to automatically extend the scheme during periods of prolonged economic downturns is broken.

As a result of these and other factors, only negligible unemployed workers currently receive assistance under this scheme, and that assistance falls short of the original goal of replacing at least half of previous earnings. In addition, the system provides no assistance either to the self-employed or to those who become reemployed at lower wages.

In the light of the above findings, three broad reforms, each designed to help the unemployment insurance scheme to better meet the needs of a twenty-first century workforce. First, strengthening the central government role in this scheme by setting the standards that would require states to harmonize their eligibility criteria and benefit levels. These new standards would aim to raise average national benefit levels and average national reciprocator rates. Second, a wage loss insurance program, as part of the Unemployment Insurance program, to provide an earnings supplement for those workers who become reemployed at a wage lower than the wage they earned at their previous job. Finally, allowing self-employed workers, to be covered under this scheme.

CONCLUSION

The existence of unemployment insurance does not eliminate the costs stemming from unemployment, though it may alleviate some of the costs by helping productive, skilled members of the workforce temporarily unemployed extend their job search period (according to "Job Search Theory") to match their skills to the right job, which maximizes economic efficiency. However, the existence of an overly 'luxurious' compensation scheme may discourage skilled labour from retreating from the labour market, whilst defrauding the government by claiming they are unemployed in order to obtain social security payments. It may also discourage the unemployed from seeking employment, as the compensation gained is high enough to compensate for the lack of employment. The present scheme, that is under implementation in India need to be modified according to the changing economic conditions in the world and its ripples on the Indian economy. The coverage should be extended to nonesuch members and should simplify the procedure of getting the benefits of it.

REFERENCES

Agarwal, R.N. and Goldar, B. (1995), Economic Reforms and Employment in India Projections for the year 2001-02., in *Indian Journal of Labour Economics* (Delhi, Indian Society of Labour Economics), Vol.38, No.4, pp.577-95.

Akerlof, G. and Yellen, J. (1986), *Efficiency Wage Models of the Labour Market* (Cambridge, Cambridge University Press).

Banerjee, B. (1986), *Rural to Urban Migration and the Urban Labour Market: A Case Study of Delhi* (Bombay, Himalaya Publishing House).

Bhagwati, J. and Srinivasan, T.N. (1975), *Foreign Trade Regimes and Economic Development: India* (Delhi, Macmillan).

Bhalotra, Sonia R. (1995), *Four Essays on the Urban Labour Market in India,* D.Phil. thesis submitted to the University of Oxford.

—Centre for Monitoring of the Indian Economy (CMIE), Economic Intelligence Service. *Basic Statistics for the Indian Economy, All India* (Vol.1) and *States* (Vol.2), (Bombay), several issues.

—Government of India. *Indian Labour Statistics* (Delhi, Ministry of Labour), several issues.

Dixon, D (1992), *Unemployment: the Economic and Social Costs,* 2nd edn, Research for Action No. 1, Brotherhood of St Laurence, Melbourne.

—(2001), NSSO, *NSS Report No. 469. Employment and Unemployment Situation among Social Groups in India, 1999-2000;* National Sample Survey Organisation, September.

Ahluwalia, Montek S. (2000), "Economic Performance in States in Post-Reforms Period," *Economic and Political Weekly,* May 6: 1637-1648.

—(2005), ESI Samachar, December, News Journal of ESI Corporation.

C.P Chandra Sekhar (2006), Unemployed in a Thriving Economy, Frontline, Volume 23, Issue 5.

Suchetana Haldar (2008), "State Yet to Get its First Jobless Worker Claimant of Centre's Shramik Kalyan Yojana".

42

RURAL UNEMPLOYMENT AND ITS REDRESSAL

M. Kusuma Kumari

Unemployment is a major problem in both the developed and developing countries. A high percentage of population in these countries depend upon primary occupation. With a low resource base, low incomes and savings potential, traditional skills and attitudinal patterns. Particularly in the rural sector. Employment is the bed rock of both development and social upliftment,

If a country cannot fully utilize its own human resources, it can achieve nothing on the economic front. If a large percentage of the work force remains unemployed, it will not be able to meet even the basic needs for want of necessary purchasing power.

Countries like China have successesfully exploited, human resources for creating assets. Maximum utilization of human resources is important for planning in any country. Mere generation of employment is not going to deliver the goods.

" India lives in Villages and village constitutes the very heart of India".

" Mahatma Gandhi"

India is a land of villages. Village is an important social and economic unit in Indian society. Rural structure can be analysed under Two main classifications.

1. Social Structure
2. Occupational Structure

SOCIAL STRUCTURE

In the words of Talcott Parsons, the famous sociologist. "Social structure is the term applied in the particular arrangement of inter related Institutions, agencies, and social patterns. Social structure is composed of different interrelated Institutions. (1) Marriage (2) Family (3) Caste (4) Kinship (5) Religious customs (6) Social Literacy (7) Power Structure

OCCUPATIONAL STRUCTURE

The Occupational structure in rural India consists of three sectors. They are (1) Agriculture and allied sector (2) Industrial Sector and (3) Service Sector.

Rural India is having abundance of labour force, most of it remaining categorized unskilled.

The Other Important Features of the Rural Labour Force are

1. The total workforce was 240.57 million of which 33.66 Million was child labour below the age of 5 years, constituting 12.5 percent of the total work force. Female workers in the total work force. Female constituting 30.2 percent.
2. It is difficult to quantify unemployment at any particular point of time. The persons who are unemployed is any given reference period may get some employment later on.
3. The rural labor force suffer from limited mobility.
4. Unemployment and under employment were recorded to be wish among rural women than man. As the family income level rises female workers show a tendency to withdraw from labour force.

The rural unemployment scene has certain characteristics. There are:

1. The availability of employment in the country has not kept pace with the increase in the labour force.
2. The proportion of labour depending on wage paid employment is increasing.
3. There is a growing casulisation of wage paid labour and
4. The labour absorption capacity of the agricultural sector is declining.

Unemployment in India is in rural areas where agriculture and agriculture based activities are the main stay of life. As these operations are seasonal, rural India also suffers from seasonal unemployment. So also the rural India faces unemployment concepts like disguised unemployment usual status unemployment. These can be discussed as follows.

SEASONAL UNEMPLOYMENT

Seasonal unemployment in rural areas is a normal condition in India. Agricultural labourers in India rarely have work through at the year. Agricultureal labour in India had 237 days employment was approximately for 3 to 4 monthes. In the agricultural sector during the 1980's and 1990's, there is every reason to believe that the seasonal unemployment should have increased in recent years.

DISGUISED UNEMPLOYMENT

The Indian agriculture is characterized by the existence of considerable amount of surplus labour. How ever, no firm estimates of its size are available. From the fragmentary information that is presently available it appears that in the green revolution belt these is no disguised unemployment for the past three decades the demand for wage labour has increased in these areas and agriculture labourers have been brought from other parts of the country to meet it in all other regions pressure of growing population has been increasing on land and when one notices too many people operating tiny agricultural holdings, one feels inclined to believe that disguised unemployment still exists in these areas on a considerable scale.

USUAL STATUS UNEMPLOYMENT

Usual status unemployment in rural areas cannot be clearly distinguished from seasonal and disguised unemployment. It is this reason whey people remaining unemployment for long periods are some times counted as seasonally or disguised by unemployment. This error erops up particularly if the survey is carried out in the off season when most people in villages do not have any productive work with them. Age wise the usual status rural unemployment was the highest in the age group 15-29.

Rural unemployment has sharply accentuated in the recent years. In the absence of gainful employment opportunities in rural areas, are increasing number of rural households have faced complete collapse of their incoverss. This miserable plight of the rural households has driven an unprecedented number of farmers to commit suicide recognizing this humanitarian crisis, the Govt. of the united progressive alliance (UPA) at the centre made a commitment in this common. Minimum programme (CMP), that it would. Immediately enact an employment Guarantees Act.

According to the present estimates, the employment strategy as stated above will example attainment of the full employment in any case not before 2002 A.D. there fore special employment programmes as in the past would be continued to provide short term employment to unemployed and under employed among the poor and vulnerable

REDRESSAL OF UNEMPLOYMENT

The national rural employment programme(NREP)

The NREP was meant to help that segment of rural population which largely depends on wage employment and has virtually no source of income dewing the learn agricultural period. The programme was implemented as a centrally sponsored scheme. But its financial burden was to be shared. Between the central Govt and the State Govt's on 50:50 basis

THE RURAL LANDLESS EMPLOYMENT GUARANTEE PROGRAMME. (RLEGP)

The programme aimed at providing guarantee of employment to at least one member of the landless house hold for about 100 days in a year. Through the programme was to be fully financed by the central Govt., the implementation of the programme was entrusted to the states.

THE INTEGRATED RURAL DEVELOPMENT PROGRAMME (IRDP)

Launched in 1978-79 and extended all over the country in 1980-81 was essentially conceived as an anti poverty programme under the sixth five year plan. This programme meant to provide self employment in a variety activities like sericulture, animal husbandary and land-based activities in primary sector, weaving, handcrafts etc. is the secondary sector the assets provided under the subsidy of the Govt.

THE SCHEME OF TRAINING RURAL YOUTH FOR SELF-EMPLOYMENT (TRYSEM)

This programme was initiated in 1979 with the objective of tackling unemployment problem among the rural youth. It aimed at training about 2 lakhs rural youths every year to enable them to become self employed. Under the scheme a minimum of one third of the rural youths trained were to be women.

Jawahar Rozgar Yojana(JRY)

1989 the Govt announced a new wage employment scheme. The JRY was restructured with effect from 1999 and was renamed as Jawahar Gram Samridhi Yojana(JGSY) the object of this programme was creation of infrastructure and durable assets at the village level so as to increase opportunities for sustained employment to the rural poor.

The Employment Assurance Scheme(EAS)

The EAS aimed at providing 100 days of unskilled manual work on demand to two members of a rural family in the age group of 18 to 60 years in the agricultural lean season with in the blocks covered under the scheme.

Swarna Jayanthi Gram Swaraozgar Yojana(SGSY)

SGSY Was launched in April 1999. after restructuring the IRDP and allied schemes. It is the only self employment programme for the rural poor. The objective is to bring the self employed above the poverty line by providing them income generating assets through bank credit and Govt. Subsidy

Sampoorna Grameen Rozgar Yojana(SGRY)

SGRY was launched in September, 2001 and the schemes of JGSY and EAS were fully integrated with SGRY. SGRY aims at providing additional wage employment in rural areas.

Prime Ministers Rozgar Yojana(PMRY)

PMRY was designed to provide self employment to more than a million educated unemployed youth by setting up of Seven lakhs Micro-enterprises under the eighth five year plan.

How ever programe are implementation of these programme was solely placed on Panchayat Raj institutions. Till now these programme have not been launched on a sufficiently large scale and thus their contribution from the point of view of the reduction in the incidence of employment seems to be only marginal.

According to Ashok Rudra, three major problems which prevent pursuit of these programme on a (1) Considerable scale are the choice of appropriate works to be done. (2) Finding the resources to finance the programmes. (3) And the lack of the clarity with regard to the organization of rural works programmes meat to generate employment.

In spite of all these employment programmes generated by Govts. till the rural unemployment problem is not attended properly. This is clearly observed in the present development scenario. Production increased literacy rate increased, but unemployment problem is still a stringent problem in rural areas.

43

CHALLENGES OF UNEMPLOYMENT THE INDIVIDUAL PSYCHE

T. D. Vimala

One of the important technological marvels of the late 20th century is the development in computers and tele-communications. Both have brought positive as well as negative changes. One major negative impact is reduction of work force due to automation. This led to increasing unemployment, and the positive impact is increase in efficiency in work places. Commitment to job and loyalty to employer, which were a hall mark of employment in the past, are glaring in their decline. Now a days. one is too ready to change jobs at the slightest opportunity.

Similarly job security and the concept of permanency are no longer the norm. Today worker has to be productive and proactive. To day worker must also develop valuable and useful skills. One should be should be ready to learn new skills and should be a life long learner,(Lick 2000) has observed that today's jobs are changing at such a speed that in many cases work skills will become obsolete quickly. Employees continuing education has become the necessity for the employee to retain employment.

Increase in temporary and contractual employment, increase in the service sector, the concept of earn while learn brought changes and challenges in the work sphere.

The state of unemployment is one of the major problem in our country. In India a person is treated as unemployed if he works less than 14 hours per week

The slow economic growth, capital intensive techniques, population growth, low priority for small scales industries, defective educational system, poor human resource planning, globalization and its consequences are the some of the major reasons for unemployment.

EFFECTS OF UNEMPLOYMENT

Employment is one of the most priced possessions of an individual. It is status, identity as well as strength. Employment has many important consequences, the most among them is the earning a living. The other latent consequences of employment are

(i) The time structuring of the working day

(ii) Regular shared experiences and contacts with people outside the family,

(iii) The linking of individuals to goals and purposes,

(iv) Personal status and identity,

(v) The enforcement of activity,

Unemployment would interfere with the fulfillment of above needs and hence create frustration, low self esteem and dissatisfaction besides uncertainty.

Fryer and Payne (1986) found that unemployment leads to loss of discretionary control, problems in maintaining relationships, and further lower self esteem. Further this influences one's mental and physical health. They found that job search as a result of unemployment involves putting one self on the line and dealing with feelings about being judged harshly, evaluated critically and ultimately being rejected. He also suggested that the unemployed can be helped by devising programmers to promote feeling of self esteem, optimism and control and developing job seeking skills.

It is also found that unemployment reduce the opportunity to use his skills. Further it is observed that unemployment reduces externally generated goals, environmental clarity about job market.

Further unemployment reduces availability of money, creates anxiety about physical security and reduces one's self–concept.

Unemployment leads to loss of socially approved roll and positive self evaluation that goes with it, it creates a new position that is of lower prestige, deviant and second rate membership in society.

Unemployment has different effects on middle aged men and women, teenagers and on the grays who are experiencing long term employment.

Losing a job in middle due to the social, political, polity changes are being observed frequently. The impact of these unemployment has multiple effects like leading to violence (Sygnatur&Toscano2000), increased aggression (Catalayo 1997); their social position is effected by unemployment to they face uncertainty about the future, ambiguity to their lives of less predictable future. Leona & Feldman (1991) found that there was no essential difference between men and women in the reaction to unemployment.

In teenager the unemployment creates a lack of valued social position. Personal responsibility and social stigma are liable to be less strongly felt. The teenagers externally give justification for their unemployment displayed higher self esteem and less helplessness than those in middle age, but they develop negative impact on effective well-being. Many researchers found the long term unemployment leads to reduced levels of mental health.Hence *"Develop these personality traits learn the skills to face the challenges of unemployment."*

Personality traits and skills required to face the challenges of unemployment in the present social scenario are

(i) Self direction, Self Management

(ii) Flexible Personality

(iii) Adaptable Personality

(iv) Learning Attitude (Life long)

(v) Managing the balance between work and home

(vi) Self awareness about their personality traits

(vii) Life skills (Interpersonal relations, time management, conflict management)

(viii) Tolerance

(ix) Alert observation of employment market

(x) Being active and projective.

(xi) Learning useful marketable skills.

In this fast changing global and national scenario one is advised, not to loose focus, be optimistic and proactive and consciously protect and preserve one's psyche from delay and detraction.

INDEX